T0330980

Work, Employment and Transition

Since the late 1980s the experiences of work and employment in the former communist world have been profoundly transformed. An ideological commitment to full employment and personal and societal liberation through work in the Soviet system has given way to mass unemployment, increasing labour market inequality, profoundly changing work practices and the deepening forms of work 'outside', but articulated within, the formal economy.

Work, Employment and Transition brings together a series of essays regarding these issues, written by leading international scholars. The contributions highlight the varied and complex forms which work and employment restructuring are taking in the post-Soviet world, while making important theoretical contributions to our understanding of these transformations.

The book focuses on four main aspects of restructuring in the post-communist world.

- the influence of neo-liberal policies on the nature of employment and work
- the restructuring of workplaces and trade union politics since 1989
- the role of gender in the experience of employment change
- the role of new and alternative forms of work, and the role of household survival strategies in the informal economy.

This important new work will be essential reading for those studying transition economies, and will be of vital interest to scholars across a range of disciplines, including geography, economics, sociology, political science and business studies.

Al Rainnie is Associate Professor in the Department of Management at Monash University, Australia.

Adrian Smith is Lecturer in the Department of Geography at the University of Southampton, UK.

Adam Swain is Lecturer in Human Geography at the University of Nottingham, UK.

Routledge Studies of Societies in Transition

1 **The Economics of Soviet Break-up**
   Bert van Selm

2 **Institutional Barriers to Economic Development**
   Poland's incomplete transition
   Edited by Jan Winiecki

3 **The Polish Solidarity Movement**
   Revolution, democracy and natural rights
   Arista Maria Cirtautas

4 **Surviving Post-Socialism**
   Local strategies and regional response in eastern Europe and the former Soviet Union
   Edited by Sue Bridger and Frances Pine

5 **Land Reform in the Former Soviet Union and Eastern Europe**
   Edited by Stephen Wegren

6 **Financial Reforms in Eastern Europe**
   A policy model for Poland
   Kanhaya L. Gupta and Robert Lensink

7 **The Political Economy of Transition**
   Opportunities and limits of transformation
   Jozef van Brabant

8 **Privatizing the Land**
   Rural political economy in post-communist socialist societies
   Edited by Ivan Szelenyi

9 **Ukraine**
   State and nation building
   Taras Kuzio

10 **Green Post-Communism?**
   Environmental aid, innovation and evolutionary political economics
   Mikael Sandberg

11 **Organisational Change in Post-Communist Europe**
   Management and transformation in the Czech Republic
   Ed Clark and Anna Soulsby

12 **Politics and Society in Poland**
   Frances Millard

13 **Experimenting with Democracy**
   Regime change in the Balkans
   Geoffrey Pridham and Tom Gallagher

14 **Poverty in Transition Economies**
   Edited by Sandra Hutton and Gerry Redmond

15 **Work, Employment and Transition**
   Restructuring livelihoods in post-communism
   Edited by Al Rainnie, Adrian Smith and Adam Swain

16 **Environmental Problems of East Central Europe: 2nd edition**
   Edited by F.W. Carter and David Turnock

17 **Transition Economies and Foreign Trade**
   Jan Winiecki

18 **Identity and Freedom**
   Mapping nationalism and social criticism in twentieth-century Lithuania
   Leonidas Donskis

19 **Eastern Europe at the Turn of the Twenty-First Century**
   A guide to the economies in transition
   Ian Jeffries

20 **Social Capital and Democratic Transition**
   Edited by Gabriel Badescu and Eric Uslaner

Work, Employment and Transition

Restructuring livelihoods in post-communism

Edited by Al Rainnie, Adrian Smith and Adam Swain

London and New York

First published 2002 by Routledge
11 New Fetter Lane, London EC4P 4EE

Simultaneously published in the USA and Canada
by Routledge
29 West 35th Street, New York, NY 10001

Routledge is an imprint of the Taylor & Francis Group

Typeset in Baskerville by MHL Typesetting Limited, Coventry,
Warwickshire

British Library Cataloguing in Publication Data
A catalogue record for this book is available
from the British Library

Library of Congress Cataloging in Publication Data
Work, employment, and transition: restructuring livelihoods in post-
communism / edited by Al Rainnie, Adrian Smith, Adam Swain.
     p. cm.
    Includes bibliographical references and index.
    1. Labor market–Europe, Eastern–Congresses. 2. Labor market–
Former Soviet republics–Congresses. 3. Post-communism–Europe,
Eastern–Congresses. 4. Post-communism–Former Soviet republics–
Congresses. 5. Europe, Eastern–Social conditions–1989–Congresses.
6. Former Soviet republics– Social conditions–Congresses.
I. Rainnie, Al. II. Smith, Adrian, 1966– III. Swain,
Adam.

HD5764.7.A6 W67   2002

331.12′0947–dc21   2001045707

ISBN 0-415-24942-2

Contents

List of figures and tables   vii
List of contributors   ix
Acknowledgements   xii

Introduction: work, employment and transition   1
AL RAINNIE, ADRIAN SMITH AND ADAM SWAIN

PART I
Restructuring employment and work and neo-liberal
transitions   5

1 Employment and work restructuring in transition   7
   AL RAINNIE, ADRIAN SMITH AND ADAM SWAIN

2 The babble of euphemisms: re-embedding social protection
   in 'transformed' labour markets   35
   GUY STANDING

PART II
Workplace transformations and trade unions in
transition   55

3 Trade unions and the politics of transformation in Central
   and Eastern Europe   57
   JOHN THIRKELL AND SARAH VICKERSTAFF

4 Broken networks and a *tabula rasa*? 'Lean production',
   employment and the privatisation of the East German
   automobile industry   74
   ADAM SWAIN

PART III
Gender, work and employment in transition   **97**

5 Out with the old, in with the new? The changing experience
of work for Polish women   99
JANE HARDY AND ALISON STENNING

6 'A woman is everything': the reproduction of Soviet ideals of
womanhood in post-communist Russia   117
SARAH ASHWIN

7 Restructuring labour markets on the frontier of the
European Union: gendered uneven development in
Hungary   134
JUDIT TIMÁR

8 Gender and entrepreneurship in post-communist Hungary   155
JANET HENSHALL MOMSEN

9 Gender and labour market restructuring in Central and
Eastern Europe   170
MIKE INGHAM AND HILARY INGHAM

PART IV
New forms of employment and survival strategies   **191**

10 Sources of subsistence and the survival strategies of urban
Russian households   193
SIMON CLARKE

11 Economic strategies of surviving post-socialism: changing
household economies and gender divisions of labour in the
Bulgarian transition   213
MIEKE MEURS

12 Rethinking 'survival' in austerity: economic practices and
household economies in Slovakia   227
ADRIAN SMITH

13 Gulag Europe? Mass unemployment, new firm creation,
and tight labour markets in the Bulgarian apparel industry   246
JOHN PICKLES

Index   273

Figures and tables

Figures

1.1	East-Central Europe and the former Soviet Union.	8
1.2	Employment change in East-Central Europe and the former Soviet Union, 1989–99.	19
1.3	Labour force participation rates, 1992–7.	21
1.4	Unemployment rates, 1990–9.	24
4.1	Organisational structure of the IFA combine.	82
4.2	Organisational restructuring of *Sachsenring Automobilwerke*, 1989–93.	91
5.1	Map of Poland.	101
7.1	Hungarian study regions.	136
7.2	Regional variations in gender inequality in employment.	138
7.3	Household economic activities by household structure and settlement type, Hungary 1996.	149
8.1	Border regions in Hungary.	159
11.1	The structure of household economies in Bulgaria.	214
12.1	The Slovak Republic.	232
12.2a	High-rise apartment estates in Martin, Slovakia.	233
12.2b	Petržalka, Bratislava.	234
13.1	Map of Bulgaria.	247
13.2	Unemployment levels in Bulgaria, 1990–3.	250
13.3	Average duration of unemployment in Bulgaria, 1990–3.	251
13.4	Index of real gross domestic product, Bulgaria and Eastern Europe (1990–8).	252

Tables

1.1	Male and female employment change in East-Central Europe, 1989–96	20
1.2	Employment and unemployment changes in East-Central Europe, 1990–6 (per cent change)	22
4.1	Employment change in nine automobile component firms	85
4.2	The privatisation of parts of IFA-SAW, 1990–4	88

5.1   Employment and monthly wage by gender in Wroclaw, 1998   104
5.2   Unemployment by gender in Wroclaw and Kraków, 1997   105
7.1   The proportion of the economically active population and the
      female–male activity rate ratio by age and settlement types in
      Hungary, 1996   140
7.2   Distribution (per cent) of active earners by economic sector and
      gender in Hungary, 1980, 1996   143
7.3   Distribution (per cent) of active earners by occupation and gender
      in Hungary, 1980, 1996   144
8.1   Types of entrepreneurial activity in rural west and east Hungary, by
      gender (per cent of total)   163
9.1   Employment and participation change (per cent): 1989 to first LFS   174
9.2   Employment change (per cent): LFS data   177
9.3   Participation changes (per cent)   178
9.4   Part-time working: averages   179
9.5   Average under-employment figures   180
9.6   Self-employment averages   181
9.7   Gender bias in labour market outcomes   182
9.8   OLS regression on male and female self-employment   186
10.1 Percentage of households with money income per head below the
      official regional adult subsistence minimum   199
10.2 Components of household income as percentage of total net income
      of all household members, excluding private transfers   200
10.3 Components of household income by income group. Percentage of
      income contributed by each source for those households who have
      that income source and percentage of households with that income
      source   201
10.4 Percentage of households in poverty with different social policies   206
11.1 Sector of employment by sex, working age Rhodope population,
      1986, 1996 (per cent of total employment)   217
11.2 Sources of income, rural Rhodope households, 1986, 1996 (per cent
      of households)   218
11.3 Employment status of Rhodope working age women and men, 1986,
      1996 (per cent)   219
12.1 Average personal income in Slovakia, 1992–6   235
12.2 Average percentage of food purchased, produced and received by
      households, 1999   236
12.3 Average percentage of food purchased, produced and received by
      below median income and above median income households, 1999   237
12.4 Average percentage of various foods produced by occupational
      groups, Martin and Bratislava   239
12.5 Food expenditure of households, Martin and Bratislava   240
13.1 Decline in employment by sector: Kurdjali 1991–8   248
13.2 Production and employment in apparel, 1980–96   250
13.3 Per cent change in manufacturing employment by selected branch
      1992–8   253
13.4 Apparel employment and unemployment by obstina   255

List of contributors

Sarah Ashwin is a lecturer in Industrial Relations at the London School of Economics. She is author of *Russian Workers: The Anatomy of Patience* (Manchester University Press, 1999) and editor of *Gender, State and Society in Soviet and Post-Soviet Russia* (Routledge, 2000).

Simon Clarke is Professor of Sociology and Director of the Russian Research Programme at the University of Warwick and Scientific Director of the Centre for Comparative Labour Studies (ISITO) in Moscow. He has been researching labour and employment in Russia with his Russian colleagues since 1991. His current research projects are on 'The development of trade unionism in Russia' and 'Innovation in Post-Soviet industry'. His most recent book is *The Formation of a Labour Market in Russia* (Edward Elgar, 1999).

Jane Hardy has been researching into regional transformation in Poland since 1993 and teaches at the University of Hertfordshire.

Janet Henshall Momsen is Professor of Geography at the University of California, Davis. She has also taught at universities in England, Canada, Brazil and Costa Rica. Her most recent books are *Women and Change in the Caribbean* (Indiana U.P., 1993), *Different Places, Different Voices* edited with Vivian Kinnaird (Routledge, 1993), and *Gender Migration and Domestic Service* (Routledge, 1999). She is also editor of a series for Routledge on International Studies of Women and Place.

Hilary Ingham is Senior Lecturer in Economics at Lancaster University.

Mike Ingham is an economist and Associate Director of the Centre for Policy Studies at the European Studies Research Institute, University of Salford. He is author (with Hilary Ingham) of *The Gender Dynamics of the Polish Labour Market* (Macmillan, 2000) and co-editor (with Hilary Ingham) of *Eastward Expansion of the EU: Prospects and Problems* (Macmillan, 2000).

Mieke Meurs is Associate Professor of Economics at the American University, Washington DC. She is the author of *Many Shades of Red: State Policy and Collective Agriculture* (Rowman and Littlefield, 1999) and *The Evolution of Agrarian Institutions: A Comparative Study of Post-Socialist Hungary and Bulgaria* (University of Michigan Press, forthcoming).

John Pickles is the Phillips Distinguished Chair of International Studies at the University of North Carolina, and a member of the Department of Geography, the Curriculum for International Studies, and the Center for Slavic, Eurasian and East European Studies. He is the author (with Petr Pavlínek) of *Environmental Transitions: Post-Communist Transformation and Ecological Defense in Central and Eastern Europe* (Routledge, 2000), and editor with Adrian Smith of *Theorising Transition: The Political Economy of Post-Communist Transformations* (Routledge, 1998), and with Krassimira Paskaleva, Phillip Shapira, and Boian Koulov of *Bulgaria in Transition: Environmental Consequences of Economic and Political Transformation* (Ashgate, 1998).

Al Rainnie is Associate Professor in the Department of Management at Monash University, Victoria, Australia. He has researched and written extensively on employment, industrial relations and small firms as well as labour and restructuring in Poland.

Adrian Smith is a lecturer in the Department of Georgraphy at the University of Southampton. He has previously taught at the Universities of Kentucky and Sussex. He is co-editor (with John Pickles) of *Theorising Transition: The Political Economy of Post-Communist Transformations* (Routledge, 1998), author of *Reconstructing the Regional Economy: Industrial Transformation and Regional Development in Slovakia* (Edward Elgar, 1998), and a former deputy editor of *Regional Studies.*

Guy Standing works at the International Labour Organisation in Geneva and has researched extensively in Eastern Europe and the former Soviet Union. He is author of *Russian Unemployment and Enterprise Restructuring* (Macmillan, 1996) and *Global Labour Flexibility* (Macmillan, 1999).

Alison Stenning is a lecturer in the School of Geography and Environmental Sciences and associate member of the Centre for Russian and East European Studies at the University of Birmingham. Her research on the politics of local economic development in the Russian Federation and on the social and cultural impacts of economic and urban change in Poland is published in, amongst others, *Political Geography* and *European Urban and Regional Studies.*

Adam Swain is Lecturer in Human Geography at the University of Nottingham. He has been researching regional development, industrial restructuring and labour relations in Hungary, East Germany and Ukraine since the early 1990s.

John Thirkell is Honorary Senior Research Fellow in Industrial Relations at the University of Kent at Canterbury. Retired from full-time academic life, he maintains his long-standing interest, enthusiasm and concern for the organisation of work and the development of labour relations in Russia and Central and East Europe.

Judit Timár is a senior research fellow at the Centre for Regional Studies of the Hungarian Academy of Sciences in Békéscsaba. Her main publications concentrate on suburbanisation, urban-rural relationships and gender studies. She also lectures at the University of Szeged, is on the editorial boards of several geographical journals, and is a full member of the Gender and Geography Committee of the International Geographical Union.

Sarah Vickerstaff is Reader in Employment Policy and Practice in the School of Social Policy, Sociology and Social Research at the University of Kent at Canterbury. She has long-standing research interests in training policy and practice in the UK and emerging patterns of labour relations in the post-communist societies of Central and East Europe and Russia. To these she has recently added an interest in the age management policies of organisations and is currently directing a research project in this area, funded by the Joseph Rowntree Foundation.

Acknowledgements

This book arises in part out of an Economic and Social Research Council research seminar series entitled 'Restructuring Employment and Work in East-Central Europe', which ran from early 1999 until late 2000 (award number: R451 26 4873 98). We are very grateful to the ESRC for supporting this programme of meetings. We also wish to acknowledge the help and assistance of our fellow organisers of this series (Simon Clarke, Carola Frege, Jane Hardy, and Alison Stenning) and to all the participants at the seminars.

Introduction

Work, employment and transition

Al Rainnie, Adrian Smith and Adam Swain

Since the late 1980s the experiences of work and employment in the former communist world have been profoundly transformed. An ideological commitment to full employment and personal and societal liberation through work in the Soviet system has given way to mass unemployment, increasing labour market inequality, profoundly changing work practices and the deepening of forms of work 'outside', but articulated within, the formal economy. *Work, Employment and Transition* brings together a series of essays by leading international scholars working on these issues. The contributions both highlight the varied and complex forms which work and employment restructuring are taking in the post-Soviet world and make important theoretical contributions to our understanding of these transformations. Many of the essays included in *Work, Employment and Transition* have their origins in a British Economic and Social Research Council-funded research seminar series entitled 'Restructuring Employment and Work in East-Central Europe', which ran from early 1999 until late 2000. In putting together this collection of essays we are very grateful to our co-organisers of this series and to all the presenters and participants who contributed to lively and engaged discussion over five separate meetings.[1] In addition to papers presented at these meetings we have also been fortunate to be able to include additional essays from other key researchers working on employment and work issues in East-Central Europe (ECE) and the former Soviet Union.[2]

The book is organised into four main parts and it is our purpose in this Introduction to outline the core themes dealt with in these different sections. A more substantive introduction to the experiences of, and theoretical perspectives on, work and employment transformation can be found in Chapter 1. The first two chapters of the book in Part I deal with key theoretical and policy aspects of employment restructuring and the uneven national and local experience of change in Soviet and post-Soviet societies. Rainnie, Smith and Swain in Chapter 1 introduce the main characteristics of employment and work in the Soviet systems of ECE and the former Soviet Union, examine the main trends and trajectories in employment and work restructuring since the late 1980s and explore several of the key theoretical claims used to interpret these changes. In particular, they emphasise the important role of understanding change in the formal sphere of work in relation to its complex articulation with the 'informal' economies of both the Soviet and post-Soviet systems. This is an important claim developed in several of the later chapters in *Work, Employment and Transition*. The chapter examines the ways in which high levels of relatively secure employment have given way to widespread official and/or hidden unemployment; job security has been replaced by greater job insecurity; employee representation has weakened; dependency on state-owned enterprises to provide not only a monetary wage, but also social amenities in kind, has been replaced by greater differentials in the value of formal wages and, for the unemployed, reliance on low-value state benefits and on varied informal legal and illegal income-generating activities. Chapter 2 by Guy Standing furthers some of these claims through a specific focus upon the key policy prescriptions articulated through the dominant neo-liberal agenda of western advisors, western governments and multi-lateral institutions. Standing examines several of the 'keywords' of transition as a means to unpack the dominant discourses used in implementing the neo-liberal agenda. Standing's 'deconstruction' of this 'babble of euphemisms' provides a way for him to begin to unpick the neo-liberal project and, in particular, its lack of concern for economic and distributive justice. By drawing upon Karl Polanyi, Standing provides a critical treatment of the need to 're-embed' the labour market and its institutions back in society, with justice as a key motif used in that process.

Part II of *Work, Employment and Transition* focuses attention on the way in which industrial workplaces have been transformed and the role that trade unions have played in transition. Chapter 3 by John Thirkell and Sarah Vickerstaff provides a cross-national analysis of the evolution of trade union policy and position in relation to economic transformation. They argue that the interests of trade unions have been directly influenced by the politics of the attempted economic reforms adopted or avoided by governments in the different countries, and they explore the implications of the various strategies adopted. Chapter 4 by Adam Swain examines the role of inter-organisational networks in the transformation of East German automobile enterprises and workplaces. Through an examination of external investment, privatisation and the introduction of 'lean production' techniques the chapter argues that interpretations of German unification as involving the disembedding of industrial networks casts employees and regions in the new *Länder* as victims of external economic relations. Through the lens of the automobile industry Swain examines the ways in which broken networks and a *tabula rasa* served to create an idealised set of economic practices which served the interests of West German capital.

Part III includes five chapters dealing with various aspects of the transformation of gender relations and employment restructuring in post-Soviet societies. Two of the chapters in this section (Jane Hardy and Alison Stenning (Chapter 5) and Sarah Ashwin (Chapter 6)) provide analyses of the mechanisms by which women's gender oppression in the workplace and between 'public' work and the domestic sphere are being transformed. Ashwin explores the articulation between Soviet and post-Soviet 'gender orders' in Russia to argue that rather than women wanting a full return to the home and 'old patriarchal' values, Russian women endorse a combination of traditional and more egalitarian ideas regarding their role and that of men. By contrast, through their study of women in work in Polish enterprises with inward investment, Hardy and Stenning investigate the ways that firms and workplaces are restructured, with differential impacts on women, and that new job opportunities expand in growth sectors such as retailing. A regional dimension to gender restructuring is added in the contributions from Janet Henshall Momsen (Chapter 8) and Judit Timár (Chapter 7) on Hungary. Through exploring the changing labour market position of women (Timár) and women's entrepreneurship (Henshall Momsen) in peripheral Hungarian border villages, both chapters explore the importance of the uneven regional impacts of transition on the gendered experiences of work and employment. Finally, in this section, Mike Ingham and Hilary Ingham (Chapter 9) provide an economic analysis of women's disadvantage in the labour market in which they highlight the varied experience across countries and the complexity of developments within particular economies.

Part IV provides four chapters examining the emergence of 'new' forms of work, their articulation with economic practices established under the Soviet systems (and before) and the role that 'informal' work and 'survival' strategies play in positioning households and individuals in the emergent labour markets of the region. Chapter 10 by Simon Clarke provides a critique of the claim that the solution to the decline of income and non-payment of wages in Russia lies in the household subsistence economy. Rather he finds these claims wanting and argues that there has not been a substantial change in the sources of household income, which are still predominantly waged income from primary employment and welfare benefits. Indeed, he argues that household food production does not make any significant contribution to compensate for lost income. Clarke concludes, in a powerful rebuttal of received wisdom, that an effective minimum wage and a social wage for those unable to gain employment would be the most appropriate forms of policy in the Russian labour market. These claims regarding the relative importance of household survival strategies are examined further by Mieke Meurs in Bulgaria (Chapter 11) and Adrian Smith in Slovakia (Chapter 12). In her study of households in the Rhodope region of Bulgaria, Meurs argues that the use of the subsistence economy by households should be seen not as adapting to austerity brought by transition, but as a truncation of income earning activities which result in reliance upon mechanisms to ensure the simple reproduction of the household. In a similar way to Clarke and Meurs, Smith finds that there is little overall evidence that domestic food production and land usage are used by urban households in two contrasting Slovak regions as a survival strategy. Rather he finds that the historical and cultural continuity of land usage must be seen in different ways from the functionalist reading dominant in much of the literature on survival strategies, and explores the articulation and co-constitution of household economic practices. Finally, the contribution by John Pickles (Chapter 13) explores in a wide-ranging manner the links between the growth of mass unemployment in a peripheral Bulgarian region, new forms of work in a burgeoning and internationalised apparel sector and links and articulations with household economies. In exploring the social constitution of the formal economy,

Pickles stresses 'the complexity (and social and historical depth) of "peasant-worker" household economies that have played an important role in the particular form of cheap wage economy that has emerged' (p. 264). Wages and uncertain work regimes in the apparel sector are, he argues, underwritten by other forms of family income generation.

Together, then, the chapters in *Work, Employment and Transition* provide a wide-ranging treatment of the dynamism, complexity and contestation of labour market and work transformations in the post-Soviet world. The chapters stress the importance of theoretical rigour as well as empirical depth and a key argument emerging is the concern to move beyond neo-liberal and naïve institutionalist prescriptions for employment restructuring towards more nuanced and, crucially, socialised notions of the transformation of livelihoods in post-Soviet East-Central Europe and the former Soviet Union.

Notes

1   Our co-organisers were Simon Clarke, Carola Frege, Jane Hardy, and Alison Stenning.
2   The chapters by Janet Henshall Momsen and John Pickles were not presented as part of the seminar series and were independently commissioned. We are very grateful to Janet and John for agreeing to contribute chapters to the volume.

Part I

Restructuring employment and work and neo-liberal transitions

1 Employment and work restructuring in transition

Al Rainnie, Adrian Smith and Adam Swain

In Moscow. . . the plan for economic transformation to capitalist markets was described by officials and the press in a representationally impoverished form as, simply, 'the big bang' (English original). This mystical, invisible, sonar boom, imported by economists from Harvard, was supposed to provide for three hundred million Russian people [*sic*] some kind of cosmic rebirth out of the ashes of seventy years of Soviet rule. Heralded as the beginning of the new era, it seemed to the average citizen, on the contrary, to lead society ever deeper into a black hole.

(Buck-Morss 1995: 466)

[I]t seems reasonable to ask what it might mean to call the countries of eastern Europe 'capitalist'. Does it mean that collective and communal and feudal and individual and family processes of production (some of which might be the same thing, and many of which co-existed with the pre-sumptively hegemomic state sector) no longer exist? Does it mean that non-market exchange networks and barter systems that were in place before 1989 are no longer operative or are not now being created to deal with new problems of privation and scarcity, problems associated with a new economic and social order?

(Gibson-Graham 1996: 244)

Introduction

Since the late 1980s, the countries of East-Central Europe (ECE) and the former Soviet Union (Figure 1.1) have been party to one of the most dramatic economic experiments in the 'modern' world. Encouraged by a proselytising community of neo-liberal economists, and almost forced by international financial institutions (IFIs) through conditionality clauses attached to lending programmes (Gowan 1995, Wedel 2000), national governments have widely deployed liberal industrial, employment and social policies. Designed to engineer a shift from, what was seen as, an overly rigid state-planned system under the Soviet model, these policies have aimed to introduce market capitalism. While many key proponents of these

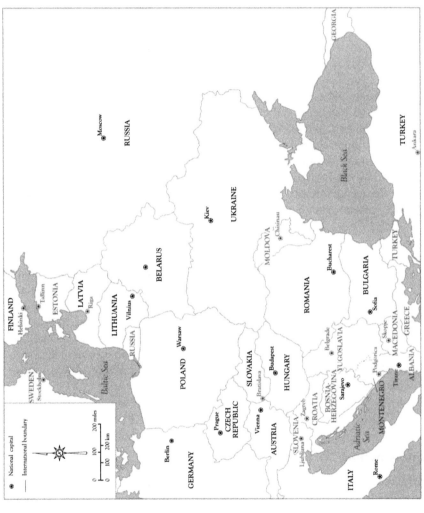

Figure 1.1 East-Central Europe and the former Soviet Union.

policies have argued that they will be the basis for economic rejuvenation after the stagnation and slowdown witnessed in the 1980s, the experience of many economies has been somewhat different. A key result of the introduction of liberal economic policies in the 1990s has been the dramatic decline in GDP, which in turn has led to a reduction in employment and investment. The result has been that by the end of the 1990s of all the countries in the region, only Poland, Hungary and Slovenia had reached, or were close to reaching, their respective 1989 GDP levels (Dunford 1998, Dunford and Smith 2000). In the context of this economic collapse labour markets and the organisation of work have been transformed and continue to undergo dramatic change across the region. While the experience of work and employment varied from country to country (Pollert 1999) there were a number of common trends: high levels of relatively secure employment gave way to widespread official and/or hidden unemployment; job security was replaced by greater job insecurity; employee representation weakened; dependency on state owned enterprises to provide not only a monetary wage, but also social amenities in kind, was replaced by greater differentials in the value of formal wages and, for the unemployed, reliance on low-value state benefits and on varied informal legal and illegal income generating activities. This has been described as a transition from a low work intensity, mass underemployment system to one that will increasingly be characterised by highly intensive work practices and mass unemployment driven by the pressures of international competition (Rainnie and Hardy 1999: 166).

These trends have led some (Elster *et al.* 1998: 196–8) to suggest that, far from resembling West European and Anglo-American capitalism, emergent forms of capitalism in ECE and the former Soviet Union more closely resemble those found in Latin America. In particular Elster *et al.* (1998) suggest that post-Soviet systems share two features with Latin America: the prevalence of 'uncivil' economic activities and a form of economic dualism involving an under capitalised nascent private sector operating on a short-term time scale interwoven with large demonetised state and privately owned enterprises. However, such a crude East–West dichotomy is questioned by analysts such as Beck (2000) who has posited the possibility of the Brazilianisation of the West with the unintended consequences of neo-liberal policies being the spread of temporary and insecure employment, discontinuity and loose informality. According to the adherents of the liberal transition model the persistence of official or unofficial mass unemployment and impoverishment could simply be explained by the persistence of enduring rigidities in the labour market. As such, transition advocates demanded further liberalisation and privatisation as well as reform of social security systems, poverty abatement and social services (see World Bank 1996).

Our aim in this chapter is to reflect critically on these theoretical and policy developments and their key employment outcomes. We wish to suggest that the largely negative impacts of liberal transition policy provide the basis for us to rethink how we understand work and employment in East-Central Europe and the former Soviet Union. In this sense, this chapter deals with two sets of 'transitions' – those enacting and creating the substantive experience of work and employment restructuring *in transition*, and those pointing to *a transition in the ways we think and theorise* work and employment in the post-Soviet world. A starting point is to question the validity of the notion of 'transition'. Such a concept implies a clearly delineated path from an understood starting point to an agreed end state (Stark 1992b, Smith 1998, Pickles and Smith 1998). Only in the wildest dreams of neo-liberal analysts does such a situation exist. We prefer to understand the process taking place as 'transformation' – one in which there are simultaneously stark continuities with the past, as well as emergent forms of new economic practices (see Smith and Pickles 1998, Grabher and Stark 1997). Reworking our *conceptions* of post-socialist labour market and employment dynamics is a task which is taken further by many of the contributions in *Work, Employment and Transition*. Our aim in this chapter is therefore to set the scene for these contributions and to review the key evidence concerning employment and work restructuring.

Theorising transitions and employment restructuring

Post-Soviet governments in ECE and the former Soviet Union sought to raise living standards towards those perceived to exist in Western Europe by enhancing their economies' international competitiveness and by integration into the global capitalist system. Accordingly, a transition model involving a rapid all-encompassing shift from the authoritarian centrally planned Soviet system to a democratic market economy gained political and academic currency (see Sachs 1990). According to this model, state policies were to stabilise the economy through austerity measures, to marketise trade by removing administrative controls and subsidies, to privatise state-owned enterprises and to internationalise their economies by reducing trade barriers.

The transition model was based on two pieces of received wisdom, one that concerned the nature of the Soviet system and the reason for its disintegration and the other concerned the perceived operation of capitalist systems. First, implicit in the liberal transition model was the view that the Soviet system centred on an omnipotent, irrational, statist economic system which was destined to collapse owing to its inherent economic inefficiencies. According to this argument the absence of market discipline, and specifically of so-called 'hard budget constraints' (Kornai 1992), meant the planning system allocated resources irrationally. In particular, state-owned enterprises were said to be overstaffed and the labour force underutilised (Sachs 1990). Second, proponents of the liberal transition model argue that the central dynamics of the capitalist system are self-generating, and in time self-regulating, commodity markets. Consequently the success of any transition to capitalism depended on the formation of a governing coalition committed to releasing social actors from the dead hand of state intervention (see Smith and Swain 1998 for a critique of this state-market dualism).

According to the transition model, state policies were required that would unleash the rationalising power of the market and reallocate capital and labour from less to more competitive economic activities. The absence of both labour and capital markets, inappropriate incentive structures and corporate governance were to receive most attention as they were regarded as barriers to the rational allocation of the factors of production (Sachs 1990, World Bank 1996). Above all, however, the labour market and specifically labour were to bear the brunt of so-called transformation costs through the reduction of real wages (Amsden *et al.* 1994). The model anticipated that the large inefficient state-owned industrial enterprises would shed labour thereby transforming a supposedly inflexible internal labour reserve into a supposedly flexible external one that in turn would supply labour to a thriving community of new privately-owned small and medium sized companies (see Smith 1997 for a critical examination of these claims). In this way a labour market would emerge in which labour power would become a commodity to be traded like any other. Commodification of labour would in turn refashion the sectoral and geographical pattern of employment as the labour process within firms was reorganised.

As an alternative to the liberal approach, we suggest in this chapter that the advocates of the transition model based their labour market policy upon two false assumptions. First, neo-liberals assumed that the Soviet system was devoid of labour market functions whereas we know that, for example, through informal networks based on reciprocity, labour was traded and that within state-owned enterprise internal labour reserves meant there was a degree of labour 'flexibility' present (Clarke *et al.* 1993). Both such mechanisms enabled enterprises to offset somewhat the rigidities of the plan and to meet plan targets. Second, according to the liberal transition model, labour could reasonably be expected to behave like other commodities by rationally adapting to emerging market signals. Adherents of the liberal transition model therefore see labour markets, like markets for other commodities, as inherently self-regulating. However as evidence from Russia and elsewhere has shown (Clarke 1998) labour market change is unpredictable because labour is a unique commodity form interacting with other arenas of social action, for example the domestic economy or other forms of non-wage labour (Polanyi 1957). Equally, labour markets cannot be self-regulating depending as they do on labour market regulations varying in type from formal legal frameworks to patterning through cultural conventions concerning work, its value and place in broader society.

Furthermore, we are also critical of several of those commentators who have developed approaches in opposition to the orthodox neo-liberal transition model. First, we are critical of those that have advocated the 'East Asian' model of statist development (Amsden *et al.* 1994) as an alternative to neo-liberal 'Shock Therapy' as it is based on a particularly brutalising form of exploitative labour relations (Pollert 1999). Second, although evolutionary or institutional perspectives (see especially Stark 1992b, Grabher and Stark 1997) have played an important role in showing that change in ECE is not so much a closed transition to a given end point – the market economy – as a series of open-ended transformations in social relations, they do share with orthodox accounts a narrow focus on capital to the exclusion of labour. As a result such accounts tend to under-emphasise the labour process, the representation of labour, the changing conventions surrounding work and non-work, and alternative non-wage forms of labour. Equally, evolutionary approaches share three conceptual problems with orthodox neo-classical accounts. First, they explain evidence as the outcome of rather abstract evolutionary processes that are therefore validated *ex post*. As such these approaches cannot explain processes which show how economic reorganisation has taken place (cf. Pollert 1999). Second, they are 'capitalcentric' in two senses: they demonstrate a fixation with capital as opposed to labour and tend to ignore non-capitalist economic and work practices (cf. Smith 2000). Third, they overplay agency (for example Elster *et al.* 1998) at the expense of structural constraints and their interactions with strategic action. There are also dangers of slipping into some sort of Third Way form of analysis positing an acceptable form of capitalism some way between neo-liberal fantasies and a command economy, whilst paying due regard to the embedded legacies upon which transforming economies must build (Pollert 1999).

Our criticism of the liberal approach is also based on expanded notions of the economy and of labour markets and 'work'. Here we draw on the writings of Trevor Barnes (1996) and J.K Gibson-Graham (1996) and others who propose a re-conceptualisation of capitalism and other economic systems in which they are no longer regarded as single binding entities (see Smith 2000). In so doing we hope to point towards an approach that emphasises the contested transformation of labour processes, the organisation of labour representation, the continuities that exist between the Soviet and post-Soviet periods, the significance of non-wage, non-commodified work, and the gendered nature of labour market trans-formations. Such a framework also implies recognition of the complex, contradictory and geographically uneven nature of employment change and awareness of the varied forms of work that co-exist in the region without reducing the 'informal' household sphere to that of 'formal' sector employment relations.

However, we wish to begin by providing an overview of work and employment change in the Soviet and post-Soviet eras. First, we examine the nature of work and employment in the Soviet system and the role it played in the transformation of societies committed to 'socialist' alternatives to capitalism. We highlight that in addition to the state-owned economic sector there existed in that sector and on its margin a multiplicity of non-Soviet economic action which has important implications for our thinking about work transformations more recently. Second, the chapter provides an overview of the key changes in employment and work in post-Soviet economies, focusing both upon national specificities – especially between states in East-Central European and the former Soviet Union – and cross-regional similarities. This part of the chapter includes an overview of employment change, the changing nature of employment and unemployment, and the gendered nature of labour market change. Furthermore, understanding these changes demands an understanding of the role of foreign investment in encouraging specific geographical and sectoral patterns of employment change, the changing remuneration of workers including an increasing reliance on multiple sources of formal and informal income and in the former Soviet Union the non-payment of wages, and the role of state and non-state institutions, especially trade unions, in regulating labour markets.

Employment and work in the Soviet system

> Soviet industrialization imitated the capitalist model; and as industrial-
> ization advanced the structure lost its provisional character and the Soviet
> Union settled down to an organization of labour differing only in details from
> that of the capitalist countries.
>
> (Braverman 1974: 12)

In order to gain an understanding of the contemporary transformations of
employment and work in East-Central Europe and the former Soviet Union it is
important to situate change and continuity in the light of the past. This section
therefore outlines some of the key characteristics of employment and work in
Soviet societies according to institutional and evolutionary analysts and then
begins to outline the elements of an alternative.

As in the west, the Soviet labour process separated the conception and
execution of production in order to concentrate knowledge in the hands of
supervisors who could control and co-ordinate production. However, the efficient
co-ordination of work was rarely achieved leading to a reliance on informal
bargaining in which individual influence, as much as the system, shaped
individualised experiences of work. Consequently, the Soviet labour process was
constantly being reorganised because of the unevenness of work and technology
(Burawoy 1985).

In addition to its fluidity, there were four key elements to the Soviet labour
process. First, as under capitalism, work was the site of conflict as workers were
dominated by management (Bahro 1978) and alienated from their work. Mandel's
(1992) interview with an assembly-line worker at an automotive factory in
Moscow is striking for the parallels to similar studies in the west (see for instance,
Beynon 1984). However, owing to the variability of the experience of work, the
workplace was a very individualistic environment in which collective forms of
resistance and solidarity were largely destroyed (Mandel 1992). It has been argued
that the labour process was depoliticised as there was a general failure to build
institutions that could co-ordinate the interests of workers and bosses and
establish rules of how work should be carried out (Stark 1992a). Resistance
generally took an individual character, in the form of coping strategies, from
withholding and concealing work effort to verbal resistance to supervisors and
including corruption, absenteeism and theft. However, as we shall see, the
situation was actually a little more complicated than this.

Second, the Soviet labour process was governed by a despotic factory regime
(Burawoy 1985). Workers were almost entirely dependent on the state-owned
enterprise not just in the sphere of work but also in many areas of their lives.
Enterprises played an important role in social reproduction so that membership of
the labour collective was for most the only avenue to opportunities (career and
political advancement and scarce products), welfare services, and freedom from
harassment from disciplining organs of the state (Kornai 1992). Mostly this
dependency was 'managed' through informal bargaining in which influence and

contacts were the best measure of an individual's power with formal line management largely irrelevant. A further aspect of the despotic regime was the absence of any genuine institutionalisation of workers' interests. Thus whilst there was indeed a system of trade unions it did not represent workers nor defend their rights but was used by the state as another organ of labour supervision and discipline (Godson 1981).

The despotic factory regime was often combined with a piece-rate wage system (Haraszti 1977, Burawoy 1985, 1988). The very low level of basic pay and piece rates forced workers to do anything to exceed quantity norms in order to earn a living wage. Consequently, supervisors perpetually increased norms as workers met them. Whilst employment was secure the insecurity of income forced workers to work harder and harder. However, more than that, since the piece-rate worker can control the speed of work, the worker was turned into a machine (Haraszti 1977), who was forced to internalise the labour process so that he – significantly piece-rate workers usually were male and women workers usually time-rate workers – became fixated by the constraints to work, such as by his fellow workers. Moreover, the allocation of 'good' and 'bad' work was arbitrary and there was no consultation over changes to production organisation. Burawoy (1985) calls this the dictatorship of norms and foremen, a regime which created a brutal labour process in which competition with fellow workers concealed the exploitative hierarchical relations.

The third key element of the Soviet labour process was the failure of the system to place the power of how work was done into the hands of supervisors (Clarke *et al.* 1993). This in turn helps to explain why piece-rates were so significant in Soviet enterprises; it forced the internalisation of the labour process and reflected the inability of supervisors to control the nature of work. Thus control over the nature of work was ceded to workers for a number of significant reasons. The development – to a greater or lesser extent – of the 'second economy' also created a partial market for labour (Stark 1992a). Thus whilst the extent to which labour remained a commodity varied, it gave workers power versus the enterprise by undermining their dependency and giving them a certain degree of power of 'exit' – moving to another state-owned enterprise – or partial 'exit' – by establishing a secondary means of income – and 'voice' – by being able to bargain with management over how work was done.

Because of the shortage economy management, supervisors and workers were faced with constant disruptions, uncertainties and unevenness of production. Supplies were unreliable and frequently of poor quality, technology was old and prone to breakdowns, the uneven development of technology resulted in production bottlenecks, and the need to meet targets towards the end of months and years would result in periods of 'storming' (Stark 1988). As a result supervisors and workers were forced to substitute and improvise which affected the labour process through 'a flexible allocation of labour on the shop floor' (Stark 1988: 329). Informal networks developed between workers and supervisors, and between different supervisors, which acted as ephemeral institutions based on the principle of reciprocity (Heidenreich 1992, Grabher 1994). At the shop-floor level labour and tools were often reciprocally exchanged within and between shops. This had the result of creating a segmentation of employment – a core group of workers who could do several jobs, repairing tools or correcting faulty components, and a peripheral group or 'internal reserve army' who could be relied upon to step in when they were rushing to meet the plan (Clarke 1993).

This brings us to the fourth element of the Soviet labour process. The despotic factory regime and the workers' considerable control over the organisation of work generated, in spite of the antagonistic relationship, a feeling of mutual interest between managers and workers (Mandel 1992). This often resulted in the creation of alliances between enterprise management, supervisors and workers in which work effort was withheld (Burawoy 1988). However, often these alliances were punctuated by ritualistic arbitrary 'scapegoating' for the system's failures which encouraged managers and workers to accept the situation and remain as anonymous as possible. In reality problems were ignored and were covered up as management and workers conspired to 'paint socialism' (Burawoy 1992).

In addition to these central characteristics of the labour process and experience of work in the Soviet system derived from institutionalist political economy approaches there are several additional elements which we wish to highlight. First, while some evolutionary or institutionalist approaches tend to extend their critique of neo-liberal orthodoxy little further than positing that the wrong kind of capitalism was being prescribed to replace the Soviet system, for Pollert (1999) searching for an alternative right kind of capitalism, be it 'associative democracy' or the 'developmental state', is a flawed strategy. In Pollert's reading, capitalism (like the Soviet system) is inherently unstable, based on conflicting interests in the relations of production and capable only of reaching transient forms of stability. Furthermore, Pollert concentrates on the role of labour in transformation, a factor which is usually ignored or views workers as passive victims trapped in a despotic regime. Pollert on the other hand stresses both structure and the agency of labour, and the dialectical relationship between them.

Secondly, then, and most clearly in the case of Poland, a dialectic of development in the Soviet system consisted of cycles of crisis, revolt, reform and repression. Successive attempts to deal with economic crisis by savage increases in the price of basic foodstuffs in a desperate attempt to subordinate consumption to the needs of production, triggered revolt in 1956, 1970, 1976 and again with the rise of Solidarnosc in 1980. Furthermore, as successive crises were growing deeper the revolt they engendered threatened the existence of the whole political structure (Hardy and Rainnie 1996: 72). Consequently, it is a mistake to see worker organisation in Soviet style systems as completely trapped in despotic regimes. Pankow (1993: 57) argues that Polish state-owned enterprises, particularly after 1956, were scenes of permanent social conflict, sometimes hidden, sometimes open: 'They [workers] try, with varying consistency, to rebuild a true worker representation. . . . Sometimes this representation takes the form of workers' councils, at other times the form of independent trade unions.'

Although it would be an independent trade union, Solidarnosc, that would finally sound the death knell for the Soviet system in Poland, workers' councils have played an important role throughout ECE. Councils were established in Poland in the crises of the 1950s and 1960s, but the concept is not unproblematic. Hardy and Rainnie argue that there are three varieties – syndicalist, technocratic and co-administration – which rise and fall in importance depending on the level and strength of working-class opposition to the regime. For Vickerstaff and Thirkell (2000), in the Soviet Union and Bulgaria, self-management and the development of councils emerged in the 1980s in response to the recognition of economic retardation and the need for *perestroika*. The developments are therefore politically contingent and dependent.

This is important because, as Thirkell and Vickerstaff (this volume) argue, the role of trade unions in the various countries before 1989 has an important influence on the process and pattern of change after 1980. This is most clear in the case of Solidarnosc in Poland though it is vital to understand the ideological shift that the movement has undergone in the 1990s (Rainnie and Hardy 1999). However, this point simply serves to underline our proposition that the role of labour and labour process change are fundamental to an understanding of the process and outcome of transformation. Furthermore, as Thirkell *et al.* (1998: 8) argue, the evolution of the Soviet model varied markedly within East-Central Europe and the former Soviet Union.

Third, most existing analyses of work and employment in the Soviet systems mask the diversity of economic practices which constitute particular societal forms through their articulation with one another (see Gibson-Graham 1995, Smith 2000, and Chs 11–13). Such practices range from the development of the so-called 'second economy', which clearly articulated with the Soviet system through allowing plan storming, and the 'double burden' of women in which the domestic division of labour was closely intertwined with that of the formal planned economy, to economic practices constituted 'outside' the formal economy such as the use of household plots for food production and the retreat to the private. As Creed (1998) has so clearly shown, these economic practices had their own importance, but were also central to the very operation of the Soviet system. Through the complex articulation of the 'formal' and 'informal' economies of ECE the experience of the Soviet system became, to use Creed's (1998) words, 'domesticated' – economic relations became co-constituted through household, informal and formal economic practices (see also Smith 2000). Such claims, therefore, mark an important epistemological distinction between neo-liberal and (some) institutionalist arguments concerning the workings of the Soviet system, on the one hand, and non-essentialist and more complex readings, on the other.

Finally, in addition to a segmented and authoritarian labour process, work and employment in the Soviet system were also highly gendered. While Soviet societies had a formal commitment to equality, Meurs (1998) has argued that in many respects this was 'imagined equality'. 'Imagined equality' results from the failure of the Soviet systems to address the gendered nature of these societies. While there was formal commitment to expanding women's education opportunities, to increasing women's participation in formal politics and to increasing equality through the expansion of employment opportunities for women, a number of contradictions constrained the effects of these goals. In particular, within the workplace women experienced a gender division of labour. Women were often concentrated in low-paying 'service' oriented jobs and the state administration, or in poorly paid industrial work deemed suitable for women (such as in the textile and clothing sector (see Pine 1996)). Women were often concentrated in jobs requiring few qualifications and were under-represented in highly paid industrial jobs at the core of the Soviet economy. Consequently, the expansion of women's employment opportunities under the Soviet system created a further level of segmentation in the workforce. In addition, the expansion of formal work took place with little or no consideration given to the household and the domestic division of labour. The consequence was, as many feminist writers have documented (see for example Einhorn 1993), a 'double burden' for women which further constrained the formal commitment to equality.

Labour and the disintegration of the Soviet system

In the late 1980s the various Soviet systems began to disintegrate and the changes that followed on from this had profound, if gradual, impacts on the nature of work and employment. In fact disintegration is slightly misleading because to varying degrees collapse was accelerated by increasing integration into the world economy from the 1970s onwards, at a time when recession-ridden Western economies could export only further economic worries. However, in concentrating on the changes that took place, it is important not to overlook the considerable resistance to change that was widespread among many constituent institutions of the system. The Soviet economic system was one in which state enterprises were to an increasing degree autarchic entities as attempts were made to free themselves from the irrationality of the plan. As the plan itself was undone and enterprises were uncoupled from one another atomisation and autonomy merely increased. In consequence there was an absence of mechanisms to enforce reform, which was itself meant to create a market co-ordinating mechanism. The result was the development of autarchic 'islands' (Clarke *et al.* 1993). Thus the transformation of work, in which management could (re)establish control over the labour process, depended on management not only being given the juridical right to behave more like owners but also on management being convinced of the worth of playing such a role. Where this failed the legacy of the mutual co-interest amongst enterprise managers, supervisors and core workers often meant that management sought to employ strategies that prevented reform, such as by seeking to find 'work' for their workers rather than enforce strict financial criteria (Clarke *et al.* 1993).

We have seen that under the Soviet system labour power was never entirely decommodified but the crux of the post-Soviet transformation of work has been the commodification of labour power – turning labour power into profitable labour power. Commodification depends on turning the 'fictitious' commodity of labour into a 'real' one (Polanyi 1944: 72–3). This is achieved in four ways: the institutionalisation of a shared belief in the idea of labour as a commodity, the buying and selling of labour on a market, the generation of real magnitudes of demand and supply, and the creation of labour market regulatory mechanisms and institutions.

Under the Soviet system all members of the labour collective, management, supervisors and workers, were considered to be employees of the state. The creation of commodified labour power therefore depended, first, on the creation of an antagonistic relationship in the workplace as members of the enterprise were differentiated into employers and employees and ascribed very different rights within the workplace. This differentiation of labour was deepened as management sought to relate responsibilities to specific jobs. An internal labour reserve was transformed into an internal labour market in which members of the enterprise sought the new positions and management began to 'buy' internal labour. The reverse side of needing to institutionalise management prerogatives was the equal need to institutionalise and regulate workers' interests as a way of concealing exploitation and dispersing resistance. The differentiation of people who had all been employees of the state generated resistance, expressed in the creation of new labour representative bodies such as workers' councils. In Hungary, for example, by June 1990 more than 160 workers' councils had been set up in opposition to the traditional trade union structure (Burawoy 1992).

The creation of employers gave management the right to 'hire and fire'. Labour power could thus be bought on an external market. However, decision making of such a sort depended on new mechanisms for measuring the worth of labour power. These measurements were used as a pretext for reducing staffing levels and creating an external pool of unemployed labour. The result was the creation of local labour markets which became steadily more segmented. The threat of unemployment, and the difficulty in gaining employment elsewhere (due to labour shedding and the preponderance of 'company towns') undermined the power of those in work and facilitated management's control over the labour power of which it was now the buyer. Thus having had to buy labour, management had an incentive to seek control over how labour power was expended.

Employment and work in 'transition'

The creation of an external market for labour power since the late 1980s has produced a dramatic transformation of labour and work in post-Soviet societies. In the ten years of 'transition' since 1989 every country in ECE and the former Soviet Union for which data are available saw a reduction in employment, sometimes of dramatic proportions (Figure 1.2).[1] Loss of formal employment has been most severe in the Balkans, many parts of the former Soviet Union and in Hungary, which have all seen levels of job loss in excess of 20 per cent. Less severe employment decline (between 10 and 20 per cent) has been seen in some parts of the former Soviet Union, such as Belarus and Lithuania, and in Poland and the Czech and Slovak Republics. While more recently some economies, such as Croatia, Hungary, two of the three Baltic

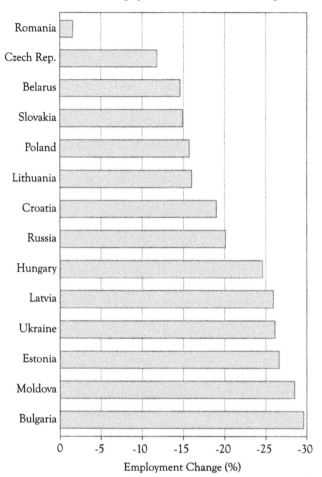

Figure 1.2 Employment change in East-Central Europe and the former Soviet Union, 1989–99.

Source: ILO Labour Statistics

states and Poland, have witnessed an increase in year-on-year employment, in none of these economies have employment levels returned to anything like that reached in the late 1980s.

Employment decline has also been a gendered process (UNICEF 1999). Female employment decline has been much greater than male job loss (Table 1.1). Between 1989 and 1996 male employment fell by nearly 9 per cent while female employment dropped by 13 per cent. According to ILO data, just over 7.2 million women lost jobs over this period, compared to just over 4.5 million men. However, what is also clear is that the gendering of employment decline has worked differently across the countries reported. In those economies where female employment loss has been highest, the experience for many women has

Table 1.1 Male and female employment change in East-Central Europe, 1989–96

Country	Gender	Total employment change (000s)	Ratio of male to female employment change
Former	male	−185.7	−2.38
Czechoslovakia	female	−442.5	
Estonia	male	−17.7	−2.57
	female	−45.5	
Hungary	male	−565.9	−1.48
	female	−837.8	
Lithuania	male	−71.0	−2.44
	female	−173.3	
Macedonia	male	−111.8	0.58
	female	−64.7	
Poland	male	−1644.0	0.98
	female	−1607.0	
Russia[a]	male	−1963.0	−2.09
	female	−4108.1	
Total	male	−4585.8	−1.59
	female	−7265.7	

Source: Elaborated from ILO (1997).

Notes
[a]   Data are for period 1992–96.

been early withdrawal from the labour force through premature female retirement (Paukert 1995) and increasing non-participation.

Overall employment decline has occurred within the context of a dramatic reduction in labour force participation throughout the region and in female formal economic activity rates (UNICEF 1999). Figure 1.3 plots data on labour force participation rates, defined as the percentage of the total working age population who are active (either employed or unemployed and seeking work), between 1992, 1993 and 1997 for selected countries. Overall falls in labour force participation rates between base year and point of final observation have occurred in Bulgaria, the Czech Republic, Hungary, Poland, Slovenia, and Russia, although some variation exists between these two points in some of these countries. The most dramatic decline in labour force participation is found in Hungary and Slovenia, suggesting in the case of Hungary at least that the dramatic fall in employment has been connected to a similarly dramatic decline in labour force participation – a mass withdrawal from the labour market. Falling labour force participation is also clearly concentrated amongst women (UNICEF 1999).

However, the relationship between employment change and increasing non-participation in the labour force varies across the countries of ECE and the former Soviet Union (Table 1.2). The table shows change in employment (expressed as a proportion of the initial labour force) between 1990 and 1996 (unless otherwise stated) and the change in the rate of unemployment over the same period (see

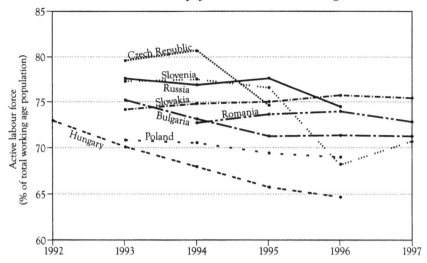

Figure 1.3 Labour force participation rates, 1992–7.

Blanchard *et al*. 1995). The table also reports the ratio of employment change to change in the unemployment rate. A ratio of 1.00 indicates that all workers who lost jobs, assuming no change in the working age population, entered unemployment. A result of less than 1.00 indicates that workers who lost jobs became non-participants in the labour market, either through early retirement or through dropping out of the formal economy. Two main experiences are apparent. First, in Hungary, Lithuania, Latvia and Bulgaria a dramatic employment loss has not been translated automatically into increased official unemployment, although unemployment rates *are* high in Bulgaria and Hungary. The experience in these countries clearly suggests a mass withdrawal from the formal labour market. However, increasing non-participation does not involve individuals sitting idly by as the waves of the transition to capitalism pass by. One way in which declining formal labour market participation has been compensated is through a return to the domestic economy, which has been historically important in societies such as Hungary and Bulgaria (Sik 1994, Begg and Meurs 1998, Smith 2000, see also Chs 11–13).

The second main way in which employment and unemployment rates interrelate is evident in Slovakia and Poland, and to a lesser extent in Russia and Estonia. In these countries there is a much closer equivalence between the fall of employment and the increase in unemployment rates, suggesting that workers losing jobs have moved into unemployment rather than having dropped out of the labour market or been absorbed by the private sector.

Clearly changes in participation and employment change work differently across the post-Soviet countries. Yet, differential, but increasing, non-participation in the labour market is significant in a number of respects. First, non-participation within the context of limited unemployment and welfare benefit provisions (often limited to 12 months or less entitlement to

Table 1.2 Employment and unemployment changes in East-Central Europe, 1990–6
(per cent change)

Country	Change in employment	Change in unemployment	Ratio
Russia[a]	−10.63	8.3	0.78
Estonia[b]	−10.75	7.9	0.73
Latvia[c]	−13.17	6.2	0.47
Lithuania[a]	−12.57	5.2	0.41
Bulgaria	−19.64	11.5	0.58
Czech Republic	−6.36	2.8	0.44
Hungary	−26.75	8.9	0.33
Poland	−13.58	11.3	0.83
Slovakia	−12.07	12.0	0.99

Source: Elaborated from ILO (1996, 1997)

Notes
Figures are expressed as % change from initial level relative to initial labour force.
[a]   Data are for 1991–96.
[b]   Data are for 1990–94.
[c]   Data are for 1992–96.
A ratio of 1.00 means that all workers who lost jobs entered unemployment, assuming that there was no change in the working-age population. A result of less than 1.00 means that workers who lost jobs became non-participants in the labour market, either through early retirement or through dropping out of the formal economy.

unemployment benefit) results in a reliance on economic practices outside the formal economy and the emerging capitalist wage relation. Second, the role of the 'informal' economy is important because it raises serious theoretical questions about how we understand the diversity of economic practices that constitute work and employment in 'post-communist transition'. This is a point that several of the chapters in this volume dealing with 'survival strategies' explore further.

Unemployment and labour market exclusion

Large-scale employment loss throughout ECE and the former Soviet Union has also translated into the emergence of mass unemployment. Unemployment is important in two respects, not only because of its negative effects on economic growth through overall reductions in demand for goods, but also because of its occurrence in societies in which until 1989 there was a commitment to full employment. The development of unemployment derived from ILO estimates in a number of post-Soviet countries between 1990 and 1999 is shown in Figure 1.4. Where possible the labour force survey estimate of the unemployment rate has been used. Three main trends are evident. First, many of the countries of the former Soviet Union (except the Baltic States) have witnessed *relatively* low overall rates of unemployment, although recently labour force survey estimates for Russia indicate an unemployment rate of nearly 13.5 per cent and rates are rising in most cases. Second, throughout much of the 1990s, the Czech Republic also experienced relatively low unemployment rates (generally around 4 per cent), although rates are now increasing as a result of open unemployment through labour shedding in enterprises. Finally, the majority of Central and South-East European states have seen the emergence of mass unemployment, with some fall-off in one or two cases (such as Hungary and possibly Bulgaria) in recent years.

There is also very strong evidence of increasing long-term unemployment (longer than 12 months) which accounts for something like 62 per cent of those unemployed in Bulgaria, 52 per cent in Hungary, 54 per cent in Romania, and 53 per cent in Slovenia and Slovakia (OECD various years). Those in older age groups (50–54 years old for women and 50–59 for men) are relatively more represented in the long-term unemployed in these countries. Furthermore, women represent a disproportionately large component of the unemployed in eight out of the 13 ECE countries for which there are reliable data.

One explanation for enduring long-term unemployment in ECE is the level of regional mismatch within an economy between new job creation and job losses (World Bank 1996: 66–77, Cornia 1996: 9–10). Indeed, this perspective has become the dominant explanatory discourse used to claim that labour market flexibility has not gone far enough in ECE. As the 1996 World Development Report argued:

> Moving to a market system involves a vast reallocation of labor resources across firms, sectors, and regions. Yet the labor markets inherited from central planning ... effectively sacrificed labor mobility for greater individual security. ... In a market system employees move between employers, between types of work, and between places. ... Income transfers (for example, unemployment benefits) in transition countries therefore need reform, not only to reduce poverty and contain costs but also to assist mobility. This means, in particular, supporting the unemployed and getting enterprises out of the business of delivering social benefits. Otherwise, labor will remain immobile, raising the costs of transition by creating pockets of poverty in declining regions, and by pressuring enterprises and governments to defer necessary restructuring.
>
> (World Bank 1996: 66)

Such claims have permeated the neo-liberal literature on labour market transformation and 'structural unemployment' in ECE (see Commander and Coricelli 1995, Cornia 1996). The World Bank (1996: 72–7) has argued that in enabling 'people to help themselves' wage rates should be reduced in 'declining' regions to further encourage mobility. The social benefits and services provided by enterprises that were such an essential part of 'regional lock-in' under state socialism (see Smith 1998) also need to be dismantled it is argued. Declining labour market rigidity is therefore an issue of increasing the geographical flexibility and mobility of labour. The fact that labour mobility

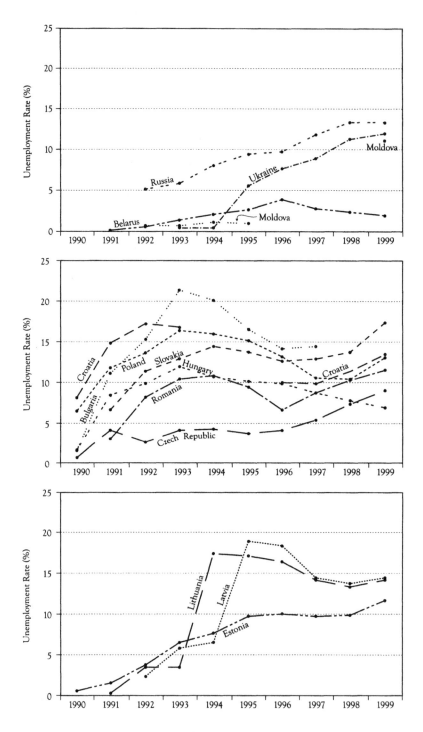

Figure 1.4 Unemployment rates, 1990–9.

tends to lead to the depopulation of declining regions, the loss of those with transferable skills and the flexibilities needed to form the basis for rejuvenated regional growth, and that reducing wages and welfare benefits further leads to mass impoverishment, seem lost on the proponents of the neo-liberal agenda.

Clearly, mass unemployment and the shedding of labour is a highly uneven process, embedded within its own geography of local labour market conditions and regulations. Also it is unlikely that job 'mismatch' can ever be 're-matched' within the context of the peripheralisation of regional economies with few job opportunities. Mobility is unlikely to solve the problem and in fact may even exacerbate the crisis of peripheral regions. Depopulation may well reduce unemployment rates for some areas, but problems of long-term unemployment associated with mass impoverishment are unlikely to have the effect of promoting the rejuvenation of local economies. In Slovakia, for example, just under 40 per cent of those who are registered as unemployed have been so for more that 12 months (Ministry of Labour, Social Affairs and Family of the Slovak Republic 1999) and there is evidence that the length of unemployment is much greater in the more peripheral regions that also have high unemployment rates (Smith 1998). Continuing unemployment within the context of a state fiscal crisis and temporal constraints on the receipt of welfare payments is resulting in a decline in the number of people covered by official unemployment benefits to as low as 22 per cent of those registered as unemployed in Slovakia in 1995 (UNICEF 1997: 7). The consequence is a large-scale reduction in levels of social welfare across the region. According to an analysis of 28 indicators of social and welfare change between 1989 and 1995, deteriorations were experienced in 41 per cent of indicators in Central Europe, 83–86 per cent of indicators in South-Eastern Europe, the Baltic States and the Caucasus, and 93 per cent in the western Commonwealth of Independent States (UNICEF 1997: 9–10). It is within this context of divergent labour market dynamics that the day-to-day 'reproduction' of labour power becomes problematic. It is also within the context of mass unemployment that alternative, and potentially non-capitalist, economic practices may be relied upon in order to sustain economic livelihoods, which is a point developed in several chapters in *Work, Employment and Transition*. But what all this evidence points to is the profound unevenness of employment and work restructuring during 'transition'. While commodification of labour power has proceeded apace, increasing income inequality, social polarisation and long-term unemployment have become central parts of emergent capitalist labour markets in ECE and the former Soviet Union.

Trade unions and transformation

In the early stages of transformation trade unions (both new independent and reformed Stalinist) played a vital role in shepherding the process of transformation. Both governments and unions embraced tripartite structures in the early stages providing a protective umbrella to cover processes that were accelerating unemployment and poverty. This despite the fact that in many cases tripartite structures were empty vessels. Government and unions were represented but employers assocations were to all intents and purposes absent. New small firms and foreign investors were mostly not interested in formal employers' organisations, leaving only a declining representation for state-owned enterprises. In some ways the commitment to tripartism also represented an attempt by western agencies to export western models of industrial relations, models which to some extent were already in disarray. However, by the mid-1990s governments were becoming increasingly less committed to such mechanisms, leaving Pollert (1999: 213) to conclude that whilst tripartism and continental European models of centralised national and sectoral bargaining have been encouraged and formally embraced, the reality is fragmented enterprise and workplace bargaining with a weak intermediate level of industry bargaining. If the major drivers of work transformation were to be foreign direct investment, privatisation and small firms then each would in their different way present new (and old) trade union structures with a set of problems.

Although small firms and entrepreneurialism have iconic status in neo-liberal ideology, the reality of transformation is that though providing a growing and considerable amount of employment, small firms are not the dynamic drivers of the new economy (Smith 1997, Piasecka and Rainnie 2000). However, small firms in ECE do seem to share some characteristics with their counterparts in the West. They fulfil a variety of roles (Rainnie 1993) mostly determined by the activities of large firms and/or the state, but most are often in precarious or marginal positions. This leaves workers in small firms in often low-paid and uncertain employment on the edge of the informal economy. Consequently, trade unions have made little headway in organising in these sectors.

Deep restructuring has been more evident in firms with foreign direct investment (FDI) than in privatised or state-owned enterprises (SOEs) (Pollert 1999). However, the level of inward FDI in ECE and the former Soviet Union has been somewhat limited and the picture is far from clear as to the effects on employment and labour process change. There are contrasting experiences of restructuring within and between sectors (Pavlínek and Smith 1998, Swain 1998, Hardy 1998) with some serious questions about the extent of transfer of work organisation and human resource management practices. However, Pollert (1999) concludes that survey evidence suggests that across a range of MNCs industrial relations have become difficult or trade unions have simply had to comply with management wishes. Even MNCs whose country of origin has strong works council traditions have been found to avoid unions. In the service sector, British supermarkets with partnership agreements are also refusing to recognise trade unions in Central Europe. This is particularly important given that employment in the retail sector is going to be one of the major carriers of 'flexible' employment patterns for women into the Central European context.

The relationship between trade unions and the state has become increasingly problematic as the case of tripartite structures has demonstrated. Although, as Vickerstaff and Thirkell (this volume) argue, the process and pattern of privatisation was heavily influenced by the extent and form of trade union involvement, the post-privatisation experience has not been favourable for trade union organisation (Hardy and Rainnie 1996). Furthermore, as successive governments have privatised industries and restructured health and education services then they have increasingly found themselves in conflict with sections of the population who had been in the forefront of support for transformation. Trade union leaders have been accused of being schizophrenic in these circumstances, or in the case of Poland being Janus-like (Pollert 1999, Rainnie and Hardy 1999). European Union (EU) accession will only serve to increase pressures on public expenditure and attack subsidies threatening to escalate conflict between organised labour and the state. Paradoxically this brings workers in ECE into line with their counterparts around the world (Fairbrother and Rainnie 2001).

In general, where trade union organisation exists, the main institutional development is a hybrid system of fragile tripartism, fragmented enterprise unionism and weak industry level regulation (Pollert 1999: 229). However, as the fragile consensus over restructuring comes increasingly under pressure, then the pattern of transformation will crucially depend on how workers and their organisations react to the changes that are still to come.

The future of employment and work in post-socialism

The most important thing today is for economic units to maintain – or, rather, renew – their relationship with individuals, so that the work that people perform has human substance and meaning, so that people can see into how the enterprise they work for works, have a say in that, and assume responsibility for it. Such enterprises must have – I repeat – a human dimension; people must be able to work in them as people, as beings with a soul and a sense of responsibility, not as robots, regardless of how primitive or highly intelligent they may be.

(Václav Havel, first published in Czech in 1986, quoted in Miller and Rose 1995: 459)

Economic reforms must be accompanied by a social system that safeguards human rights and prevents social upheaval ... [by protecting] those most likely to suffer in the transition.

(President Václav Havel, June 1990, quoted in Offe 1996: 233)

These two quotes from Václav Havel before and after he became President of Czechoslovakia (and subsequently of the Czech Republic) illustrate the two sides to the shift from a labour shortage under state socialism to a work shortage in post-socialism: the nature of the conditions for those who remain in paid work in some form, and the prospects for those (of whom many of which are the same people) who have been excluded, wholly or partially, from the world of paid employment since 1989. Above all the future of employment and work in ECE and the former Soviet Union will be shaped by the shift away from the 'quintessentially production-centred, or "productivist"' state socialist societies peopled by "worker-citizens"' (Offe 1996: 235). As Offe has suggested, the sphere of paid work was ideologically and institutionally central to the workings of state socialism. Activity levels were high by international standards, and the labour collective perhaps exceeded the family as the fundamental social unit providing not only work but also social goods as well as social status and identity. Accordingly, the end of the Soviet system may well be accompanied, enforced or otherwise, by an end to the centrality of paid work to societies in ECE and the former Soviet Union. Moreover, the social and cultural fluidity that has accompanied the transition may provide scope for beginning to re-imagine the role of work and employment in the future.

Such a re-imagining of the role of work begins with the need to rethink ideas about 'the economy' and 'capitalism' in response to epistemological challenges posed by the demise of metanarratives for the economism and productivism of much political economy (Thrift 1998: 27) and the increasing geographical stretching and complexity of economic practices. Trevor Barnes (1996), for example, has developed a sustained critique of neo-classical and orthodox Marxist economic theory. He argues that Marxist political economy shares with neo-classical economics particular features with Enlightenment thinking. In particular, he suggests that Marxist theory (within the context of the sub-discipline of economic geography) was based on a notion of privileged knowledge and a rational, universal and essentialist concept of the subject, features which he argues are no longer tenable.

In beginning to elaborate new ways of conceptualising the economic, Barnes draws on the work of, amongst others, J.K. Gibson-Graham (1995, 1996). Gibson-Graham engage with feminist and non-essentialist Marxist thinking about identity and difference to argue for a re-envisioning of capitalism. Gibson-Graham suggest that critical political economy has been cast in capital-centric ways which has inadvertently regulated and reinforced visions of 'capitalist hegemony'. Thus Gibson-Graham treat capitalist hegemony as a discursive artefact which simultaneously constitutes and drives capitalism as well as constitutes and marginalises anti-capitalist and non-capitalist practices. In a similar way Buck-Morss (1995) argues that the 'capitalist economy' was invented as an object of representation during the 18th century. She argues that the economy was representationally mapped in a particular way as a whole, which could be seen from the outside, that served to present the economy as an autonomous object possessing agency independent from individual and collective economic actors (Buck-Morss 1995: 440).

Gibson-Graham argue that the effect of this form of representation is to present capitalism as an all-encompassing essential cause of social behaviour. They also argue that whereas the discursive construction of varieties of capitalisms might superficially present capitalism as plural, it actually serves only to reinforce the core notion of capitalism as all encompassing. Instead, Gibson-Graham argue that capitalism as a centring totality has to be represented as comprising multiple, unstable and shifting identities. In this way capitalism is not to be regarded as a cause driving social change but as a representation of the product of a multiplicity of causes. This is an anti-essentialist formulation of social causation in that whilst events can be 'over determined' there is ultimately no one cause in the last instance as everything causes everything else. Gibson-Graham suggest that a shift away from thinking about capitalism as hegemony to capitalism as difference demands focusing on *the articulation that exists between capitalist and non-capitalist practices*. In order to do this they seek to distinguish between capitalism as a specific form of social relations and processes of surplus appropriation and redistribution through class relations that may or may not be capitalist (see also Smith 2000, 2001).

Thrift (1998) argues that the emergence of discussion about the identity and representation of 'the economic' amongst social theorists is mirrored in the world of business and management. He identifies the emergence of 'soft capitalism' in which a new managerial discourse, which he terms the 'new managerialism', evangelised by a cadre of academics, business gurus and management consultants, has an increasingly formative impact on the conduct of economic practices. Thrift suggests that new managerialism frames and forces an increasingly complex and uncertain economic world in which the 'learning' business organisation is based on a refusal to accept received wisdom.

At this point the discussion about reconceptualising the economic is extended to include rethinking ideas about work, as well as the role of work and employment in society. Thus Thrift argues that the new managerialism discourse seeks to embody its metaphors, including religious metaphors (Kostera 1995: 335), in its employees through the organisation of work (Thrift 1998: 41). Thus new managerialism treats business organisations as cultural entities and the performance of work as constitutive of workers' subjectivity.

In a similar vein, Václav Havel's clarion call before the collapse of state socialism for humanising work was answered by what has been termed the 'management education project' in ECE and the former Soviet Union (Kostera 1995: 349) – a project which is fundamentally concerned with the transformation of our conceptions of labour and work in post-Soviet systems. Kostera (1995: 332) uses religious metaphors to liken management educators and consultants to missionaries seeking to transfer management models to ECE to 'a religious mission: the capitalist West transmitting its managerial religion to the eastern "heathens"'. Also she likens business administration to religion, business organisation to religious institutions and economic rationality to God and argues that the management models sought not only to organise but also to provide the co-ordinates of being and acting in the world. Whilst Kostera treats the management education project as a colonising crusade, Dunn's (1999) study of attempts to impose US management practices in a Polish food processing firm shows that these practices are always negotiated, distorted and transformed by workers.

Two broad positions in connection with the future of employment and work in ECE and the former Soviet Union and our conceptualising of change are therefore suggestive. On the one hand, concern for the relational quality of identity, embodiment and performativity reasserts both the expressive and constitutive role of employment and work since 'the workplace is a principal site of identity formation' (Miller and Rose 1995: 427). For some, like Václav Havel in the quotation above, this development is potentially a source of guarded celebration as work is invested with social meaning and personal desires through which employees elaborate their identity (Miller and Rose 1995). For others, the workplace is regarded in a less benign light in which employees are subjected to increasingly invasive knowledges and technologies which reduce the scope for contestation, negotiation and resistance (du Gay 1996). As Thrift (1998: 60) puts it in connection with management fads: 'for all the caring rhetoric, lean can just as easily be mean and learning can mean stomach churning'. On the other hand it has been posited, in what has recently been termed the 'end of work debate' (Strangleman 2001), that employment and work-based meaning and identities are in the process of being corroded in advanced industrial societies.

While Beck (2000), amongst others (see for example Bauman (1998) and Gorz (1999)), centre their attention on the 'end of work' in the industrialised West, the uneven development of labour market exclusion, mass unemployment and increasingly flexibilised labour markets in ECE and the former Soviet Union is suggestive of a *partial* convergence with the experiences they each describe. What they point to, however, as do Gibson-Graham in a different way, is the importance of reconceptualising work and employment. Whether this is through forms of 'multi-activity' or through imagining and enacting diverse and emancipatory economic practices outside of emergent capitalism (Community Economies Collective 2001, Smith 2001), such a rethinking opens the possibility to move beyond neo-liberal policy prescriptions as well as overly circumscribed institutionalist analyses. What each of these sets of claims suggest, in their different ways, is a radical rethinking of work, employment, livelihood and transformation in post-Soviet societies.

Acknowledgement

We would like to thank Tim Strangleman for introducing us to and discussing with us the burgeoning recent literature on the future of work and employment.

Note

1   This section draws in part upon, and updates, the analysis in Smith (2000).

References

Amsden, A., Kochanowicsz, J. and Taylor, L. (1994) *The Market Meets its Match: Restructuring the Economies of Eastern Europe*, Harvard: Harvard University Press.

Bahro, R. (1978) *The Alternative in Eastern Europe*, New Left Books: London.

Barnes, T. (1996) *Logics of Dislocation*, Guilford Press: New York.

Bauman, Z. (1998) *Work, Consumption and the New Poor*, Open University Press: Buckingham.

Beck, U. (2000) *The Brave New World of Work*, Polity Press: Cambridge.

Begg, R. and Meurs, M. (1998) 'Writing a new song: Path dependency and state policy in reforming Bulgarian agriculture', in I. Szelenyi (ed.) *Privatizing the Land: Rural Political Economy in Post-Communist Societies*, Routledge: London, pp. 245–270.

Beynon, H. (1984) *Working for Ford*, Penguin: London.

Blanchard, O., Commander, S. and Coricelli, F. (1995) 'Unemployment and restructuring in Eastern Europe and Russia', in S. Commander and F. Coricelli (eds) *Unemployment, Restructuring, and the Labor Market in Eastern Europe and Russia*, Washington, D.C.: World Bank, pp. 289–329.

Braverman, H. (1974) *Labor and Monopoly Capital*, Monthly Review Press: New York.

Buck-Morss, S. (1995) 'Envisioning capital: political economy on display', *Critical Inquiry* 21: 434–467.

Burawoy, M. (1985) *The Politics of Production*, Verso: London.

Burawoy, M. (1988) 'Piece rates Hungarian style', in R. Pahl (ed.) *On Work*, Blackwell: Oxford, pp. 210–228.

Burawoy, M. (1992) 'A view from production: The Hungarian transition to capitalism', in C. Smith and P. Thompson (eds) *Labour in Transition*, Routledge: London, pp. 180–197.

Clarke, S. (ed.) (1998) *Structural Adjustment without Mass Unemployment? Lessons from Russia*, Cheltenham: Edward Elgar.

Clarke, S. (1993) 'The contradictions of the Soviet system', in S. Clarke, P. Fairbrother, M. Burawoy and P. Krotov, *What About the Workers? Workers and the Transition to Capitalism in Russia*, London: Verso.

Commander, S. and Coricelli, F. (eds) (1995) *Unemployment, Restructuring, and the Labor Market in Eastern Europe and Russia*, Washington, D.C.: World Bank.

Community Economies Collective (2001) 'Imagining and enacting noncapitalist futures', *Socialist Review*, forthcoming.

Cornia, F. (1996) 'Public policy and welfare conditions during the transition: An overview', *MOCT-MOST* 6: 1–17.

Creed, G. (1998) *Domesticating Revolution: From Socialist Reform to Ambivalent Transition in a Bulgarian Village*, University Park, PA: Pennsylvania State University Press.

Dunford, M. (1998) 'Differential development, institutions, modes of regulation and comparative transitions to capitalism: Russia, the Commonwealth of Independent States, and the former German Democratic Republic', in J. Pickles and A. Smith (eds) *Theorising Transition: The Political Economy of Post-Communist Transformations*, London: Routledge, pp. 76–111.

Dunford, M. and Smith, A. (2000) 'Catching up or falling behind? Economic performance and regional trajectories in the "new" Europe', *Economic Geography* 76 (2): 169–195.

Dunn, E. (1999) 'Slick salesmen and simple people: Negotiated capitalism in a privatised Polish firm', in M. Burawoy and K. Vedery (eds) *Uncertain Transition: Ethnographies of Change in the Postsocialist World*, Rowman and Littlefield: Lanham, pp. 125–150.

Einhorn, B. (1993) *Cinderella Goes to Market: Citizenship, Gender and Women's Movements in East-Central Europe*, London: Verso.

Elster, J., Offe, C. and Preuss, U.K. (1998) *Institutional Design in Post-Communist Societies: Rebuilding the Ship at Sea*, Cambridge University Press: Cambridge.

Fairbrother, P. and Rainnie, A. (2001) 'The state we are in (and against)', paper presented at the Employment Research Unit annual conference, University of Cardiff, September.

Du Gay, P. (1996) *Consumption and Identity at Work*, Sage: London.

Gibson-Graham, J.K. (1995) 'Identity and economic plurality: Rethinking capitalism and "capitalist hegemony"', *Society and Space* 13: 275–282.

Gibson-Graham, J.K. (1996) *The End of Capitalism (As We Knew It): A Feminist Critique of Political Economy*, Blackwell: Oxford.

Godson, J. (1981) 'The role of trade unions', in L. Schapiro and J. Godson (eds) *The Soviet Worker: Illusions and Realities*, Macmillan: Basingstoke, pp. 106–129.

Gorz, A. (1999) *Reclaiming Work: Beyond the Wage-Based Society*, Polity: Cambridge.

Gowan, P. (1995) 'Neo-liberal theory and practice for Eastern Europe', *New Left Review* 213: 3–60.

Grabher, G. (1994) 'The disembedded regional economy: The transformation of east German industrial complexes into western enclaves', in A. Amin and N. Thrift (eds) *Globalization, Institutions, and Regional Development in Europe*, Oxford University Press: Oxford, pp. 177–195.

Grabher, G. and Stark, D. (eds) (1997) *Restructuring Networks in Post-Socialism: Legacies, Linkages, and Localities*, Oxford: Oxford University Press.

Haraszti, M. (1977) *A Worker in a Workers' State*, Penguin: London.

Hardy, J. (1998) 'Cathedrals in the desert? Transnationals, corporate strategy and locality in Wroclaw', *Regional Studies* 32 (7): 639–652.

Hardy, J. and Rainnie, A. (1996) *Restructuring Krakow: Desperately Seeking Capitalism*, Mansell: London.

Heidenreich, M. (1992) 'Ostdeutsche Industriebetriebe zwischen Deindustrialisierung und Modernisierung', in M. Heidenreich (ed.) *Krisen, Kadar, Kombinate: Kontinuität in ostdeutsche Betrieben*, Edition Sigma: Berlin, pp. 335–365.

International Labour Organisation (1996) *Yearbook of Labour Statistics*, Geneva: ILO.

International Labour Organisation (1997) *Yearbook of Labour Statistics*, Geneva: ILO.

Kornai, J. (1992) *The Socialist System: The Political Economy of State Socialism*, Oxford: Clarendon.

Kostera, M. (1995) 'The modern crusade: The missionaries of management come to eastern Europe', *Management Learning* 26 (3): 331–352.

Mandel, D. (1992) 'A view from within: Interview with a soviet auto worker', in C. Smith and P. Thompson (eds) *Labour in Transition*, Routledge: London, pp. 149–179.

Meurs, M. (1998) 'Imagined and imagining equality in East Central Europe: Gender and ethnic differences in the economic transformation of Bulgaria', in J. Pickles and A. Smith (eds) *Theorising Transition: The Political Economy of Post-Communist Transformations*, London: Routledge, pp. 330–346.

Miller, P. and Rose, N. (1995) 'Production, identity and democracy', *Theory, Culture and Society* 24: 427–467.

Ministry of Labour, Social Affairs and the Family of the Slovak Republic (1999) *Social Policy of the Slovak Republic*, Bratislava: Ministry of Labour, Social Affairs and the Family of the Slovak Republic.

Offe, C. (1996) *Modernity and the State: East, West*, Polity: Cambridge.

Pankow, W. (1993) *Work Institution in Transformation*, Friedrich Ebert Stiftung: Warsaw.

Paukert, L. (1995) 'Economic transition and women's employment in four Central European countries, 1989–1994', *ILO Labour Market Papers* no. 7, International Labour Organisation, Geneva.

Pavlínek, P. and Smith, A. (1998) 'Internationalization and embeddedness in East-Central European transition: The contrasting geographies of inward investment in the Czech and Slovak Republics', *Regional Studies* 32 (7): 619–38.

Piasecka, E. and Rainnie, A. (2000) 'Small firms and local economic development in Poland', *Journal of Southern Europe and the Balkans* 2 (1): 25–37.

Pickles, J. and Smith, A. (eds) (1998) *Theorising Transition: The Political Economy of Post-Communist Transformations* London: Routledge.

Pine, F. (1996) 'Redefining women's work in rural Poland', in R. Abrahams (ed.) *After Socialism: Land Reform and Social Change in Eastern Europe*, Berghahn.

Polanyi, K. (1957 [1944]) *The Great Transformation: The Political and Economic Origins of Our Time*, Boston: Beacon.

Pollert, A. (1999) *Transformation at Work, in the New Market Economies of Eastern Europe*, Sage: London.

Rainnie, A. (1993) 'The reorganisation of large firms subcontracting', *Capital and Class*, 49.

Rainnie, A. and Hardy, J. (1999) 'Global strategies, local firms, working lives', in M. Upchurch (ed.) *The State and Globalisation*, Mansell: London.

Sachs, J. (1990) 'Eastern Europe's economies: What is to be done?' *The Economist* 13 January: 21–26.

Sik, E. (1994) 'From the multicoloured to the black and white economy: The Hungarian second economy and the transformation', *International Journal of Urban and Regional Research* 18 (1): 46–70.

Smith, A. (1997) 'Constructing capitalism? Small and medium enterprises, industrial districts and regional policy in Slovakia', *European Urban and Regional Studies* 4 (1): 45–70.

Smith, A. (1998) *Reconstructing the Regional Economy: Industrial Transformation and Regional Development in Slovakia*, Cheltenham: Edward Elgar.

Smith, A. (2000) 'Employment restructuring and household survival in "post-communist transition": Rethinking economic practices in Eastern Europe', *Environment and Planning A* 32: 1759–1780.

Smith, A. (2001) 'Culture/economy and spaces of economic practice: Positioning households in post-communism', unpublished ms.

Smith, A. and Pickles, J. (1998) 'Introduction: Theorising transition and the political economy of transformation', in J. Pickles and A. Smith (eds) *Theorising Transition: The Political Economy of Post-Communist Transformations*, London: Routledge, pp. 1–22.

Smith, A. and Swain, A. (1998) 'Regulating and institutionalising capitalisms: The micro-foundations of transformation in Eastern and Central Europe', in J. Pickles and A. Smith (eds) *Theorising Transition: The Political Economy of Post-Communist Transformations*, London: Routledge, pp. 25–53.

Strangleman, T. (2001) *The End of Work as the Future of Work? A Sociological Reflection*, Paper presented to the BSA Annual Conference, Manchester, April.

Stark, D. (1988) 'Rethinking internal labour markets', in R. Pahl (ed.) *On Work*, Blackwell: Oxford, pp. 325–345.

Stark, D. (1992a) 'Bending the bars of the iron cage: Bureaucratisation and informalisation in capitalism and socialism', in C. Smith and P. Thompson (eds) *Labour in Transition*, Routledge: London, pp. 41–72.

Stark, D. (1992b) 'Path dependence and privatization strategies in East Central Europe', *East European Politics and Societies* 6 (1): 17–54.

Swain, A. (1998) 'Governing the workplace: The workplace and regional development implications of automotive foreign direct investment in Hungary', *Regional Studies* 32 (7): 653–671.

Thirkell, J., Vickerstaff, S. and Petkov, K. (1998) *The Transformation of Labour Relations*, Oxford University Press: Oxford.

Thrift, N. (1998) 'The rise of soft capitalism', in A. Herod, G. Ó Tuathail and S.M. Roberts (eds) *An Unruly World? Globalization, Governance and Geography*, Routledge: London, pp. 25–71.

UNICEF (1997) *Children At Risk in Central and Eastern Europe: Perils and Promises*, UNICEF MONEE Project Regional Monitoring Report no. 4, Florence: UNICEF.

UNICEF (1999) *Women in Transition*, UNICEF MONEE Project Regional Monitoring Report no. 6, Florence: UNICEF, available at http://www.unicef-icdc.org/monee/pubs.htm.

Vickerstaff, S. and Thirkell, J. (2000) 'Instrumental rationality and European integration: Transference or avoidance of industrial relations institutions in Central and Eastern Europe', *European Journal of Industrial Relations* 6 (2): 237–251.

Wedel, J.R. (2000) 'Tainted transactions: Harvard, the Chubais Clan and Russia's ruin', *The National Interest*, No. 59: 23–34.

World Bank (1996) *World Development Report 1996*, New York: Oxford University Press.

2 The babble of euphemisms

Re-embedding social protection in 'transformed' labour markets

Guy Standing[1]

Introduction

Francis Bacon is often regarded as the father of modern scientific method, and among his aphorisms is the warning about the *idols of the marketplace*. He recognised that the words and terms we use shape the way we think and reflect our beliefs, often not based on any reality or knowledge. Raymond Williams (1976) put this in modern idiom when he drew up a long list of 'key words'. These tell us a lot about the era in which we live, and the dominant ideology of the time.

The language that permeated the 1980s and 1990s was delightfully loaded. One key word was a prefix – 'post', as in post-socialist, post-modern, post-Fordist, post-industrial, and post-transformation. Any term beginning with 'post' should suggest that the person using the term does not know where s/he is or where s/he is going. Perhaps it was appropriate. For the 1990s was an extraordinary decade, in which all certainties became dogmas or crumbled into yellowing parchments, bookshelves of earnest prose, left unread, unadmired and uncopied. This was mainly on the political left, but gradually it spread to the libertarians of the right. In September 1998, we had the delightful spectacle of two European Prime Ministers and one US President holding a much-publicised seminar peering into the mist trying to find 'the Third Way'. They were soon joined by a German Chancellor, and then by Brazilian and South African Presidents. In 2000, they tried *progressive governance* instead, but the Third Way had stuck.

Through looking at euphemisms used during the 1990s by policymakers, international organisations and a host of academics, commentators and earnest middle-aged 'consultants', this chapter is a plea for a new radical vision, one that puts distributive justice and *equality* firmly back at the centre of the debate about the type of society and economy that should be pursued in the 'post-twentieth' century. It starts, as the sub-title of the chapter might suggest, by recalling a central insight of Karl Polanyi (1944) in his *The Great Transformation*.

Liberally reinterpreted, Polanyi argued that periods of stability and societal security are followed by periods of economic and social upheaval, during which new forms of inequality and insecurity evolve. In such periods, the economy is dis-embedded from society. But gradually the inequalities and inequities threaten the sustainability of the economic system, because the losers become fed up and develop awkward habits that disturb the sleep of the winners. At that stage, contrary to crude versions of Marxism, the state takes steps to re-embed the economy in society, by introducing new mechanisms for redistribution that reduce inequalities to a functional level, a level that enables the economic dynamism to continue while providing enough people with enough economic security to make them tolerate or support the overall system. Clearly, writing in the 1940s, Polanyi saw the welfare state as re-embedding the economy after the Great Depression and the Second World War.

Since the 1980s, one may well conclude that globally we have been experiencing a Second Great Transformation. It has not been pretty. As developed at length elsewhere (Standing 1999a), essentially *both* mainstream models of socio-economic development pursued from 1945 until the 1970s collapsed or corroded under the strains of social, economic and technological change. From an historical point of view, one of the great ironies of the 1990s may well turn out to be that with the collapse of state socialism there was a rush to introduce social policies based on welfare state capitalism precisely at the time when the latter was losing its capacities and legitimacy. Compounding the sense of irony, there has been a wonderful, if tragic, spectacle whereby the libertarians and supply-side economists – the Chicago school of law and economics – have been rushing around using all sorts of tactics to persuade new political and financial elites in eastern Europe and the former Soviet Union to adopt neo-liberal models that have fizzed with much more ideology than institutional common sense. Many statesmen have obliged with corresponding zest.

To use less loaded language, the 1990s were a decade of experimentation in social policy. Although the avowed architect of *shock therapy*, the Polish Deputy Prime Minister, at the beginning of the decade warned that this was not a time for experiments because people were too poor for that, experimentation is precisely what we have seen. The bulk of this chapter will try to look at what went on in terms of the 'key words' of the continuing debates over 'post-communist' transformation and labour market changes.

Sequencing, shock therapy and state desertion

'After eight years, the process of post-communist transformation is largely complete'.
(Aslund, 1998)

The 1990s began well in East-Central Europe. The bright young economic advisers to bright untried politicians felt that they had a model, which some said had been tried and found to be successful in Bolivia and elsewhere. The euphemism they concocted was a wonder in itself – *'shock therapy'*. This conveyed the reasonable message that one must be harsh to be kind. Sometimes one also heard the virile term 'big bang', to capture the sense that many changes had to take place simultaneously. But it was neither the scale nor the speed that distinguished it. The critical part was the *sequencing* of policy changes that underlay the approach.[2] Price *liberalisation* was to be the first big bang. Of course, because the region's economy was characterised by huge monopolistic 'total enterprises', and because of 'monetary overhang', this unleashed price rises that threatened to become hyper-inflationary. So, the second phase of *stabilisation* had to be more draconian than if restructuring had preceded the price liberalisation. This stabilisation was actually a nice word for deflation, and – for those of a conspiratorial bent of mind – a justification for very heavy cuts in 'state spending'. For the liberal reformers, this had to be a good idea anyhow, because the 'state' was associated with a system that people had overthrown.

What transpired, as we know, was *state desertion* – one euphemism eschewed by the majority of participants in the debates during the 1990s. In some countries, it was just about possible to succeed if there was a reasonable public infrastructure in place, a strong national culture and assurances of adequate foreign financial and technical assistance. However, in many more countries these changes have had disastrous longer-term effects, to which we will return. In any case, cutting public spending, either directly by fiscal policy or indirectly by monetary policy, which resulted in unpaid salaries and so on, led to severe declines in national output, coupled with steeply rising poverty, mass unemployment, extremely rapid growth of economic inequalities and rising morbidity.

Nobody who promoted the reform strategies that were followed openly predicted any of these aspects of 'stabilisation'. Indeed, prominent economic advisers and international agencies systematically denied many of the outcomes. Later, as the evidence piled up, they attributed the 'regrettable' outcomes either to statistical illusion or to insufficiently rapid reforms, or a mixture of both. Some gave the trends a scientific name, such as 'the transformation recession', as if it were normal, predicted and even desirable.

During the phase of stabilisation, while old systems of social support were being wound up or left to rot, there was to be the introduction of a 'social safety net'. If one were to give prizes for best euphemism, this would have to be a candidate. Who could possibly be against a safety net to catch all those people who fell off the stabilising economy? In fact, the term contained a germ of a longer-term agenda for social policy. For some, it did mean introducing a welfare state either along Bismarckian or Beveridge lines. For others, and these have come to dominate the pressure emanating from the international community, it was a seemingly neutral way of tip-toeing towards the ultimate dream of full *privatisation of social policy*. Although I return to this, two euphemisms that gained popularity in the early and mid 1990s were 'targeting' and 'selectivity', as in 'targeting limited resources selectively to help the truly needy and deserving'.

After stabilisation in the sequencing of transformation came *privatisation*, meaning the transfer of state enterprises to private ownership coupled with the spread of *de novo* private firms. Only then, according to the shock therapists, would *restructuring* occur, because only then would there be a *hard budget constraint* guiding enterprise managements. Along with other commentators and economists, I argued in the early and mid 1990s that enterprise and institutional restructuring should have preceded price liberalisation, that the subsequent transfer of ownership should have been the opportunity to create a genuinely 'post-capitalist' economy, based on economic democracy and distributive justice, and that instead of a selective, conditional social security system there should have been a new form of universalism (Standing 1996). However, in fact, under the watchful eyes of the International Monetary Fund (IMF), the World Bank, the G7, the European Bank for Reconstruction and Development (EBRD) and the European Union (EU), shock therapy evolved into a neo-liberal 'revolution' that is still in progress.[3]

There was one other euphemism belonging to the macro-economic strategy that should also be highlighted – the 'budget deficit'. It seemed for a time that the IMF was setting a target of 5 per cent as the legitimate deficit. But for countries trying to gain entry into the European Union, the Maastricht Treaty level is 3 per cent and for some brave Ministers of Finance it must be reduced to 'zero'.[4] Whatever the target, it requires 'austerity' measures, most of all large and continuing cuts in 'public spending'. Clearly, any sensible person could see that public spending should be reduced, if not eliminated. It 'crowds out' private investment, which must be bad.[5]

One can detect several trends that flowed from the persistent campaign to cut budget deficits faster and more than previous governments had done or than had been done in neighbouring countries. First, since deficits arise from spending being greater than revenues, there were sharp cuts in spending. One way of reducing spending is to hold down salaries in the public sector, while cutting the level of employment more slowly. Unfortunately, this creates a problem – morale, efficiency and integrity in the public services drop. If salaries of civil servants and tax collectors drop to 30 per cent of the levels received by businessmen and private sector workers, leaving them unable to feed their families, it should not be surprising if they fill their pockets by other means. If teachers' salaries drop even lower, it should not be surprising if they moonlight, avoid/evade taxes and neglect their teaching in 'public' schools.

As spending is cut in various ways, tax and contribution rates have to rise to increase public revenue. Unfortunately, this further encourages the payers to meet with the civil servants to split differences. Revenues fall further, tax rates rise further, and the circle persists. But the problem, well known as it is, is further complicated because a large part of the 'public deficit' arises not from high current public spending but from rising debt repayments. An irony of the late 1990s was that, if you took away that factor, some governments would have been running 'budget surpluses' or would have been much closer to the magical 'zero' that some pundits love so much.[6] The trouble has been compounded by the fact that much of the government debt was built up in a period of very high interest rates due to the high inflation of the early 1990s. Meanwhile, governments plunged on with deflationary monetary and fiscal policy (particularly the latter) that intensified social hardships and restrained economic growth. Even in Russia and Ukraine, where there is much noise about the need to improve tax collection, actual tax revenue is quite high as a percentage of GDP by comparison with industrialised market economies.

Of course, one cannot interpret the macro-economics of the reforms without recognising the ideological agenda. Analysis and evaluation are complicated, in that the ideology has shaped the reforms in an almost Darwinian fashion, giving little attention to the supposedly short-term 'transitional' human costs, in the interest of creating an economic and social environment for the survival of the fittest. Towards the end of the decade euphemisms that had a quiet start at their outset were treated with more gravitas – words like 'strain' and 'sustainability'.[7]

Most significantly of all, at the end of the century there was official discomfort over the 'Washington consensus' that had shaped economic, social and labour reforms in Central and Eastern Europe, just as it had shaped 'structural adjustment' programmes in developing countries. The World Bank's former Chief Economist, Stiglitz, attacked that approach and – predictably – spoke of the 'post-Washington consensus'. Given his subsequent resignation, it is not yet clear whether the claim that it has changed its approach amounts to a real change.[8] But one point is clear – the euphemisms are changing.

Perhaps the most influential of the new breed is *social capital*, an almost infinitely elastic notion that could become a prime candidate for the prize for best euphemism of the early 2000s.[9] It is a means of bringing back 'the State' into acceptable discourse, yet it does so cleverly by not alarming those hostile to a 'large State' by referring to 'capital'. To say that countries in eastern Europe have floundered economically because they have not invested in the State does not guarantee the same nods of approval as to state that they have failed because they have not invested in social capital.

Labour market developments

While economic and political 'transformations' and 'transitions' were taking place, labour markets evolved in most countries of the region. The way they evolved varied, and there were sharp differences between central European countries such as the Czech Republic and Hungary and eastern European countries including all the Commonwealth of Independent States (CIS). To assess social policy developments and options, one needs to identify the main labour market trends, however schematically. The key words have included 'unemployment', 'black economy', 'informal economy', 'administrative leave', 'wage arrears', 'benefit, pension and tax arrears', 'minimum wage', 'real wage rises' and 'unemployment benefits'. Let us consider just a few of them.

Unemployment

All commentators expected unemployment to rise in the early 1990s. In many countries, it rose to double-digit levels, and in some it rose to over 25 per cent. However, in several countries unemployment officially remained extremely low by any standards, even though national income and output were dropping by more than 50 per cent. Or at least we were supposed to believe that unemployment was minimal. In this regard, one should differentiate between eastern and central European 'transformations'. Let us concentrate on the biggest and most strategic countries. For much of the 1990s, several international organisations, including the IMF, World Bank and Organisation for Economic Cooperation and Development (OECD), blithely told the world, again and again, that the unemployment rates in Russia and Ukraine were less than 2 per cent, as they were supposedly in almost all CIS countries. Prominent economic advisers to governments and such bodies told the world the same story, that there was a soft budget constraint or that workers were being very flexible, preferring to take wage cuts rather than lose their jobs. This picture suited governments, and advocates of the economic strategy – because they could claim policies were succeeding – and it suited the international financial agencies because they did not have to allocate resources to policies to deal with mass unemployment.

There was a deeply disturbing dishonesty in this story. No industrial country in history has had a major slump without mass unemployment. It was no different in those countries of Eastern Europe. I and colleagues were visiting dozens of enterprises in Russia, Ukraine and elsewhere at the time, and *everywhere* they were slashing employment, visibly shrinking as centres of human activity over successive visits. You had to be blind or worse to believe that there was no 'disemployment'. If you went into the streets of St Petersburg, Ivanovo, or many other cities, you saw beggars and ex-workers selling old clothes. Even the official employment figures showed sharp declines in employment, despite repeated claims to the contrary.

The fact is that most of those eased out of employment did not *register* as unemployed. This does not mean that they were thriving in the 'grey', 'informal' and 'black' economy, as has been suggested by some wishing to support the old story. To some extent, in some countries labour force surveys have shown that when non-registered unemployed are counted, the actual unemployment rate is several times the registered rate. For instance, in Ukraine even in 1998 the official registered unemployment rate was 1.5 per cent. Labour force survey data gave a figure of 10.7 per cent. More significantly still, as we know, several million people (mainly young and middle-aged men) have died prematurely in the two big countries of Eastern Europe, while suicides, morbidity and imprisonment among the unemployed have helped to keep down the official rates of unemployment there and elsewhere.[10] Millions of others were unemployed but were not counted as such.

Other reasons for real unemployment being higher than recorded unemployment include the extensive use of 'early retirement' – a euphemism very familiar to Western European policymakers. In some countries, anyone becoming unemployed in their 50s has been likely to find their way into classification as 'retired early'. Indeed, in some countries, including Russia, a woman becoming unemployed at age 54 automatically is excluded from figures on registered and total unemployment. This has been one reason for the gross distortion of unemployment, because whereas someone of any age (even in their 70s) who is employed is counted as employed, all those above the early retirement age who are unemployed, or who state that they want and are looking for a job, are classified as outside the labour force. One recalls hundreds of 'early retirees' standing or lying in Nevski Prospect in St Petersburg and in other streets elsewhere. Most had their hands out or were holding out old clothes or Coca-Cola bottles to obtain some money, with which to 'enjoy' their early retirement.

There is still a great deal of confusion about unemployment in the whole region. Too much is read into recorded levels and trends in 'registered' unemployment.[11] One suspects that the registration numbers are not good proxies either for total unemployment or for trends in it. In some countries, such as Poland, it seems that labour force survey estimates are reasonably close to the registered totals. In others, notably Russia, Ukraine and other CIS countries, the differences have been huge and variable. One suspects that the labour force data are unreliable as well, although some statistical offices have made great strides in collecting information. Cross-national comparisons of registered rates are surely dubious. And if we recognise that 'employment' figures are also suspect, and likely to become more so in more flexible and heterogeneous labour markets, we might conclude that citing percentage rates to one decimal point is less than impressive scholarship.

Administrative leave

Into this slightly fuzzy world stepped new euphemisms. One reason for unemployment not rising by as much as one might have expected was the imaginative use of 'administrative leave'. For firms required to pay severance pay of several months wages if they made workers redundant, it was much less costly just to tell the workers to take 'leave', while leaving their work history book on the premises. For their part, the workers dared not 'quit', because that would disentitle them to severance pay and jeopardise their right to unemployment benefit. Moreover, with the IMF-inspired 'tax-based incomes policy', it paid enterprises to keep the number of 'dead souls' as high as possible, because this lowered the average wage (total wage bill divided by number of workers on the books, which determined whether they paid tax) and allowed them to pay themselves and their core workers higher wages.

In Russia, Ukraine and elsewhere, we have found that about a third of workers in many industrial enterprises were on such 'administrative leave'. Adding such workers to the unemployment figures – and deducting them from the employment figures – would give a more accurate estimate of real unemployment. They had no prospect of returning to jobs, yet they had no right to claim unemployment benefits either. Their impoverishment was the reality of this 'flexibility'. Of course, some died, some became socially ill and thus removed from the 'active labour force', some went into crime, went into prison and out of the 'active labour force', and some went into the 'informal economy'. But there is no evidence to suggest that in those or other countries in the region large numbers of the workers who have become dis-employed have gone into *thriving* informal activities providing them with high incomes and security.

The informal sector

The notion of informal sector has had a chequered history, with numerous alternative terms competing with it, such as 'the uncivil economy'. Two observers can see the same picture, and one can say, 'the economy is in a less serious state than it seems because most of those not in employment are in the informal sector', while the other can say, 'the situation is grave, with more and more people trying to survive in the informal sector'. The trouble is that too much is compressed into a single notion. Those who presume that all those in 'informal' – non-recorded – activities are hand-to-mouth survival activities cannot demonstrate that this is the case. And those who purport to believe that national income and employment are understated because of the oversight of a vast amount of productive informal activities are merely revealing a bias. We simply do not know. The notion becomes an all-purpose term to mean whatever we wish, good or bad.

There is little doubt that with growing diversity in forms of production and forms of labour relationships, and with more flexible labour markets, simple models based on standard employment conceived in terms of full-time, stable, unionised labour are likely to be misleading. However, we need to disaggregate types of work, types of remuneration and types of survival activity. There is no such entity as a homogeneous informal sector, and social scientists do their analysis and their field a disservice to present papers and reports making assertions about 'the informal sector'.

Wage arrears

In the aftermath of the deep 'stagflation' or 'transformation slump' of the early 1990s, along came a new euphemism, which has distorted politics and social policy in Eastern Europe since about 1995 – 'wage arrears'. If a firm in any country has no funds, has no work for its workers and has no prospect of having work or funds, the workers are or should be called unemployed. The huge phenomenon called wage arrears, affecting many millions of workers, is a misnomer. It is widespread in Russia, Ukraine, Serbia, Kyrgyzstan, and elsewhere.

Unless enterprises and government authorities can be persuaded to face the fact that people in places where there is no work and no money to pay them are really unemployed, then economic, labour market and social policy will all continue to be misdirected. An enterprise that could survive if it had 200 workers that has instead 1,000 because it dare not make 800 redundant is in an impossible position. In the end, the probability must be high that all 1,000 will be in the streets. Moreover, if the workers and the governments think that the problem is finding funds to pay wages for doing something for which there is no tangible or marketable outcome they will try to borrow to pour money into an unsustainable process.

Minimum wages

While unemployment has been distorted in these imaginative ways, in most countries across the region several other euphemisms have made their contribution to a dis-embedded social policy. Wages are a good place to start. The old wage-tariff system of the Soviet era was an intricate edifice, where 'leveling' was more fiction than either apologists or critics liked to admit. Then along came the reformers, and one of the well-meaning measures was 'the minimum wage'. This was never what it pretended to be. Conceptually, it is an old social democratic instrument for protecting the low-paid in the labour market, and was embraced by some policymakers in the region as part of a 'socially regulated labour market' (a term much used in the early 1990s). But the neo-liberal economic advisers to 'reformist' governments, the main international financial agencies and their protégés in the region did not like minimum wages, seeing them as socialistic or as labour market 'rigidities'. A rigidity is anathema for our reformers.

The main trouble is that the minimum wage has never been what most people outside the transformed countries think it is. At best, it has been a measure to limit the level of some social transfers, such as unemployment benefits and family benefits. Governments were under pressure to cut public (state) spending, and one way of keeping social spending down was to allow the level of the minimum wage in real terms to fall continuously to levels at which it was impossible to live. And then we had the situation when a government proposed to double the national minimum wage and the head of an international financial agency stood up and denounced it – when the doubling would have meant that the minimum wage would have been raised to about 20 per cent of the income needed for 'physiological survival'.[12]

While the minimum wage has mostly been a bad joke, analysis of labour market trends and refinement of policy needs have been hampered or distorted by the realities surrounding 'wages'. To give an example, you may read 'real wages rose by 10 per cent last year'. For several reasons, the one point on which one could be reasonably confident is that they did not rise by 10 per cent last year. Often, wage payments take place, quite literally, under the table, or bonuses and non-wage forms of remuneration are given to some high-income groups much more than they report. At the same time, there is ample evidence that many lower-income workers do not receive all the wages that are reported. For instance, the Russian Goskomstat statistics report contractual wages, not what workers actually receive. A result is that some economists have claimed that labour markets *must* be tight, because real wages have risen. Or they have argued that high unemployment is due to 'wage rigidity', because real wages have not fallen. So, wage developments have been mysterious. Perhaps the biggest difficulty is that because the money wage was such a low proportion of total remuneration in the old system, a monetisation of wages would reveal a rise in 'wages', while a withering of enterprise-based benefits and facilities would imply a deterioration.

Active labour market policy

Another candidate for best euphemism of the decade is 'active' labour market policy. It is juxtaposed with 'passive' policy. Active has a virile aura, whereas passive has an aura of inadequacy. Originally, the term 'active labour market policy' was used in the Rein-Meidner Swedish model to mean 'counter-cyclical' policy. In the 1980s and 1990s it came to mean almost any measure to remove the unemployed from the unemployment pool. Numerous politicians, commentators and social scientists have used the term in a casual, all-embracing and uncritical way. An irony of active policy is that often the reality has been that a state bureaucrat is the active party, leaving the unemployed person to accept directions on what he or she must do in order to receive some income transfer. The person becomes passive. By contrast, the 'deplorable' passive policy of giving a benefit to someone without obligations actually allows that person to be active, by making choices.

Typically, so-called active policy includes labour market training schemes, obligation to participate in 'public works' (a euphemism in itself), employment or wage subsidies, and (often) labour supply-reducing policies such as early retirement. Lots of positive tendencies are attributed to these. Yet if we inspect reality with a slightly jaundiced perspective, or just as trained social scientists, we should feel uncomfortable. Claims about the 'success' of many of these policies are usually unverified and even unverifiable. Most are subject to high *deadweight effects* – the activities, if economically viable, would have taken place anyhow – or high *substitution effects* – those placed in the schemes or subsidised jobs merely substitute for others. Often the introduction of employment subsidies is a direct encouragement to lower labour efficiency.

Case studies can reveal farcical anomalies. Several years ago, when asked by the Russian Federal Employment Service to devise a labour market information system for it, we tried to identify what constituted 'public works'. In one oblast, local farms were provided with subsidies to help them pay sheep shearers, and one could guess where the money ended up. In another oblast, a major insulin producer arranged with the local employment office to receive a subsidy to enable it to lay off workers and convert to produce vodka with the remainder. This was classified as an active labour market policy. One could multiply such cases, and certainly cite examples of training schemes that scarcely deserve the name or positive connotations linked to the term. Active they may be; useful should not be presumed.

Dis-embedded social policy

We need not repeat a description of the character and features of the social protection system of the pre-transformed economies, other than to state that it was comprehensive, enterprise or organisation-based, and ultimately limited in quality. Since then there have been many changes. In order to assess the direction of those changes, it is useful to recall the stylised facts that testify to the medium-term effects of the transformations. Between 1989 and 1996 (or the latest dates for which relevant data are available):

- Male life expectancy at birth declined in Azerbaijan, Belarus, Bulgaria, Estonia, Latvia, Lithuania, Kazakhstan, Kyrgyzstan, Moldova, Romania, Russia, and Ukraine. It may have declined in several other countries for which there are no data.
- Female life expectancy at birth declined in most of those countries, albeit by less.
- Marriage rates plunged in *every* country for which there are data (25), and the divorce rate rose in most of them (18).
- The birth rate fell in *every* country (except Croatia); the share of births outside marriage rose in *every* country.
- In several major countries the population fell, in several cases to a large extent.
- Abortion rates have been high, in six countries abortions exceeding the number of live births; in Russia and Romania there are two abortions for every live birth.
- Kindergarten enrolment rates plunged in most countries; primary school enrolment rates fell in 22 countries, rising in only two; technical secondary school enrolment rates, while remaining high in central Europe, fell all across eastern Europe and the CIS.
- The crime rate rose sharply in most countries – more than doubling in central European countries and in some others; the proportion of youths convicted of crimes rose very sharply in most countries; homicide rates have doubled in some.
- In every country for which there are data, earnings inequality increased, as measured by Gini coefficients.

Are these the statistics of success? [13]

The 1990s was a decade in which two rhetorical stances dominated social policy in central and eastern Europe. To call it a struggle between two schools of thinking would be giving too much credit to those favouring 'social insurance', because those favouring the privatisation of social policy were leading all the charges and had the rather important advantage of being backed by powerful forces from outside the region.

The limitations of social insurance of either the Bismarckian or Beveridge variety have been much greater in the transformed economies. If up to half of economic activity is 'informal' and if half the workforce are in and out of jobs, or unemployed for long periods, or receiving wages that fluctuate wildly, or receiving payments in forms that do not look like 'wages', it should be hard to imagine the vast majority of the population building up entitlements and making regular contributions to Pay As You Go (PAYG) schemes.

In trying to capture the dynamics of social protection and labour market policy in transforming economies it helps to recall Polanyi's (1944) *patterns of social integration*, and in particular the mechanisms of reciprocity and redistribution. Social insurance has, at its best, the intention of achieving reciprocity based on contributions matching benefits; its redistributive role has always been modest, being mainly over the life cycle. It has also promoted a sense of social solidarity. It is rather ill-suited to a highly flexible, fragmented labour market.

By contrast, the neo-liberal model that has come mainly across the Atlantic during the 1980s and 1990s, based on libertarianism and the *new paternalism*, essentially seeks to disembed social policy from society and turn it into an arena for self-regulating markets. In its celebration of the liberty of the individual, it rejects the solidaristic character of social policy and rejects the legitimacy of redistribution. Let the market decide. And for the losers, they must prove they are *deserving poor* as opposed to *undeserving poor*, and if they do that they can rely on a charitable state and the philanthropic kindness of the rich (who are, unless proven by the courts to be otherwise, deserving rich because, following Nozick (1974), justice is only a question of contractual propriety).[14]

Whatever their philosophical and social policy foundations, most social transfers have moved in similar directions – with greater selectivity, more restrictive conditions for entitlement, lower levels of benefit and resort to more means-testing, behaviour-testing and arbitrary decision-making at the local level. Meanwhile, a new euphemism swept through the corridors of power throughout the region – the Big C – Chile. The mystique surrounding the Chilean pension scheme is one of those historical oddities that are fascinating.[15] Gradually, there has evolved faith in *three-tier pensions* and multi-tier social benefits of other kinds. Chile has not been the only model being copied, but it has been enormously influential. Essentially, what one sees being introduced in countries as dissimilar as Hungary, Kazakhstan and Poland is a system in which there is a low, basic, means-tested state pension, with a mandatory private scheme for all those in formal employment and a voluntary third tier, dependent on individual or collective agreements (leaving space for a fourth tier in which an individual takes out a voluntary personal savings scheme).

One sees somewhat similar tierism in health services and in schooling, and one can anticipate it spreading to other social services. Essentially the partial privatisation is passing on more of the costs and risks to 'users', or ordinary people. The resultant insecurity and lack of coverage for the poor, the regularly unemployed and those in 'flexiworker' statuses has already produced a highly fragmented social structure, in which the affluent are detaching themselves from an increasingly selective, residual welfare system and in which the flexiworkers and marginalised are being detached from it by lacking the entitlements to its nominal schemes. The poor are being left dependent on charity, on means-tested assistance that is hard to obtain and often scarcely worth obtaining, and on their wits, their willingness to resort to petty crime, begging, prostitution and other 'unsocial' means of survival.

Unemployment benefits

Most countries have introduced unemployment benefits. We assume that these are sums of money given to the unemployed to compensate them for becoming unemployed, to enable them to look for alternative employment and to give them an income on which to survive. Unfortunately for the unemployed, that is not quite what has happened. In all countries where unemployment benefits were introduced (beginning in Hungary in 1986), there has been a steady stream of *conditions* introduced, limiting entitlement to them. At the same time, more of the workforces of most countries have found their experience and status resulting in them not qualifying for benefits. Finally, even if they do qualify for benefits, the level has been held down to very low levels.

In Russia, according to the statistics, the average benefit has been equal to the minimum wage.[16] Yet the minimum wage has been about 16 per cent of the physiological survival minimum. Moreover, many employment offices have not been provided with the funds with which to pay the benefits, so they have gone unpaid, or in some cases the claimants have been offered old shoes or coats or bread in lieu of benefits. Yet the statistics report the average, because they report what is supposed to be the case at the limit (i.e., the benefit must be at least equal to the minimum wage). Only those unemployed in relatively affluent areas and those capable of finding ways through the bureaucracy in such areas have been ensured benefits. Most of the unemployed are effectively marginalised and subject to such income insecurity that they become detached from the mainstream of society.[17]

In other countries, the number of months during which an unemployed person could receive benefits has been steadily cut. In Poland, immediately after the duration was cut from twelve to six months, the unemployment rate improved dramatically. One can be confident that cuts in eligibility duration elsewhere have had similarly 'beneficial' effects.

In various countries, the notion of *quitting* one's job has been used to block a person's entitlement to unemployment benefits. So, you could go to work for six months, not be paid and 'quit' in disgust, and you would promptly be blocked from receiving benefits. You would become one of the growing body of 'undeserving poor' – a nineteenth-century euphemism that crept back into reputable discourse in the 1990s.

Thus unemployment benefits have become a residual mechanism, a means of control and a means of segregating the marginalised. A man or a woman who cannot find legitimate employment must either act as a 'blackleg', helping to drive down wage rates by accepting any employment for whatever wage is offered, or opt for informal activity that has the effect of fuelling the *de novo* economy, eroding the legitimacy and capacity of the social security system and acting as a disciplining device for those in jobs.[18] Or, of course, they could drift into the fastest growing market of many economies – the criminal market, which has been an unintended device for accelerating accumulation in previous economic transformations (as in Chicago in the USA of the 1930s). Or they could drift off the human stage by dying or falling prey to one or other of the revived social illnesses that have emerged in many communities.

Above all, with the drift to selectivity, privatisation and multi-tierism, the most crucial development has been the growth in the number of people dependent on *means-tested social assistance* benefits of one kind or another. The rise in numbers has been extraordinary, and the proportions of the population *dependent* on means-tested benefits have reached very high levels (Standing 1997–98). The trend is continuing. In July 1998, for instance, in Slovakia the Social Assistance Act came into effect, making most state benefits means-tested.

It is also worth reiterating a point we all know yet too often neglect: the *poverty rate* is a euphemism. If governments or their advisers do not like the numbers or trend in the numbers of people who fall below the *poverty line*, or do not wish to fund schemes to support too many people, the definition of poverty can be improved.[19] The trouble is that a euphemism is a term concealing a real meaning. The notion of poverty is inherently nebulous, and can be manipulated in many ways. In any country one could devise numerous rates of poverty, and in most that is what happens. Most revealing is the difference that emerges between 'consumer basket' measures and self-assessments ('Leiden measures'). For instance, in Hungary one survey found that over a third of the population defined themselves as poor, whereas only 6 per cent were counted as poor through having incomes below the minimum pension (Andorka and Zsolt 1997). The EBRD were even more encouraging, reporting in 1998 that only 2 per cent of the population were in poverty (EBRD 1998). In Ukraine, the official poverty rate has fluctuated, but whereas a majority used to consider themselves in the 'middle class' now a majority of the adult population considers themselves to be in the poor working class. In Russia, whereas recently the official poverty rate was 21 per cent, opinion polls have regularly found that over half the population consider themselves as poor.

Poverty is pervasive deprivation, and if the social support system is dismantled people's *insecurity* becomes an impoverishing experience even if their money income would enable them to buy that bundle of goods and services used to define the poverty line. One of the most intriguing findings in the region has been that in Uzbekistan the Russians have been dying to a much greater extent than native Uzbeks in response to the impoverishment process. One way of interpreting this is that the Russians lack the institutional support network of *reciprocity*, so vital in communities under stress.

Although one should develop this theme at much greater length than is possible in this chapter, the key point about the drift to social assistance is that means-testing, behaviour-testing and conditional social assistance are impoverishing in themselves. They are regulatory devices. Most means-tested schemes everywhere have a low *take up rate*, i.e., a low proportion of those eligible to receive them actually do receive them. The reasons for this are well known, and the term 'take up' is actually slightly misleading, suggesting that everybody not taking the benefits do this voluntarily, when in fact many do not receive them because they are disqualified by some bureaucrat or are ignorant or are prevented from obtaining them because of the cost of travel to a distant office, or some other such reason. One cannot imagine any economist or other social scientist believing that complex, conditional, 'selective' schemes could work well in a huge country with an undeveloped administrative apparatus. Therefore, encouraging such countries to adopt complex 'tested' schemes must reflect other motives.

The spread of targeting has been rapid and pervasive. Evaluations of its efficiency or equity have lagged. One valuable examination of the Mahalla social assistance scheme in Uzbekistan found that there was little correlation between household income and probability of receipt of benefit (Coudouel *et al.* 1998). To some extent, this might have been because income is not a reliable proxy for 'welfare', as measured by Sen-type capabilities, although receipt was also unrelated to children's nutritional status. But if that is the case, schemes based on income tests will display systematic targeting inefficiency, even *if* the objectives of targeting were clearly determined (Atkinson 1995). Some social scientists might suggest that such drawbacks could be overcome by decentralisation and administration by local authorities and non-governmental organisations. But this route allows scope for arbitrary and subjective discretion by local rulers or interests.

Latently, targeting in social policy is an ideological tool. The privatisation and multi-tierism of social policy are part of the vision of an individualistic society. Yet Central and Eastern European and CIS countries have become societies on the edge. If they go on as they have been going in the 1990s, deep-rooted fragmentation beckons. The billionaires will be detached from their surroundings – mocking the system, sending their money into the international financial markets and bypassing any national regulatory system – while the middle class will wallow in their passive existence of consumerism and the losers will either sink into the shadows of anomie and social illnesses or become willing recruits of the gangs seeking retributive justice. The *mafiosation* of the labour market and of society will be deep, perhaps until the sons and daughters of the successful rogues adopt the manners and style of the natural rulers. Of course, this is an exaggeration.

Re-embedding social policy in flexible economies

The values of the market are in danger of being out of control, and it is essential to re-embed the economy in society as soon as possible. Historically, a great transformation reaches a stage when the inequalities and insecurities have grown to such an extent that they threaten to undermine the economy's sustainability. This was the situation globally as the century came to an end. In Central and Eastern Europe, even more than in less 'transformed' or less 'post-' regions, re-embedding will depend on how social relations are *patterned*. If a fragmented, individualistic society is to be overcome, policymakers will have to devise ways of ensuring elements of social solidarity and socio-economic *security*, and ensure that distributive justice is steadily improving. As argued elsewhere (Standing 1999a), this will require a particular mix of institutional developments and fiscal policy. Three measures will surely become crucial, once critics of current trends reflect on the inadequacy of trying to create welfare states along the lines of one or other variant developed in the last 50 years in other parts of Europe.

First, social solidarity and redistributive justice will not occur or be sustained unless there are strong collective institutions to give voice to the vulnerable and socially deprived. This will have to go beyond the types of neo-corporatism that have been tried over the past few years (Standing 1997). So-called 'tripartite governance' of social and labour market policy is not promising. *Representation security*, through *voice regulation* of the economy, labour markets, social services and social protection generally, will require trades unions to evolve into something more relevant to the flexible, informal economies taking shape, and those that do evolve will do so through joining forces with *representative non-government organisations* in new citizenship associations, probably local in character and surely democratic, to represent today's and tomorrow's employed, unemployed, others working but not recognised as such, and those on the edge of society. Without collective voice to put pressure on the winners, no economic system will redistribute more than a residual amount to placate the losers. One term that might be appropriate for the sort of development that is required is *solidaristic individualism*. Redistribution does not occur unless the winners fear that the losers will make life too uncomfortable for them. Solidarity does not mean charity, it means rights recognised as universal.

Second, the means of redistribution must be in tune with the era of globalisation. There is an inherent tendency in the global 'free market' economy for the functional distribution of income to shift from labour to capital. In many places the incidence of tax on labour has been rising, the incidence on capital has been declining; subsidies for workers and ordinary consumers have been cut, but subsidies to capital have been rising remarkably. The only feasible way of overcoming these tendencies is *economic democracy*, through enabling society to ensure the surplus is redistributed to the citizens of an integrated society. There is a long way to go before mechanisms are in place, but surely no re-embedding can occur without powerful moves in that direction.

Third, there is a need to renew *universalism* as the principle of social protection. The reality of the future will surely be flexible labour markets and economic informalisation, characterised by people combining a variety of activities in a variety of statuses, and by firms multiplying and turning over, here today, gone tomorrow, back in a different guise the day after, while big enterprises switch profit centres, sub-contract activities, contract out their employment function and so on. Of course, there will long be some big corporations and many people will be in stable career employment. But making that latter image the norm is neither practical nor desirable. Society should be such as to facilitate and celebrate diversity of life styles and work styles.

It is in that seemingly rarefied context that the fundamental requirement for distributive justice will be *equal basic security*, for otherwise the flexibility will continue to be a winner-takes-all, loser-loses-all world, in which fragmentation will grow and in which the winners will vote to strengthen the policing of the poor while the middle class will vote to erode the state transfers and services, and basic security, of one minority group after another, none of which alone would have enough voice to check the erosion, and once having lost themselves would be reluctant to come to the defence of the next group in the line for cuts.

In the scenario of flexibility and informalisation, making income security the basis of social policy must be the crucial part of any 'post-' strategy or vision. A basic *citizenship income* as a right is even more appropriate in the chaotic circumstances of central and eastern Europe than elsewhere. The arguments for this are presented elsewhere, and will not be repeated here. Suffice it to assert that neither social insurance nor multi-tierism with means testing as envisaged by the neo-liberal policy agenda offers the prospect of income security or solidaristic social policy. And suffice it for me to end by urging all those sympathetic to the goal of making basic income security for all a reality early in this new century to join us in an organisation dedicated to supporting efforts in that direction, BIEN (Basic Income European Network).

No sensible person would argue for going back to the nastiness and stagnation of state socialism. Critics of what has been called the transformation still need to make that point, because those adopting the mantle of intellectual leaders of the reform process have continued to have a tendency to answer criticisms by using labels that refer to the past. However, the critics are gaining confidence, and will gain much more once an alternative decent vision of distributive justice has been articulated.

As for what has gone on, it would be misleading to suggest that social policy reform has lagged behind the economic and political transformation in the region (World Bank 1996). The changes have been substantial and have been introduced at an extraordinarily rapid rate, in a flurry of legislation, 'decrees' and regulatory devices introduced by less transparent means. In general, they have pushed most countries in the direction of something close to what Richard Titmuss (1963) called the residual welfare state or what Esping-Andersen (1990) called the liberal welfare regime. The state has increased the degree of socio-economic differentiation through its social protection policies and social services policies. Targeting on the poor is divisive. As Titmuss remarked, benefits that are just for the poor will be poor benefits.

Intellectually, this is an exciting stage of the social and economic restructuring process. This has been the first revolution in history led by international financial capital and international financial agencies. There has been an effort to put on a mask of 'therapy' to match the traumatising experience of the 'shock'. No one should doubt that many of the spokesmen and directors of the agencies and organisations involved in steering the reform process are concerned about the poverty and insecurity that have spread. Yet laws of finance are not the laws of society. The failure in the early 1990s was a lack of socio-economic strategy, a lack of integration of social and economic policy. Ironically, while the rhetoric focused on *liberty, rights* and *democracy*, it was the failure to promote and protect *economic and social rights* that has made the transformation such a mess. The task now is to rectify the imbalance, putting economic and social rights at the heart of the post-post-transformation.

Notes

1 This chapter does not represent the views of the International Labour Organisation, and should not be attributed to the ILO.
2 This was part of the so-called 'Washington consensus' and 'structural adjustment programmes'.
3 When wise commentators wish to criticise the international financial institutions with a sense of delicacy, they refer to the need to reposition the 'financial architecture'.
4 In April 1998 in Poland, Leszek Balcerowicz, reinstated as Minister of Finance and Deputy Prime Minister, stated that he wanted to cut the budget deficit from the current 3.5 per cent of GDP to zero by 2003.
5 This is a lovely euphemism. The image is of a fat bully (public) pushing the virile youth (private) out of the swimming pool. The simplistic dualism of private and public has been unfortunate.
6 Russia was criticised for running a budget deficit of over 6 per cent in the late 1990s. But more than half the deficit was accounted for by interest payments. By the first quarter of 1998, excluding the latter, the government was running a budget surplus of about 1 per cent of GDP, but the interest payments were nearly 5 per cent of GDP. The debt has been mostly short maturing, so placing a heavy continuing burden.
7 The idea of strain is an interesting one. It is supposed to measure the scale of required resource reallocation for 'transformation'. It has been defined as the distance between two vectors of prices and quantities at the outset and at the level deemed to identify the country as fully adjusted. See, for instance, Daianu (1997). One might wonder whether one could define an appropriate vector by which to define an 'undistorted' economy.
8 For an assessment, see Standing (1999b). This was published in September 2000 in *Development and Change*.
9 After writing this paper, I read Ben Fine's (1999) critique of the notion of social capital, and share his scorn.
10 The statistics and analysis behind the statements made in this and preceding paragraphs are elaborated elsewhere. See, for example, Standing (1996, 1998).
11 Even the UN Economic Commission for Europe has tended to do this, although in most respects it has been the best international body in terms of its reporting of developments. In its 1999 report it stated that in most of the countries unemployment had been falling since 1993, until 1998 when it started to increase. This came from relying on the registration data (UNECE 1999: 128). Later in the Report it has a short section recognising differences, but certainly not all the reasons for doubting both sources of information.
12 There are no prizes for guessing which country and which international agency were involved. In several countries the minimum wage has been less than 10 per cent of the official subsistence minimum, in several others it has hovered around 20 per cent of that.
13 Just one more caught my attention. Anders Aslund recently described Georgia as in a 'boom'. At the time, the GDP was 32 per cent of what it had been in 1989, according to the EBRD. When an economy has shrunk to such levels, the growth rate could be quite high and the population would still be very poor!

14 The charitable act creates a hierarchical bond, making a moral debtor of the recipient, which is intrinsically humiliating. I owe this point to Zsuzsa Ferge.

15 One of the most ironic experiences this writer had during those years was being ushered into the World Bank office in Kiev in 1994 and finding a Chilean as its head, an enthusiast about the Chilean reforms, with a map of Chile on the wall behind his huge desk. His office had previously been the office of the First Secretary of the Ukrainian Communist Party.

16 There is no reason for this being the case. The complex formula for calculating unemployment benefits gives the appearance of a modern rational system. In practice, it has never worked like that.

17 An anecdote may be permitted. In 1997, the woman in charge of one Russian city's employment service told me that she was beyond despair. In the previous three months, 23 of the registered unemployed had committed suicide. They no longer wanted the shoes being offered as unemployment benefits. Of course, this is an extreme case. But it is reality.

18 Some papers have used the term *de novo* firms, somehow implying that these are decent, legitimate and healthy, whereas 'privatised state enterprises' are suspect. *De novo* has a nice ring about it. You can roll it round your mouth and savour the effect when you say how important it is to promote them.

19 An example of improvement was in Russia. Initially, to be classified as poor an adult had to be unable to afford 64 kilos of meat a year. When the poverty rate started to climb dramatically, some wise men realised that actually adults only needed 54 kilos a year. When poverty still remained high, some wiser men put their heads together, clicked their fingers and said that, of course, an adult only needed 27 kilos of meat a year. Similar recalculations were done with eggs, milk, vegetables and so on.

References

Andorka, R. and Zsolt, S. (1997) 'Poverty dynamics during the transformation', in European Bank for Reconstruction and Development, *Inequality and Poverty in Transition Economies*, London: EBRD.

Aslund, A. (1998) 'Post-communism report card', *Financial Times*, August 5.

Atkinson, A.B. (1995) 'On targeting social security: Theory and western experience with family benefits', in D. van de Walle and K. Nead (eds) *Public Spending and the Poor*, Baltimore: Johns Hopkins University Press.

Coudouel, A., Marne, S. and Micklewright, J. (1998) 'Targeting social assistance in a transition economy: The Mahallas in Uzbekistan', *Innocenti Occasional Papers EPS 63*, Florence, UNICEF.

Daianu, D. (1997) 'An economic explanation of strain', in J. Bachaus (ed.) *Issues in Transformation Theory*, Marburg: Metropolis.

Esping-Andersen, G. (1990) *The Three Worlds of Welfare Capitalism*, Cambridge: Polity Press.

European Bank for Reconstruction and Development (EBRD) (1998) *Transition Report 1998*, London: EBRD.

Fine, B. (1999) 'The development state is dead – long live social capital?', *Development and Change*, 30 (1): 1–19.

Nozick, R. (1974) *Anarchy, State and Utopia*, New York: Basic Books.

Polanyi, K. (1944) *The Great Transformation*, New York: Farrar and Reinhart.

Standing, G. (1996) *Russian Unemployment and Enterprise Restructuring: Reviving Dead Souls*, Basingstoke: Macmillan.

Standing, G. (1997) 'Labour market governance in eastern Europe', *European Journal of Industrial Relations*, 3 (2): 133–159.

Standing, G. (1997–98) 'The folly of social safety nets: Why basic income is needed in eastern Europe', *Social Research*, 64 (4): 1339–1379.

Standing, G. (1998) 'Societal impoverishment: The challenge for Russian social policy', *Journal of European Social Policy*, 8 (1): 23–42.

Standing, G. (1999a) *Global Labour Flexibility: Seeking Distributive Justice*, Basingstoke: Macmillan.

Standing, G. (1999b) 'New development paradigm or Third Wayism? A critique of a World Bank rethink', paper delivered at a Conference on Welfare State Transformations, European University Institute, Florence, March 26.

Titmuss, R. (1963) *Essays on the Welfare State*, London: Allen and Unwin.

UN Economic Commission for Europe (1999) *Economic Survey of Europe*, Geneva, Economic Commission for Europe.

Williams, R. (1976) *Keywords*, New York: Oxford University Press.

World Bank (1996) *World Development Report: From Plan to Market*, Washington, DC, World Bank.

Part II

Workplace transformations and trade unions in transition

3 Trade unions and the politics of transformation in Central and Eastern Europe

John Thirkell and Sarah Vickerstaff

Introduction

This chapter aims to set out the changing significance and role of trade unions in the post-socialist era in Central and East Europe (hereafter CEE) and Russia with particular reference to the development of politics and political processes in the region. There have of course been several aspects of the political transition, including the development of a plurality of political parties and the establishment of elections. The interests of trade unions, however, have been directly influenced by the politics of the attempted economic reforms adopted or avoided by governments in the different countries; such reforms have of course been promoted by western governments and the international financial agencies and constitute a significant aspect of the politics of transformation. The chapter charts the changing importance and role of trade unions in post-socialist politics through four stages.[1] The first, and very significant phase, was the place of trade unions in the crises which led to regime changes and the extent to which they were strategic actors in the transformation process. The second stage typically involved the establishment of new Labour Codes and trade union support for economic reform strategies. The third phase was one of social partnership comprising the development of tripartite forums of one sort or another. In the fourth and continuing stage the earlier consensus on the reform process has been broken and there is a tendency for governments to try to marginalise trade unions from the political process. This discussion does not provide detailed empirical material on the current status of trade unions in CEE, in terms of issues such as membership levels, involvement in collective bargaining or their role within the enterprise (for this kind of information, see Pollert 2000, Thirkell, Petkov and Vickerstaff 1998: 75–91, Standing 1997: 140–5, Mason 1995). The aim, rather, is to address the broad questions of the role of trade unions in the processes of political transition and their trajectories in the CEE region and to pose questions as to the future position of trade unions in the politics of these transforming societies, taking Bulgaria, the Czech Republic, Hungary, Poland, Slovakia and Russia as our basis for discussion. The chapter concludes by considering the possible strategies trade unions in CEE could adopt and the prospects for their success.

Trade unions and regime change

In the unitary political system of the socialist states, with their centrally planned economies, trade unions were the largest mass membership organisation and as is well known their primary function was to facilitate the fulfilment of economic plans decided by the Communist party. In practice this meant promoting production. For this their main resource was the distribution of social funds and other welfare benefits to the workforce. Their secondary protective function centred on ensuring adherence to the standards set out in Labour Codes and other regulations (Petkov and Thirkell 1991: 36). In the unitarist political model there was no expectation that trade unions could (or should) function as autonomous political agencies. The first major challenge to this was the emergence in Poland of Solidarity, the prototype of the independent alternative to the established communist trade unions. It was a social and political movement as much as an industrial trade union (Thirkell, Scase and Vickerstaff 1995: 15).

Although the process of political change in the Soviet Union was a protracted one the outstanding feature of regime change elsewhere in CEE was the rapidity of what became a domino process. There were, however, significant differences between countries in the nature of the extrication process and of the agencies active in it. The first question for our concern is the role, if any, of the trade unions in the process of political change. Stark (1992) has argued for a connection between the processes of political extrication in Czechoslovakia, the GDR, Hungary and Poland and the different forms of privatisation adopted in those countries. He conceptualises this as 'path dependence' reflecting the nature of the situation and the agencies active or inactive in the process. In relation to the trade unions the issue is whether their initial place in the post socialist arena can be linked to their role in the process of regime change and the conditions under which extrication occurred.

It is clear that there are important differences between countries. In Poland there was an economic crisis while in Bulgaria there were conditions of ethnic and industrial conflict and the possibility of civil war. In Poland the electoral outcomes gave Solidarity the status of leading agency in the political arena. In Bulgaria the role of the established union CITUB and the new independent union Podkrepa in the crisis secured their recognition as primary agencies. In Czechoslovakia and Hungary there were no financial crises at the time of regime change. In Hungary, the established unions were excluded from the bargained political process within the elite, and the influence of the new alternative unions was very weak due to their hostile agendas. In the regime collapse that occurred in Czechoslovakia the accompanying changes in the trade unions gave them a secondary or supporting place in the political process. On the other hand, in Russia, the miners' strikes undermined perestroika but the established unions abstained from the political process; although leaders of new alternatives (sometimes termed the 'workers movement', Clarke, Fairbrother and Borisov 1995) often became engaged in the actions of alternative political organisations. These alternative unions in Russia, arising mainly from the base, have failed to establish firm institutional bases, 'although a significant number of [disillusioned] workers put their faith in the new workers' movement' (Clarke, Fairbrother and Borisov 1995: 1). The Russian sociologists Gordon and Klopov, discussing the possibilities for the development of the market and of democracy took the position that 'the role of the workers' movement and the movement of labour collectives will be vital' (1992: 51). In practice the political process in Russia assumed

> a lobbyist character. . . . The political forces that have had a serious chance of success have been those that represent the interests of one of three large economic formations: the military-industrial complex, the agro-industrial complex, and the fuel and energy complex, and the different trade unions collaborate with the complexes in the political lobbying process.
>
> (Buketov 1995: 35)

The argument here is that the role of trade unions and the nature of political conditions in the initial phase of regime change had an influence on the subsequent extent to which trade unions continued as leading agencies in the political arena. The strength of the trade unions at this level in the different countries was reflected in the methods subsequently adopted for privatisation as will be shown below. There were also differences in the abilities of different trade union movements to resist certain reform measures in the field of labour relations. In this first phase of redevelopment and development the significance of different trade unions was derived from the nature of the political process.

Early consensus: economic reform and 'pluralist' labour relations

Throughout CEE the trajectory of national politics has been the initial context for post-socialist trade union development. Three features of the transformation created the space for trade union evolution: the political changes legitimised the existence of new alternative trade unions, for example Solidarity in Poland and Podkrepa in Bulgaria; the Communist Party was forced to withdraw from its base in the enterprise creating the opportunity for the old trade unions to reform themselves; and legislative innovations such as the right to association and to strike and the recognition of collective bargaining prefigured the establishment of market economy institutions. These features of 'pluralist' labour relations systems were imitated and transferred from western Europe and were anticipatory of actually functioning market mechanisms. Reformers and neo-liberal apologists saw these developments as necessary to 'depoliticise' the enterprise and create a boundary between the economy and the polity (for example, Aslund 1992: 70; for further discussion see Vickerstaff and Thirkell 1999: 2–3).

At this stage the issue of economic reform was closely associated with regime change. Reform involving macroeconomic stabilisation came to be the core issue in the national political arena. In the political process the newly elected political agencies were to endorse the neo-liberal policies advocated by the international financial agencies, sometimes categorised as shock therapy. Politicians judged (for example in Poland and Czechoslovakia) that popular support for the market economy, especially the prospect of the availability of the consumer goods with which the market was associated, could help maintain political consent through the hardships that this type of economic reform would necessarily entail, for at least a limited period (Thirkell, Petkov and Vickerstaff 1998: 19, 26).

In this phase trade unions regarded it as necessary to support economic reform strategies and there was an initial consensus with governments, the focus of trade union activity was primarily towards the national political stage. The issue of consent, more graphically termed social peace, was undoubtedly a continuing concern of governments and the international financial institutions on which they were dependent for financial assistance. This relationship of dependence has in varying degrees been a significant factor in the political and economic development of most CEE countries. As Waller has pointed out in the changed political system: 'the political parties, as parliamentary structures, tend to have only weak links to organised interests in society, or indeed to established and stable constituencies of any kind' (1994: 24). In these conditions trade unions, with their mass memberships, came to be accepted by governments (and international agencies) as essential or necessary partners in the process of economic reform. The political context is illustrated by Polish Minister of Labour Kuron's remark in March 1993 that 'the trade unions are the only mass organisations in Poland with any real power. . . . We're pushing them to the wall. It is only a matter of time before they revolt' (quoted in Waller 1994: 33).

In conditions of economic crisis Solidarity maintained its role as an agency in the political process contributing to the fall of the Suchodska government in 1992. Similarly, in Bulgaria, the loss of trade union support led to political changes in 1990 and 1992. Waller has commented that 'both Solidarity and Podkrepa have moved between the roles of party and pressure group' (1994: 24). In Czechoslovakia and Hungary, by contrast, the more favourable economic conditions, some incremental progress and the absence of widespread industrial unrest were accompanied by a less central and critical role for the trade unions. The political and economic crises in Russia, on the other hand, did not lead to an increase in the role of the trade unions as a strategic agency.

The differences between trade unions in the various countries are also reflected in the privatisation strategies of different governments in the region (for a more developed discussion see Thirkell, Petkov and Vickerstaff 1998: 58–74). Offe has made the distinction between resource-based and rights-based approaches to ownership change (1996: 108). This can be further developed by dividing rights-based approaches into those that privilege the rights of enterprise insiders and those that focus on the more populist approach of citizens' rights. In Poland, Bulgaria and Russia the mechanisms of 'self-management' developed in the 1980s led to a much clearer sense by enterprise insiders of their special rights to a share in owning their enterprises. In Poland and Bulgaria, trade unions were able to mobilise to an extent around these ownership issues. In Poland, the legacy of a powerful and organised working class meant that neither governments nor many enterprise managers were in a position to ignore the need to mobilise consent for privatisation strategies (Thirkell, Petkov and Vickerstaff 1998: 72). In Czechoslovakia, by contrast, the government faced little challenge from trade unions and was able to speed ahead with privatisation on the populist voucher-based method. In Hungary, the legacy of decentralised management in the 1980s and the relative weakness of trade unions led to a largely management-led process over which government continually struggled to regain control.

These differences were also reflected in early debates about which new mechanisms of labour relations should be instituted. The German and Austrian systems of labour relations provided attractive models to copy, the extension or imposition of institutions from West Germany into the East suggested that mechanisms might be transferred (although in practice in East Germany this has been far from straightforward, see for example, Hyman 1996a). In Hungary, despite trade union opposition, Works Councils were established, although government failed in its original intention to make the Councils the agent for collective bargaining. In Bulgaria, by contrast, the trade unions were able to resist Works Councils altogether at this early stage. Subsequently, however, CITUB's position changed in the context of accession to the European Union:

> Working Councils are a useful source of information on the strategic perspectives of the company, especially in the financial sphere, technological innovations and administrative structure, closure of parts or whole enterprises. . . . Through such forms of participation employees and trade unions get the opportunity to demonstrate their own opinions and positions practically on all issues of the development of the enterprise.
>
> (KNSB 1997: 16)

At this point it is possible to see that the initial place of trade unions in the post-socialist arena can be linked to their role in the process of political extrication, which in turn is related to the nature of enterprise reforms in the 1980s. In Poland and Bulgaria the trade unions were much more active agents on the national political stage than their counterparts in Hungary, Czechoslovakia or Russia.

Social partnership and tripartism

Following from this period many trade union centres accepted some shared responsibility for the reform process and entered into dialogue with governments in tripartite forums of one sort or another. Governments (and sometimes representatives of international agencies) consulted with the 'social partners' on their economic and other related reforms. This led in some countries, for example Hungary and Bulgaria, to further institutionalisation, but also increasing pluralisation (or fragmentation), of trade unions. However, the importance of the parties in these forums differed and generally the employers (who were mainly representatives of state organisations) counted for less than the trade unions. As a result the core of the process was often bipartite, although coalitions between employers and trade unions sometimes occurred. In the period up to 1994 the content of tripartite discussions focused upon wage restraint and employment policy issues institutionalised in the form of national collective bargaining. In their review of the period Héthy and Kyloh conclude:

> Thus it can be argued that despite the roles that have been theoretically assigned trade unions and employer associations have not really been involved in the discussion of economic and social reform strategies. Rather the main components of these strategies continue to be determined between senior government officials and the international financial institutions. Any negotiations that subsequently take place with employers and trade unions on economic and social policy are confined to the narrow parameters that the predetermined economic reform programme permits. Dialogue with the social partners takes place only regarding the details rather than the scope or pace of reform (1995: 38).

For both governments and trade unions there were dilemmas in the process of social partnership. Governments might be deflected from their transformation strategies while unions might lose 'their precarious legitimacy as the representatives of employee interests' (Deppe and Tatur 1995: 4). Such dilemmas underlay the tensions of the tripartite process in CEE. Thirkell, Petkov and Vickerstaff (1998: 89) offer one answer to the question of why trade unions co-operated:

> For both pragmatic and political considerations, most trade unions expressed their support from the inception of the most difficult period of macro-economic stabilization. This support enabled them to participate in negotiation of the terms of price liberalization and anti-inflationary policy, which marked the start of monetary reform. This participation in turn stimulated the development of mechanisms for the representation of interests of different branches and occupational groups ... and established the trade unions as a major strategic agency at national level. Refusal to give support would have been vulnerable from a political point of view from the outset of transition, as there was an accepted parallel between economic reform and democratization of the societies in the East.

However, from the middle of the 1990s the consequences of economic reform and the shift in its focus came to affect the policies of the trade unions at the national level and to erode membership at the base. Continuation of the neo-liberal reform model led to an increasing need for trade unions to focus on social policy issues. This was illustrated by events in the Czech Republic where the economic transformation appeared well advanced. As a result Prime Minister Klaus in 1994 claimed that as the economic transformation had been completed it would now be succeeded by the social transformation, involving particularly health and pension provision. Although the timing varied between the countries, there were similarities in the sequencing of the different elements of the neo-liberal model of reform after the achievement of macroeconomic stabilisation. At the national level, trade union movements were reluctant to endorse this aspect of the reform package and social policy became a contested issue at the national level, for example in Hungary and the Czech Republic.

The relationship between the consequences of the implementation of the structural aspects of economic reform, especially ownership change and restructuring, and the effects on trade union membership became increasingly apparent. Unemployment, ownership change and the restructuring of large enterprises, the shift to employment in the service sector and in small firms all took their toll on trade union membership. Although density started at a much higher base than that found in western market economies, reductions in trade union membership were increasingly apparent. In 1995 evidence from the ILO on trade union membership showed that there were some eighty trade union confederations and national federations in the ex-socialist countries, representing a considerable pluralisation or fragmentation of union membership. Falls in trade union membership were recorded in Bulgaria, the Czech Republic, Hungary, Poland, Russia and Slovakia. However, the estimated densities ranged from 40 per cent in Poland and 45 per cent in the Czech Republic and Hungary to 60 per cent in Bulgaria and 75 per cent in Russia. The dynamics of the downward trend are indicated in survey evidence that by 1997 density in Hungary had fallen to 25 per cent (Neumann 1997: 200) and the informal estimates of specialists that by 1999 density in Bulgaria had fallen to 35 per cent and in Slovakia to 50 per cent.[2] In the early period of transformation it was necessary for the trade unions to orient themselves to the national political stage but it became increasingly obvious that this strategy could not ensure their survival as mass organisations. The impact of restructuring, privatisation and the new market economy became more intensely felt as trade union membership declined and many new areas of employment remained non-unionised. Economic conditions were increasingly important in determining the trade unions' scope for development.

Post 1995: the political and economic hegemony of the neo-liberal model

In the period after the regime changes governments were faced with a series of political and strategic choices about the form and pace of economic reform. The varying conditions and the internal balance of political forces in the different countries influenced the timing and form of these changes. All were to a greater or lesser extent subject to the influence of the policies promoted by the international financial agencies on behalf of western capitalism. Internal economic crises (in Bulgaria in 1996 and the Czech Republic and Russia in 1997–8) did not alter the direction of the model of economic reform although it might affect the timing of particular aspects. Equally the replacement of governments in elections, as in the Czech and Slovak Republics, Poland and Bulgaria, did not shift the basic adherence to neo-liberal policies. As the European Bank for Reconstruction and Development (EBRD 1999: 104) review in 1999 commented:

In the transition countries, reforms have tended to generate a political backlash in a majority of cases. In 14 of the 21 countries in the region that held competitive elections, incumbents had lost control of the government in the second election. Yet these electoral reversals have not led to reform reversals, nor have they generally halted further progress in reform.

After 1994 the 'false dawn' of tripartism became increasingly apparent as the hegemony of the neo-liberal model became clear; the initial consensus on the reform process between governments and trade unions was broken. This arose out of the trade unions' refusal to endorse the social policy reforms of the neo-liberal model, which constituted the second stage of the 'transition'. It also became apparent that growing numbers of employers were ignoring the new Labour Codes and that there was a general erosion of labour standards. Some trade union centres moved to a more confrontational stance towards government and some have found themselves pushed to the periphery of the reform process and progressively marginalised at the political level. In this fourth phase the structural changes outlined in the previous section underlie the processes affecting the role and place of trade unions. The significance of the effects of particular economic contingencies and their political consequences on these general trends can be illustrated by reference to the Czech Republic, Hungary, Bulgaria and Slovakia.

In the Czech Republic Klaus's political position had seemed secured by the programmatic pattern of economic development established under his leadership. After initial support for tripartite processes Klaus sought to restrict its significance as much as possible (Myant, Slocock and Smith 2000: 729–33). However, the proposals for pension reform provoked demonstrations, which led to consultations with the trade unions. This and economic problems led in 1996 to a large increase in the representation of the Social Democrats and their eventual electoral success in 1998. The progress of tripartism has been contingent on the political and economic fortunes of the government. In March 1997 the tripartite process came to a halt over the issue of public sector pay but by the summer economic crisis had forced Klaus to revive tripartite processes again (Thirkell, Petkov and Vickerstaff 1998: 164.) However, as Pollert (2000: 26) points out, even with the election of a Social Democratic government:

> the labour movement has failed to press for any fundamentally different course of restructuring from the free-market route implemented by the predecessor government. Disillusion is expressed in the oscillations of party political support, together with the rising popularity of the CP, but there is no evidence that any political party has any major alternative policies.

Hungary has been widely publicised in the literature for the development of tripartite institutions at the national level, building upon some anticipatory frameworks from the late 1980s and consolidated in the post-socialist government as a result of the taxi drivers' strike and blockade of 1990. Thereafter the institutions of the Social Security Boards and Health Insurance Boards in 1993 'constituted a very important step in the institutionalisation of the social partners' role in social policy' (Thirkell, Petkov and Vickerstaff 1998: 164) and also served to strengthen the successor unions. The election of the Socialist government in 1994, to replace the right-wing government that had been in power since 1990, created expectations that the unions' influence on government policy would increase. However, an economic crisis removed the hope of a longer term Social Pact as the scope for political exchange had disappeared. Writing in 1997, Thirkell, Petkov and Vickerstaff (1998: 167) concluded that the institutionalisation of the tripartite process 'appears most evident in Hungary'. However, the dependence of tripartism on electoral politics was shown by the defeat of the Socialist Party in the election of April 1998. Abolition of the Social Security and Health Insurance Boards was one of the first acts of the new government (Andor 1998: 36). Subsequently this was followed by the erosion of the national tripartite forum so carefully fostered for nearly a decade.

In Bulgaria in the first half of the 1990s the tripartite process had been significant in securing social peace, in the revision of the Labour Code in 1993 and in the institutional consolidation of social partnership at national level. However, following the election of the Socialist government at the end of 1994 the new government's strategy was to pursue aspects of economic reform without tripartite involvement. Subsequently, the economic crisis in late 1996 was accompanied by political demonstrations, the fall of the Government and the imposition by the international financial institutions of a Currency Board to control inflation. This economic and political crisis required some revival of the tripartite process. The government sought to secure the participation of the trade unions and the employers to maintain social peace as far as possible and at the expert level the trade unions participate in the political process (Ribarova 2000). However, the government retains the right to decide and implement policy and in 1998 it passed legislation on Social Security despite the opposition of trade unions and employers. This is in contrast with the situation in Poland in which Solidarity as a trade union was able to challenge successfully the Social Security proposals of the Solidarity Government. Slovakia has seen the continuation of regular, but sometimes interrupted tripartite processes in a country where the maintenance of social peace has a high political value. The main trade union confederation turned against the government and its policy in 1996 and the previous pattern of tripartite dialogue was revived only after the 1998 elections were won by the democratic coalition (Sorenova 2000: 139). It is clear from this discussion that the fortunes of tripartite arrangements in this region are politically dependent:

> The perceived threat (and actual threats in Bulgaria and Poland) to social peace in response to macro-economic stabilisation were significant factors in the early development of tripartite processes, so that governments made strategic choices, encouraged by the IFI [International Financial Institutions], to co-opt trade unions into the tripartite process ... economic crises, as in Bulgaria in 1996/7 and in the Czech Republic in 1997, tend to

foster the need for consent through tripartism whilst also making agreement more difficult as was seen with the failed social pact in Hungary in 1994/5.

(Thirkell, Petkov and Vickerstaff 1998: 166)

Governments' motivation to engage in social partnership is largely to share the blame for economic hardship, when it comes to the development of social policy governments have often tried to marginalise trade union influence.

Politics and the representation of interests

It was argued earlier that the magnitude of trade union membership compared with that of the political parties (except the Communist parties in Bulgaria and Russia) gave them a special importance in the political processes of the early transition period. Patterns of electoral party politics have gradually been established and this leads to the question of the relation of trade unions to political parties and to the representation of interest in societies. In 1993 Ost argued that 'in state socialism there are no clearly defined societal interests waiting for the chance to capture the state. . . . The Leninist state prevents the formation of independent interests by nationalizing the economy' (1993: 458). In their review of ten years of transition the European Bank for Reconstruction and Development still judged the process of representation in the political processes as incomplete:

> In many transition countries, political parties, labour unions and lobbies do not yet effectively represent collective interests as in other systems. As a result demands have generally not been filtered through organisations with broad mandates. . . . In some cases, firms have been able to put their representatives in high public office. This leaves politicians vulnerable to capture by interest groups that became wealthy in the transition.
>
> (EBRD 1999: 106)

In general the representation of interests by trade unions has been more direct or complete than by political parties. Zhelev (1999: 29) has argued that 'the political parties in transitional Bulgaria are not earthed, they have no social basis because the social groups and strata whose interest they seek to present and defend are not yet in place and this will only happen at the end of the transition period'. A key informant familiar with local political organisations interviewed in 1997 affirmed that industrial workers were no longer active in the Socialist/Social Democratic Party although they had been a key stratum in local Communist Party organisations. Henderson, however, argues for an alternative view of political development in the Czech Republic as shown by the election of 1998 where 'it was however social class, education which really defined the Czech party system' (1998: 14) particularly the cleavage between the social democrats and Klaus and the right. On the other hand, in Hungary the level of party identification is much lower than in Western Europe (Ilonszki 1998: 165).

The issue for national trade unions of relations with political parties has been a continuing one, which has varied significantly over time and reflecting the changing salience of issues in the political arena and the outcomes of the electoral process. The decline of tripartism after 1995 and the accompanying shift of power to the political arena were a stimulus for trade union centres to develop or re-establish links with political parties as in Hungary and the Czech Republic (Thirkell, Petkov and Vickerstaff 1998: 169–70, Myant, Slocock and Smith 2000: 730). However, Héthy (1999: 11) comments about Hungary that:

> such open political affiliations have in my view caused more tensions between trade unions and the political parties than produced positive dividends for the unions. The presence of union leaders in the parliamentary benches of the Socialists seemed to have no positive impact – from the perspective of the unions – on the work of either parliament or the government.

An illustration of the shifting basis of the relations between political and trade union organisations is that at the end of 1999 the link between the Solidarity trade union and the Solidarity political organisation, which had been a central feature of the political transformation in Poland since 1989 (and was organisationally important in the election of 1997) was reported to have been broken. In the Russian Federation it has been judged that the Communist Party's 'attempts to improve links with trade unions were scarcely successful with the unions fearing once again the party's deathly embrace. The gulf between party and unions was strongly evident in for example the union day of action on 27 March 1997' (Sakwa 1998: 132). However, while Mandel (1997: 45) acknowledges the weakness of unions in Russia, Ukraine and Belarus, he reminds us that given the 'general weakness of popular social forces (indeed all social forces) the unions are the strongest social forces in the society'. One can therefore conclude that in CEE union membership is in decline but relative to other organisations of civil society remains significant and a potential source of interest representation in the political sphere.

Conclusions: perspectives on politics and trade unions

Electoral politics are established but it would be premature to assume that the transition economies are yet free of the economic crises which have motivated national governments to seek the co-operation of national trade unions at such crisis points. On the other hand, the real or potential threats to social peace from mass strikes, which were a potent factor earlier in the political process in the transition countries, seem unlikely to materialise although the threats of action in key sectors, as well as enterprise protests, may well continue and develop. However, at the national level the consultative discussions on economic and social policies between governments and trade unions as organisations with large memberships, may well continue in appearance, if not much substance, legitimised as an aspect of the social dialogue fostered and encouraged by the prospect of European Union accession (for discussion on the prospects for such consultation see Myant, Slocock and Smith 2000, Vickerstaff and Thirkell 2000b). One example of the consultation process may be the minimum wage, which can affect pensions and a wide range of social and other benefits, which are important for a wider social constituency beyond the workplace.

It is hardly surprising that in this light and the more general conditions of political and economic transformation that most trade union confederations have focused their energies on the national political stage. However, throughout the countries of the region it appears that it does not matter which government or party is in power, the hegemony of the neo-liberal model of economic reform remains unchallenged and as a result the scope for unions to extract employment and social policy concessions is largely undermined. It thus becomes vital for trade unions to develop new survival strategies and to reassess their organisation below the national level. However, responding to members' interests at the level of the enterprise is increasingly difficult in conditions of economic recession and the absence of political support in most countries. This raises the question of which strategies trade unions in CEE should follow.

Hyman (1996b) offers a framework of alternative trade union identities, which he argues were particularly significant in contemporary Europe. This provides a starting point for considering the options facing trade unions in CEE. Hyman provides five alternative trade union identities: the guild built around an occupational élite; the friendly society focused upon the individual worker; the company union or productivity coalition; the social partner involved in political exchange with government; and the social movement with the aim to be a mass campaigning organisation (1996b: 70). It is possible to identify examples of each of these identities in trade unions in the post-socialist era.

There are examples of occupational élites such as the air traffic controllers in Russia and the railway workers in Hungary. The distribution of social welfare through the trade union was a significant institutional benefit of union membership before regime change. Although the general trend has been for the withdrawal of national institutional support for the continuation of such benefits, the practice has continued in some firms and sectors and so provides a basis for the individual's attachment to the trade union. CITUB in Bulgaria, for example, has provided individual services to its members in areas such as pensions and health insurance. In Slovakia on the other hand, trade unions tried to restore their earlier role in company social policy by promoting a measure to require employers to establish an enterprise Social Fund to cover issues such as holidays and accidents. It is reported that this failed to help unions to sustain membership levels (Sorenova 2000: 137–8). Hence, the friendly society model cannot necessarily cement the unions' position. The company union or productivity coalition is a partial way of conceptualising the role of trade unions under socialist planning and case study evidence provides many examples of a continuation of a community of interest in some enterprises especially in Russia and in the case of employee-owned enterprises (Clarke 1996, Pickles 1998, Vickerstaff and Thirkell 2000a). This model seems highly dependent upon forms of ownership in CEE and Russia and might be expected to wither as privatisation to owners external to the enterprise proceeds. As discussed above political exchange and social partnership have a chequered history in the region. Commentators agree that there is no general trend towards the institutionalisation of tripartism in the region (Myant, Slocock and Smith 2000, Cox and Mason 2000). For the trade unions concentration on national tripartite forums runs the risk of neglecting their membership at enterprise level, which ultimately supplies the negotiating power needed to extract any concessions from governments. Solidarity has been the prototype of a social movement with a mass following in the past but would find it difficult to regain its previous support in the current climate. No other union in CEE has shown the potential, or the inclination, to be a mass campaigning organisation. Although in the absence of other major interest organisations in civil society this role could be sought, it would require, however, a greater degree of agreement between different trade union centres than is evident at present.

In CEE a major issue is the co-existence of such trade union identities. A limitation of Hyman's scheme is that it does not capture the dynamics of the situations in CEE where the simultaneity of transitions in both economic and political spheres exercise substantial influences on trade unions and their scope for strategic choice. As the discussion above indicates, the impact of government on labour relations issues is largely pragmatic and unpredictable, driven by short-term political and economic considerations. At the same time, trade unions face an increasingly heterogeneous economy in terms of different ownership and control patterns and related management strategies.

The problem in trying to predict likely future outcomes for trade unions in CEE is that transformation is not an incremental process. Nor is there a single transformation either between or within countries in the region. As we have seen, short-term political considerations and conditions weigh heavily on trade unions' room for manoeuvre. There is no reason to expect that this situation will change in the short to medium term.

> In the 'absence of stable configurations of political and economic agents' (Swain and Hardy 1998: 588) the state's role in labour relations is politically contingent on electoral considerations and outcomes, the leverage of the International Financial Institutions and other more domestic considerations such as the bargaining power of local elites. In other words, the state's role is largely pragmatic and unpredictable.
>
> (Vickerstaff and Thirkell 1999: 10)

The pluralist institutions of labour relations so hurriedly adopted in the immediate post-regime change period in most countries are only weakly institutionalised. Labour Codes and national tripartite agreements may exist but there are no stable institutions to enforce them (Standing 1997: 156, Makó and Simonyi 1997: 223–7, Mason 1995: 363). Or, as in the case of Russia, reform of the Labour Code promises to worsen workers' rights and working conditions (The Union Messenger 2000).

The conditions at enterprise level are hardly more auspicious. Here trade unions face many different varieties of emerging capitalism involving a plethora of different ownership and control structures (from foreign direct investment and control, joint ventures, domestically owned and controlled through to a variety of insider-dominated ownership forms and continuing state ownership). This often noted fragmentation of organisational forms and work experiences in CEE may reflect the emergence of competing labour relations systems within each country, or as Makó and Simonyi have put it, that large numbers of people in these countries 'are not under the "umbrella" of the labour relations system' (1997: 237). Hyman has commented in another context that: 'The agenda of trade unions may be defined as the expression in action of the interests which they seek to represent' (1996b: 59). In the current situation in CEE countries it may not be simple for trade unions to represent clear interests around which their members can rally. Incomplete marketisation is accompanied by incomplete structuration of interests and their representation. Anticipatory politics and institutionalisation modelled on liberal market economies cannot substitute for the articulation and representation of real interests. The strategies of trade unions will have to vary according to the sector or situation they are in. There may well be 'islands of pluralism' in which trade unions are able to maintain their right to collective bargaining and representation of the workforce. In many other instances trade unions will have to fight even to approach the workforce and here services to members may be an appropriate strategy.

In reviewing the future prospects for trade unions in CEE it may be useful to consider the findings of extensive research on the factors influencing union membership in western European countries over the period 1950–1995. Ebbinghaus and Visser (1999) concluded that institutional variables were very important and especially union-led unemployment schemes and whether or not, and to what degree, unions' position in the workplace was recognised or institutionalised. The establishment of consultative forums, such as works councils, could provide a solid basis for trade union activity at enterprise level. The European Union provisions on consultation and the provision of information at the workplace may provide some, albeit weak, underpinning for such institutions (Vickerstaff and Thirkell 2000b). Although comparative research on works councils in eastern Germany and Hungary reminds us of the contrasting effects of institutional legacies in different contexts (Frege 1998, Tóth 1997). However, it is necessary to conclude that in CEE states have not been positive or active agents for labour relations institutionalisation.

In the early phases of political and economic transition trade unions played an important national role because of their actual or potential strength to mobilise opposition. However, the new freedoms and rights gained in this period are poorly institutionalised, pluralist mechanisms of industrial relations were developed but are not enforced. Economic conditions now provide the main pressure on trade unions and the early advantage of Solidarity in Poland or CITUB and Podkrepa in Bulgaria, due to their roles in the path of extrication from communist rule, have been all but lost. However, in a context of an underdeveloped civil society and the consequent poor articulation of interests, representation by trade unions, although limited and politically and economically contingent, is comparatively direct.

Notes

1 This paper draws on ongoing research projects for which the following funding is gratefully acknowledged: the project Labour Relations in Eastern Europe: Restructuring and Privatisation funded by the Economic and Social Research Council from 1992–96; research visits to Russia (1996/7), Hungary and Bulgaria in 1998 funded respectively by the Nuffield Foundation; the University of Kent Social Sciences Faculty Research Committee and the British Academy East European Exchange Agreement. We would also like to acknowledge the contribution of Grigor Gradev, Co-Ordinator of the ETUC Task Force for the South East Europe Stability Pact (formerly Director of Research, Confederation of Independent Trade Unions in Bulgaria) for his information on current trade union policies and his critical assessment of our ideas.
2 Information from research collaborators, Grigor Gradev, Co-Ordinator of the ETUC Task Force for the South East Europe Stability Pact (formerly Director of Research, Confederation of Independent Trade Unions in Bulgaria) and Ludovit Cziria, Deputy Head of Research at the Slovak Institute of Labour.

References

Andor, L. (1998) 'New striker in old team: The 1998 parliamentary elections in Hungary', *Labour Focus on Eastern Europe*, 60: 28–44.
Aslund, A. (1992) *Post Communist Economic Revolutions: How Big a Bang?* Washington: Center for Strategic and International Studies.
Buketov, K. (1995) 'Russian Trade Unions in 1994', *Labour Focus on Eastern Europe*, 50: 224–40.
Clarke, S. (1996) *The Russian Enterprise in Transition*, Aldershot: Edward Elgar.
Clarke, S., Fairbrother, P. and Borisov, V. (1995) *The Workers' Movement in Russia*, Aldershot: Edward Elgar.
Cox, T.M. and Mason, R. (2000) 'Interest groups and the development of tripartism in East Central Europe', *European Journal of Industrial Relations*, 6 (3): 325–347.
Deppe, R. and Tatur, M. (1995) 'Trade union configurations and transformation policy in Poland and Hungary', paper given to ICEES 5th World Congress, Warsaw, August 6–11.
Ebbinghaus, B. and Visser, J. (1999) 'When institutions matter: Union growth and decline in Western Europe, 1950–1995', *European Sociological Review*, 15 (2): 135–158.
European Bank for Reconstruction and Development (EBRD) (1999) *Transition Report 1999: Ten Years of Transition*, London: EBRD.
Frege, C.M. (1998) 'Institutional transfer and effectiveness of employee representation: Comparing works councils in East and West Germany', *Economic and Industrial Democracy*, 19 (3): 475–504.
Gordon, L.A. and Klopov, E.V. (1992) 'The workers' movement in a post socialist perspective' in B. Silverman, R. Vogt and M. Yanowitch (eds) *Labour and Democracy in the Transition to a Market Economy*, New York: M.E. Sharpe, pp. 27–52.
Henderson, K. (1998) 'Social democracy comes to power: The 1998 Czech elections', *Labour Focus on Eastern Europe*, 60: 5–25.

Héthy, L. (1999) 'Under pressure: Workers and trade unions in Hungary during the period of transformation 1989–1998' in the International Labour Organisation (ILO) technical cooperation project *Strengthening Trade Unions in Central and Eastern Europe*, Budapest: International Labour Organisation, pp. 1–35.

Héthy, L. and Kyloh, R. (1995) 'A comparative analysis of tripartite consultations and negotiations in Central and Eastern Europe' in R. Kyloh (ed.) *Tripartism on Trial: Tripartite Consultations and Negotiations in Central and Eastern Europe*, Budapest: ILO, pp. 1–48.

Hyman, R. (1996a) 'Institutional transfer: Industrial relations in Eastern Europe', *Work, Employment and Society*, 10 (4): 601–639.

Hyman, R. (1996b) 'Changing union identities in Europe', in P. Leisink, J. van Leemput, and J. Vilrokx (eds) *The Challenges to Trade Unions in Europe*, Cheltenham: Edward Elgar, pp. 53–73.

Ilonszki, G. (1998) 'Representation deficit in a new democracy: Theoretical considerations and the Hungarian case', *Communist and Post Communist Studies*, 31 (2): 157–170.

KNSB (Confederation of Independent Trade Unions in Bulgaria) (1997) Programme for the Fourth Regular Congress of KNSB, 28–30 November, Sofia.

Makó, C. and Simonyi, Á. (1997) 'Inheritance, imitation and genuine solutions: Institution building in Hungarian labour relations', *Europe-Asia Studies*, 49 (2): 221–243.

Mandel, D. (1997) 'Unions in Russia, Ukraine and Belarus; A case study', *Labour Focus on Eastern Europe*, 58: 44–86.

Mason, B. (1995) 'Industrial relations in an unstable environment: The case of Central and Eastern Europe', *European Journal of Industrial Relations*, 1 (3): 341–367.

Myant, M., Slocock, B. and Smith, S. (2000) 'Tripartism in the Czech and Slovak Republics', *Europe-Asia Studies*, 52 (4): 723–739.

Neumann, L. (1997) 'Circumventing trade unions in Hungary: Old and new channels of wage bargaining', *European Journal of Industrial Relations*, 3 (2): 183–202.

Offe, C. (1996) *Varieties of Transition: The East European and East German Experience*, Cambridge: Polity Press.

Ost, D. (1993) 'The politics of interest in post communist East Europe', *Theory and Society*, 22: 453–486.

Petkov, K. and Thirkell, J. (1991) *Labour Relations in Eastern Europe: Organisational Design and Dynamics*, London: Routledge.

Pickles, J. (1998) 'Restructuring state enterprises: Industrial geography and eastern European transitions', in J. Pickles and A. Smith (eds) *Theorising Transition: The Political Economy of Post-Communist Transformations*, London: Routledge, pp. 172–196.

Pollert, A. (2000) 'The Czech labour movement a decade after 1989', *Labour Focus on Eastern Europe*, 66: 8–33.

Ribarova, E. (2000) 'Social rights in Bulgaria under reform', *South East Europe Review*, 3 (5): 45–50.

Sakwa, R. (1998) 'Left or right? The CPRF and the problem of democratic consolidation in Russia', *Journal of Communist Studies and Transition Politics*, 14 (1 & 2): 129–158.

Sorenova, M. (2000) 'The development of trade unions in Slovakia during the past decade', *South East Europe Review*, 3 (2): 131–142.

Standing, G. (1997) 'Labour market governance in Eastern Europe', *European Journal of Industrial Relations*, 3 (2): 133–159.

Stark, D. (1992) 'Path dependence and privatisation strategies in East-Central Europe', *East European Politics and Society*, 6: 17–51.

Swain, A. and Hardy, J. (1998) 'Globalization, institutions, foreign investment and the reintegration of East and Central Europe and the former Soviet Union into the world economy', *Regional Studies*, 32 (7): 587–590.

The Union Messenger (2000) 'Russian labour 2000', translated by D. Mandel, *Labour Focus on Eastern Europe*, 66: 47–54.

Thirkell, J., Petkov, K. and Vickerstaff, S. (1998) *The Transformation of Labour Relations: Restructuring and Privatisation in Eastern Europe and Russia*, Oxford: Oxford University Press.

Thirkell, J., Scase, R. and Vickerstaff, S. (1995) 'Changing models of labour relations in Eastern Europe and Russia' in J. Thirkell, R. Scase and S. Vickerstaff (eds) *Labour Relations and Political Change in Eastern Europe: A Comparative Perspective*, London: UCL Press, pp. 7–29.

Tóth, A. (1997) 'The invention of works councils in Hungary', *European Journal of Industrial Relations*, 3 (2): 161–181.

Vickerstaff, S. and Thirkell, J. (1999) 'Theorising labour relations in Central and Eastern Europe: Legacies, transference and strategic choices', paper given to the BUIRA Conference, DeMontfort University, Leicester, 1–3 July.

Vickerstaff, S. and Thirkell, J. (2000a) 'L'importance de la continuité sociale et politique de l'entreprise en Europe centrale et orientale', in B. Lestrade and S. Boutillier (eds) *Les Mutations du Travail en Europe*, Paris: Editions L'Harmattan, pp. 325–343.

Vickerstaff, S. and Thirkell, J. (2000b) 'Instrumental rationality and European integration: Transference or avoidance of industrial relations institutions in Central and Eastern Europe?', *European Journal of Industrial Relations*, 6 (2): 237–251.

Waller, M. (1994) 'Political actors and political roles in East-Central Europe', in M. Waller and M. Myant (eds) *Parties, Trade Unions and Society in East-Central Europe*, Ilford: Frank Cass, pp. 21–36.

Zhelev, Z. (1999) 'Post-communism – an incredible era', *South East Europe Review* Special Issue: The 10th Anniversary of the Fall of the Berlin Wall: 29–37.

4 Broken networks and a *tabula rasa*?

'Lean production', employment and the privatisation of the East German automobile industry[1]

Adam Swain

> *Tabula rasa . . . fig.* A clean slate; a mind having no ideas (as in some views of the human mind at birth).
>
> (*The New Shorter Oxford English Dictionary, Vol. 2. N-Z,* 1993, 3198)

> For investors in the automobile industry, the economic and social *tabula rasa* of eastern Germany provides an almost ideal field for experimenting with the most advanced management practices and production techniques. In the eastern German plants, the European versions of the new management fetish of 'lean production' will be pioneered.
>
> (Grabher 1994: 192)

Introduction

The unification of Germany in 1990 precipitated a deep depression in the former German Democratic Republic (GDR) followed by a period of rapid recovery between 1992 and 1995. However, between 1995 and 1999 economic growth slowed once more and the economic convergence that had been taking place between the eastern and western *Länder* was halted. Orthodox neo-liberal economists explained the post-unification depression as a transitional adjustment as production factors were reallocated according to market discipline from less to more profitable activities. *Contra* this approach, heterodox economists argue that the deep recession and the absence of a sustained convergence between the two economies was caused by the particular transition policies adopted in the GDR. They argue that monetary union between the GDR and the Federal Republic of Germany (FRG) and rapid privatisation resulted in the destruction of industrial networks, the paralysis of indigenous growth potential, and dependence on exogenous capital. This explanation suggests that the German 'transition to capitalism' erased the legacies of the GDR, created a *tabula rasa* and permitted new state institutions and market entrants to build a new economy as if by design.

This chapter problematises this explanation in two ways. Firstly, the chapter argues that German unification did not erase legacies nor produce a *tabula rasa*.

The chapter suggests that existing networks of agency and mobilisation amongst employees and managers in state-owned enterprises survived unification. Equally, new networks linking centres of employment in industry to new trade union structures circumscribed the power of the privatisation agency and private investors. Consequently, the 'new economy' was the outcome of conflict and negotiation involving not only the privatisation agency and private investors but also employees, trade unions and regional state institutions. Accordingly, some commentators argue that this conflict undermined employee and trade union power (see, for example, Hyman 1996, Fichter 1997) whilst others suggest trade union and employee power was successfully institutionalised and articulated (see, for example, Turner 1997, 1998, Frege 1998).

Secondly, the chapter suggests that the notion of a *tabula rasa* was a powerful metaphor deployed by the privatisation agency and private investors to force the economy in the new *Länder*[2] to conform to their idealised abstract models of how capitalist economic practices should be organised. Thus the *tabula rasa* may be seen in the context of what has been termed 'virtualism', the process by which the economy is forced to conform to abstract idealised economic models produced by academic economists (Carrier and Miller 1998). The notion of a *tabula rasa* pre-explained transition policies designed to disembed and disintermediate economic and social activities that previously took place within the confines of huge industrial combines and within localities. The notion of a *tabula rasa* also extended into the workplace to justify the imposition of particular models of management practice, such as 'lean production'. The idea of a *tabula rasa* was a means to construct a malleable space-economy inhabited by social actors lacking the capacity to contest, to negotiate and to self-organise. In other words the *tabula rasa* metaphor is a corollary to the notion of a 'transition to capitalism'; the teleological idea that capitalism can be normatively built by design (for a critique, see especially Stark 1995).

The chapter explores these issues through an examination of the privatisation and restructuring of the automobile industry and specifically the privatisation of *VEB-Sachsenring Automobilwerke* (VEB-SAW) which produced the infamous Trabant in the industrial town of Zwickau in south-west Saxony. The first section critically examines the arguments that have been offered as explanations for the post-soviet deindustrialisation of the former GDR. Section two opens the discussion of the automobile industry by considering the organisation of the industry during the soviet era since this conditioned the restructuring of the industry during *'die Wende'*.[3] This is followed by a discussion of the privatisation of the automobile industry following unification. Section three examines the long and complex and contested privatisation of VEB-SAW. This is followed by some concluding remarks.

Explaining the de-industrialisation of the former GDR: broken networks and a *tabula rasa*?

For some, the evisceration of the GDR following the breaching of the Berlin Wall on 9 November 1989, culminating less than a year later in unification with the

FRG, was the apotheosis of the 'transition to capitalism'. The GDR party-state contractually undertook to dissolve itself and merge with the FRG. Moreover, the dismantling and replacement of the soviet system was executed through external legal *fiat* and political legitimation (Offe 1996). This mode of extrication produced what has been termed a *tabula rasa*, at least in the political domain (Elster *et al.* 1998: 25), which enabled the unconstrained selection of a radical strategy of economic reform designed to engineer a comprehensive, rapid, and simultaneous 'transition to capitalism' (Pickel 1992: 178). The treaty on monetary, economic and social union that was concluded between the GDR and FRG on 1 July 1990 inserted the GDR into the world economy and submitted domestic producers to foreign market competition and 'hard budget constraints'. Under the influence of the FRG (Seibel 1997: 286), the *Treuhandanstalt* (THA), which had been established in March 1990 to administer and restructure state-owned industry, became the legal owner of state enterprises in June 1990 and adopted a strategy of rapid privatisation, restitution or liquidation of state-owned property. Monetary and social union and privatisation established the accelerated pace of transition and the colonial-style structural dependence the GDR had on the FRG prior and subsequent to unification (Pickel 1992: 182).

Advocates of neo-liberal 'shock therapy' expected *'die Wende'* to result in a rational re-allocation of capital and labour from less to more efficient economic activities (for a critique see Ch. 2). Accordingly, the THA pursued a privatisation programme that involved the monetary valuation of assets and the sale of those assets to corporate institutions. Enterprises without positive capital value were to be liquidated. As unemployment was interpreted either as a temporary consequence of disguised underemployment or non-economic employment inherited from the soviet economic system, privatisation was accorded primacy over employment (Offe 1996: 153). The 'transition to capitalism' in the new *Länder* involved an unparalleled devaluation and the de-industrialisation of the GDR space-economy. Thus by the end of 1991 industrial production had fallen to a third of the 1989 level (cited in Offe 1996: 153). Despite widespread economic migration to western Germany and the growth of employment in service sectors, around three million east Germans were either officially registered as unemployed or were prematurely retired, placed on job-training programmes or ceased to seek employment (Dunford 1998: 102). With total unemployment, registered and unregistered, estimated at 40 per cent for much of the 1990s the development policy in the new *Länder* was labelled 'catastrophic' (Offe 1996). Neo-liberals explained this employment catastrophe as the consequence of weak political leadership allowing labour costs in the new *Länder* to converge with those in the old *Länder* much more rapidly than the convergence in productivity levels.

Two alternative explanations for the de-industrialisation of the new *Länder* have been asserted, both derived from institutional economics. The first explanation emphasises the precise manner in which the new *Länder* were inserted into and articulated with the German and international economic hierarchy and the absence or inappropriateness of the social institutions needed to regularise the market economy. Dunford (1998: 103–5) identifies five reasons connected to the conditions attached to German unity that explain the de-industrialisation of the GDR. First, monetary union at an exchange rate of 1 *Deutsche Mark* to 1 *Ost Mark* protected individuals' savings (and therefore had political benefits) but rendered East German output uncompetitive. Second, monetary union combined with the break up of the CMEA severed east German producers from their suppliers and customers and forced them to compete in the western market for which they were ill prepared. Third, monetary union led to price convergence resulting in rapid inflation in the cost of east German goods and services. Fourth, social union, which involved extending FRG labour law to the east, led to wage convergence that reduced the productivity of east German producers. Finally, Dunford (1998) suggests that the dissonance that existed between the institutions, structures and patterns of behaviour in the GDR and FRG economies, and especially the differences in sectoral and geographic specialisation, exacerbated the shock to the GDR economy.

The second explanation for the de-industrialisation of the GDR extends Dunford's final point by focusing on the manner in which economic action is socially embedded in networks (see, for example, Begg and Pickles 1998, Grabher and Stark 1997, Smith and Swain 1998, Thrift and Olds 1996). Stark and Bruzst (1998), in their comparison of industrial and policy networks in Hungary, the Czech Republic and the new *Länder*, demonstrate the importance of network relations and the power of abstract economic theory put into practice by institutions (Carrier and Miller 1998). Neo-liberal property transformation strategies were based on the theoretical assumption that a capitalist's capacity to act is derived from their legal entitlement to property ownership. Stark and Bruzst's economic theory contends that assets possess network properties with the result that capitalists' capacity to act depends not on their legal entitlement to ownership but on their ability to mobilise or control assets through network relations. They examine property transformation in the three countries and explain their divergent developmental capacities in terms of the variability in the adaptability of policy and industrial networks. This variability is in turn explained according to the institutionalisation of what they term 'inclusive deliberation' and 'extended accountability'. They conclude that weak bureaucratic control over privatisation in the Czech Republic and Hungary preserved industrial networks which served to buffer individual enterprises from market discipline and enabled them to remain in business. However, in the new *Länder* strong bureaucratic control over privatisation or in other words 'state-led denationalisation' (Offe 1996: 153), failed to take the network properties of individual enterprises into account and consequently undermined what were already weakly developed industrial networks (Voskamp and Wittke 1991).

The privatisation of state-owned industry in the new *Länder* meant the THA had an unparalleled formative impact upon the economy. Privatisation in the new *Länder* was administered by a single centralised bureaucratic agency (Stark and Bruszt 1998: 88–9). Moreover, as all the GDR's other institutions (government ministries, local authorities, trade unions, etc.) had been dissolved (Seibel 1997: 286) the THA was unchallenged by any rival institutions and was therefore largely unaccountable. The THA was a holding company that assumed ownership of around 7,000 industrial enterprises. It also owned the 126 highly centralised industrial combines (which also provided social functions such as healthcare and housing) and in order to privatise these combines the THA dissolved them to create around another 7,000 individual companies. In total the THA's enterprises employed around four million people.

The THA employed 4,300 officials to value, audit, monitor and privatise its 14,000 holdings. These officials were mostly either civil servants from the old *Länder* or private consultants seconded from West German management consultancy or accountancy firms. Ironically the internal organisation of the THA imitated the GDR industry ministries (Seibel 1997: 287, 301). This organisational structure meant already minimal inter-enterprise links between individual enterprises were broken whilst vertical links to the centre were maintained. Another aspect of privatisation that imitated soviet planning was the way privatisation, and the mitigation of the social impacts caused by it, involved setting crude aggregate targets which were used to measure progress (Grabher 1997: 111). In such crude terms the THA can be considered to have been successful since by the time it was wound up at the end of 1994 around 11,500 enterprises had been privatised (including almost 2,700 'management-buy-outs' (MBOs)), and more than 3,500 firms had been liquidated (THA 1994). The fixation with surrogate measures of success established an accelerated timetable for privatisation and imposed a crude efficiency based on the elimination of short-term costs even at the expense of future growth. Similarly, the THA's success in managing the social impacts of privatisation was measured according to legally unenforceable promises of capital investment and job creation made by investors. Thus investors in the new *Länder* promised to invest DM198bn and create or safeguard 1.46 million jobs.

Crucially then the operation of the THAs had a powerful formative impact on the economy in the new *Länder*. The THA was permitted not only to transform property ownership in increasingly abstract ways but also had other important formative effects. In particular the THA's intervention in enterprises through auditing and monitoring transformed economic practices relating to, for example, employment, logistics and marketing, and involved the imposition of crude management models, based on turnover per employee to measure an enterprise's efficiency. In this way the operation of enterprises had to correspond with the premises of the consultants who worked for the agency (cf. Miller 1995: 13). The THA was therefore the primary institution involved in replacing one idealised economic system organised around the state with another idealised economic system organised around markets based on abstract notions such as *homo economicus* and *laissez-faire* capitalism which bear little relation to actual economic practices.

The most profound formative impact the THA had on the economy involved the dis-embedding of the economy through the wholesale 'disintermediation' and 'reintermediation' of inter and intra-enterprise production networks and value chains.[4] This involved the disaggregation of state-owned enterprises and the externalisation of economic activities that were once contained within them (cf. Carrier 1998: 4). As a result economic activities formerly internal to the enterprise became constituted through transient market relationships. Initially the THA dissolved the 126 combines and attempted to privatise enterprises through the sale of shares in 'going concerns'. Later the THA became increasingly proactive in splitting up existing enterprises (or individual factories or production shops[5]) and recombining assets in permutations to suit potential investors. This resulted in the creation of 'empty shell' companies, legal successors to GDR enterprises and as such inherited their liabilities but which contained no assets. The liberated assets were in turn recombined to create companies possessing specific employment levels or building facilities demanded by investors. In practice investors were invited to notify the THA of their requirements following 'mail shots' and the agency constructed custom-made companies that met those requirements. Thus the THA's financial experts engaged in increasingly abstract forms of ownership, to institutionally cleanse 'brownfield' industrial sites, involving the speculative manipulation of risk, debt, assets and markets in conjunction with private investors.

Analyses derived from institutional economics of economic development in the new *Länder* argue that the disintermediation of formal and informal social and economic networks resulted in the destruction of endogenous economic growth potential (Albach 1993). Thus Grabher (1994: 182) states that the THA:

> . . . probably also paralysed the potential for developing a social infra-structure for new economic activities. The loss of supportive tissue goes beyond simply the loss of personal ties, but represents, above all, the demise of the entrepreneurial skills and experience related to the development of *ad hoc* solutions within the informal networks.

As a result the second economy failed to act as an engine for economic growth since within two years of unification half of the GDR's 185,000 private entre-preneurs had ceased trading (Koch and Thomas 1997: 245). Equally it is argued that the reintermediation of production networks and value chains, in which 80 per cent of the THA's holdings were sold to companies in the old *Länder* (Koch and Thomas 1997: 246), produced particular forms of economic development in the new *Länder*. Grabher (1994: 191) argues that this resulted in 'truncated industrialisation' involving the construction of 'capitalism without capitalists'. In particular he argues that whilst demand-led sectors such as construction and food, beverage and tobacco developed regional networks much investment in other sectors resulted in 'cathedrals-in-the-desert' with limited local forwards and backward linkages. This created a 'disembedded' regional economy dominated by branch plants which were nodes in increasingly unstable market-governed transnational production networks. Stark and Bruszt (1998: 163) conclude that: '[T]he economy of contemporary East Germany shows little sign of the vibrant associational life linking networks of producers through lines of competition and cooperation'.

Moreover, it is argued that the disembedding and disintermediation of industrial networks produced a socio-economic *tabula rasa* in the new *Länder* on which the THA and private investors could impose, unchallenged, new industrial practices on a disorganised and docile society. Thus Grabher (1997: 130) suggests that the 'proper implementation [of new industrial practices such as lean production] ... presupposed a far-reaching paralysis of pre-existing formal economic relations and informal networks'. Elsewhere in the same paper, Grabher (1997: 125–126) argues that private investors required a *tabula rasa* involving the 'vigorous demolition of the old *social* web and *cultural* standards' (emphasis in original) to implement organisational and technical changes.[6]

However, this argument is problematic for three reasons. First, this analysis is prone to oversimplification and the denial of the complexities and contestation involved in economic practices. The conceptualisation of 'broken networks' and 'cathedrals-in-the-desert' having produced a *tabula rasa* renders social actors in the east German space-economy without agency, lacking in the capacity for contestation, negotiation and self-organisation, and which are acted upon by hegemonic external actors (Dunn 1999, and Ch. 13). Second, by overemphasising ruptures with the past, the idea of a *tabula rasa* reduces the significance of path dependency and pre-explains the elimination of legacies. By implication the presence of a *tabula rasa* permits a 'transition to capitalism'. Thus, metaphors such as institutional 'cloning' (Grabher 1994: 177) or institutional xeroxing or that unification resulted in a 'square one' (Koch and Thomas 1997: 246) serve only to deny the role of contestation and negotiation in economic change. Third, the notion of a *tabula rasa* serves the self-understanding of the THA and private investors as they sought to construct a new capitalist economy in the new *Länder*. Thus, like so many economists who find the *tabula rasa* so attractive (Stark 1995: 69), the THA regarded the presence of a *tabula rasa* as likely to attract private investors which sought to implement new business practices in a malleable environment.

Privatising the East German automobile industry: disembedding and disintermediation

The ruling Socialist Unity Party (SED) in the GDR attached little priority to the development of the automobile industry with the result that investment in the sector was relatively low and varied considerably from year to year (Leptin and Melzer 1978: 68). After the formation of the GDR the 25 per cent of the pre-war German automobile capacity that fell within the borders of the new state was nationalised. The Audi motor works located in Zwickau were nationalised as *VEB-Sachsenring Automobilwerke* (VEB-SAW) and began producing the Trabant in 1958. The factory at Eisenach which was part of what later became known as BMW was nationalised as *VEB-Automobilwerke Eisenach* (VEB-AWE) and produced the Wartburg. These two state-owned producers, together with Barkas-Werke in Karl-Marx-Stadt,[7] which produced motor vans, joined a number of suppliers and enterprises producing commercial vehicles and motorcycles to form the automobile VVB employing 200,000 workers (von Schleinitz 1993: 70). As a result of nationalisation and central planning the production of cars increased from 22,000 in 1955 to 214,000 in 1985. However, whilst other soviet bloc countries modernised their automobile industries in the 1960s through the CMEA international car production system, based on a technology licensed from Fiat, the industry in the GDR stagnated.

In 1977 the SED regime reorganised the structure of the vehicle building industry and allocated higher levels of investment in a bid to modernise the industry (Preusche *et al.* 1992: 23). The automobile VVB was replaced by three vehicle building combines (*Industrie-Fahrzeug-Anlagen Kombinate* (IFA-Kombinate)) specialising in the production of passenger vehicles, commercial vehicles and motorcycles (Mickler and Walker 1991: 6). Together the three IFA combines comprised 95 VEBs and employed a total of 195,000 workers.[8] The largest of the combines produced passenger vehicles (*IFA-Personenkraftwagen* (IFA-PKW)), employed 65,000 workers and incorporated the three assembly VEBs (see Figure 4.1). Following reorganisation, the SED regime launched a major investment programme designed to modernise the industry (Lungwitz 1991: 4) which resulted in the construction of a new assembly plant, a new engine plant and two international technology transfer agreements (Swain 1992: 83). In 1977 Peugeot-Citroën undertook to build a new plant in Mosel, 8km north of Zwickau, to produce drive shafts for the Trabant. In 1984 VW undertook to construct a new engine plant which opened in 1988 in Karl-Marx-Stadt to produce a new VW designed engine for the Trabant. The new engine plant was connected to the introduction of a new model of the Trabant which was produced at a new small assembly plant, which employed 1,800 workers located adjacent to the new drive shaft plant in Mosel.

When economic, monetary and social union took place on 1 July 1990 IFA-PKW was capitalised and transformed into *IFA-Personkraftwagen* AG, a public company limited by shares wholly owned by the THA. Prior to monetary union the FRG government indicated its willingness to permit the THA to subsidise continued car production until 1993. However, monetary union and trade liberalisation in east and central Europe led to a collapse in the demand for the Trabant and the Wartburg.[9] It having been estimated that a DM100 million subsidy per year was required to maintain production of the Wartburg alone, the THA embarked on a strategy to end production of the Trabant and Wartburg and to privatise or liquidate IFA-PKW AG. This was to be achieved by partnering the two main assembly plants with VW and GM and the sale of component producers to companies in the old *Länder*. This strategy also prevented overcapacity and reduced competition for car producers in the old *Länder* (Turner 1998: 77).

In December 1989 IFA-PKW SAW, the producer of the Trabant, entered into a joint venture with VW to establish temporary small-scale assembly of the Polo and later the Golf model. The THA owned the majority of the joint venture but VW assumed management control. SAW's most modern production facility and 1,250 of the 10,800 workforce were transferred to the joint venture. Assembly of the Polo commenced in May 1990 and employment grew to 1,900 workers assembling up to

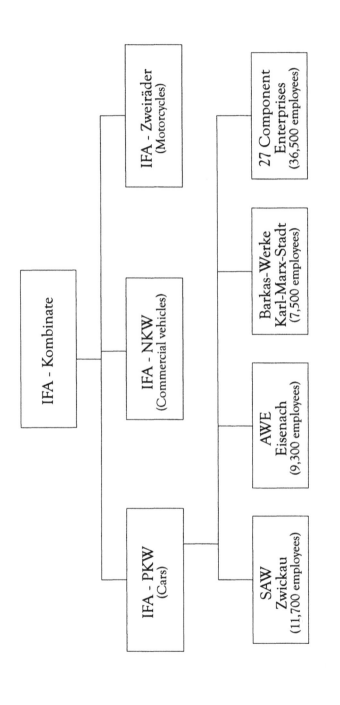

Figure 4.1 Organisational structure of the IFA combine.

380 vehicles per day. Production of the Trabant ceased on 3 April 1991. The THA guaranteed the joint venture's losses in return for VW deciding to make significant additional investment in the locality. In this way the joint venture maintained the workforce whilst the new factory was built. VW established a wholly owned subsidiary, VW Sachsen, to purchase a site adjacent to the existing facility and invest more than DM4.6 billion in a 'greenfield' factory to employ 5,800 workers assembling 250,000 Golfs to open in 1994. VW regarded the new plant as an opportunity to experiment with 'lean' forms of production (Turner 1998: 68). Once the new plant was fully operational it was expected VW Sachsen would purchase the joint venture and its assets transferred for closure or incorporation. VW's involvement with IFA AG was extended in 1991 with the takeover by VW Sachsen of two further facilities. First, VW took over and extended the IFA engine works at Chemnitz (formerly Karl-Marx Stadt) which it had built in the late 1980s. Secondly, VW took over an engine component plant that had formerly formed part of AWE. The assumption by the THA of various liabilities together with investment subsidies provided by other public agencies amounted to a total public subsidy to VW of between DM500–600 m, almost 20 per cent of the total investment. Whilst there were initially no legal guarantees attached to the THA's financial support, as VW's investment timetable slipped in response to recession in the old *Länder*, the THA negotiated employment and investment commitments. In the end the two new factories became fully operational in 1997 by which time VW had invested less and employed fewer people than had been expected initially.

The producer of the Wartburg, IFA-PKW AWE, was partnered with GM in March 1990. A joint venture, majority owned by the THA but managed by GM, involved the transfer of 250 from AWE's 9,300 workforce to the joint venture to assemble 50 Opel Vectras per day in an existing building. Also a partially built plant adjacent to AWE's main site was leased to the joint venture which completed the building of the factory according to GM's specification. The factory was designed to assemble 150,000 Astras and Corsas employing 2,000 workers. The THA, through the joint venture, assumed those costs above and beyond what it estimated the construction of a 'greenfield' factory would have cost. Production of the Wartburg was terminated on 10 April 1991 and AWE was placed in liquidation. The new GM plant opened in early 1993, employing 1,800 people, and was designed as an exemplar of high productivity 'lean production' (Turner 1998: 76–81).

Termination of the Trabant and Wartburg assembly lines, together with the gradual disaggregation of the automobile combine, severely affected the component producers. Deprived of their traditional market, these enterprises now depended on the THA's ability to secure a privatisation or permit the enterprise to remain in business until such time as a privatisation could take place. As enterprises lacked a market, finance, skills (especially marketing and innovation) and technology, the THA argued for rapid sale to existing component firms from the old *Länder*. In a number of cases the THA prevented enterprises from becoming independent firms through MBOs (Lungwitz and Kreißig 1992). The privatisation of component producing enterprises took place in two phases.

The first phase from late-1989 to end-1992 was buoyed by the investments by VW and GM. This was enhanced as both companies had signalled that their investments in the new *Länder* were to be guided by ideas about 'lean production' and were to involve localised supplier networks as a response to the greater efficiency of Japanese-owned transplants in Europe and North America. There were a number of large privatisations as established German component producers, such as Bosch, sought facilities in the new *Länder* to supply the entire European car market. Other companies made smaller investments in facilities close to Zwickau and Eisenach to supply the new plants on a 'just-in-time' basis. The second phase of privatisation took place after 1992, when the most attractive enterprises had already been sold, and involved disaggregating enterprises into profit centres for asset sales to small investors and the creation of 'empty shell' companies to liquidate inherited liabilities. As enterprises were prepared for privatisation or liquidation, employment fell dramatically. In a study of nine automobile component producers, employment fell by 4,213, from 7,161 in 1990 to 2,948 (including short-time workers) in 1992 with employment expected to fall still further once privatisation had been completed (see Table 4.1). *In toto*, IFA-PKW combine's workforce fell from 31,470 people in July 1990 to 754 in December 1992 (von Schleinitz 1993: 81).

The privatisation of the automobile industry was legitimated not only by the evident uncompetitiveness of the GDR automobile industry, but also by a widespread acceptance within the west German automobile industry that outmoded production and labour practices needed to be restructured (Schamp 1995). German car makers sought a response to the widely held view that Japanese producers had identified a new, more efficient way of producing motor cars. Equally German car assemblers faced overcapacity, and intensified competition in the industry following the opening of new low-cost production locations in the Iberian peninsula and subsequently in east and central Europe. Following the publication of *The machine that changed the world* (Womack *et al.* 1990), German managers framed their response to these threats around a model of management enunciated in the book termed 'lean production' which the authors argued would supplant traditional mass and craft production (cf. Thrift 1998). The book was regarded as a 'bible' by managers (Cooke 1993) and 'lean production' became highly influential in German industry in the late 1980s and early 1990s (Auer 1997: 22–24).

'Lean production', based on practices pioneered by Toyota, emphasises technical and organisational rationalisation and participatory forms of work organisation. In particular, the authors argue that greater efficiency can be achieved by organising workers into teams and outsourcing much of the value chain to a network of key suppliers. Whereas the old *Länder* were regarded as having too many institutional barriers to permit the successful deployment of new manufacturing principles (Cooke and Morgan 1998: 52–53), following unification the new *Länder* were presented as an ideal laboratory in which to experiment with 'lean production' techniques (Fichter 1997: 105). Moreover, as 'lean production' focused on the organisation of work within firms and the

Table 4.1 Employment change in nine automobile component firms

Enterprise	Ownership	Products	Employment at currency union	Employment including short-time workers	Expected employment after restructuring
1.	Privatisation imminent	sound dampers	400	200	200
2.	Privatisation in progress	small metal parts	179	179	80
3.	THA owned	gearbox	200	81	n/a
4.	Ready for privatisation	bumpers;	200	83	c.150
5.	Enterprise divided into parts for privatisation	metal parts clutches; dashboards; wheel parts	2,500	800	500
6.	Privatisation in progress	bumpers; springs	650	450	117
7.	Privatisation expected	pressed metal parts	1,015	621	240
8.	Privatisation in progress	pistons; breaks; springs	1,110	254	125
9.	THA owned	parts for electric vehicles	907	280	150
Total			7,161	2,948	

Source: Lungwitz and Kreißig (1992: 181).

external networks among firms, privatisation of industry by the THA permitted experimentation. Thus the metaphorical *tabula rasa* in the new *Länder*, in which networks of social actors inherited from the state system had supposedly been erased, served as an opportunity to construct a new economy that conformed to the premises of a new model of industrial production.

The politics of privatising *VEB-Sachsenring Automobilwerke*

The metaphorical *tabula rasa* was by no means an inevitable outcome of the disintegration of the soviet system but had to be produced by the THA. Thus the THA sought to disaggregate SAW in order to construct as far as possible a *tabula rasa* on which VW and its suppliers could impose new forms of industrial organisation. Equally, the THA's privatisation of SAW and VW's attempts to introduce 'lean production' involved contestation and negotiation within the context of inherited social relations of production. This meant that whilst the THA and investors sought to paralyse institutional legacies, they could not paralyse social relations nor impose their will without contestation and negotiation. Whilst SAW was disaggregated some informal networks amongst former employees were maintained and new informal networks such as amongst trade union members were established. We first examine the THA's attempts to erase the legacies of SAW through its disaggregation before considering workers' and managers' responses.

SAW was transformed in July 1990 into a wholly owned subsidiary of IFA AG that in turn was owned by the THA. However, even before capitalisation, the ownership of SAW's two most modern production facilities had been transferred to other companies. In December 1989 ownership of SAW's most modern assembly plant, including a paintshop, which had been constructed in the late 1980s with VW technology, was transferred to the joint venture established by the THA and VW. VW intended to use the investment in Zwickau as an opportunity to experiment with 'lean production'. Only 25 per cent of the value chain was to take place in the factory compared to 43 per cent at its headquarters plant at Wolfsburg in the old *Länder*. This demanded close co-operation with a select group of 'first tier' suppliers of sub-assemblies. Eight 'just-in-time' projects were established in close proximity to the plant in which suppliers synchronised their production lines to permit continuous delivery straight to the VW assembly line. Experimenting with 'lean production' was also to involve the introduction of team working as a means of intensifying work. In January 1990 a further plant, built in 1981 with technology licensed from Peugeot-Citroën to produce drive shafts, was demerged from SAW to form an independent enterprise *Gelenkwellenwerk Mosel* (GWM) owned by the THA. In May 1991 this enterprise was sold to the British owned automobile component company GKN, a long-time supplier to VW, which became one of the 'just-in-time' suppliers.

Once production of the Trabant ceased in April 1991, the remainder of SAW was broken up to form a series of new companies (THA 1992: 8). SAW was divested from IFA AG, which became an 'empty shell' and was liquidated, to form *Sachsenring Automobilwerke Zwickau* (SAZ), an independent company owned by the THA. As SAZ was the legal successor to SAW and not an 'empty shell', it inherited SAW's DM600 million debt (the THA subsequently assumed half of this debt liability). The team of management consultants sent in by the THA to restructure SAZ's corporate profile identified four profit centres. The automotive engineering profit centre comprised the supply of car parts to VW and accounted for 75 per cent of turnover.

In June 1991 the THA sanctioned a DM70 million investment in new technology which allowed SAZ to assemble pressed parts supplied from VW's headquarters plant in Wolfsburg to complete bodies for VW's temporary assembly operation in Mosel. SAZ also provided a number of sub-assemblies comprising parts shipped in from the old *Länder* before final delivery to VW's plant at Mosel. The other three profit centres were based on service functions provided to investors who had purchased or leased buildings from SAZ, including VW. By the beginning of 1992 around 85 per cent of SAZ's turnover was derived from business with VW. The risk associated with such dependency was demonstrated in early 1992 when it was announced that the assembly of bodies was to be transferred to VW's new factory in late 1992. This meant SAZ's DM70 million investment a year earlier became obsolete. Moreover, as VW's new factory was commissioned so SAZ began to supply fewer and fewer parts to the factory and all but a few hundred workers were placed on short-time working. In time VW accounted for 99 per cent of SAZ's sales.

Whilst this restructuring took place employment dropped precipitously. The workforce fell from over 11,000 on 1 January 1990 to 8,000 in April 1991. Once production of the Trabant ceased, employment at the firm fell even more rapidly. Between April 1991 and January 1992, 6,500 jobs were lost as SAZ's workforce fell to 1,500. In early 1993, having failed to meet the threshold (a measure of turnover per employee) that the THA had set to establish viability, officials abandoned hope of a sale of shares in a 'going concern' and responsibility for the enterprise was transferred to the THA's asset recovery and liquidation department. In November 1993 SAZ became an 'empty shell' company with the loss of 1,200 jobs, whilst some of its assets and 280 employees were transferred to a new company, *Sachsenring Automobiltechnik*. This company, owned by two engineers from the old *Länder*, specialised in producing plastic and metal parts, steering and electrical systems and axles as well as special vehicles. By 1997 employment at the new company had increased to 800 and the company had become only the third company in the new *Länder* to be publicly quoted on a German stock market.

The privatisation and liquidation of SAW, and subsequently SAZ, also involved transferring its most modern and valuable assets not as 'going concerns' but as bundles of assets without liabilities to new firms. This permitted private investors to recruit new workforces with the result that they did not have to take over legal responsibility for existing labour contracts nor the costs of severing them. Thus whilst SAZ inherited debt and accumulated operating losses (SAZ made a loss of DM70 million on a turnover of DM360 million in 1991) its assets were sold, or to minimise risk, leased to private investors. By the end of 1991 more than 14 automotive firms had acquired 165,000 square metres and leased a further 70,000 square metres of SAW's site. Excluding VW, they planned to invest nearly US$150 million and create 3,500 jobs (see Table 4.2). These firms included major German component producers, such as Siemens and Dr. Meleghy, which supplied VW's assembly plants in the old *Länder*. Of SAW's four original sites, the one in Mosel to the north of Zwickau was taken over by VW and GKN, a site in Zwickau became an industrial park comprising automotive-related companies, a further site housed job training facilities and SAZ occupied most of the final site. Ultimately 19 privatised companies employing 5,800 took over parts of SAW (THA 1992: 8).

SAZ's assets, then, were decentralised through a network of new private investors, liabilities were centralised first in SAW and later in SAZ to be assumed by the state once liquidation took place in late 1993 (Stark 1996). However, whilst the THA sought to paralyse and erase institutional legacies by disembedding and disintermediation of intra- and inter-enterprise networks, it was constrained by the social relations of production with the result that there were important continuities and the emergence of new forms of reintermediation.

Table 4.2 The privatisation of parts of IFA-SAW, 1990–4

Investor	Activity	Planned workforce	Planned investment (US$m.)
VW*	car assembly	5,800	5,000
GKN (UK)	drive shafts	800	34
Hoppecke	batteries	400	20
Dr. Meleghy	dies, mouldings, pressed parts	400	20
Varta	batteries	300	20
Gillet	exhausts	200	14
Spedition Rolf Schellecke	logistics	72	10
Siemens	sub-assembly of electrical components	300	8
Naue Johnson (US)	seats	240	7.5
Siebenwurst	machine tools	100	3
Benteler	pressed parts	33	3
Sachsenring Automobiltechnik	components	280	n/a
SASIT	tools	90	n/a
SAQ**	training	55	n/a
Total		9,370	5,139.5

Source: after *Automobil-Produktion* (1992: 55–56).

Notes
* This includes the joint venture between VW and the THA as well as VW Sachsen.
** A temporary employment training company.

The THA's claims to property rights over SAW and later SAZ were not unfettered owing to the emergence of a coalition of the management, the works council and the company's supervisory board which resisted plans for privatising the firm. The coalition emerged during the soviet era when they were commonplace as enterprises sought to minimise the contradictions of the state plan (Hyman 1996: 626). In contrast to the majority of the THA's holdings, the size and importance of SAW meant there was continuity in the personnel running the enterprise. The existing management remained in place after the THA assumed ownership of SAW and the one manager (from the old *Länder*) who was parachuted into the company was said by THA officials to have 'gone native'. Furthermore, owing to its size, by law a supervisory board had to be established. This board included amongst its membership nationally prominent trade union officials as well as *Land* politicians who sought to protect the local industrial base. Throughout the four years during which SAW and later SAZ were disaggregated management, supported by the supervisory board, sought to transform the company into a major car component producer. This contrasted with the THA's view that it should focus on providing services to automotive firms. This dispute culminated in early 1993 with a thwarted attempt at a management buy out

(MBO), with the financial support of Deutsche Bank, to frustrate a team of 40 auditors which had been sent in by the THA to divide the company into nine profit centres prior to their privatisation.

In December 1990, following the extension of West German industrial relations law to the new *Länder*, a works council was elected, led by the same individual who had headed the equivalent institution under the SED regime. Owing to the size of SAW the works council comprised 39 members of which seven by law had to be relieved of normal working duties. All works council members, like most of the workforce, had joined the West German metalworkers' trade union, IG Metall, which moved into the new *Länder*. Additionally IG Metall members at the enterprise elected shop stewards. These new institutions within the enterprise transformed a tradition of labour activism during central planning (which involved a refusal to participate in official trade union structures) into a collective consciousness amongst workers who strongly identified with the enterprise, the locality and the automobile industry. Indeed it was believed the enterprise could at last be run by and in the interests of employees – a rhetorical claim during the soviet era.

The works council leader enjoyed good relations with management and was intimately involved in developing the company strategy (Jürgens *et al.* 1993: 238). Whilst such co-operation between management and the works council led in many cases to the 'co-management' of company restructuring (Hyman 1996: 627, Frege 1998: 478–80, Fichter 1997: 100) and the works council acting as an extension of the personnel department, at SAZ co-management took the form of collective resistance. For example, management supported workers' demands for the establishment of a temporary employment and training company (ETC) to cushion the effects of mass redundancies and placing workers on short-time working. Initially the THA refused to permit SAZ to set up such a company. However, after the intervention of the deputy president of IG Metall, demands for SAZ to be allowed to set up an ETC grew. This culminated in a sit-in by over 1,000 workers in May 1991 which resulted in management ignoring the THA and establishing *Sächsische Aufbau- und Qualifizierungsgesellschaft* (SAQ) as a wholly owned subsidiary. Subsequently the THA decided to support SAQ financially.

Whilst it has been argued that ETCs provided a cheap and politically advantageous way of reducing the workforce to entice private investors (Knuth 1997: 75) SAQ provided retraining and temporary employment for 2,000 former SAW workers up to the end of 1993 and politically mobilised the town. In particular the establishment of SAQ was regarded as a successor for the works council and for IG Metall. SAW employees transferred to SAQ remained within the regional collective bargaining framework, retained their membership of IG Metall and were entitled to elect a works council of their own. Also the creation of SAQ led to the establishment of around 400 ETCs elsewhere in the new *Länder* (Knuth 1997: 76). More broadly the dispute at SAZ formed part of IG Metall's campaign adopted by the *Land* of Saxony, to protect core industrial regions (Wever 1997: 218). This resulted in ATLAS, a regional development and industrial policy initiative, which allowed the *Land* to identify strategic industrial enterprises, such as SAZ, which received additional state support (Seibel 1997: 298–9). Thus the struggle to set up SAQ ensured that SAZ remained in existence for longer than would otherwise have been the case, resulting in the establishment of *Sachsenring Automobiltechnik*.

The privatisation and liquidation of SAW and SAZ not only involved disintermediation but also reintermediation as existing networks were transformed and new networks of firms were established. Reintermediation was the outcome of the THA's and private investors' strategies that built on the long tradition in the automobile industry in the town. VW's investment in Mosel, for example, built on the technology transfer agreement with SAW in 1984 and links it had established through procuring parts, including engines, from the combine since the early 1970s. Equally, VW's experiments with 'lean production' resulting in greater outsourcing led to the emergence of a local supply network. The cluster of 13 local component companies employed 2,500 people and ensured that the locality remained an important site in the international automobile industry. Thus SAZ and subsequently *Sachsenring Automobiltechnik*, for example, continued to supply various VW plants in Germany and beyond. Moreover, supply linkages existed within the cluster of companies and included transactions that once took place within different parts of SAW prior to unification (see Figure 4.2).

The decentralisation of production and employment involved in the disaggregation of SAW altered the balance between management and labour in the plants. Management attempted to introduce new working arrangements that sought to reduce the influence that works councils had in the old *Länder* over recruitment, rostering and manning levels. This focused on the introduction of team working, which management sought to present as a modern version of the soviet brigade system, in which workers worked for the common good of the enterprise (Turner 1998: 75–6). Also in contrast to SAZ and VW, which were unionised, belonged to the employers association, Gesamtmetall, and were bound by collective bargaining agreements, some of the new firms were weakly ununionised and did not join Gesamtmetall. Whilst some joined other employers associations and were bound by collective bargaining in other sectors, many firms were not members of any association and paid salaries which were lower than stipulated in regional tariff agreements (see Ettl 1995). As these firms were small, employees were legally entitled only to small works councils often with no member relieved of normal working duties. In some instances works councils 'co-managed' the plant and resented interference by IG Metall. In part this was a consequence of increased competition between plants and works councils within companies because many produced parts that were also produced at their company's higher cost plants in the old *Länder* (Mickler *et al.* 1994: 277). In several cases firms in the local network of suppliers had established no works council at all (Turner 1998: 75).

Although the majority of private investors purchased assets rather than 'going concerns' and thus did not take over an existing workforce and their labour contracts, most recruited former SAW employees (80 per cent of VW's employees had worked for SAW). The collective identification that existed amongst SAW

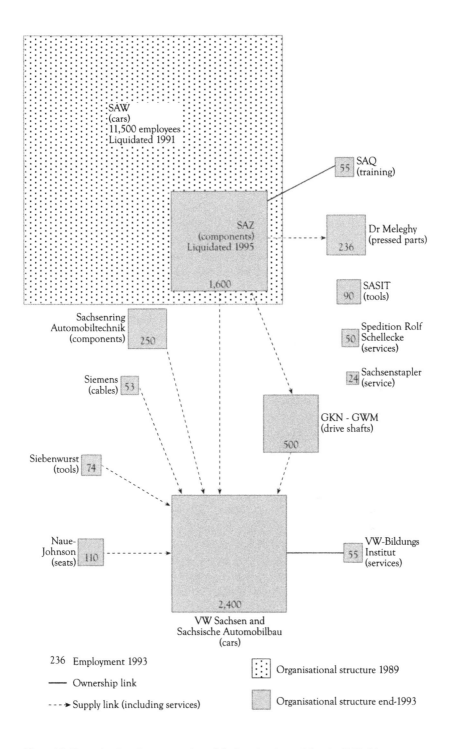

Figure 4.2 Organisational restructuring of *Sachsenring Automobilwerke*, 1989–93.

workers prior to unification was transformed after the disaggregation of the firm into identification with the trade union. SAW workers were at the forefront as IG Metall recruited 70,000 of the 90,000 people working in the metal industry in the Zwickau region. Also *Sachsenring Automobiltechnik*, which emerged from SAZ remained very highly unionised (Turner 1998: 74). Moreover, through the auspices of the trade union the works councils in the new automotive firms were in close contact. Indeed the outsourcing of elements of the value chain to local suppliers by VW encouraged the establishment of links among employees of the firms. As a result the new employers were not able to introduce new working practices without contestation and negotiation. Thus despite the argument that the works council and employees at VW did not resist 'lean production' (Mickler *et al.* 1994: 278) the works council supported by IG Metall were involved in the design of team working and successfully limited the amount of outsourcing. Therefore, even though many works councils were weak and employment in the metal industry fell to 22,000 by the end of 1993, IG Metall enjoyed a strong presence in the region. This was demonstrated in May 1993 when workers at VW and GKN were asked by the union to strike with 25,000 workers in 44 engineering plants after Gesamtmetall revoked a collective bargaining agreement in the first official strike in the new *Länder* since before 1933 (Turner 1997: 118).

Conclusion

This chapter argues that the notion that unification produced a *tabula rasa* casts employees and regions in the new *Länder* as victims of external economic relations and needs to be critically problematised. The chapter suggests that the THA and private investors attempted to refashion economic practices according to virtual idealised models of how the economy should be organised. This involved the disembedding of economic practices through the disintermediation and reintermediation of state-owned enterprises and value chains. The chapter suggests that the privatisation and restructuring of the automobile industry was planned in the context of the model of management practice called 'lean production'. This model became highly influential in Germany at the time of unification and had particularly powerful formative effects on the economy as it links the organisation of production networks to the organisation of work within individual firms. However, whilst disembedding and disintermediation sought to paralyse institutional legacies, the case study of *Sachsenring Automobilwerke* demonstrates that the construction of a new 'lean' automobile industry was embedded in inherited social relations. These social relations had been produced through a long history in Zwickau of working in the automobile industry under both capitalist and non-capitalist relations of production. Consequently networks of social actors survived, more-or-less transformed, the 'transition to capitalism' to negotiate and contest the restructuring of the industry and its localities. This meant that both the THA and individual investors were unable to impose their designer models of how the automobile industry should be organised without negotiation and struggle with managers and especially employees and their trade union.

Notes

1 This chapter is based on fieldwork visits to Germany in 1992 and 1993. The fieldwork involved 39 semi-structured interviews in English or German with managers, IG Metall trade union representatives, works council representatives and employees of automotive assembly and component firms. Interviews were also conducted with local and *Länder* economic development officials, officials of the THA and national IG Metall officials. I am grateful to Nick Marshall for allowing me to use a transcript of an interview he conducted with an SAZ employee in 1993. I would like to acknowledge the financial support from the ESRC for the original research. I would also like to thank Andrew Leyshon and Adrian Smith for helpful comments on earlier drafts of this chapter.

2 The 'new' *Länder* refers to the five federal states that joined the Federal Republic of Germany on 3 October 1990. The 'old' *Länder* refers to the federal states that formed the Federal Republic of Germany prior to 3 October 1990.

3 *'Die Wende'* literally means 'the turning' and refers to the ending of the soviet system symbolised by the breaching of the Berlin Wall on 9 November 1989, the adoption of a market economy with monetary, economic and social union on 1 July 1990, and unification with the Federal Republic of Germany on 3 October 1990.

4 I have borrowed these terms from Leyshon's study of digital music networks (Leyshon 2001).

5 Disintermediation also took place within enterprises between different production sites and shops and was not wholly caused directly by the THA. Thus migration to the old *Länder* served to reinforce the dislocation within enterprises as migration primarily involved the most highly skilled workers in the workers' brigades (Stark and Bruszt 1998: 90).

6 See Grabher (1995) for a somewhat different discussion on *tabula rasa* in the context of institutional change in East Germany and Hungary.

7 Karl-Marx-Stadt reverted to Chemnitz following unification.

8 IFA-Nutzkraftwagen (IFA-NKW) produced commercial vehicles and comprised 26 VEBs employing 50,000 workers whilst the third production system produced motorcycles (IFA-Zweiräder) and consisted of seven VEBs employing 15,000 people.

9 Both models were essentially designed in the 1950s and were under powered and notoriously unreliable. The Trabant, especially, became the object of ridicule and emblematic of the inadequacies of the planned economy not only in the GDR but also throughout the Soviet bloc.

References

Albach, H. (1993) *Zerrissene Netz: Eine Netwerkanalyse des ostdeutschen Transformationsprozesses*, Berlin: Edition Sigma.

Auer, P. (1997) 'Institutional stability pays: German industrial relations under pressure', in L. Turner (ed.) *Negotiating the New Germany: Can Social Partnership Survive?* Ithaca: Cornell University Press, pp. 15–32.

Automobil-Produktion (1992), April.

Begg, R. and Pickles, J. (1998) 'Institutions, social networks and ethnicity in the cultures of transition: Industrial change, mass unemployment and regional transformation in

94   *Adam Swain*

Bulgaria', in J. Pickles and A. Smith (eds) *Theorising Transition: The Political Economy of Post-Communist Transformations*, London: Routledge, pp. 115–146.

Carrier, J. G. (1998) 'Introduction', in J. G. Carrier and D. Miller (eds) *Virtualism: A New Political Economy*, Oxford: Berg, pp. 1–24.

Carrier, J. G. and Miller, D. (eds) (1998) *Virtualism: A New Political Economy*, Oxford: Berg.

Cooke, P. (1993) 'The experiences of German engineering firms in applying lean production methods', in ILO, *Lean Production and Beyond*, Geneva: ILO.

Cooke, P. and Morgan, K. (1998) *The Associational Economy: Firms, Regions, and Innovation*, Oxford: Oxford Univesity Press.

Dunford, M. (1998) 'Differential development, institutions, modes of regulation and comparative transitions to capitalism', in J. Pickles and A. Smith (eds) *Theorising Transition: The Political Economy of Post-Communist Transformations*, London: Routledge, pp. 76–111.

Dunn, E. (1999) 'Slick salesmen and simple people: Negotiated capitalism in a privatised Polish firm', in M. Burawoy and K. Verdery (eds) *Uncertain Transition: Ethnographies of Change in the Postsocialist World*, Lanham: Rowman and Littlefield, pp. 125–150.

Elster, J., Offe, C. and Preuss, U.K. (1998) *Institutional Design in Post-Communist Societies: Rebuilding the Ship at Sea*, Cambridge: Cambridge University Press.

Ettl, W. (1995) 'Arbeitgeberverbände als Transformationsakteure: Organisations-entwicklung und Tarifpolitik im Dilemma von Funktionalität und Repräsentativät', in H. Wiesenthal (ed.) *Einheit als Interessenpolitik: Studien zur sektoralen Transformation Ostdeutschlands*, Frankfurt: Campus Verlag, pp. 70–77.

Fichter, M. (1997) 'Unions in the new Länder: Evidence for the urgency of reform', in L. Turner (ed.) *Negotiating the New Germany: Can Social Partnership Survive?* Ithaca: Cornell University Press, pp. 87–111.

Frege, C. (1998) 'Institutional transfer and effectiveness of employee representation: Comparing works councils in East and West Germany', *Economic and Industrial Democracy*, 19 (3): 475–504.

Grabher, G. (1994) 'The disembedded regional economy: The transformation of East German industrial complexes into western enclaves', in A. Amin and N. Thrift (eds) *Globalization, Institutions, and Regional Development in Europe*, Oxford: Oxford University Press, pp. 177–195.

Grabher, G. (1995) 'The elegance of incoherence: Institutional legacies in the economic transformation in East Germany and Hungary', in E. Dittrich, G. Schmidt and R. Whitley (eds) *Industrial Transformation in Europe: Processes and Contexts*, London: Sage, pp. 33–54.

Grabher, G. (1997) 'Adaptation at the cost of adaptability? Restructuring the Eastern German regional economy', in G. Grabher and D. Stark (eds) *Restructuring Networks in Post-socialism: Legacies, Linkages, and Localities*, Oxford: Oxford University Press, pp. 107–134.

Grabher, G. and Stark, D. (eds) (1997) *Restructuring Networks in Post-socialism: Legacies, Linkages, and Localities*, Oxford: Oxford University Press.

Hyman, R. (1996) 'Institutional transfer: Industrial relations in eastern Germany', *Work, Employment and Society*, 10 (4): 601–639.

Jürgens, U., Klinzing, L. and Turner, L. (1993) 'The transformation of industrial relations in Eastern Germany', *Industrial and Labor Relations Review*, 46 (2): 229–244.

Knuth, M. (1997) 'Active labour market policy and German unification: The role of employment and training companies', in L. Turner (ed.) *Negotiating the New Germany: Can Social Partnership Survive?* Ithaca: Cornell University Press, pp. 69–86.

Koch, T. and Thomas, M. (1997) 'The social and cultural embeddedness of entrepreneurs in Eastern Germany', in G. Grabher and D. Stark (eds) *Restructuring Networks in Post-socialism: Legacies, Linkages, and Localities*, Oxford: Oxford University Press, pp. 242–261.

Leptin, G. and Melzer, M. (1978) *Economic Reform in East German Industry*, Oxford: Oxford University Press.

Leyshon, A. (2001) 'Time, space and (digital) compression: Software formats and the geographical reorganisation of the music industry', *Environment and Planning A* 33(1): 49–77.

Lungwitz, R. (1991) 'Zwischen Kollaps und Ausfstieg der Automobilzulieferindustrie in der neuen Bundesländer', *Informationsblatt Nr. 9*, Chemnitz: WISOC.

Lungwitz, R. and Kreißig, V. (1992) 'Sozialer und wirtschaftlicher Wandel in der Autombilzulieferindustrie der neuen Bundesländer', in M. Heidenreich (ed.) *Krisen, Kader, Kombinate: Kontinuität und Wandel in ostdeutschen Betrieben*, Berlin: Edition Sigma, pp. 173–185.

Mickler, O. and Walker, B. (1991) *Auf dem Weg zu Marktökonomie und innerbetrieblicher Demokratisierung? Die ostdeutsche Automobilindustrie im Prozeß der Anpassung und Modernisierung*, ms, Institute of Sociology, University of Hannover.

Mickler, O., Engelhardt, N., Lungwitz, R. and Walker, B. (1994) 'Ein Aufstieg wie Phönix aus der Asche? Der Wiederaufbau der ostdeutschen Automobilindustrie die Konflikte der Betriebsräte', in R. Hoffmann, N. Kluge, G. Linne and E. Mezger (eds) *Problemstart: Politischer und sozialer Wandel in der neuen Bundesländern*. HBS-Forschung, vol. 15, Köln: Bund-Verlag, 263–80.

Miller, D. (1995) 'Consumption as the vanguard of history: A polemic by way of an introduction', in D. Miller (ed.) *Acknowledging Consumption: A Review of New Studies*, London: Routledge, pp. 1–57.

Offe, C. (1996) *Varieties of Transition*, Cambridge: Polity Press.

Pickel, A. (1992) 'Jump-starting a market economy: A critique of the radical strategy for economic reform in the light of the East German experience', *Studies in Comparative Communism*, 25 (2): 177–191.

Preusche, E., Lungwitz, R. and Falkenberg, U. (1992) *Historie des DDR-Automobilbaus als Zeuge der Innovationsblockade durch politische Machtstrukturen*, Chemnitz: WISOC.

Schamp, E.W. (1995) 'The German automobile production system going European', in R. Hudson and E.W. Schamp (eds) *Towards a New Map of Automobile Manufacturing in Europe: New Production Concepts and Spatial Restructuring*, Berlin: Springer, pp. 93–116.

von Schleinitz, F. (1993) 'IFA-Kombinat PKW Karl-Marx-Stadt: Vom internationalen Markt abgekoppelt', in *Kombinate: Was aus ihnen geworden ist*, Berlin: Verlag Die Wirtschaft, pp. 69–82.

Seibel, W. (1997) 'Privatization by means of state bureaucracy? The Treuhand phenomenon in Eastern Germany', in G. Grabher and D. Stark (eds) *Restructuring Networks in Post-socialism: Legacies, Linkages, and Localities*, Oxford: Oxford University Press, pp. 284–304.

Smith, A. and Swain, A. (1998) 'Regulating and institutionalising capitalism: the micro foundations of transformation in Eastern and Central Europe', in J. Pickles and A. Smith (eds) *Theorising Transition: The Political Economy of Post-Communist Transformations*, London: Routledge, pp. 25–53.

Stark, D. (1995) 'Not by design: The myth of designer capitalism in eastern Europe', in J. Hausner, B. Jessop and K. Nielsen (eds) *Strategic Choice and Path-dependency in Post-socialism*, Cheltenham: Edward Elgar, pp. 67–83.

Stark, D. (1996) 'Networks of assets, chains of debt: Recombinant property in Hungary', in R. Frydman, C.W. Gray and A. Rapaczynski (eds) *Corporate Governance in Central Europe and Russia. Volume 2: Insiders and the State*, Budapest: Central European University Press, 109–150.

Stark, D. and Bruzst, L. (1998) *Postsocialist Pathways: Transforming Politics and Property in East Central Europe*, Cambridge: Cambridge University Press.

Swain, A. (1992) 'Eastern Europe and the global strategies of automobile producers', Discussion Paper No. 11, *Change in the Automobile Industry: An International Comparison*, Department of Geography, University of Durham.

THA (1992) *Treuhand Agency Sales Offer: Sachsenring Automobilwerke Zwickau GmbH*, Berlin: THA.

THA (1994) *Monats-information der THA (Stand 30.06.1994)*, Berlin: THA.

Thrift, N. (1998) 'The rise of soft capitalism', in A. Herod, G. Ó Tuathail and S.M. Roberts (eds) *An Unruly World? Globalization, Governance and Geography*, London: Routledge, pp. 25–71.

Thrift, N. and Olds, K. (1996) 'Refiguring the economic in economic geography', *Progress in Human Geography*, 20 (3): 311–337.

Turner, L. (1997) 'Unifying Germany: Crisis, conflict, and social partnership in the East', in L. Turner (ed.) *Negotiating the New Germany: Can Social Partnership Survive?* Ithaca: Cornell University Press, pp. 113–136.

Turner, L. (1998) *Fighting for Partnership: Labor and Politics in Unified Germany*, Ithaca: Cornell University Press.

Voskamp, U. and Wittke, V. (1991) 'Industrial restructuring in the former German Democratic Republic (GDR): Barriers to adaptive reform become downward development spirals', *Politics and Society*, 3: 341–371.

Wever, K.S. (1997) 'Renegotiating the German model: Labor-management relations in the new Germany', in L. Turner (ed.) *Negotiating the New Germany: Can Social Partnership Survive?* Ithaca: Cornell University Press, pp. 207–225.

Womack, J.P., Jones, D.T. and Roos, D. (1990) *The Machine that Changed the World*, New York: Rawson Associates.

Part III

Gender, work and employment in transition

5 Out with the old, in with the new?

The changing experience of work for Polish women

Jane Hardy and Alison Stenning

Introduction

The rapid transformation to a more market oriented economy after 1989 has brought about profound restructuring of the Polish economy. The implementation of shock therapy in 1990 resulted in a dramatic fall in industrial production of 25 per cent and a sharp increase in unemployment to 11.8 per cent in 1991.[1] By 1998, however, Poland was regarded as the 'tiger economy' of Eastern and Central Europe (ECE). The 6.1 per cent growth rate of the Polish economy was significantly ahead of those of comparable economies such as Hungary (1.3 per cent) and the Czech Republic (3.9 per cent) (EBRD 1998). The effects of this rapid growth, however, have been unevenly spread and accompanied by an increase in poverty and marked disparities in income and wealth, differentiated by class, gender, generation and geography.

Much of the literature on transformation has been gender blind. One school of thought, however, has unequivocally argued that women have born the brunt of transformation in suffering disproportionately from unemployment and encountering difficulties in finding new work (Einhorn 1993, Hübner, Maier and Rudolph 1993, Czerny 1998, Ruminska-Zimny 1999). While this is the case in all East-Central European economies, in Poland these tendencies have been bolstered by an ideological backlash spearheaded by the Catholic Church to return women to the home (Plakwicz 1992, Pine 1995, Lobodzinska 1996, Knothe 1999), manifest in the banning of abortion in 1993. Gregory *et al.* (1998), however, have argued that the effects are more ambiguous and that other factors may offset this dismal picture, in particular the opportunities offered by the rising service sector and the informal sector, and evidence of a growing number of women entrepreneurs (Mroczkowski 1997, and Ch. 9).

While there has been much juggling with figures, there has been much less written on how the experience of women in work has changed as their firms or workplaces are restructured or as they move into new jobs in the growing sectors such as retailing. It is argued that three factors have shaped the restructuring of women's work in East-Central Europe, both in terms of the number of jobs available and the form and content of that work. First, there is a spatial dimension in that those regions which are at the forefront of transformation and where processes such as privatisation are most progressed and levels of foreign investment highest are likely to see a faster rate of change, which should in theory at least, open up better labour market possibilities. Second, at the level of the individual firm, foreign investment has had a profound effect on state-owned enterprises (SOEs) either by directly changing ownership through the privatisation process or, equally importantly, by changing the nature of competition in which the firm operates. Third, the impact of foreign investment, particularly greenfield developments, and other new private business will determine the number of new jobs in a locality and the form and nature of new employment opportunities. In this chapter we examine how the interplay of these three factors has transformed both opportunities for employment and the nature and conditions of work for women in two regions of Poland.

Case studies

The case study work was carried out in Wroclaw and Kraków, both regarded as leaders of transformation, where privatisation is well progressed and levels of foreign investment and private sector growth relatively high (Figure 5.1). Both cities were dominated by heavy industry, steel in Kraków and engineering in Wroclaw, yet traditionally women worked in light industry. Both Wroclaw and Kraków have particularly high numbers of women working in the public sector. These cities have a higher than average number of institutions of further and higher education and possess regional concentrations of health facilities and administrative functions. In addition, their status as tourist centres has increased the number of women employed in the service sector such as retail, hotel and catering relative to other regions. The impact of restructuring on gender has a clear spatial aspect as economic histories have a regionally diverse effect on local economies (Pine 1995).

Two of our case study workplaces are former SOEs. Cigarettski produces Polish and American cigarettes for the Polish and Russian market and was privatised in 1995 after being purchased by a major US transnational tobacco company. Fridgski is a white goods producer assembling refrigerators and washing machines, employing 4,000 workers in 1998. The firm was floated on the Stock Exchange in 1997, and in 1999 a French white goods producer purchased a majority of shares. A strong Solidarity trade union that has negotiated and contested the privatisation process at every stage meant that restructuring has proceeded at a much slower pace than in Cigarettski.

The third case study is a major foreign food retailer, which opened a store in Wroclaw in 1998 and employed 700 workers. At the time of undertaking this research, employment in this sector was highly controversial and access to other major foreign food retailers was hampered by a government investigation into employment abuses under the Labour Code. Although we have to be cautious about drawing strong conclusions, as other food retailers from other countries are likely to provide a different employment experience, the interviews do nevertheless enable us to discuss the experiences of women in one workplace and raise some general issues about working in foreign supermarkets.

Figure 5.1 Map of Poland.

Semi-structured interviews were carried out with women in the production and retail sectors in the three workplaces, exploring their experiences of changes at work. The interviews covered a range of topics including working patterns, pay, training, labour relations and employment history. Discussions with the interviewees concluded with more general questions regarding the women's attitudes and beliefs regarding the changing opportunities for them and their families. Women were interviewed in pairs where possible, or groups of up to six and the interviews were recorded. In the case of the SOEs the interviews were organised either by the Solidarity trade union or by management, which suggests some bias in the selection. In the case of the foreign-owned food retailing the interviews were set up by a trainee personnel officer. In both places we were able to speak to a cross-section of women in terms of ages and type of employment within the workplace. Where possible interviews were also carried out with managers and trade union representatives in the workplaces and regions.[2]

The chapter is structured as follows: the first section looks at the changing position of women in the labour market in Poland as a whole and then draws out the particular patterns of women's employment in Kraków and Wroclaw. The following sections look at the changing experience of women in the case study workplaces through exploring five themes: the continued gendering of employment; modernisation and management changes; flexibility; restructuring the social wage, the job security and wages trade-off and changing employment opportunities; and assessments of transformation.

From plan to market in Poland

In spite of ideological, legislative and social policy efforts to secure positions of equality for men and women in communist societies, extensive discrimination against women persisted. Processes of gender-based labour market segmentation and stratification accompanied women's access to paid work across ECE. Women dominated employment in finance and insurance, the health service, education, trade and public administration, but even in these sectors men held the most senior positions. Women constitute just one-third of the total of senior positions, which includes members of parliament, higher executives and managers (Knothe 1999). Where women worked in production they were concentrated in lower priority light industrial sectors of the economy such as textiles and consumer goods production (Hübner *et al.* 1993). Overall, women's wages were lower, approximately 70 per cent of those of men (Hübner *et al.* 1993). There were undoubtedly some advantages of working to women, including entitlements such as free health care, paid retirement and paid vacations, but it is important to note, however, that access to these benefits varied widely between workplaces and regions (Domanski 1997, Ciechocinska 1993, Hardy and Rainnie 1996). Further, pension policies also reinforced gender and class inequalities in the workplace, and consequently women's financial situation became worse in retirement because the pension is based on pay levels and number of years worked (Calasanti and Zajicek 1997).

Since the beginning of the transformation in 1990 the arrival of foreign investment in East Central Europe and Russia is having profound implications on the number and type of jobs and the nature of work. Due to higher levels of FDI, in general workers in countries such as Poland and Hungary have experienced the impact of foreign investment through changing employment opportunities and the restructuring of work more markedly than in Russia and other CIS economies. By 1997, for example, inflows of foreign investment in Poland were second only to the Russian Federation and accounted for 30 per cent of total inflows in the region. However, the legacy of the role of women in the labour force in Poland under the previous regime has meant that foreign investment has had an impact on employment and the nature of work in specific ways. For example, the greatest concentration of foreign investment has been in food, beverages and tobacco and light industry, and as women workers are concentrated in these sectors of industry it is their workplaces that are likely to face more rapid and deeper processes of restructuring at work.

The restructuring of state-owned enterprises, with or without the direct participation of foreign investors, also has specific implications for women workers. Adaptation to the market has more often than not accelerated a trend established in the 1980s whereby firms have focused on core operations and divested the social functions of the firm (Ciechocinska 1993, Hardy 1998). Privatisation has increased the impetus to efficiency and productivity and has led some employers to regard women as relatively expensive as a result of their domestic commitments. This has resulted in both overt and covert discrimination in the labour market. The perception that women are less employable derives from the fact that many of what are regarded as the costly social services that remain on the statute books (such as child care) are oriented to them. In terms of the provisions in the welfare code, the employment of women is viewed by employers as potentially problematic, even if women's employment rights and privileges are not observed in practice (Ruminska-Zimny 1999). This overt and covert discrimination is reflected in the higher levels of female unemployment in the 25 to 34 age group (30 per cent as against 23 per cent for men) which suggests that some employers are choosing not to employ young women, wary of their future maternity and family obligations (Knothe 1999). Further, Flecker *et al.* (1998) suggest that the technological upgrading of labour intensive industries in western-owned enterprises, in which women comprise the majority of the workforce, has resulted in their removal from production. This is because craft and vocational areas, less affected by technological change, are overwhelmingly dominated by men, whilst the upgrading of routine, largely women's, work leads to an intensification incompatible with other responsibilities which may include other jobs as well as domestic tasks.

More recently there has been an explosion of foreign investment in the retail sector, which had been fully privatised by 1995. This sector is currently going through a process of concentration, which is attributable to the activity of a few foreign firms that have expanded their activities in Poland from the mid-1990s onwards. PAIZ (Polish Agency for Foreign Investment) reported foreign investment in the trade sector as exceeding US$2.1 billion in 1998. Although investment started in the mid-1990s, 1995 saw an acceleration in the pace of development of foreign retail chains and in particular, French and German investment in the construction of supermarkets and hypermarkets. It is estimated that by the end of 2001 there will be 170 foreign hypermarkets in Poland, compared with just 27 in 1996. Such is the scale of expansion that it was estimated that by 2000 the shares of foreign food retailers exceeded 40 per cent of the market. Firms appearing on the Polish market during this period included the French companies Leclerc (1995), Auchan (1996), Geant (1996) and Carrefour (1997), Alkauf-Ahold, HIT and Stinnes from Germany and Billa from Austria (*Warsaw Voice*, 21.2.99). In October 1998 the UK supermarket chain Foodco opened its first hypermarket in Wroclaw and plans twelve more stores before 2001.

In the West, the rise of service sector employment in areas such as retailing created new opportunities for women to work and it is argued that the changes in employment practices introduced by foreign food retailers (including part-time and flexible work) offers better opportunities for combining work and household responsibilities in ECE as well. Such an argument rests on the notion that part time work is an active choice (Walsh 1999). However, a cross-European study of women in the food retailing sector (Perrons 1998) argues that this flexibility represents a new form of precariousness and works in the interest of employers rather than women workers. Within East Central Europe Pollert's (1995) case study of changes in retailing brought about by foreign investment in the Czech Republic contends that the work processes of women have been intensified with the result that older established women have left their jobs leaving young women without family commitments in place.

Women in the labour market in Wroclaw and Kraków

In many ways, Kraków and Wroclaw can be seen as microcosms of the national picture. Table 5.1 shows that the largest sectors of employment for women in Wroclaw are in manufacturing, trade, education and health. Women workers make up 37.4 per cent of workers in manufacturing and comprise 51.8 per cent of those in trade (including retail) and 82.5 per cent of the labour force in health.

Table 5.1 Employment and monthly wage by gender in Wroclaw, 1998

Sector	Males		Females		Average wage (zloty)*
	no.	*%*	*no.*	*%*	
Agriculture, hunting, forestry and fishing	311,141	51.5	293,369	48.5	865.18
Mining	1,084	83.6	213	16.4	895.3
Manufacturing	58,606	62.6	34,900	37.4	888.56
Electricity, gas, water	5,315	75.9	1,686	24.1	1243.42
Construction	30,014	89.0	3,737	11.0	877.21
Retail and wholesale trade	31,620	48.2	33,850	51.8	838.56
Hotels and restaurants	2,312	36.3	4,056	63.7	607.06
Transport and communications	19,167	70.0	8,181	30.0	957.55
Financial services	3,440	30.3	7,904	69.7	1256.22
Real estate services	13,990	52.4	12,673	47.6	897.86
Public administration legal	5,186	42.6	6,981	57.4	1185.74
Education	11,135	31.4	24,308	68.6	879.29
Health and welfare	6,524	17.5	30,751	82.5	752.49
Miscellaneous municipal services	7,167	49.5	7,316	50.5	754.59

Source: Adapted from *Rocznik Statystczny Wojewodztwa Wroclawskiego* published by Urzad Statystczny We Wroclawiu 1998.

Notes
*   Exchange rate £1 = 5 zloty; average wage in public sector = 865.18 zloty; average wage in private sector = 931.44 zloty.

Table 5.2 Unemployment by gender in Wroclaw and Kraków, 1997

		Wroclaw		Kraków	
		% change unemployment on prev. year	% total unemployed	% change unemployment on prev. year	% total unemployed
Total	1995	–	–	–	–
	1996	−15.5	–	−21.0	–
	1997	−22.7	–	−30.9	–
Males	1995	–	39.9	–	42.3
	1996	−27.4	33.9	−31.7	36.6
	1997	−30.7	30.4	−34.3	34.8
Females	1995	–	60.1	–	57.7
	1996	−7.7	66.1	−13.1	63.4
	1997	−18.6	69.6	−28.9	65.2

Source: Authors' calculations from *Rocznik Statystczny Wojewodztwa Wroclawskiego* and *Rocznik Statystczny Wojewodztwa Krakówskiego*.

Those sectors in which women are concentrated receive lower than average wages. A similar pattern is also found in Kraków where women are concentrated in health, education, finance, hospitality and administration (all over 60 per cent), but make up just 36.5 per cent of manufacturing employment in the region. The official statistical material makes it difficult to differentiate within sectors, such that although women make up only around 52 per cent of the workforce in trade and repairs in both regions, it is likely that women dominate in 'trade' (retail and wholesale) whilst men dominate in 'repairs'. Moreover, the size of the manufacturing sector fails to allow us to discriminate between light and heavy industrial work and to assess the gender balance within these sub-sectors.

Although we have argued that Wroclaw and Kraków are at the forefront of transformation, Table 5.2 shows that between 1995 and 1997 men's unemployment has fallen much more rapidly than women's and that women now make up 69.6 per cent and 65.2 per cent of the unemployed in Wroclaw and Kraków respectively compared with 60.1 per cent and 57.7 per cent just two years before. In these areas, at least, this would support the contention that women are facing increased difficulties in finding work. This is a notion reinforced by the observation that in 1995 when women nationally accounted for 55 per cent of the total unemployed, they comprised almost 70 per cent of those unemployed for over two years (Glowny Urzad Statystyczny 1996). These average figures mask the fact that there are marked disparities between unemployment rates in the cities (municipalities) and the small towns and villages where unemployment rates are significantly higher.

The continued gendering of employment

The gendering of employment patterns discussed earlier was evident in all of the case study workplaces. In line with the national picture in light consumer goods, the two former SOEs employed large numbers of women. In Fridgski, 40 per cent of the workforce were women, with the largest number in the 41 to 50 age group. In Cigarettski, where privatisation had taken place earlier and processes of restructuring were more advanced, the number of women as a percentage of the workforce had fallen from 45 per cent at the beginning of the privatisation process in 1995 to around 35 per cent by 1999, largely as a result of women bearing the brunt of redundancies. In both factories women were employed primarily on the production line, doing light cigarette assembly work and packing or assembling refrigerators or washing machines. Men tended to work predominantly as team leaders or in jobs that required 'special skills' such as maintenance or were deemed to be dangerous such as working in the paint shop.

Foodco employed 700 workers, 670 of whom were shopfloor or warehouse workers. All checkout operators were women, and attractive young women were involved in the promotion of new food and goods on the shop floor. Both men and women were attached to specialist departments, but while men were predominant in the alcohol and meat departments as this was deemed to be heavy work, women worked in the dairy and clothing sections. Outside of the specialist departments men were employed primarily in security, warehouse and in management functions.

What clearly emerged from all the interviews was that working was not a choice for women. Although full-time housekeeping may have had some appeal to some women given the memory of combining domestic work, childcare and paid work under the conditions of the 1980s,[3] the reality was that the financial survival of the family was predicated on two wages. Many of the women interviewed had taken employment breaks earlier in their work histories in order to raise families, but for financial reasons had returned to work when the children were no longer entirely dependent. Although many women enjoyed their jobs, experienced job satisfaction and benefited from the social nature of work, these were bonuses and secondary to the primary financial motive. The need to work was illustrated by the fact that several women, particularly from small towns, travelled as far as 40 km to do part-time work in Foodco. Questions regarding the notion of choice implicit in many debates about women working in West European economies were deemed irrelevant and often met with incomprehension.

Whilst the gendered division of labour between and within workplaces had persisted from the socialist to post-socialist era, all of the women interviewed had experienced significant changes to their working practices and conditions over the last decade. Some of these resulted from the women choosing or being forced through redundancy to change jobs but many more were the consequence of the restructuring of existing workplaces in response to wider processes of social and economic transformation. Although the form and intensity of restructuring varies both between and within sectors and workplaces, it is possible to identify a number of emerging themes.

Modernisation and management change

In the two manufacturing plants – Fridgski and Cigarettski – the changes that have taken place have been brought on by privatisation and increasing competition within both Polish and global markets as a result of processes of marketisation and internationalisation. Both the white goods and cigarette sectors have been targeted by foreign firms, which now manufacture and market their products in Poland. This intensification of competition has resulted in growing pressure for product quality and efficiency and both plants have adopted ISO standards. This, coupled with an emphasis on marketing and sales within the plants' management teams, has had an impact on the structure of management and the organisation of work. Both Fridgski and Cigarettski had introduced western management techniques, which was reflected in the introduction of new departments and functions, in particular, Human Resource Management (HRM) and Marketing. While this has led to increased opportunities for younger educated women, it has also resulted in an increasing polarisation of wages, working conditions and opportunities between white-collar and shopfloor workers. In Fridgski middle and senior managers were given a 300 per cent salary increase in January 1998, while shopfloor workers experienced an increase of 20 per cent in line with inflation. Solidarity reported being continually exhorted by management to keep wages down in exchange for maintaining current employment levels. Since Cigarettski was bought by a global tobacco corporation the opportunities for training, foreign travel and job satisfaction have increased dramatically for management. For shopfloor workers, pay had remained relatively stable but the introduction of new machinery had led to a greater intensity of work because of the need to concentrate harder (Rainnie and Hardy 1999) and was subject to constant supervision.

In both workplaces, the modernisation of product and process technology has had a major impact on shopfloor workers. In Fridgski, investment in a new washing machine line in 1996 had improved the quality of work but at the same time placed increasing pressure on women to become proficient in new technologies, to produce to a higher quality and to work at a faster pace. Women have very much been on the sharp end of increasing productivity, with auditors from outside the department constantly checking quality and the pace of work. Production line workers suggested that work was more stressful because the ever-present threat of redundancy meant that they were fearful of not 'coming up to scratch'. In Cigarettski, the ongoing modernisation of production lines and consequent increases in productivity encouraged rounds of voluntary redundancies in which up to 80 per cent of those taking early redundancy packages have been women. In line with the findings of Flecker *et al.* (1998), the reasons cited for leaving were increased stress, fear of new technology and newly emerging conflicts between work and home. For those women still working in Cigarettski, the introduction of new technology raised fears about their ability to acquire new skills and for their jobs in the future.

The greenfield investment in the foreign-owned retail sector offered the possibility of introducing western working practices *ab initio*, without having to negotiate with unions or change long-established routines. While adapted to local labour codes, management techniques and the administration of the labour process have largely been imported by the western parent firm. According to a trainee manager, western recruitment techniques were acting as a barrier to employment from the start, because applicants were required to complete detailed forms. This posed a problem because under the old system, most older Polish workers had been allocated employment and therefore had no experience of such an application process. Further, younger workers had been socialised within an education system which had still not caught up with the needs of a restructured and competitive labour market. Indeed Foodco's trainee manager reported having virtually abandoned the application form as a criterion by which to judge applicants.

The women interviewed at Foodco stressed the use of western human resource management techniques in contrast to Polish-style labour relations with personnel departments that had previously had only an administrative function. Two issues were highlighted. First, workers at Foodco talked about the emphasis on customer care and identified this as a new concept in Poland. In a highly competitive market where food retailers sold similar products, customer.care and customer service were the frontiers of the new competition. The main criterion for recruitment was attitude and flexibility and, once employed, explanation, exhortation, exercises and role play were all part of the extensive training given to employees to inculcate notions of customer care and to cultivate new skills and attitudes. This experience at Foodco is supported by the slogan of one of its competitors – a French hypermarket – 'Nasz zawod – sluzyc Panstwu!' ('Our job is to serve you'), reinforced by young women responding to customer needs and queries dressed as cheerleaders and travelling on rollerskates. The emphasis on customer service and care had increased the monitoring and supervision of employees as well as training them in new skills and attitudes.

Second, the women interviewed were emphatic about the need for a trade union, because they had no way of resolving grievances or arbitrating conflicts. A number of issues were raised where they would have liked some trade union intervention – eight-hour shifts without a break, the provision of drinks machines, and the better planning of hours. Ironically, the case study firm in the home country had signed up to a Partnership Agreement with a major union, but had no union in its Polish stores. The local Solidarity trade union official suggested that foreign retailers were generally hostile to trade unions, and this was evidenced by the fact that they had already taken one foreign retailer on the same site to court for sacking an employee who had joined a union.

As in the two former SOEs, the management structure offered opportunities for educated women (and men) on company training schemes. However, there was an upper age limit of 29 which precluded educated but older women and entry was highly competitive. In 1998/99 there were 600 applicants to become management trainees, 50 were tested at the Polish headquarters and six were eventually selected. Jobs in firms with foreign investment were especially attractive for men and women with higher education. For them foreign companies offer good career prospects including higher wages and opportunities to learn western-style management techniques. This labour segment is, however, narrow and competitive and the best jobs specify young people between 25 and 30, most often with degrees in economics or law and fluent in at least one foreign language. Women in these jobs had to adapt to busy work schedules and reported frequent travel, long working hours and/or work at weekends. Competitive pressure meant that they felt they had to choose between a career and a family, echoing contemporary stories from the west.

Flexibility

The pattern of work has remained largely unchanged in the former state-owned enterprises. In Fridgski, the shifts were standard for Polish firms ranging from 6am–2pm, 2pm–10pm, 10pm–6am and once workers had been assigned a particular shift there was little tendency to change. This suited the interviewees who were able to make permanent domestic and childcare arrangements. In contrast, in Cigarettski, where changes were more profound, the shift pattern had markedly improved since being bought up by a foreign firm. Whereas previously the women interviewed had worked a fairly irregular shift pattern, which included some Saturdays, under foreign ownership none of the women worked Saturdays and shift patterns were regular, changing on a permanent rotation from week to week. The factory worked on a three-shift system (morning, afternoon and evening), with each shift working as a team or brigade. However, women could not swap shifts to accommodate domestic or other commitments and flexibility was only introduced into the system by women taking leave, compassionate or otherwise.

In all these workplaces then there was little flexibility for employees despite the use of shift work. This also meant, however, that employers could not and, by all accounts, did not disturb the regular work patterns to call women into work at short notice disregarding domestic and other commitments (which may include other jobs). However, the situation was very different in the food retail sector. Flexibility and uncertainty in working patterns were the cornerstones of employment in Foodco. In line with other large food retailers, sales information is used to help make decisions about not only check-out opening and product replenishment but also staff scheduling. Staff were brought in and out of the store as demand dictates and attitudes to flexibility, particularly with regard to unsocial hours, were a central part of the interview and appointment process. After opening in 1998 a number of staff were given permanent contracts, which were then retracted under the threat of redundancies. As one women explained:

> They said they would have to reduce hours otherwise some people would have to be dismissed. We didn't want them to do that. We wanted everyone to work. Especially now when it's so hard.

Apart from managers and department managers, all workers were on fractional contracts. The Polish Labour Code states that a full-time contract is 176 hours per month and any additional hours worked have to be paid at an overtime rate, which is 50 per cent higher than the normal hourly rate. Because Foodco gave workers contracts which were 50 or 75 per cent of a full-time 176 hour contract, they could then be asked to work additional hours at normal rates of pay which kept labour costs down and maintained a high degree of flexibility. Therefore Foodco was able successfully to comply with the Labour Code while circumventing the necessity of paying overtime. Schedules and rotas changed every month to fit with the expected level of demand and the number of hours and times worked on a daily and monthly basis varied considerably from one month to the next. Hours worked varied daily, from four- to twelve-hour shifts. There is no regular pattern within the shift system and one woman complained of working 88 hours one month and 130 hours the next. Given that all women expressed a desire to work as much overtime as possible, there was a great deal of slack in the system which suggested that flexibility worked for employees and managers alike. However, this flexibility and variation was not driven by the employees and took little or no account of the women's desire, need or availability for work. Part-time work was not an active choice but was, in fact, the only contract on offer for the majority of workers. No account was taken of the distance travelled to work, such that one woman travelled 40km for a four-hour shift, whilst another who lives in close proximity to the store was allocated longer, six-hour shifts. Neither were there any concessions for unsociable hours. Although the women interviewed were prepared to be very flexible in the hours worked, the lack of transport, low car ownership and long distances to small towns meant that early morning and late night shifts involved long journeys and practical difficulties. As mentioned before, the women complained that the absence of a trade union meant that there was no mechanism for alleviating these shift difficulties.

It is not only temporal flexibility that has become an issue in contemporary working practice. Employees are increasingly expected to be functionally flexible. While women workers in Fridgski performed the same task on a more or less permanent basis, Cigarettski was beginning to introduce functional flexibility policies. In this firm, the women did not know from day to day on which piece of machinery they would be working. This was seen as positive in as much as it introduced variability into the working pattern, but the negative side was that they were not formally trained in the use of new equipment and had to pick up the techniques as they went along.

Restructuring the social wage

Providing workers with additional services, facilities or access to scarce products over and above the regular wage was a typical characteristic of employment under the previous regime, in all sectors of the economy. However, it should be noted that access to these facilities was differential. The best and most extensive facilities were provided by heavy industries or strategic SOEs, which were male-dominated (Hardy and Rainnie 1996). However, for women, who shouldered the lion's share of the domestic burden, this 'social wage', which would not have been affordable or accessible outside the workplace, was essential for managing domestic life. Access to services as diverse as housing, infrastructures, consumer goods, information, transport, childcare, health care, recreation, leisure and culture were all provided and controlled by workplaces to differing degrees. The way in which the social wage was generally provided most comprehensively by large SOEs was borne out in our contemporary examples.

In Fridgski, the employers continued to provide extensive social functions including two holiday homes, one on the coast and one in the mountains (used by 1,300 children in 1998), a nursery for 120 children, summer camps and a health centre with a physiotherapist and gynaecologist. Crucially, free transport was provided from a number of small towns and villages for each shift. All of these facilities were well-used by the women interviewed. Eight out of twelve of the interviewees had, for example, used the holiday homes in the previous year. However, continuing provision was in doubt. In particular, divesting the health centre had been mooted as a possibility in 1997, but was contested successfully (at least temporarily) by the active Solidarity union in the plant. Solidarity argued that the physical nature of the work at Fridgski demanded that the facilities be maintained, not least because the costs to the employers in terms of absence for hospital appointments and sick leave more than justified the continuance of in-house facilities. Notwithstanding the maintenance of the health facilities, Fridgski had already divested some of its social services – the number of crèches and kindergartens has been reduced – and it is not clear how long the remaining facilities will be supported in the light of the purchase of the majority of the shares by another foreign investor.

Under the previous regime, employees at Cigarettski also had access to a wide variety of social facilities including health care, housing and holiday homes. However, most of these were divested in the early 1990s and this process had accelerated since privatisation in 1996 with the women interviewed identifying, for example, a crèche that had been converted to an office following privatisation. None of the women interviewed had used the facilities offered by the enterprise, but all had accessed zero per cent loans provided by the employers. This trend of the conversion of in-kind social provision to monetary opportunities is indicative of the trend across the country. As a result of legislation in 1998 the Polish Labour Code now states that all workplaces must offer a social fund, jointly administered by trade unions and management, from which employees can borrow for a whole range of reasons from children's weddings, to house repairs and holidays. Access to these funds is effectively by right – if you ask, you will be given a loan.

In stark contrast to both Cigarettski and Fridgski, workers in Foodco received no benefits in addition to their salary, with the exception of a subsidised canteen. In particular Foodco provided no transport and there were no arrangements for pensions. This marked difference in social wage provisions between the former state-owned enterprises and new foreign-owned private enterprise demonstrates quite clearly the influence of ownership form on conditions of work. Though foreign and privately owned, both Cigarettski and Fridgski possess a legacy of significant social wage provision which has been maintained, though restructured, in the post-communist period. Foodco, in contrast, has no such legacy in Poland and has not built in-kind benefits into its employment terms, notwithstanding their presence in their UK parent company.

The job security and wages trade-off

One of the clearest tendencies identified in the interviews was an apparent trade-off between wages and job security. The women working in Fridgski and Cigarettski felt that in terms of pay and conditions their jobs were better than those of their friends. Wage levels were high enough to live on and they still received in-kind payments through the social wage, especially in Fridgski. Women at Cigarettski considered themselves well paid, receiving both regular salaries and bonuses at Christmas and Easter, neither of which were performance related. The interviews in both Cigarettski and Fridgski were, however, dominated by fears of imminent redundancies. Modernisation, job loss and insecurity were part of the everyday vocabulary of these workplaces and the women were very fearful of losing what they saw as 'good jobs'. In Fridgski, this climate of fear had encouraged a wariness and mistrust between workers in a workplace up until recently characterised by co-operation and camaraderie. In Cigarettski, the women repeatedly wondered whether they would still have a job in weeks to come.

In Foodco, the situation was more complex. Women had security in the sense that they had permanent contracts, which guaranteed a minimum number of hours which ranged from 80 to 120 per month. The issue here was that all the women would have worked full time if they had been allowed to do so; this was driven by sheer financial necessity. The opportunity to work additional hours and the amount of overtime available lay in the gift of the managers whose shift rotas were driven by the need to cope with uneven demand at different times of the year.

In the Wroclaw region, wages and conditions of work in flagship foreign investments in manufacturing, employing largely male workers, were generally above average for the locality. However, as we will see below, the opportunities for work at Foodco, and other foreign-owned retail firms like it, were not seen as entirely positive. From the perspective of employment in former SOEs, jobs at hypermarkets were seen as being characterised by low pay levels and poor working conditions.

Changing employment opportunities and assessments of transformation

Much has been written, both in the academic and popular media, about the difficulties faced by women in a restructured labour market, and these concerns were reflected in the women's responses when asked how they felt about how employment opportunities had changed for themselves, their friends and families.

All of the women talked of the difficulties of finding new employment, many speaking from personal experience. Half of the interviewees at Foodco had been made redundant from employment in small firms or SOEs that had gone bankrupt, the other half had held a string of badly paid service sector jobs. They all reported applying for many jobs and several of the women had experienced involuntary unemployment of between nine and twelve months. Many of the interviewees found potential employers setting an upper age limit for applications and, as we have seen, complex application processes were a deterrent to applying. Women reported having to travel further to find work and found that the jobs available offered increasingly worse pay and conditions. The women at Fridgski and Cigarettski all felt that they would find job hunting difficult on account of their age, lack of higher education and specialised skills – only one of the women interviewees at Cigarettski had ever had another job. These women, reflecting the relatively good pay and conditions in former SOEs, derided the opportunities available in the growing foreign-owned retail sector (primarily supermarkets and hypermarkets) held up as a positive employment pathway for women (see Gregory *et al.* 1998).

Most of the women talked of mixed opportunities for the next generation. Some of their children had found good jobs in foreign or new private firms; others, especially those with technical or vocational educations, had failed to find employment altogether. In Cigarettski, the women stressed heavily that employment prospects for young people were almost non-existent in comparison to their youth, ten to twenty years ago. This pattern was as true for young men as for young women. It was felt, however, that increasingly some employers, in addition to discriminating against older workers, expressed a preference for men over women as a result of women's need for more family-related leave. Many of the interviewees related reports of some employers explicitly asking young women about their intentions of having children and many cited job advertisements which explicitly excluded women from applying. But while both these practices contravened the Polish Labour Code many private firms appeared to flaunt national labour regulations.

In general, the women interviewed had been disappointed by the consequences of reform and transformation. Many noted that they had expected so much more and that the impacts had been more mixed than they had expected. Most identified improved choice in shops as a benefit, but balanced this against increased prices, which made such choice inaccessible to the majority.

Conclusion

This chapter began by identifying a gap in the literature on women and employment in East Central Europe. Whilst many authors have already noted that women tend to suffer disproportionately from redundancy and long-term unemployment, little work has been carried out which has focused on the changing experiences of women in work, save for optimistic prognostications that new jobs in expanded sectors (especially retail) might provide some positive opportunities for women's labour market participation. What this research has demonstrated is that the changes of the last ten years have significantly altered the conditions of work for women who have retained employment. Privatisation, the increasing influence of foreign investment, the importance of new skills for a new era and the restructuring of workplaces in the light of increasing competition have all transformed the working practices and conditions of workers.

This research has furthermore suggested that the transformations of work since 1989 have been gendered and, specifically, have affected women in particular ways. The restructuring and increasing absence of the social wage hits women harder as it is women who bear the burden of childcare and domestic commitments. The loss of nursery places and of privileged access to medical care, for example, impact more on women as it is primarily wives and mothers who carry responsibility for meeting these needs. The total absence of in-kind service provision (in particular transport and childcare facilities) in new foreign-owned workplaces, such as Foodco, makes managing the home–work balance increasingly difficult.

Balancing women's double shift of work and home is complicated still further by the technological speed-up and the demands of learning new skills that typified all of the case study workplaces. In addition to losing many of the 'fringe benefits', women testified to experiencing considerably more stress at work. The patterns of work had changed, the pace of work had intensified and women no longer felt so secure in their work. These changes at work have been coupled with the increasing burdens of domestic life – many of the women interviewed also had primary care responsibilities for ageing parents, unemployed children and invalided husbands and all suggested that everyday tasks such as shopping, visiting the doctor and travelling within the city had become more difficult. The loss of the social wage and the restructuring of welfare systems exacerbated this still further.

Nostalgia for work in the 'old economy', which promised security, a range of non-wage benefits and continuity has not been eased by the realities of work in the new economy. Those women still working in former SOEs derided the opportunities of new work and those working in the expanded retail sector rarely expressed much satisfaction with their work. Both sets of women bemoaned the low wage, flexible and part-time nature of the opportunities offered them in the new economy, which detracted from the permanency of employment. Whilst women in Cigarettski and Fridgski felt the ever-present threat of redundancy, none felt the growing opportunities in the expanded service sector offered them a real and attractive alternative.

This chapter has explored the employment experiences of women working in three workplaces in two regions in Poland. Not only is Poland seen as the most successful 'transition economy', but Kraków and Wroclaw are also lead regions within Poland. Both regions are characterised by a range of employment opportunities and by vibrant economies. The labour markets of these two regions are much stronger than many others, most particularly than those in small towns and on Poland's eastern border. This notwithstanding, it is likely that the influence of privatisation and growing domestic and international competition have impacted further on Kraków and Wroclaw than on more peripheral regions. As such, though unemployment may be higher in other regions, the restructuring of working conditions is unlikely to have been so profound.

This chapter has also focused only on women working in the privatised and private economy. As we saw earlier, under communism, many women in East Central Europe worked in the public sector – in health, education and public administration. As Polish reforms have progressed, these sectors are becoming the new focus of restructuring and employment transformation. The research reported here suggests that the remaking of working conditions is a clear and significant result of wider transformations and that these changes are evidently gendered. There is a need, therefore, for further research, which explores the passage of such restructurings in different employment and different regional contexts.

Acknowledgement

This research was funded by a grant awarded by the Nuffield Foundation.

Notes

1   Shock therapy is the term given to the Balcerowicz Programme implemented in 1990, which comprised a package of macroeconomic reforms such as raising interest rates, limiting government borrowing and cutting the money supply (Slay 1994).
2   Although there are other unions active in both regions, Solidarity was the only union in the two former SOEs.
3   The 1980s was the second decade of unsuccessful reform of the Polish economy. As a result the 1980s were a period of widespread shortages where goods could be obtained only by queuing, bribery or on the black market. The greater share of these difficulties fell to women and on average women had to queue for two hours a day to buy the basic necessities.

References

Calasanti, T.M. and Zajicek, A.M. (1997) 'Gender, the state and constructing the old as dependent: Lessons from the economic transition in Poland', *The Gerontologist*, 37 (4).

Ciechocinska, M. (1993) 'Gender aspects of dismantling the command economy in Eastern Europe: The case of Poland', in V.M. Moghadam (ed.) *Democratic Reform and the Position of Women in Transitional Economies*, Clarendon Press: Oxford, pp. 302–326.

Czerny, M. (1998) 'Economic recovery in peripheral regions of Poland: The case of Eastern Poland', paper presented at the *Conference of European Urban and Regional Studies*, Durham, September.

Domanski, B. (1997) *Industrial Control Over the Socialist Town: Benevolence or Exploitation*, Praeger, Westport: Connecticut.

EBRD (1998) *Transition Report: Economic Transition in Central and Eastern Europe, the Baltic States and the CIS*, European Bank for Reconstruction and Development: London.

Einhorn, B. (1993) *Cinderella Goes To Market: Citizenship, Gender and Women's Movements in East Central Europe*, Verso: London.

Flecker, J., Meil, P. and Pollert, A. (1998) 'The sexual division of labour in process manufacturing: Economic restructuring, training and "women's work"', *European Journal of Industrial Relations*, 4 (1): 7–34.

Glowny Urzad Statystyczny (Central Statistical Office) (1996) *Rocznik Statystyczny* (Statistical Yearbook), GUS: Warsaw.

Gregory, A., Ingham, M. and Ingham, H. (1998) 'Women's employment in transition, 1992–94: The case of Poland', *Gender, Work and Organisation*, 5 (3): 133–147.

Hardy, J. (1998) 'Cathedrals in the desert? Transnational corporate strategy and locality in Wroclaw', *Regional Studies*, 32 (7): 639–652.

Hardy, J. and Rainnie, A. (1996) *Restructuring Krakow*, Cassell-Mansell: London.

Hübner, S., Maier, F. and Rudolph, H. (1993) 'Women's employment in Central and Eastern Europe: Status and prospects', in G. Fischer and G. Standing (eds) *Structural Change in Central and Eastern Europe*, OECD: Paris.

Knothe, M.A. (1999) 'Poland's economy in transition: A gender perspective', *Trade Sustainable Development and Gender*, UNCTAD: New York.

Lobodzinska, B. (1996) 'Women's employment or return to "family values" in Central and Eastern Europe', *Journal of Comparative Family Studies*, 27 (3): 519–544.

Mroczkowski, T. (1997) 'Women as employees and entrepreneurs in the Polish transformation', *Industrial Relations Journal*, 2 (2).

Perrons, D. (1998) *Flexible Working and the Reconciliation of Work and Family Life – Or A New Form of Precariousness*, European Commission: Brussels.

Pine, F. (1995) 'Kinship, work and the state in post-socialist Poland', *Cambridge Journal of Anthropology*, 18 (2): 47–58.

Plakwicz, J. (1992) 'Between church and state: Polish women's experience', in C. Corrin (ed.) *Superwomen and the Double Burden*, Scarlet Press: London.

Pollert, A. (1995) 'Women's employment and service sector transformation in Central Eastern Europe: Case studies in retail in the Czech Republic', *Work, Employment and Society*, 9 (4): 629–655.

Rainnie, A. and Hardy, J. (1999) 'Global strategies, local firms, working lives: Restructuring of Polish state owned enterprises', in M. Upchurch (ed.) *The State and Globalization*, Mansell: London.

Ruminska-Zimny, E. (1999) 'Globalization and gender', in *Transition Economies, Trade, Sustainable Development and Gender*, UNCTAD: New York.

Slay, B. (1994) *The Polish Economy: Crisis, Reform and Transformation*, Princeton UP: Princeton.

Walsh, J. (1999) 'Myths and counter-myths: An analysis of part-time female employees and their orientation to work and working hours', *Work, Employment and Society*, 13 (2): 179–203.

Warsaw Voice, 21.2.99, 'To buy or not to buy?', available at http://www.warsawvoice.com.pl/v539/Busi06.html.

6 'A woman is everything'

The reproduction of Soviet ideals of womanhood in post-communist Russia[1]

Sarah Ashwin

Introduction

At the beginning of the transition era, there was a good deal of speculation over whether the collapse of communism would precipitate a return to so-called traditional gender roles in Russia. In particular, a number of Western and Russian commentators predicted that women would succumb to the call of the home, leaving the labour force voluntarily as soon as they had the option of doing so (for example, Pilkington 1992: 200, Funk 1993: 322, Lissyutkina 1993: 276). The logic of such predictions was that since women's inclusion within the Soviet labour force had occurred under pressure, it had not brought the emancipatory gains usually associated with female employment. As one Russian commentator put it

> There can be no doubt that working outside the home and being paid for their labour is one of the main conditions for women's emancipation. . . . However, women's working outside the home can be transformed from an important means of liberation into a very powerful instrument for their enslavement. . . . That was precisely what occurred in our country.
>
> (Voronina 1994: 46–7)

The idea that Soviet women were coerced into work has led commentators such as Larissa Lissyutkina to argue that, 'Emancipation for Soviet women is not based on a demand to work. On the contrary, liberation is perceived by many as the right not to work' (Lissyutkina 1993: 274). Other commentators have argued more generally that a return to traditional values would actually be welcomed by many Russian women. For example, the feminist writer Nina Gabrielyan claimed that a large number of women had responded positively to the 'replacement of the socialist pseudo-egalitarian mythology' with the 'old patriarchal' one because they were tired of 'pseudo-emancipation' which left them torn between work and home (quoted in Morvant 1995: 5). This chapter scrutinises such claims through an analysis of the nature of the Soviet legacy in terms of gender ideology. The argument that women want a full return to the home and 'old patriarchal' values is rejected, in favour of the idea that women tend to endorse a combination of traditional and more egalitarian ideas regarding their role and that of men. This reflects the confusion within the officially sanctioned roles of men and women in the Soviet era, which were themselves a blend of traditional and revolutionary norms.

Understanding the nature of local gender ideologies is important because they form an important part of the normative framework in which people take decisions regarding employment and the household. As the anthropologist Henrietta Moore has argued:

> Economic processes such as the differentiation of tasks by gender, discussions between husbands and wives over income distribution . . . are actually a set of practical activities which operationalise gender ideologies. They are therefore in some sense the outcome of local ideas regarding the appropriate behaviour of men and women.
>
> (Moore 1994: 92)

The influence of gender ideology on behaviour has recently been recognised in literature using the concept of distinct 'gender orders', to explain different patterns of male and female employment between nations and between cultures.[2] For example, the idea of different gender orders is employed by Angela Dale and Clare Holdsworth (1998) to explain why, even though both sets of women face the same institutional constraints, British ethnic minority women tend to work full time, while white women are more likely to work part time. The idea of the gender order has also been built on by Birgit Pfau-Effinger (1998, 1999), who uses a version of it to explain cross-national differences in patterns of full-time and part-time working among women as well as divergent attitudes to maternal employment. In addition to examining the nature of the dominant gender ideologies with regard to the employment of women and the domestic division of labour in contemporary Russia, this chapter also attempts to analyse their implications in terms of women's employment behaviour.

The argument presented here is based on two sources. First, data from an on-going research project funded by INTAS.[3] This project is designed to examine gender differences in employment strategies through longitudinal qualitative research which traces the labour market activity of specially selected groups of men and women through a consecutive series of semi-structured deep interviews. The four groups selected are defined by a series of distinct labour market transitions at the beginning of the research. Equal numbers of men and women (thirty in each group) have been selected and are being interviewed at six-month intervals for a period of three years which began in March 1999. The research on the four different groups is being carried out in four separate cities. The groups are: new entrants to the labour market, graduating from a university and a technical training institute (in Ul'yanovsk); those confronting the labour market involuntarily as a result of the acute financial difficulties of their employer (in Moscow); those who are unemployed and seeking work through the employment service (in Samara); and those whose incomes are so low that they qualify for state social assistance (in Syktyvkar). This chapter is based on data from the first two rounds of interviews. Each interview is referred to by three numbers: the first indicates the city;[4] the second, the respondent; and the third, the stage of the research. The second source of data used here is 20 deep interviews with female blue-collar workers carried out in Samara in July 1997. The women interviewed were either working at garment factories, the large foreign-owned chocolate factory in the city, or in catering. Fourteen of those interviewed were aged between 30–50, and the rest were in their early twenties.

The Soviet gender order

In order to understand the Soviet legacy in terms of gender ideology, it is necessary first to understand the nature of the Soviet gender order. The Soviet state promoted and institutionalised a distinctive gender order in which the roles of men and women were defined according to the perceived needs of the communist state.[5] Involvement in work was to be central to the identity of all Soviet citizens: over time the labour collective became the main locus of social integration and distribution within Soviet society (Ashwin 1999a). In the case of women, their role was defined as worker-mothers who had a duty to work, to produce future generations of workers, as well as to oversee the running of the household. In return for this they received 'protection' from the state in their capacity as mothers, as well as independence through their access to paid work. But although women were integrated into the workforce *en masse*, early Bolshevik dreams of the transfer of domestic functions from the private to the public sphere were never realised except to a limited extent in the realm of child-care.[6] This meant that women workers were still expected to perform their traditional domestic role: none of the Bolsheviks, not even Aleksandra Kollantai, challenged the idea of domestic work as inalienably female (Ashwin 2000: 11–12), and essentialist understandings of the division of labour within the household remained a feature of official thinking until the end of the Soviet era. This acceptance of supposedly natural sexual difference on the part of the new communist elite informed both the terms on which women were integrated into the labour force (as second-class workers), and what was expected of them as wives and mothers.[7]

Men, meanwhile, had an at once more limited and higher status role to play. They were to serve as leaders, managers, soldiers, workers, while the state assumed responsibility for the fulfilment of the traditional masculine roles of father and provider, becoming, in effect, a universal patriarch to which both men and women were subject. In the early post-revolutionary period, the new Bolshevik authorities perceived the traditional patriarch as a bulwark of the old regime, a little Tsar whose influence needed to be restricted. Initially, the state struggle with the patriarch was conducted through a combination of legislation and coercion which served to undermine male prerogative within the family (Kukhterin 2000). After the compromise with the new Soviet family in the 1930s this campaign was relaxed, but the private power of men continued to be regarded with suspicion. This distrust found its expression in a notable silence about the male domestic role. While mothers were glorified, Soviet men were not allowed to compete with the father-figures who led the Party.[8] Male self-realisation was thus to be confined to the public sphere, where their dominance continued to be seen as legitimate and 'natural'.

The extent to which official discourse and institutional arrangements influenced subjective understandings in the Soviet period is difficult to assess. Obviously, it is not possible retrospectively to untangle the various influences on the formation of male and female gender identities in order to assess the precise role of the state in shaping these. Nonetheless, the life history data available suggests that there was a remarkable congruity between the ideal of the Soviet woman propagated by the state and that accepted by individual women. That is, women tended to accept that a woman should work, take responsibility for the household, and be a mother, though the generally accepted social norm was for women to have at least one child, rather than the five to ten required to earn a medal from the state (Ashwin 1999b, Kiblitskaya 2000a).[9]

In the transition era, however, the institutional and ideological underpinnings of Soviet-approved gender relations and identities have been removed. First, work is no longer a state-imposed duty. Economic inactivity is an option for both men and women, while the capitalist evil much dwelt on by Soviet propagandists – unemployment – is now an unwelcome reality in Russia. Now, rather than emphasising women's duty to work, members of the political elite are more likely to argue that in an era of high unemployment women should leave the jobs for the boys.[10] Second, motherhood has been redefined as a private responsibility. While in the Soviet era motherhood was portrayed as a service to the state, and recognised as such through a social policy which supported the mother and child unit as an indivisible whole, now the state has reneged on its paternal role as the protector of mother and child (Issoupova 2000). This, of course, implies that there is greater pressure on men to perform the role of providers, as can be seen in the following quotation from a 1996 magazine article:

> Today our Russian post-Soviet fathers have gained the chance to occupy an appropriate place in the family. As soon as the economy became market-oriented, it required the development of traditional male qualities, and a man obtained the possibility of returning to his normal and natural role. His destiny is now in his own hands. . . . He can (if he wants, if he gets up from the sofa and makes an effort) provide for his family. Now he himself must take responsibility for the children, and not delegate it to Big Daddy: the state.
>
> (*Materinstvo*, no 1, September 1996: 91, quoted in Issoupova 2000: 42)

These changes in state policy appear to be conducive to a return to the so-called traditional family consisting of a male breadwinner and non-working wife, thus perhaps lending credence to the predictions noted in the introduction.[11] Clearly, it will be very difficult for men to become sole breadwinners in an era of economic collapse but, this practical problem aside, have such policy reversals had an impact on the norms and expectations of men and women? The following section will attempt to answer this, focusing on the case of women.

The persistence of Soviet ideals of womanhood

The qualitative evidence in terms of women's perception of their roles is remarkably consistent. While the issue of generalisation is always problematic with qualitative data, this is to some extent off-set by the detail of the responses. When women who work in different industries, in different parts of Russia, with different levels of skill and education express their views in similar terms (often using almost identical expressions) it is a strong indication that the views in question are widely shared. In addition to qualitative material, I also use quantitative data from our INTAS study in the following sections. The numbers involved here (240 respondents) and the nature of the sample (non-random) mean that these figures need to be treated with caution, though on many issues the consistency of the responses is striking.

Work

How do Russian women of the post-Soviet era see their role? First, as has been shown before, there is no evidence to suggest that they perceive 'liberation . . . as the right not to work'. Surveys have consistently shown that, even if women had the financial possibility of staying at home, the majority of them would continue to work (for details see Ashwin and Bowers 1997: 25–26). In our current INTAS research, 80 per cent of women said that they would continue to work if they had the financial possibility of not working, as against 72 per cent of male respondents. Meanwhile, qualitative studies have shown that work is crucial to women's sense of identity; provides them with sense of meaning, of being needed and socially useful; and is a source of companionship and support, even when the work itself is unpleasant and provides little intrinsic satisfaction (Ashwin and Bowers 1997, Gruzdeva 1995, Kiblitskaya 2000b, Zdravomyslova 1996).

There is little new in this. The interesting finding from our INTAS research concerns younger women. These women have grown up in a climate in which 'traditional' values are valorised both in political discourse and certain forms of popular culture and they therefore might be expected to be less committed to work than older generations. Nonetheless, 90 per cent of our young female respondents (as opposed to 80 per cent of men in the same group) said that they would work if they had the financial possibility of not working. Our largest group of young respondents are the graduates from the university and technical training institute in Ul'yanovsk who, having invested in their education, would be expected to be more committed to work than those who are less educated. Indeed, 93 per cent of female respondents in this group said that they would work if they had the financial possibility of not working, as opposed to 74 per cent of men in the same group. Nonetheless, between 75–100 per cent of female respondents under 35 in the other city samples gave the same answer. The major difference between older and younger women was in the reasons they gave for wanting to work. As can be seen from the following quotations, young women said that they would continue to work because of their fear of boredom and social isolation. The consistency in their reasoning is notable:

> You exaggerate a bit if you sit at home, you find a fifth corner in the flat already. No, generally speaking, it's impossible to sit at home (2-26-2).

> Yes, I would work. I always said that. Even if I had a super-millionaire as a husband, or, I don't know, got some kind of inheritance . . . I can't sit at home. I hate to sit within four walls, doing nothing. I can do nothing all day – but that's only for one day, two at the most (2-32-2).

> What [else] is there to do? You'd die of boredom. It [work] is in its own way a rest from resting (2-46-2).

> I would work. Because if you don't work it in any case means staying at home. It means no acquaintances, no new acquaintances. It seems to me that it is very hard and you become like part of the furniture (2-35-2).

> Of course I'd work, because it's a way out into the light and a chance to socialise with people (2-57-2).

> I would work. I've thought about that a lot, by the way. When I see films where they show a husband completely supporting his wife, I don't know, on the one hand it's good that you don't have any financial problems. . . . But on the other hand, what can you spend the whole day doing if you don't work? Some kind of work at least, it's necessary, otherwise you'd crack up (2-31-2).

While younger women stressed that work was a way to meet people and to avoid boredom or madness, older women (who know far more about the reality of what goes on within the dreaded 'four walls') placed more emphasis on the fact that it gave them a sense of social significance, financial independence and a rest from housework (all quotations taken from Moscow factory workers):

> I think that work is a necessity. Work helps you to feel that you are a woman. Well and money, of course, that's important. Take me, for example, I think that at home I am on the whole *nothing* [*nichto*] (1-16-1).

> It's unconditional. When my husband . . . has got a bit more money, he says: stay at home. I say: no way. No way. Home – it means the floor cloth. I don't want that. Not under any circumstances (1-52-1).

> I would like to have my own pay. . . . so that no one could say to me, 'you stay at home' and have the right to reproach me with anything (1-58-1).

Thus, although the justifications for wanting to work vary between different age groups, the idea that work is an important part of a woman's life is held by a sizeable majority of women regardless of age. The housewife ideal does not seem to be catching on. Indeed, the Ul'yanovsk research group sensed that their female respondents were framing their answers in opposition to post-Soviet 'neo-traditionalist' opinion, even though they did not explicitly identify this adversary in their comments. (Meanwhile, the same research team also noticed that their young male respondents, though generally supportive of the idea of their future wives working, talked about this in a lordly tone, suggesting they expected to have the ultimate right of decision in this matter; 'let her work' was a common formulation.)

Women's desire to remain in work is reflected in the employment statistics. Contrary to predictions, women's economic activity has fallen by almost exactly the same as men's between 1992 and 1998: 8.3 per cent, as against 8.1 per cent for men (Goskomstat 1999: 8). The reduction in overall economic activity rates is accounted for by the withdrawal from labour market activity of the young and those of pension age, and only to a very limited degree by the exit of women from the labour force (Clarke 1999a: 118). It should also be noted that women are far less likely to leave their jobs voluntarily than men (Clarke 1999b: 179). Nor do they seem to be more vulnerable to unemployment: according to the internationally comparable Labour Force Survey data, in October 1998 51 per cent of the unemployed were men, and 49 per cent were women (Goskomstat 1999: 28).[12] Clearly, this is not the whole story. Women spend longer unemployed than men (Ashwin and Bowers 1997, Katz 2000), and there is a great deal of anecdotal evidence that discrimination and sexual harassment are rife in the Russian labour market. Meanwhile, women earned 65–70 per cent of men's wages in the Soviet era, and this gap has certainly not narrowed in the transition era: indeed, Katerina Katz (2000) estimates that it has increased. It may therefore be the case that women are experiencing 'downward mobility' in the transition era, but at the same time they are retaining their presence in the workforce. They show no signs of retreating into the home, and nor does it seem they would rush to do so were their prospects of finding a male breadwinner to improve.

Household and family

Where young and old women are similar is in their negative characterisations of 'home', which, as can be seen from the quotations in the previous section, is portrayed as a potential prison, while men are portrayed by some older women as would-be gaolers. Nevertheless, women tend to accept that running the household is their responsibility. A clear majority (65 per cent) of women in our INTAS research said that the woman should be responsible for running the household, with 32 per cent saying that this should be a joint responsibility. Moreover, the qualitative responses of those who did not explicitly say that the household was a feminine responsibility sometimes revealed tacit acceptance of a traditional domestic division of labour, as can be seen in the comments of the following young woman:

> Whoever's got the bigger brain should be the one to answer for the running of the household. If, for example, we trusted my father to run the household, we'd all, on the same amount of money, have died of hunger by now. He goes to buy onions and he buys the most mangy onions in the market. . . . It's not even really that the brain should be bigger in those kind of areas, but that whoever is more practical should run the household. For some people it's the husband, for some the wife, but it's more often wives. . . . I would, of course, hope that I'd have the sort of husband who'd buy good onions [laughs], who'd do everything so well. . . . But he can even be useless in that area – if he brings in good money I'll go along with it (2-41-2).

Unsurprisingly, virtually no one thought that men should assume responsibility for the household.[13] In the under-35 age group the proportion of women thinking that the woman should be responsible for running the household fell to 53 per cent (as opposed to 41 per cent of men in the same age group). It is possible that this reflects a shift towards more egalitarian values among the young, but given the small numbers involved it is difficult to read too much into this result. Overall, what was striking in the tone of qualitative responses of those who thought that women should take responsibility for the household was the degree to which they saw this as *natural*.

But although the majority of women adhere to essentialist ideas regarding the domestic division of labour, their views on childcare run counter to the ideology of the male-breadwinner/female-carer model. This perhaps reflects the fact that, while the Soviet authorities never challenged the idea that women were responsible for the domestic sphere, they were too greedy for female labour power to endorse the idea of private motherhood. Instead, they 'struggled' to get women to use state childcare, which served the dual function of allowing women to work and ensuring that children were correctly socialised (Issoupova 2000). It seems that state propaganda was effective in this regard for many women, given the chance, will expatiate enthusiastically on the virtues of kindergartens, as can be seen in this comment from one of the respondents in my Samara study:

> Kindergartens are interesting for children. They mix with other children, they develop there. For example, my son had problems with his speech. Well, at the kindergarten they have a speech therapist and he was given special help, and by the time he entered the first class at school he could speak and he could read. It really surprised me. I couldn't have taught him to do that if I'd have stayed at home with him. . . . So I think kindergarten is very important. The children should have proper teachers – what's a nanny? Nannies are no good. And with their mother – they're going to arrive at school knowing nothing. And those early years are very important in development, I think. It's a very serious question. (Forty-three-year-old cook in Samara café)

The taken-for-grantedness of sending children to kindergarten is dramatically illustrated by the comments of one 22-year-old worker from one of the Samara garment factories, who, asked if she would consider staying at home if her (putative) husband could afford to keep her replied: 'I wouldn't want to sit at home ... it would be boring – the children wouldn't be at home, and my husband wouldn't be at home. It would be boring alone there.' Clearly, the idea that she might stay at home to look after her children *herself,* in preference to sending them to kindergarten, did not even occur to her! There is, however, a division of views on this question. Fifty-two per cent of female respondents in the INTAS study with children of pre-school age thought that kindergarten was the best option for their child (along with 44 per cent of male respondents), and many of those were as enthusiastic as the cook quoted above. A number of respondents even justified their answer with comments that would have been deeply gratifying to Soviet ideologues. One man, for example said that even if the mother stayed at home 'some kind of kindergarten, even if just for a while, is very necessary. Children learn a lot there, *to live in a collective,* and in terms of education' (4-2-2, emphasis added). Twenty four per cent of mothers did, however, think that being at home with them was the best option for their children, with a similar proportion of fathers wanting maternal care for their pre-school children (28 per cent). Meanwhile, 6 per cent of parents of pre-school children felt that their children were best off with their grandmother, and 18 per cent favoured the 'other' option, which usually implied that they endorsed a combination of mother and kindergarten.

The importance of social norms regarding motherhood and childhood have been emphasised by Birgit Pfau-Effinger (1999), who argues that a purely institutional analysis is not adequate to explain different patterns of women's labour participation in different countries. She bases her argument on a comparison between the Netherlands, Germany and Finland. In the Netherlands and Germany the pre-industrial 'male-breadwinner/female-home-carer' model was culturally influential, so that 'the idea of private motherhood and childhood survived at least in part' (p. 68). Meanwhile, in Finland the pre-industrial 'family economic model' of small farming, where all members of the family worked, was modernised into what Pfau-Effinger terms the dual breadwinner/state carer model. The resulting differences in the relative acceptability of mothers of pre-school children working, Pfau-Effinger argues, go a long way towards explaining the differences in the patterns of female labour participation between these societies. In its inculcation of the value of public childcare, therefore, the Soviet state can be said to have had a profound impact on the norms that govern the labour market behaviour of Russian women. The lack of strong support for the ideal of private motherhood, and the prevalence of the idea that kindergartens are actually a superior form of childcare, is a major cultural obstacle to the institution of a male-breadwinner/female-home-carer model in Russia.

Combining work and home

The literature on women in the Soviet era paid a good deal of attention to women's 'double burden' of work and housework, and the tone of such discussion often implied that women were victims of this state imposition. But life history interviews with women suggest that the Soviet ideal of the woman who successfully combined home and work was not an alien imposition, but something to which many women aspired (Ashwin 1999b). Their gender identity was not forged solely at work; to be a good woman was to combine work and home effectively. This often involved making compromises in one sphere or other, but women do not tend to talk about this with resentment, but rather as an accepted part of life. For example, the majority of the women I interviewed in the Samara study who had families related having made adjustments in their working lives in the Soviet era for the sake of their dependants. A typical example was that of a glazer from the chocolate factory who had given up the four-year course she was attending at a Moscow food institute after one and a half years because 'there was no one else to look after my mother-in-law... [and] she was a very good woman. I can even say she replaced my mother. I couldn't have behaved differently.' Meanwhile, a skilled seamstress at the garment factory reported that she had been forced to give up her position as forewoman because it entailed working night shifts and she was a single mother. A particularly striking form of the Soviet art of juggling home and work was the 'kindergarten career move' of mothers (often of children with bad health) who, as one worker explained, went to work at the kindergarten attended by their child:

> They'll get a job as anything, a nanny, a teacher if their education allows it, a cook, a cleaner. That way they can be around their child – they don't have to think, for example, 'Am I going to send him today? Is he well enough or not?'. I know of a few cases like that; some even go on and get a job at the school when their child moves on there.

That women would choose to take a job at a kindergarten to be near a sick child, rather than attend to that child at home, highlights not only the strength of the normative pressure on women to work in the Soviet era, but also their willingness to structure their work lives around the needs of their family.

Under communism, such juggling was facilitated through state childcare provision, and the ready availability of work which increased women's chances of finding a job close to home, with a suitable shift system. During the transition era, however, it has become increasingly difficult for women to pursue 'convenient work' strategies (Yaroshenko 1999). Since 1991 pay has become increasingly important in the labour mobility of both men and women, while women have become less likely to cite working hours and conditions as a reason for leaving a job – though they are still more likely to cite such factors than men (Clarke 1999b: 167–78). Therefore, in contemporary conditions, a convenient work strategy is likely to be adopted only where a woman has a partner or spouse with relatively high and stable earnings. This is well illustrated by the account of this 27-year-old respondent from Sytyvkar:

> It was necessary after maternity leave to go to work somewhere, [and] I went to a kindergarten; then it seemed to me to be the most convenient option, mainly in order to be near my son. . . . There were also privileges for the workers at the kindergarten, their children could attend for free, though now they've changed it all and you have to pay. There were wage delays there as well, but you can wait, especially if your husband's providing everything (4-1-1).

Although taking a very low-paid job for the sake of convenience is an option fewer and fewer women can afford, accepting what could be termed a sub-optimal job (in terms of status, career prospects and in some cases pay) in order to reconcile work with household responsibilities is still common.[14] (In our INTAS research we have found a small number of men who also do this, although the most notable examples are widowers with dependent children who have been forced to take on a 'female' role). Thus, rather than completely changing their approach to combining work and family in the transition era, women's emphasis has shifted. Now, as will be seen in the following section, ensuring the survival of the household through earning money is often more pressing than finding time for housework.

What women expect from men

Women's readiness to sacrifice career development in order to fulfil what they perceive as their domestic responsibilities reflects the fact that they expect men to be the *main* (but not sole) breadwinners. Asked who should take primary responsibility for providing for the family, 72 per cent of female, and 79 per cent of male, respondents in our INTAS study said that it should be the man. Given that women generally earn less than men, it is not surprising that many men do manage to live up to their implied obligation to earn more. Sixty per cent of our married male respondents and 64 per cent of married female respondents said that a man was responsible for breadwinning in their family. Unsurprisingly, among never married, divorced and widowed respondents this proportion was lower, with 50 per cent of divorced men in our study saying that a woman (who could be their former wife, mother or new girlfriend) was responsible for providing for their family, and 93 per cent of divorced women saying that a woman had this responsibility. Although the numbers of female main breadwinners in households containing married couples are not that high (15 per cent, with 21 per cent saying that the woman shares responsibility for providing for the family), it could well be that divorce is most likely to occur where a husband fails to fulfil his masculine obligations. Our research does suggest women find it difficult to deal with male failure to provide.[15] For example, one male respondent who, after a long period unemployed had managed to find a low-paid job, had been left by his wife between the first and second stages of our INTAS study because 'she couldn't stand it' (3-22-2). Meanwhile, another had suffered a similar fate before our study began:

> A man should earn more... At the factory when I got 190, she got 82, but then everything changed and she began to get one and a half times more, and began to reproach me, while my mother-in-law urged her on, and the result was those differences between us. Because of the fact that I started to earn less than her at the factory. Continual reproaches. So we split up (3-15-2).

This, of course, also poses major problems for the men who fall short of the male breadwinner ideal, although in some cases doing what would be required to live up to this role can present what are perceived as even more serious challenges to masculine identity.[16]

Although on the face of it the numbers of men failing to fulfil their perceived obligations are not that high, female anxiety about the issue is more widespread. Women often complain that men do not take their responsibility to provide seriously, and for this reason cannot be relied upon. For example, one woman, asked why she had named herself as the main breadwinner responded:

> Why? He [her husband] can chuck it in [his job] and lie down. I can't do that. Generally speaking he's working at the moment, but, judging by the fact that he didn't work until this month, I don't even know how to put it. I've got a sense of responsibility, perhaps. I've got the kind of work that I can't just drop. I've got stable earnings and I cling on to that job. But him he's got work at the moment, then he won't have it, and that means that we'll once again live on my pay (3-43-2).

The idea that women have a more developed sense of responsibility with regard to household survival was encountered reasonably frequently. For example, half of the married women in my Samara study suggested that women took on greater responsibility for household survival than men, typical comments being:

> Now mainly women work [laughs]. Women try to earn money but men, [breaks off]... men, somehow don't really try and, how can I put it? ... Either they don't get paid, or they can't find work. Women try.... Perhaps we ourselves, women, are guilty. We've spoilt them perhaps.... I just compare all of our husbands, and those with live-in lovers – in general none of them work, no, they work, but they don't get paid, generally. And so we have to work, to labour (machine operator, chocolate factory, 43 years old).

> Our men – it's not that many of them who take responsibility for feeding the family. There's lots of women at work whose husbands don't even work. ... And all the same I think it's more difficult for women to find work. I think that men can always find a job somewhere. They can find work. Perhaps not

prestigious, not what they want, but something that will bring in a few kopeks. But they load everything onto women's shoulders (glazer, chocolate factory, 40 years old).

This sense that men are unreliable reinforces women's attachment to the labour market, but it is also a major cause of marital discord. The norms surrounding the breadwinner role are a key area of conflict in contemporary gender relations in Russia, for although men and women ostensibly share the same aspirations, achieving these is now more difficult than ever.

This sense of a male 'responsibility deficit' is not confined to fears about men's ability to provide financially. Another complaint was lack of male involvement in the home, in terms of 'help' provided and participation in decision making, a view best summed up by one of the respondents from my Samara study:

> Everything is on women's shoulders. The woman is the leader. With money, in financial questions. Women decide everything. Men don't want to do it because it's difficult. Only a woman can work out how to divide it up, where to spend it, what it's possible to do without. . . . Everywhere the wife is the leader (cook, Samara café, 43 years old).

Although some women complained that their husbands were not 'leaders', it does not seem that these women would like to be dictated to by a breadwinner who would confine them to the 'four walls'. Instead, the substance of the complaints tends to reflect a yearning for a sober breadwinner who shares some of the responsibility for the well-being of the household. Interestingly, this is very close to the view of the ideal husband portrayed by mainstream publications of the late Soviet era, when concern about the failure of women to perform their demographic duty led to a minor re-evaluation of the male role and greater emphasis being placed on the need for male 'help' in the home.[17] The problem is that this model was conflict-ridden even in the era when it was underwritten by state policy; it is unlikely to flourish now such support has been withdrawn.

Conclusion

Rather than ushering in a return to the so-called traditional family, the post-Soviet era has seen a reproduction of the Soviet-style family in which women share the burden of breadwinning, yet play the primary role within the domestic sphere. Given that the majority of women want both to work and consider that they should take responsibility for running the household, this can be seen as a choice rather than an imposition. But this situation is not without its tensions. Women's bearing of the 'double burden' is based on the assumption that men will perform the role of *main* breadwinner. Even in the Soviet era, a substantial minority of men were unable to live up to this role (Kiblitskaya 2000a), and now the difficulty of their doing so has increased dramatically. This has major implications because, as has been seen, women are able to choose only 'convenient work' strategies, which allow them to balance the demands of work and home when their partners have decent, stable incomes. The inability of many men to discharge their 'duty' in the present situation therefore raises the question of the durability of the prevailing gender ideology. This is also called into question by evidence that a more egalitarian approach to breadwinning is gaining ground among younger women.[18] Changes in behaviour, however, will not occur overnight, for, as the experience of women in the West in the last few decades reveals, even if Russian women do move towards the idea of shared roles, it will be some time before they receive the male co-operation required to put such ideas into practice.

Notes

1   The quotation in the title comes from one of my female respondents in the West Siberian mining settlement where I carried out my doctoral research. She argued that, 'I always say a woman is everything: she is a mother, a wife, a lover, a laundress, a cook, and everything else. She does everything'. See Ashwin (1999b) for more details about this respondent, whom I refer to as 'Marina the *medalistka*'.
2   The gender order can be defined as the historically constructed pattern of power relations between men and women and definitions of masculinity and femininity in a given society (Connell 1987: 98–9).
3   This project is entitled 'Gender differences in employment strategy during economic transition in Russia', grant no. INTAS-97: 20280. Along with interview transcripts, in preparing this chapter I have used analytical reports prepared for the project by Natalya Goncharova, Marina Ilyina, Ol'ga Isupova, Marina Kiblitskaya, Irina Kozina, Tanya Lytkina, Elena Omel'chenko, Irina Popova, Irina Tartakovskaya and Sveta Yaroshenko.
4   Numbers 1–4: Moscow, Ul'yanovsk, Samara, and Syktyvkar respectively.
5   The following account of the Soviet gender order is based on Ashwin (2000), where its content and contradictions are explored in greater detail.
6   As is well known, by the end of the Soviet era female labour participation was close to the biological maximum. The figures were impressive even taking into account lower retirement ages and the fact that the Soviet figures defined as economically active women on maternity leave, which by the end of the Soviet era could last up to three years. It should also be noted that there was virtually no provision for Soviet women to work part time.
7   For a full account of the terms of women's integration into the labour force see Filtzer (1992: 177–203).
8   Stalin was a particularly jealous guardian of the paternal role (for details see Ashwin 2000), but the official neglect of the private role of men persisted throughout the Soviet era. For example, in 1984 G. Bragrazyan charged journalists with 'praising women to the hilt, almost singing hymns to their honour, and letting fathers slip to the periphery of our consciousness' (*Pravda*, 2 September, 1984, quoted in Attwood (1990: 168)).
9   For a discussion of men see Kukhterin (2000).
10   One of the most notorious expressions of this was the comment of the (then) Russian Labour Minister, Gennadi Melikyan, who, when asked in 1993 about

measures to combat female unemployment, replied, 'Why should we employ women when men are out of work? It's better that men work and women take care of the children and do housework. I don't think women should work when men are doing nothing' (quoted in Morvant 1995: 5).

11 The use of the term 'traditional' is problematic in this context. The male-breadwinner/female-carer model is not 'traditional' in Russia, in the sense of being the dominant pre-revolutionary model. On the eve of the Russian revolution 80 per cent of the Russian population were peasants, and peasant women worked within the context of the peasant household. As one study of Russian peasant women's work concluded, 'work, paid and unpaid, was the focal point of existence for peasant women as well as for men' (Glickman 1992: 69). Moreover, on the eve of the revolution the participation of women in industry was quite high: in 1913, though they were heavily concentrated in the textile industry, women constituted a third of the industrial labour force, rising to half during WWI (Lapidus 1978: 164–5). Male heads of household were considered to have the right to control women, but most men in Tsarist Russia could not afford to keep a non-working wife.

12 Goskomstat began conducting a labour force survey in 1992. According to these figures, which provide a far more reliable picture of unemployment levels than the registered unemployment statistics, there have always been marginally more men unemployed than women. But this has not prevented certain feminist scholars from peddling the fallacy that unemployment in Russia has a 'female face'. See, for example, Bridger et al. (1996: 51), Khotkina (1994), Sperling (1999: 43). It seems that this results from a confusion regarding the relative reliability of the Labour Force Survey and registered unemployment statistics, possibly reinforced by a tendency to perceive women as victims.

13 Interestingly, however, despite women's fear of being confined at home by their husbands, men revealed themselves to be slightly less conservative than women, with 47 per cent saying that women should be responsible for the household and 43 per cent that it should be a joint responsibility. What they mean by this, however, is another question.

14 Women's desire to reconcile work and family suggests that a sizeable proportion of Russian women would prefer to work part time were it to become a more widely available option (though many of those who would like such work would probably not be able to afford to take it).

15 See Meshcherkina (2000) for an interesting account of women's investment in preserving the male breadwinner norm. She argues, on the basis of her study of New Russians, that both women and men are contributing to the reproduction of this norm, and that both feel uncomfortable when it is disrupted.

16 See Kiblitskaya (2000b) on men's interpretation of their role. She argues that being a successful male breadwinner sometimes conflicts with other determinants of masculine status such as professional status (bringing home the bacon can mean taking on what is perceived as a demeaning job), and male comradeship (not having any personal money, and not being free to drink with workmates, is a sign of the cardinal sin of being 'accountable to the wife').

17 See Irina Tartakovskaya (2000) on the gender relations promoted by *Izvestia* in 1984.

18 As well as being less likely to see running the domestic sphere as a purely female responsibility, women under 35 are also somewhat less likely to think that the

man should take responsibility for providing for the family (60 per cent, as opposed to an average of over 80 per cent in the older age groups). Men in the younger age group are just as traditional as their older counterparts regarding this issue, however, 85 per cent of them thinking that they should be responsible for providing for the family.

References

Ashwin, S. (1999a) *Russian Workers: The Anatomy of Patience*, Manchester: Manchester University Press.

Ashwin, S. (1999b) 'Russia's saviours? Women workers in transition from communism' in M. Neary (ed.) *Global Humanisation: Studies in the Manufacture of Labour*, London and New York: Mansell, pp. 97–126.

Ashwin, S. (2000) 'Gender, state and society in Soviet and post-Soviet Russia' in S. Ashwin (ed.) *Gender, State and Society in Soviet and Post-Soviet Russia*, London and New York: Routledge, pp. 1–29.

Ashwin, S. and Bowers, E. (1997) 'Do Russian women want to work?' in M. Buckley (ed.) *Post-Soviet Women: From the Baltic to Central Asia*, Cambridge: Cambridge University Press, pp. 21–37.

Attwood, L. (1990) *The New Soviet Man and Woman: Sex Role Socialisation in the USSR*, Basingstoke: Macmillan.

Bridger, S., Kay, R. and Pinnick, K. (1996) *No More Heroines? Russia, Women and the Market*, London: Routledge.

Clarke, S. (1999a) *New Forms of Employment and Household Survival Strategies in Russia*, Coventry, Moscow: ISITO/CCLS.

Clarke, S. (1999b) *The Formation of a Labour Market in Russia*, Cheltenham: Edward Elgar.

Connell, R. (1987) *Gender and Power: Society, the Person and Sexual Politics*, Cambridge: Polity Press.

Dale, A. and Holdsworth, C. (1998) 'Why don't minority ethnic women in Britain work part-time?' in J. O'Reilly and C. Fagan (eds) *Part-time Prospects: An International Comparison of Part-Time Work in Europe, North America and the Pacific Rim*, London: Routledge, pp. 77–95.

Filtzer, D. (1992) *Soviet Workers and De-Stalinization: The Formation of the Modern System of Soviet Production Relations, 1953–1964*, Cambridge: Cambridge University Press.

Funk, N. (1993) 'Feminism East and West', in N. Funk and M. Mueller (eds) *Gender Politics and Post-Communism: Reflections from Eastern Europe and the Former Soviet Union*, New York and London: Routledge, pp. 318–330.

Glickman, R. (1992) 'Peasant women and their work', in B. Farnsworth and L. Viola (eds) *Russian Peasant Women*, New York, Oxford: Oxford University Press.

Goskomstat (1999) *Statisticheskii byulleten*, 3, 53, Moscow: Goskomstat Rossii.

Gruzdeva, E. (1995) *Zhenskaya bezrabotista v Rossii (1991–1994gg.)* Moscow: IMEMO RAN.

Issoupova, O. (2000) 'From duty to pleasure? Motherhood in Soviet and post-Soviet Russia' in S. Ashwin (ed.) *Gender, State and Society in Soviet and Post-Soviet Russia*, London and New York: Routledge, pp. 39–54.

Katz, K. (2000) 'Labour in transition: Women and men in Taganrog, Russia', paper presented at the ICCEES IV world congress in Tampere, Finland, 29 July–3 August 2000.

Khotkina, Z. (1994) 'Women in the labour market: Yesterday, today and tomorrow', in A. Podsadskaya (ed.) *Women in Russia: A New Era in Russian Feminism*, London and New York: Verso, pp. 85–108.

Kiblitskaya, M. (2000a) 'Russia's female breadwinners: The changing subjective experience', in S. Ashwin (ed.) *Gender, State and Society in Soviet and Post-Soviet Russia*, London and New York: Routledge, pp. 55–70.

Kiblitskaya, M. (2000b) 'Once we were kings: Male experiences of loss of status at work in post-communist Russia', in S. Ashwin (ed.) *Gender, State and Society in Soviet and Post-Soviet Russia*, London and New York: Routledge, pp. 90–104.

Kukhterin, S. (2000) 'Fathers and patriarchs in communist and post-communist Russia', in S. Ashwin (ed.) *Gender, State and Society in Soviet and Post-Soviet Russia*, London and New York: Routledge, pp. 71–89.

Lapidus, G. (1978) *Women in Soviet Society: Equality, Development and Social Change*, Berkeley, Los Angeles and London: Berkeley University Press.

Lissyutkina, L. (1993) 'Soviet women at the crossroads of perestroika', in N. Funk and M. Mueller (eds) *Gender Politics and Post-Communism: Reflections from Eastern Europe and the Former Soviet Union*, New York: Routledge, pp. 274–286.

Meshcherkina, E. (2000) 'New Russian men: Masculinity regained?' in S. Ashwin (ed.) *Gender, State and Society in Soviet and Post-Soviet Russia*, London and New York: Routledge, pp. 105–117.

Moore, H. (1994) *A Passion for Difference: Essays in Anthropology and Gender*, Cambridge: Polity Press.

Morvant, P. (1995) 'Bearing the double burden in Russia', *Transition*, 1, 16, 8 September 1995, pp. 4–9.

Pfau-Effinger, B. (1998) 'Culture or structure as explanations for differences in part-time work in Germany, Finland and the Netherlands?' in J. O'Reilly, and C. Fagan (eds) *Part-Time Prospects: An International Comparison of Part-Time Work in Europe, North America and the Pacific Rim*, London: Routledge, pp. 177–198.

Pfau-Effinger, B. (1999) 'The modernisation of family and motherhood in Western Europe', in R. Crompton (ed.) *Restructuring Gender Relations and Employment: The Decline of the Male Breadwinner*, Oxford: Oxford University Press, pp. 60–80.

Pilkington, H. (1992) 'Behind the mask of Soviet unity: Realities of women's lives', in C. Corrin (ed.) *Superwomen and the Double Burden: Women's Experience of Change in Central and Eastern Europe and the Former Soviet Union*, London: Scarlet Press, pp. 180–235.

Sperling, V. (1999) *Organising Women in Contemporary Russia: Engendering Transition*, Cambridge: Cambridge University Press.

Tartakovskaya, I. (2000) 'The changing representation of gender roles in the Soviet and post-Soviet press', in S. Ashwin (ed.) *Gender, State and Society in Soviet and Post-Soviet Russia*, London and New York: Routledge, pp. 118–136.

Voronina, O. (1994) 'The mythology of women's emancipation in the USSR as the foundation for a policy of discrimination', in A. Podsadskaya (ed.) *Women in Russia: A New Era in Russian Feminism*, London and New York: Verso, pp. 34–56.

Yaroshenko, S. (2000) 'Gender differences in employment strategies in Russia. Results from the first stage of research', *mimeo*.

Zdravomyslova, E. (1996) 'Problems of becoming a housewife', in E. Haavio-Mannila and A. Rotkirch (eds) *Women's Voices in Russia Today*, Aldershot: Dartmouth Publishing Company.

7 Restructuring labour markets on the frontier of the European Union

Gendered uneven development in Hungary

Judit Timár

Introduction

The socio-economic changes taking place in East Central Europe have brought about considerable shifts in the current position of women and men compared to the past. One area in which such changes have been experienced concerns the position of men and women in the labour market. The level of employment, wage differences and vertical and horizontal gender segregation are influenced not only by the emergence of the market economy, the pace of economic restructuring, and the external effects of globalisation and European integration, but also by institutional, cultural and social frameworks. However, macro-economic and macro-social transformations are experienced by individuals at the level of locality. For example, Walby's (1994) conception of differentiated patriarchy permits the recognition of the diversity of women's situation between different areas or localities without giving up the concept of male domination and female subordination (Perrons 1998). Therefore, in evaluating paid work in relation to the division of labour in the household, as an important element of patriarchy, a first step should be to shift the emphasis of analysis from the national level to the examination of sub-national spatial differences.

Following this approach, the most important arguments developed in this chapter are as follows. First, spatial inequality in Hungary's labour market affects women and men differently. Second, levels of gender inequality in paid work are most severe in regions and settlements increasingly falling behind in the process of capitalist development. Third, accession to the European Union (EU) is likely to have little positive impact on the gendered nature of the uneven spatial development in the labour market. This chapter therefore examines how economic activity, occupational restructuring and unemployment created differing situations for women and men in different places in Hungary.

The chapter relies on national and regional statistical data as well as the results of a case study examining settlements in one county in south-east Hungary. In addition, the difficulties people living in 'backward' rural areas have to face will be illustrated from ongoing research in two contrasting regions,[1] three villages located in Györ-Moson-Sopron County, one of Hungary's most advanced counties in the north west and located next to the Austrian border and three villages in Békés County, one of the most 'backward' counties in the south east near the Romanian border (Figure 7.1). These villages can be paired across the contrasting two regions with Méhkerék in Békés and Jánossomorja in Györ-Moson-Sopron being the most advanced villages in the border zones with frontier stations and a several thousand-strong population. Zsira in Györ-Moson-Sopron County and Körösnagyharsány in Békés County illustrate ageing villages, each with a population of under one thousand, high unemployment figures and unfavourable accessibility. Finally, Györújbarát and Szabadkígyós represent villages enjoying prosperity through suburbanisation. As part of a broader study, 35 women living in some sort of relationship in the six villages have so far been interviewed about their own and their partners' family backgrounds, places of work, education, division of labour in the household, their survival strategies, and their own role in them, their evaluation of the period of transition and its effects, and how they consider the position of their settlement and region affects their lives. The labour market chances of the inhabitants of the villages studied are as varied now as they are likely to remain after accession to the EU. At the same time, however, women's disadvantageous position in the competition for paid work and the inequalities of household divisions of labour have turned out to be widespread and a common experience for women after the collapse of communism.

The geography of gender inequality in employment

In order to measure the relative economic activity of men and women, it is useful to use an indicator to assist in the evaluation of Hungarian conditions in an international context. Perrons's (1998) regional analysis of 12 EU member states, which involves the use of the female-male activity rate ratio,[2] provides a good starting point. As Hungary has only recently started reporting data conforming to international statistical norms, a chronological comparison concerning economic activity is not feasible. Consequently, only data from the 1996 microcensus are available.

With a female-male activity rate ratio of nearly 71 per cent, Hungary is comparable to the best performing EU member states. In comparing these countries, however, it is difficult to give a comprehensive explanation for such a relatively high level of gender equality in employment in Hungary. Perrons's (1998) summary suggests that, for example, Denmark is a model of the so-called 'social-democratic regime' characterised by the support of gender neutral citizenship (Leibfried and Ostner 1991) and this contributes to a high female-male activity ratio. According to another theoretical approach, Denmark is the embodiment of the 'weak breadwinner' model, which encourages women's participation in paid work (Lewis 1992). In contrast, the UK, which also has a high female-male activity rate ratio, is an example of a 'liberal market regime', where 'there is a formal commitment to equal opportunity but little state provision or support to facilitate equal outcomes' (Perrons and Gonäs 1998: 5). On the other hand, however, though employment of women in the UK is economically

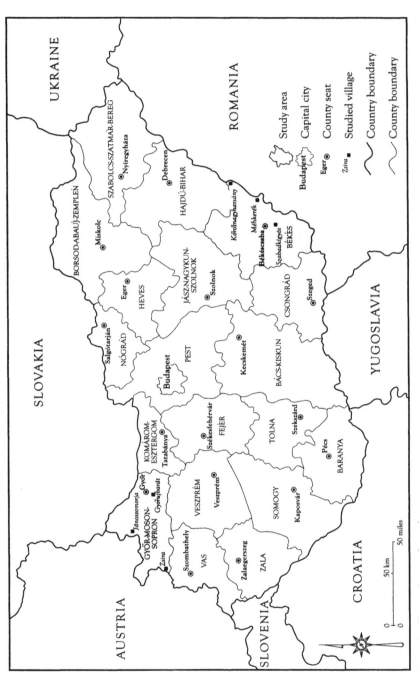

Figure 7.1 Hungarian study regions.

necessitated, many women can only attain a partial breadwinner role with only a limited income. Thus, the UK represents an example of the 'strong breadwinner model'. It appears that the factors responsible for the present Hungarian situation are similar to those at work in the former East Germany; the economic activity of men and women, counting as balanced in a European context, may be attributed to the shared inheritance of socialism.

However, these national differences support the hypothesis that the gender inequalities in economic activity in themselves cannot be explained by national institutional or regulatory frameworks (Perrons 1998). Regional-level analyses are therefore important in developing an understanding of causes and effects. The analysis that follows uses Hungarian counties as intermediate level units of administration as the basis of comparison. Larger Hungarian regions are not appropriate for detailed analysis. Comparing the counties' female-male activity rate ratios with the national average, it becomes clear that there are considerable regional differences within Hungary, even though they do not reach the level of division experienced in Italy or Greece (Figure 7.2). The question is whether the higher gender ratio is associated with economically more advanced or city regions as is the case in many parts of Europe (see Perrons 1998). Or are sectoral differences in the economy (Schmude 1996) or distinctive regional cultures (Sackmann and Haüssermann 1994) the key explanation of the regional differences, as has been argued in the southern and western parts of Germany, for example?

Due to lack of appropriate data, an elaborate study of interrelationships still awaits future research. However, data available for regional economies do clearly suggest that:

- Women's economic activity best approaches that of men's in Budapest, the most developed urban space comprising one-fifth of the country's population. The counties with the next most favourable female-male activity rate ratios are the ones with the highest level of female employment, the only exception being Komárom County, whose economy surpasses the national average, but where there is a relatively low level of male employment, as a result of restructuring, which has led to a process of gender levelling. The counties belonging to this next most favourable group and situated mainly near the western border form the most developed region alongside the central one. Csongrád County, which is close to the national average, stands out with its high urban population.
- The counties in the East of the Great Plain and partly in Northern Hungary exhibit the highest gender inequalities concerning access to paid work and are the economically most backward regions of the country, where female economic activity is the lowest.

On the whole, however, one interrelationship stands out: women's economic activity shows greater regional differences than men's and women's labour market chances are more determined by the region they live in.

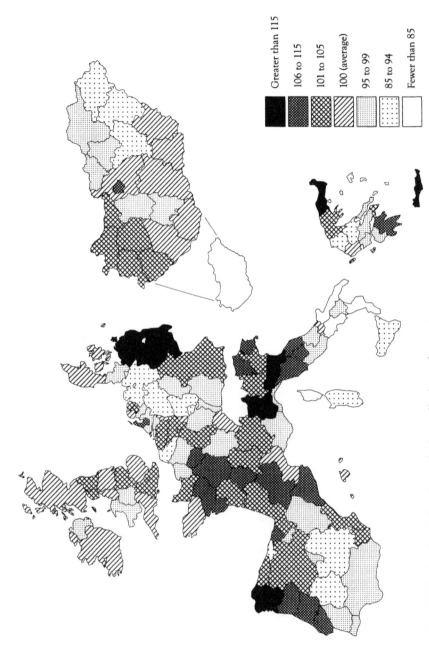

Figure 7.2 Regional variations in gender inequality in employment.

However, whether women live in villages, cities or the capital city is of significance to the levels of inequality experienced. The degree of gender equality in all four major age groups unequivocally follows the urban hierarchy: highest in Budapest and lowest in the villages (Table 7.1). The urban-rural dichotomy has long been more pronounced in the former socialist countries than in other parts of Europe due to relatively late urbanisation and the 1990s have not brought any significant improvement in this situation. Rural women thus face a twofold disadvantage in the labour market. The only age group whose level of economic activity is well below men's, without differing from city women's, is that of the 15–29-year-olds. For rural men and women alike leave school earlier than their city counterparts. However, while men either start work or become registered unemployed, rural women become what are officially labelled as homemakers in larger numbers than women in cities. In addition to that, rural women are more likely to make use of the system of childcare benefit.[3] The question is whether this is really their 'free' decision or they are forced to do so.

Some argue that childcare benefit serving as a means of either including women in, or excluding them from, the labour market and of treating them as a reserve army has played an important role in the assessment of female employment since its introduction in the socialist era. Our research shows that childcare benefit was made use of in the socialist era and since then by all the rural mothers interviewed. Today it is the only source of income for many. According to a woman in the village of Méhkerék, 'the majority of those making use of childcare benefit worked in the nearby hosiery factory', which employed 80–100 people from the village but has now closed down. However, the number of children in a household is one of the most important differentiating factors in contemporary Hungary. For example, a village mother of two said quite simply that 'I'm not going to bear another child only to get the benefit. We would've liked to have one more, but I'm not going to bear another. We can't afford it.' Still, in the most recent system of social care having a third child may be a survival strategy for low-income families without any plans concerning the long-term education of their children. Mothers of three are relatively common among the younger women interviewed. By raising at least three under-eighteens, they became eligible for 'full-time mother' status and special childcare benefit ('childcare support'),[4] and they all decided to stay at home with their children. No matter how low the benefit was, payments were regular and of key importance for the families. As a mother of four on childcare leave and with an unemployed husband in Szabadkígyós put it, 'I've been thinking about becoming a "full-time" mother. It depends on how things will be in one year, whether I'll still be needed at work. If not, childcare benefit is more than nothing.' Interestingly, though, it never occurred to the majority of women that their husbands would also have been eligible for the benefit. However, there were some whose painstaking calculations showed that they suffered less financial loss in that 'traditional' way. The decision, as one mother admits it, is far from being the result of accepting this role without a word of protest:

Table 7.1 The proportion of the economically active population and the female–male activity rate ratio by age and settlement types in Hungary, 1996

Age group	Budapest			Other cities			Villages		
	Activity rate %		Female–male activity rate ratio %	Activity rate %		Female–male activity rate ratio %	Activity rate %		Female–male activity rate ratio %
	Women	Men		Women	Men		Women	Men	
15–29	43.9	54.3	80.8	42.5	60.1	70.7	43.1	65.6	65.7
30–39	74.2	91.6	81.0	72.9	91.5	79.7	65.9	86.4	76.3
40–54	74.9	84.1	89.1	72.4	80.8	89.6	59.3	73.0	81.2
55–59	16.5	50.9	32.4	9.3	40.6	22.9	4.6	31.1	14.8
Total	36.8	48.2	76.3	35.4	47.9	73.9	28.7	55.8	63.9

Source: Calculated from *Microcensus, 1996. The Characteristics of Population and Dwelling*, Budapest: Central Statistical Office.

It would've been possible for my husband to draw the childcare benefit and for me to go back to work. But a woman was better at running a household and raising children. At least that was what I thought then. Now that it's over, I have regrets.

At a later age, however, while city women approaching retirement were able to maintain the economic activity that they had undertaken earlier in their thirties, every fourth rural woman in Hungary went into forced retirement. Indeed, along with early retirement for health reasons, forced retirement is a typical feature of the transition period and accompanied a massive loss of jobs in the early 1990s (see Ch. 1).

Migrating to more developed regions or cities would seem an obvious way of overcoming such spatial disadvantage. Many do not opt for it, however, referring to some kind of local attachment or, less commonly, to the fact that 'children need a healthier environment' as is attested to by the following woman:

> The village makes our life harder inasmuch as we have to work harder. It doesn't help us in any way. We live here, our parents lived here, too, it's difficult to break away. In the end we were stuck here completely. We kept saying we'd leave, but we never did.

What is even more important, however, is that the very people willing to migrate cannot do so. In the socialist era the only feasible way of investing the family's income was through building a house. Consequently, huge family houses were built even in villages with poor infrastructure. Costs were, and are, often reduced on the basis of several years of work by the owners and their families. With a real-estate market now emerging, such houses have become unsaleable. The problem becomes tangible when we listen to the story of a woman, herself on disability pension and her husband no longer eligible for unemployment benefit,

> The fact that we live in the country must have its disadvantages. The children would ask us to sell the house and move to the city of Gyula. They said there were better chances of employment and more entertainment facilities. In the end they gave up the idea. We never seriously considered moving, for we toiled so hard to have this place, in fact my husband did all the work by himself, that we wouldn't give it up easily. We wouldn't get enough (money) for it to buy one of the same size in Gyula, after all, it stands in a village.

In circumstances like that and without developing a market for rental housing, it will not be possible for migration to ensure better chances in the labour market for rural populations and backward areas.

Changing gender segregation in employment

The increasing participation of women in the labour market in EU member states can be linked to the restructuring of their economies towards the tertiary sector. Although female participation in the group of active wage-earners grew in Hungary in the 1980s (female wage earning activity in 1980 was 76.8 per cent of men's, and 80.1 per cent of men's in 1990), this tendency did not continue after the political change of regime. In fact the ratio fell to 79.9 per cent in 1996. The tertiary sector has acquired a considerably larger importance in Hungary too, but the underlying causes of this process are different. Privatisation, the withdrawal of the state, the radical restructuring of agriculture, the loss of Eastern markets, the collapse of certain traditional industries and the concentration of new small enterprises in the tertiary sector have together led to the restructuring of the economy resulting in a drastic cut in both female and male employment. Indeed, it is not clear yet whether the process of employment restructuring in Hungary will follow Western European tendencies or bring about a labour market typical of peripheral societies, or even produce a special Hungarian way (see Barta 1998).

However, processes operating in European market economies do not necessarily apply to gender-sectoral segregation in Hungary. In the EU member states the expansion of the tertiary sector has increased segregation. For example, the 'Duncan Index of Dissimilarity'[5] has increased, and in Greece, where the agrarian sector has an overwhelming weight, gender-sectoral segregation is lower than in any other country in the EU (Kyriazis 1998). In contrast, although segregation increased somewhat in Hungary between 1980 and 1996, it was not strongly linked to a higher proportion of tertiary-sector employment. Indeed, the situation is just the reverse: segregation increased least in Budapest where tertiarisation is most significant, whereas segregation increased the most sharply and reached the highest level in the villages (Table 7.2).

In essence, the increasing horizontal segregation of employment is very much like what we have witnessed in Western Europe and it goes hand in hand with the gender stereotyping of jobs. The concentrated employment of Hungarian women in education and health care is the most striking phenomenon in comparison with men. Although segregation is considerable in wholesale and retailing, too, it has only increased in villages and decreased in cities. In manufacturing industries in the cities, especially in Budapest, there has been significant job loss. Cutbacks here assumed such proportions that, in contrast with the situation in the past, this branch today employs more men than women. For rural women, however, it was agriculture, where an even more drastic loss of jobs took place.

Examining the female-male occupational structure, a more subtle picture emerges. Gender segregation increased here also, but changes in different settlement types were extremely varied. While in 1980 the occupational gender segregation of cities exceeded that of Budapest, not to mention villages, by 1996 the order had completely reversed (Table 7.3). Women are more dominant in white-collar occupations, with the notable exceptions of the highest-prestige and

Table 7.2 Distribution (per cent) of active earners by economic sector and gender in Hungary, 1980, 1996

Economic sector	Budapest				Other cities				Villages			
	1980		1996		1980		1996		1980		1996	
	women	men	women	men	women	men	women	men	women	men	women	men
Agriculture, hunting, fishing	2.46	5.32	0.41	0.89	8.51	14.73	2.55	7.57	33.40	36.70	9.29	21.34
Mining	0.25	0.29	0.05	0.07	1.31	4.91	0.41	1.53	0.83	4.03	0.27	1.51
Manufacturing	32.45	32.35	13.93	18.20	34.65	31.17	22.60	26.82	28.43	20.82	26.69	24.37
Electricity, gas, and water supply	0.74	1.26	1.18	1.67	1.12	2.12	2.17	4.48	0.52	1.48	1.35	3.28
Construction	3.53	12.68	1.76	9.77	2.95	12.12	1.09	8.97	1.92	11.38	0.88	10.37
Wholesale and retail trade	13.55	8.62	17.83	17.41	12.28	7.03	15.75	12.29	10.21	5.18	14.22	7.58
Hotels and restaurants	4.08	2.74	3.93	3.42	3.91	1.48	3.81	2.95	2.06	0.62	3.57	1.96
Transport, storage	6.91	13.71	6.93	12.59	4.38	10.28	4.31	11.06	4.00	10.31	5.89	12.95
Financial intermediation	1.47	0.42	5.73	2.50	1.19	0.30	3.42	1.25	0.68	0.09	2.16	0.54
Real estate and business activities	8.00	6.59	7.33	8.75	2.50	2.04	3.36	3.76	0.88	0.92	1.65	1.78
Public administration	5.14	5.13	9.54	8.15	3.90	3.99	6.75	7.05	3.12	2.98	8.56	6.69
Education	7.40	2.71	12.62	4.53	9.98	2.72	16.79	4.69	7.29	1.24	13.24	2.17
Health and social work	7.48	2.02	10.31	3.12	8.39	1.78	12.31	3.06	4.13	0.77	9.29	2.10
Other services	6.54	6.15	8.46	8.95	4.94	5.33	4.67	4.51	2.58	3.49	2.93	3.37
Total (number)	483,678	545,585	335,629	373,264	961,123	1,220,153	739,679	884,714	757,245	1,101,056	472,704	678,835
Duncan index	19.38		20.84		26.38		28.0		24.20		32.33	

Source: Calculated from *Microcensus, 1996, Changes of Employment, 1980–1996*, Budapest: Central Statistical Office.

Table 7.3 Distribution (per cent) of active earners by occupation and gender in Hungary, 1980, 1996

Occupation	Budapest				Other cities				Villages			
	1980		1996		1980		1996		1980		1996	
	women	men	women	men	women	men	women	men	women	men	women	men
Legislators and managers	5.79	12.12	6.47	10.12	4.15	10.44	4.81	8.75	2.46	5.85	3.42	4.11
Professionals	15.49	13.05	19.97	17.39	10.31	6.31	15.64	10.02	4.82	2.26	8.27	4.01
Technicians	21.61	10.47	25.77	14.02	13.83	7.73	21.86	9.23	6.56	3.47	15.36	4.95
Clerks	18.79	1.80	16.92	1.34	15.63	1.34	13.15	0.64	9.37	0.70	10.63	0.38
Service and sales workers	10.71	4.60	15.00	13.60	13.44	4.21	18.96	12.89	12.00	3.91	20.54	10.32
Agricultural, forestry	0.33	0.58	0.11	0.32	2.63	3.80	1.27	3.30	11.34	10.10	4.70	8.90
Industrial and construction	14.38	34.70	6.25	25.84	17.40	37.79	9.38	32.66	18.13	36.25	13.22	36.06
Plant, machine operation	4.08	13.48	1.18	9.70	7.72	17.01	5.53	14.00	8.92	21.19	8.50	19.72
Elementary occupations	8.81	9.20	6.43	5.07	14.88	11.37	8.90	5.63	26.42	16.27	15.07	9.61
Military	–	–	1.01	2.61	–	–	0.49	2.87	–	–	0.29	1.94
Total (number)	483,678	545,585	335,629	373,264	961,123	1,220,153	739,679	884,714	757,245	1,101,056	472,704	678,835
Duncan index	36.73		33.12		37.14		40.10		33.79		40.60	

Source: Calculated from Microcensus, 1996, Changes of Employment, 1980–1996, Budapest: Central Statistical Office.

best-paid jobs in legislation, administration and trade unions as well as business management. Getting an élite job like this still remains a male privilege.[6] On the other hand, only slightly over one-third of all rural women make a living in white-collar occupations. An increasing proportion of women (19 times more than men) work in low-status clerical and administrative jobs. It appears that in all settlement types, skilled physical jobs in industry and construction have been exchanged for occupations requiring high school or college qualifications and service-like manual jobs, thus increasing segregation especially in villages. Among physical occupations it is in service jobs and elementary occupations, at the bottom of the skill hierarchy, that women's employment is higher than men's.

What is certain then is that the occupational structure of women with regard to position and pay is less favourable than that of men. If we accept Koncz's (1994) idea that feminisation begins in occupations which have been devalued, and occupations are devalued because they have been feminised, a decrease in labour market gender inequality is least likely in villages, where the occupational gender segregation increased the most sharply. However, the experience of economic restructuring and the feminisation of employment in EU member states raise a number of issues for women's labour market position in Hungary. Jobs in the service sector, especially in economically backward EU regions, are precarious (Rodriguez-Pose 1994, Perrons 1998). Insecure employment is also experienced in the growth of women in the public sector in Hungary, but as the experience of Sweden suggests, this form of employment is especially endangered by cuts in public expenditure (Gonäs 1998). Indeed, sooner or later the countries preparing to join the EU will have to take Perrons's (1998: 21) concern into account: 'These cuts are likely to increase as countries try to meet the Maastricht convergence criteria.' It is to be feared that such convergence might lead to disadvantages in employment for Hungarian women, too, similar to those in Western Europe. Another danger, as Szalai (1998) has indicated, is that 'women, as their clients in the mushrooming welfare-service units, become ghettoised in a world where each blames the other, and none of the partners find the way out.'

Gender inequalities in unemployment

Over the last ten years it has been unemployment that has administered the greatest shock both to women and men (the unemployment rate in Hungary was 9.1 per cent in 1998). One of the most intriguing features of Hungarian unemployment is a phenomenon rare both in EU member states and former socialist countries. Women are underrepresented among the unemployed compared to the participation of women in overall economic activity. However, this general, national picture is not necessarily relevant to all regions. Among the unemployed, women outnumber men in the Central Hungary Region (54 per cent of registered unemployed persons were women in 1998, and the unemployment rate was 4.4 per cent according to the Hungarian Central Statistical Office), whereas the predominance of unemployed men can be observed in the Northern region (59.1 per cent of registered unemployed persons were men) and Northern Great Plain (58.7 per cent) struck by massive unemployment (the unemployment rate was 15.6 per cent and 14.5 per cent, respectively).

More detailed analysis is possible from the settlement size groups data in the county microcensus as well as from a database of the Labour Force Centre broken down into settlements. A study of the 1996 microcensus in Békés County showed that lower female unemployment is not universal in all parts of the county. In Békéscsaba, the county seat and the only settlement with more than 50,000 inhabitants, the situation, like that in Budapest, is the reverse. Here women constituted the numerical majority of the unemployed in spite of their lower employment level. Thus the overgeneralization that in Hungary and Békés county, respectively, women have an advantage over men concerning unemployment simply does not stand its ground in Békéscsaba, home to one in six inhabitants in Békés county.

Previous research on Békés County has attempted to explain the lower female unemployment rate (see Timár and Velkey 1998). While according to Frey (1993) one explanatory factor is the mode of economic restructuring, in our research it became obvious that the present situation was largely to be blamed on the conceptualisation of 'unemployed' and the definitions accepted by the International Labour Organisation (ILO). An analysis of who exactly belonged to statistical categories such as employed, unemployed, inactive earners or dependants has revealed that by including some groups in the economically active population (which acts as the denominator of the official unemployment rate) and by including the unemployed undertaking casual jobs in the numerator, a distorted picture of unemployment results. As each of these distortions shows women's position more favourably,[7] the official rate shows higher differences between the genders than is justified. A 'corrected' unemployment ratio was developed to evaluate the actual male and female employment situation.[8] As a result of this computation, in 1996 22.7 per cent of the males and 23.8 per cent of the females potentially endangered with unemployment at any time were actually jobless. Yet, the official male unemployment rate was 16.5 per cent whereas the female rate was 11.6 per cent (Timár and Velkey 1998). In essence, then, the present official computation of unemployment hides the real chances and problems of several social strata in difficult situations, especially women.

If our 'adjusted' rates are compared in each settlement group in Békés County the picture becomes more differentiated. Except for large villages and small towns, relatively more women are actually jobless among those potentially endangered with unemployment at any time in every settlement category. Not only in Békéscsaba but also in villages with fewer than 1,000 inhabitants, too, women constituted the numerical majority of the actual unemployed.

These villages are typically located in backward areas along the border with Romania or in the internal periphery. The inhabitants most often earn a living in agriculture, and usually do unskilled manual work locally. It would require detailed research to find out how the presumably agricultural activity of 'dependent' housewives here contributes to family income and how a large part of them would be available for paid work if they were given a chance (the probability of which is of course large). The importance of this issue is further supported by the example of a woman who said how she was forced to become a housewife after having had a job and how she had to do household farming and tend to the livestock at the same time.

> When my third and youngest child was two years old and I could've gone back to work, my father-in-law died unexpectedly and my mother-in-law was taken ill. Then my old man and I made an agreement that he went out to work and undertook more than before and I took care of his mother. I took care of her for 13 years. I stayed at home all the time as she needed round-the-clock attendance. I was very much left out of everything. Now here I am with nothing, no income at all!

In such places it is not only real unemployment that can be different from what is known as typical in the EU. The only group of employed people in Hungary dominated by females is that of those helping family members (65.8 per cent of whom are women). Thus they qualify as 'new other European women' not only because their identity is rebuilt from their East Central European past (Regulska 1997), but their work is considered to be 'atypical' in the hierarchy of forms of work established in the European Union as Vaiou (1996: 67) has argued about certain groups of Southern European women.

Changes in the gender distribution of unemployment may also be influenced by differences in the method and intensity of job search. Only the minority of the clients visiting the labour office in Békés County until 1997 were women in all settlement categories. However, the women who have chosen official methods for job searches show more endurance in struggle for work than men. The number of women no longer on unemployment benefit but still keeping in touch with the labour office hoping for a job is larger than that of men in every settlement type, except Békéscsaba. A woman with an intermediate-level degree in accounting, having lost a job relevant to her qualifications after childcare leave in the 1990s, describes the pain of finding a new job:

> After being unemployed I started working in a completely new job. The fact that I'm a nurse at an old people's home now and not an accountant is a completely different situation. I think . . . I couldn't work as an accountant as they wouldn't reimburse my travelling expenses. I found a job locally, which meant 2 years' retraining. To me it has been the biggest change of the past 10 years as I wouldn't have become a nurse if it had been up to me. The very sight of blood made me sick, let alone the idea of being a nurse. I'm sure I wouldn't have become one of my own will. But necessity is a hard taskmaster. I needed a job.

In every settlement category, there are numerically more women undertaking to participate in retraining or voluntary public work than men trying to improve their chances in the same way. This difference, however, manifests itself most characteristically in cities with better possibilities. Thus it appears that differing settlement potentials not only influence the whole population's chances of obtaining work but also affect the relative position of men and women as well as their opportunities in the labour market.

Janice Monk (1988: 16) asks in one of her former studies: 'What type of families will emerge in a traditional patriarchal society when educated women are breadwinners and uneducated men are unemployed? Is there a new division of labour within the household, or do women carry a double burden?' The present-day changes in Hungarian employment urge us to ask similar questions. What impacts will be exerted on 'private patriarchy' (see Walby 1990) by the gendered uneven development of a capitalist labour market?

The rural women we asked nearly all admitted to spending more time on housework than their husbands. However, they did not rebel against a 'traditional' domestic division of labour. Women tended to undertake 'inside' duties especially childcare, while men were largely responsible for 'outside' jobs. The manager of a mutual savings bank, for instance, told us point-blank that as well as working extremely hard together with her husband in the family's greenhouse and going to school parents' meetings, she also adapted to the shift-work of her husband. 'When he was working on the afternoon shift, I could wash as late as midnight as there was nobody around to bother me.'

Finally, there has been a differentiation of households based on the combination (or absence) of work for each partner, which can be divided into three roughly equal categories: in the first category both the husband and the wife are active wage-earners, in the second only one of them is a wage-earner (in 22 per cent of households this was the husband, in 9 per cent the wife), while in the third type neither earn a wage (Figure 7.3). In the villages of Central Transdanubia in 26 per cent of households the husband is the bread-winner with the wife receiving only either a pension or some kind of state benefit. In contrast, in the disadvantaged villages of the Northern Great Plain neither spouse is an active wage-earner in over half of the households. The significant inequalities in average wages favouring men are made worse by the present system of pensions and unemployment benefits (Frey 1993) because benefit levels are calculated on the basis of formal wages, which are also gender biased. It therefore follows that in the lives of the majority of households the male-female relationship is more significantly influenced by the fact that there are fewer active wage-earners among women, more workers in feminised and devalued jobs, and more pensioners or persons on childcare leave than by the fact that women's official unemployment rate is somewhat more favourable than men's.

These spatial aspects of women's changing position in the Hungarian labour market thus reinforce Ferge's (1999) assumption that if the state cannot or does not want to intervene in market transactions, and at the same time does not regard the problems of gender distinctions as part of its political agenda, the majority of women become losers in transition.

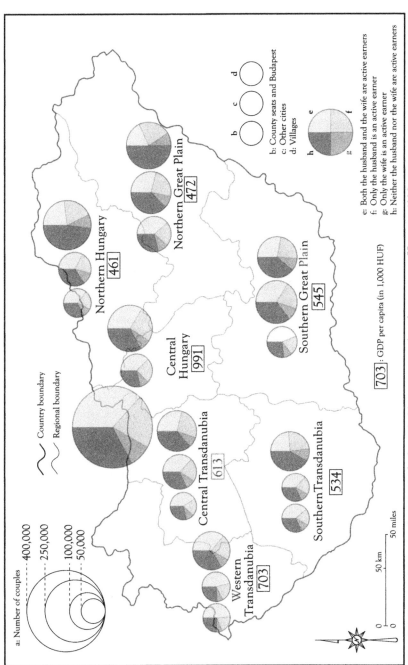

Figure 7.3 Household economic activities by household structure and settlement type, Hungary 1996.

Source: Microcensus 1996, Central Statistical Office 1997.

Approaching a single European market with spatial inequality?

The pivotal issue for the future development of the labour market in post-socialist Hungary is the possible effect that accession to the European Union will play. In forecasting the future map of regional inequalities in Hungary, the experience of current EU member states does not look promising (Dunford and Smith 2000). According to Illés (2000: 22), 'the only result of the policy of cohesion is that the level of development and the labour market position of less developed regions have not declined compared to those of the more developed ones.' His doubts concerning the reform of EU structural and cohesion policy coincide with the prognoses of others and suggest that a regionally more balanced expansion of the labour market against the backdrop of more efficient economic development is an illusory expectation.

The question also arises as to how Hungary's accession to the EU will affect the differing chances of men and women in the race for paid work. The work of Western feminist geographers suggests that women may not benefit significantly from the process of integration. Changes in the social and welfare regimes of EU member states have brought disadvantages to several groups of women and have resulted in increasing inequalities (García-Ramon and Monk 1996; Kofman and Sales 1996). Policies targeting equal opportunities and the integration of women in a Single European Market such as the Action Programmes 'maintain a partial focus on women-as-workers in the labour market and leave out of their scope important aspects of everyday life and local specialities' (Vaiou 1996: 63). The same view was reflected in the European Commission's opinion on Hungary's application for membership in Agenda 2000, where only a single sentence is devoted to the gender issue: 'In the equal treatment of men and women the Hungarian legal system already includes the main prescriptions of EU legal material' (Agenda 2000: 60).

As far as Hungarian labour market policy is concerned, specific gender issues have not been taken into consideration. The present state regulations have already given up the protection of the labour market position of those on childcare leave. At the same time the arsenal of the 'female specific' active labour market policy applied, though criticised on several points, in some West European countries has not been adopted, either. By contrast, national regional policy is trying assiduously to conform to EU practice with the aim of preparing Hungary for the future use of the Structural Funds. Accordingly, it enforces the principle of concentration and additionality and, with its own financial means, strives to support small regions similar to the ones favoured in the EU, especially those affected by long-term unemployment. The focus of job creation in such small regions is upon the promotion of innovative enterprises relying on their own resources. A regional policy like this, especially given its gender blind nature, is hardly likely to serve the interests of the women who are not in business, not able to commute under the pressure of housework, not properly skilled and heavily exploited by underpaid homework.

Politicians, officials and project managers, now busily preparing to join the European Union, have been surprisingly quick to acquire EU language, concepts and norms. Many of these norms are certainly conveyed by PHARE experts. The typical pair of a Western male expert, struggling with a limited local knowledge and hiding behind the shield of EU rhetoric, and of a Hungarian female interpreter translating his words carries a symbolic message. At the same time, the parliamentary and government commissions and departments shaping Hungary's integration policy are also controlled by men as the participation of women in political power is extremely low. Only 8.5 per cent of members of parliament are women. Among the member-states of the European Union, it is only Greece where the representation of women falls below this level, and among the 'most successful candidates for EU membership' only Slovenia was behind Hungary in 1999 (Kiss 1999). In six out of the 21 parliamentary committees, including the committee responsible for regional development, there is no woman at all. The committee for European integration consisted of three women and 23 men, and the gender division in the committee of employment is four women and 17 men (Kiss 1999).

Consequently, Vaiou's (1996: 71) argument concerning the position of women in the EU is relevant to the Hungarian situation as well: 'In this project of selective integration, marginalization and poverty continue to be the actual reality in many regions and among many social groups.' In Hungary, a significant proportion of unskilled and immobile women living in villages on the eastern and north-eastern edge of the country, far from more dynamic regions and western investors, fall into this category.

How will women's labour market chances, which are currently worse than men's and differ considerably from region to region, affect the relationship between men and women in the economically more advanced regions of the country and the more backward ones, that is in traditional villages and in urbanised settlements? We should not underestimate the importance of NGOs, where women, on a small regional or local scale, play an important role, organise partnership programmes to promote regional development, help to make use of local resources and enhance their region's competitiveness in the battle for EU funds. There is a chance that women will be able to benefit from their activity in such organisations, that the interests of women in villages can be better represented, that both urban and rural women can prepare for the changes accompanying EU membership, and that their experience on the local scale can be utilised in national policy, thus sooner or later enhancing female participation. However, an efficient protection of women's interest needs women themselves to perceive that their disadvantageous position in the realm of work is not a local phenomenon, it is rooted in general social and power relations.

Notes

1   The survey results discussed in this chapter are part of a project on household survival strategies sponsored partly by the Hungarian National Research Fund

(OTKA No. T020443). The project is being carried out in co-operation with Irén Szörényiné Kukorelli. See also Chapter 8 for a study of women's entrepreneurship in parts of the same regions.

2   The activity rate is the proportion of the population in a particular age group either employed or formally unemployed. The female–male activity rate ratio expresses the female activity rate as a percentage of the male activity rate.

3   The parent, foster parent or guardian is eligible for what is called 'childcare benefit' until their child's completion of either their third or tenth year if the child is permanently ill or severely disabled. The person receiving the benefit is not allowed to work until their child has become one and a half years old. After that they can work not more than four hours per day, or in the case where they work in their own home there is no time restriction. The benefit for a month is equal to the current minimal pension (Act LXXXIV of 1998).

4   The parent, foster parent or guardian raising three or more minors in their own household is eligible for what is called 'childcare support'. The support is to be granted from the end of the third year of the youngest child until the end of their eighth year. The person receiving the support is allowed to work not more than four hours per day, or in the case where they work in their own home there is no time restriction. The support for a month is equal to the current minimal pension (Act LXXXIV of 1998).

5   The Duncan Index of Dissimilarity is calculated as:

$$100 \times \sum_{i=1}^{N} \left| \frac{\frac{x_i}{x} - \frac{y_i}{y}}{2} \right|$$

where N is the number of occupations and x_i is the number of women in occupation i, x is the total number of women employed, y_i is the number of men in occupation i and y is the total number of men employed. The index ranges from 0 (complete integration) to 100 (complete segregation) and is based on the assumption that integration exists when the proportional representation of men and women in each occupation is the same as the proportion in the overall workforce (Kyriazis 1998: 73).

6   Especially in comparison to their high level of education, women are strongly underrepresented in managerial posts (Nagy 1999).

7   We have studied not only the rather rigid and bureaucratically interpreted category of 'registered unemployment' appearing in the Hungarian statistics and using ILO definitions, but also every unemployed person who contacted Békés County Labour Centre or any of its branch offices until 30 October, 1997. Each person is processed into the database only once. On second registration, some data are refreshed while others remain in the database. Thus, this database enables us to reproduce the individual's unemployment history. At the same time, it helps us assess the labour market position of those who previously met the requirements of a 'registered unemployed person', but who no longer do so owing to a stricter definition, in spite of the fact that their real position has not changed at all.

8   The denominator includes all active-age persons not drawing a pension or childcare benefit. They are the ones for whom becoming unemployed may be an imminent danger. We include people who do not carry on wage-earning activities in the nominator.

References

Agenda 2000. *Az Európai Bizottság véleménye Magyarország Európai Unióba történő jelentkezéséről* (The European Comission's Opinion on Hungary's application for EU membership), Budapest.

Barta, Gy. (1998) 'Industrial restructuring or deindustrialisation?', in G. Enyedi (ed.) *Social Change and Urban Restructuring in Central Europe*, Budapest: Akadémiai Kiadó, pp. 189–209.

Dunford, M. and Smith, A. (2000) 'Catching up or falling behind? Economic performance and regional trajectories in the "new Europe"', *Economic Geography* 76, 2: 169–195.

Ferge, Zs. (1999) 'Hogyan hatott a rendszerváltás a nők helyzetére?' (How did the change of regime affect the condition of women?), in K. Lévai, R. Kiss and T. Gyulvári (eds) *Vegyesváltó. pillanatképek nőkről, férfiakról*. Budapest: Egyenlő Esélyek Alapítvány, pp. 13–29.

Frey, M. (1993) 'Nők a munkaerőpiacon' (Women at the Labour Market). *Társadalmi Szemle* 3: 26–36.

García-Ramon, M.D. and Monk, J. (eds) (1996) *Women of the European Union: The Politics of Work and Daily Life*, London and New York: Routledge.

Gonäs, L. (1998) 'Has equality gone too far? On changing labour market regimes and new employment patterns in Sweden', *European Urban and Regional Studies* 5, 1: 41–53.

Illés, I. (2000) 'Az Europai Unio keleti kibővítése és a regionális politika reformja' (The Eastern enlargement of the European Union and the reform of regional politics), in Gy. Horváth and J. Rechnitzer (eds) *Magyarország területi szerkezete és folyamatai az ezredfordulón*, Pécs: MTA Regionális Kutatások Központja, pp. 21–39.

Kiss, R. (1999) 'Nők a közéletben' (Women in public life), in K. Lévai, R. Kiss and T. Gyulavári (eds) *Vegyesváltó. Pillanatképek nőkröl, férfiakról*, Budapest: Egyenlő Esélyek Alapítvány, pp. 77–94.

Kofman, E. and Sales, R. (1996) 'The geography of gender and welfare in Europe', in M.D. García-Ramon and J. Monk (eds) *Women of the European Union: The Politics of Work and Daily Life*, London and New York: Routledge, pp. 31–60.

Koncz, K. (1994) 'A nők foglalkoztatása és a pályák elnőiesedése' (Women's employment and feminisation of occupation), *Társadalmi Szemle* 7–8: 122–132.

Kyriazis, N. (1998) 'Women's employment and gender relations in Greece: Forces of modernisation and tradition', *European Urban and Regional Studies* 5, 1: 65–75.

Leibfried, S. and Ostner, I. (1991) 'The particularism of West German capitalism: The case of women's social security', in M. Adler and A. Sinfield (eds) *The Sociology of Social Security*, Edinburgh: Edinburgh University Press, pp. 164–186.

Lewis, J. (1992) 'Gender and the development of welfare regimes', *Journal of European Social Policy* 2 (3): 159–73.

Monk, J. (1988) *Encompassing Gender Progress and Challenges in Geographic Research*, Plenary Address, International Geographic Congress, Sydney, Australia, August, 1988.

Nagy, B. (1999) 'Munkahelyi előmenetel' (Employment career), in T. Pongráczné and I. Gy. Tóth (eds) *Szerepváltozások. Jelentés a nők és a férfiak helyzetéről*, Budapest: TÁRKI, Szociális és Családügyi Minisztérium Nőképviseleti Titkársága, pp. 30–39.

Perrons, D. (1998) 'Maps of meaning: Gender inequality in the regions of Western Europe', *European Urban and Regional Studies* 5, 1: 13–25.

Perrons, D. and Gonäs, L. (1998) 'Introduction: Perspectives on gender inequality in European employment', *European Urban and Regional Studies* 5, 1: 5–12.

Regulska, J. (1997) *The New 'Other' European Woman*. Invited keynote speech. Third European Feminist Research Conference Coimbra, Portugal, July, 1997.

Rodriguez-Pose, A. (1994) 'Socioeconomic restructuring and regional change: Rethinking growth in the European Community', *Economic Geography* 70, 4: 325–43.

Sackmann, R. and Haüssermann, H. (1994) 'Do regions matter? Regional differences in female labour-market participation in Germany', *Environment and Planning A* 26, 9: 1377–1418.

Schmude, J. (1996) 'Contrasting developments in female labour force participation in East and West Germany since 1945', in M.D. García-Ramon and J. Monk (eds) *Women of the European Union: The Politics of Work and Daily Life*, London and New York: Routledge,. pp. 156–85.

Szalai, J. (1998) 'Conflicts of gender and class: Paradoxes of women's occupational mobility in post-1989 Hungary'. Paper presented at the conference on 'Losers of the "Wende" – Winners of the EU', Vienna, November 1998.

Timár, J. and Velkey, G. (1998) 'Half way between the Soviet Block and the European Union: Spatial differences in women's access to jobs in Hungary'. Paper presented at the workshop on 'Women's Rights within the Context of the European Integration' at the International Institute for Sociology of Law, Oñati, Spain, 28–30 May 1998.

Vaiou, D. (1996) 'Women's work and everyday life in Southern Europe in the context of European integration', in M.D. García-Ramon and J. Monk (eds) *Women of the European Union: The Politics of Work and Daily Life*, London and New York, Routledge, pp. 61–73.

Walby, S. (1990) *Theorising Patriarchy.* Oxford: Blackwell.

Walby, S. (1994) 'Methodological and theoretical issues in the comparative analysis of gender relations in Western Europe', *Environment and Planning A* 26, 9: 1339–54.

8 Gender and entrepreneurship in post-communist Hungary

Janet Henshall Momsen

It is often considered that the transition to capitalism in East-Central Europe (ECE) has been accompanied by an employment crisis (Smith 2000). It has been estimated that there were 26 million fewer jobs in the 27 countries of East-Central Europe, and the former Soviet Union in 1997 relative to 1989 (UNICEF 1999). Of these about 14 million were jobs lost by women. In Hungary, a country of ten million people, one-third of women's jobs have gone since 1989 (UNICEF 1999). Despite this, Hungary is one of the very few countries in the region where women's officially recorded unemployment rate has consistently been less than that of men. A recent World Bank report suggests that two factors may explain this unusual feature of the Hungarian labour market: first the higher proportion of women in the government sector, which provides greater job security; and second, the higher proportion of women with college and university education relative to men in the labour market (World Bank 1999: 232). Self-employment was seen as a solution to unemployment but the particular nature of post-communist entrepreneurship and its gender aspects have rarely been considered.

Many writers considered the collapse of communism in Eastern Europe and the Soviet Union in 1989–90 to be a cataclysmic break, 'the end of History' according to Fukuyama (1992). The development of an entrepreneurial spirit is seen as a new beginning but I will argue that, at least in the case of Hungary, it also has deep roots in the past. However, the legacies approach (Szelenyi 1988, 2001, Kuczi 1998) based on pre-socialist era family history and more recent experience in the second economy, is shown to have declining but regionally variable utility as an explanation for current entrepreneurial activity.

Hungary has a very high rate of entrepreneurial activity, accounting, in 1995, for just over one-fifth of employment in non-agricultural sectors, more than twice the average for OECD countries (11 per cent) and almost the average level for Latin America (26 per cent) (Gábor 1997: 164). Gábor (1997: 159) sees this rapid growth of entrepreneurial activity since 1989 as 'too many, too small' and further argues that the development of successful small businesses has been hampered by the historical heritage of the second economy as well as by the context of the crisis of the transition. In this chapter I shall examine these issues using data from an empirical study of entrepreneurs in two rural areas of Hungary.[1]

Our working definition of entrepreneurial activity has been to include all those officially recognised and licensed as entrepreneurs. This includes sole proprietors of small businesses as well as working owners of 'corporations without legal entity' (World Bank 1999: 106), consultants and home workers. These are all included in international statistics as self-employed (Gábor 1997: 159). Fieldwork also revealed that some successful small business people are working without official licences, while some register as official entrepreneurs on behalf of other family members. In both of these cases the underlying reason is to avoid taxes. In Hungary corporate taxes are much lower than personal taxes and a 1999 World Bank Report (1999: 106) noted that 'almost 70 per cent of the registered enterprises are unincorporated partnerships commonly used to reduce taxes'. The laws relating to taxes and official self-employed status are constantly changing and even in rural areas people are very aware of the implications of these changes. For example, during the field surveys in 1998, we were told that it was no longer necessary for someone providing a few rooms for tourists to buy an entrepreneur's licence. This instability in the context of the transition, while individual economic activity and state regulations are in a continual stage of adjustment, undermines the reliability of information on self-employment.

According to official national statistics, there was a very rapid growth in the number of small entrepreneurs in the 1980s and early 1990s from 113,000 in 1980 to 211,536 in 1988, 394,000 in 1990 and 521,000 in 1991 (Róna-Tas 1994: 50 for 1980 and 1988; Lengyel and Tóth 1994: 13 for 1990 and 1991). Lengyel and Tóth (1994) show that this growth in actual entrepreneurs was coupled with a substantial rise in the proportion of working age people who could envisage setting up business on their own account from 25 per cent in 1988 to 40 per cent in 1990. There was a slight change of definition in the reported national statistics in 1992, accordingly the number of enterprises without legal entity grew from 676,804 in 1992 to a peak of 936,312 in 1995 with the subset of sole proprietors falling from 89.6 per cent in 1992 to 84.5 per cent of this total in 1995. By 1997 the total figure had fallen to 839,602 of which sole proprietors made up 78.6 per cent (World Bank 1999: 106).

Such a change of individual actions and aspirations reflected changes in official attitudes to small business. The laws that came into effect during this period enlarged the scope for entrepreneurship. Law No. 6 of 1988 on Business Societies, Associations, Companies and Ventures provided for economic associations. Law No. 13 of 1989 on Transformation of Economic Organization and Business Associations provided for the transformation of state enterprises. Law No. 5 of 1990 simplified the conditions for launching individual ventures, served as the legal protection of private property and promoted unbiased competition. The concepts of enterprise and entrepreneur were no longer vilified but became widely known and positively reported on by the mass media. At the same time the existing economy was in crisis and the formerly unknown condition of unemployment was becoming a reality (Lengyel and Tóth 1994). Thus both the improved conditions for self-employment and the expanding need for alternative forms of income were reinforcing each other.

Entrepreneurship prior to the transition

Entrepreneurs did exist during the communist period in Hungary but to a much smaller extent because of mixed messages from the state. The failure of the state to provide housing led to an expansion of privately built housing, especially in villages. Between 1971 and 1975 44.2 per cent of all homes were built by the private sector (Róna Tas 1997: 111). The Politburo in both 1968 and 1976 had allowed small private artisans to survive in order to meet some of the demand for repairs to faulty consumer durables, and to undertake plumbing and electrical services (Róna-Tas 1997: 106) but in the early 1970s the level of official criticisms and restrictions rose again. However, '[B]y 1976, the increasing discontent in the countryside over the lack of services and the ghost of the burgeoning shadow economy had persuaded the leadership to adopt a more favourable position toward private services in small towns and villages' (Róna-Tas 1997: 111).

Róna-Tas argues that the private sector of the late 1970s, despite the régime's limited support, was an economy of needs, a consolation prize for those who were unable to maintain a sufficient income from the state sector. He further points out that, based on data from the 1981 social stratification survey, 70 per cent of the full-time self-employed were men as women were too busy with their double burden of a full-time job in the state sector combined with their household chores. It should be noted that Hungarian women's workload had fallen from an average of nearly 75 hours a week in 1965 to 63 hours a week in 1977 which was still about ten hours a week more than the average for British women in 1961 (UNICEF 1999: 25). Self-employed women were most numerous in enterprises linked to household farming (41 per cent) or to renting of property (55 per cent). Men were also more likely to have the requisite skills for the most common types of work available, particularly repair of consumer durables such as televisions and cars, and construction work.

During the 1960s and 1970s many people moved back and forth between the state and self-employment. In a 1982 survey of 389 self-employed artisans and tradesmen in Eastern Hungary reported in Róna-Tas (1997) only 17 per cent indicated having chosen self-employment for material gain. A further 14 per cent said they were doing it because of conflicts at their former place of employment and half because they thought that it was a way of realising their dreams. It was generally believed that skill was the most important determinant of success. Given the acute consumer shortages there was little competition so marketing strategies were unnecessary. In 1982 laws came into operation which allowed an increase in the number of people who could work in private partnerships, permitted the private sector to do business with the state sector and liberalised the operating conditions for small family-owned businesses. This led to an expansion of part-time work, especially in internal contracting and outside consulting for state firms. These changes did not lead to an increase in hours worked but rather, as Róna-Tas (1997) points out, a redistribution of effort from the state to the private sector. Unlike the earlier reforms, these brought into the private sector those who had benefited most from the socialist economy. Consequently, when in 1985 at the Party Congress, the leadership tried to tighten its hold on the economy and restrict the private sector, the delegates baulked. The boundaries between public and private sectors became blurred and the 'private sector of needs' was transformed into a 'private sector of opportunities' weakening the power of the Party-state (Róna-Tas 1997: 163).

The entrepreneurial continuum?

Most published studies of Hungarian entrepreneurship deal with the situation in the very early years of the transition (see for example Agócs and Agócs 1993, Róna-Tas 1994 and 1997, Róna-Tas and Lengyel 1997, Lengyel and Tóth 1994, Gábor 1997). Many of these authors see close links between post-transition entrepreneurship and the private sector under socialism. Under socialism most entrepreneurs participated in the private sector part time while continuing to work in their secure state jobs. They were often able to take advantage of the equipment, facilities and even material from their state employers and did not pay tax on their income. These characteristics of pre-transition entrepreneurship provide the background for many of the complaints voiced by the self-employed at the end of the millennium, particularly resentment at having to pay taxes and to cope with competition.

Women entrepreneurs

The economic restructuring following the end of the Cold War was embedded in the simultaneous process of social and political transformation (Quack and Maier 1994) and was not gender neutral (Einhorn 1993: 127). Watson (1993: 471) argues that 'the transformation of the relationship between public and private spheres lies at the heart of the process of change in Eastern Europe, and that the exclusion of women and the degrading of feminine identity currently in train are not contingent to, but rather a fundamentally constitutive feature of, the democratization of Eastern Europe'. The transition from a command to a market economy and from a centrally planned regime to democracy was accompanied by a decline in state-provided services, an increase in pornography and prostitution, pressure from politicians and church to limit access to abortion (Gal 1994), increased public support for traditional male and female stereotypes, and a decline in the number of women in political positions (UNICEF 1999, Makara 1992, Goven 1993, Matynia 1995).

The part-time work undertaken by young mothers in much of Western Europe is generally not available in transitional economies. Thus self-employment may offer the flexibility needed by many women in order to combine their productive and reproductive work. A 1988 study found that 77 per cent of Hungarian working women wished to continue with their jobs even if given the opportunity to stay at home although ideally they would prefer part-time work (USAID 1991: 57). Denich (1990: 504) also found that it was 'necessary to understand the motivation of young employed women who look homeward in planning their futures, rather than concentrating primarily on jobs and careers'. In our western Hungary study

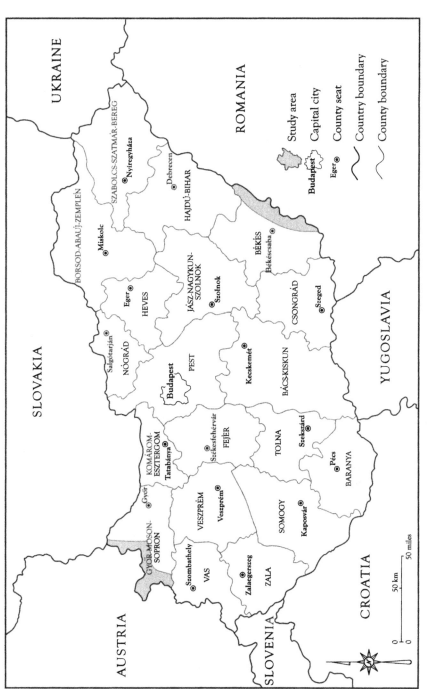

Figure 8.1 Border regions in Hungary.

area (Figure 8.1) we found several women who had chosen to give up their jobs in the city in order to stay at home with their children and to work part-time out of their houses as self-employed hairdressers or dressmakers, or on a contract basis for their former urban employer.

Rural areas have certain advantages for entrepreneurial activities. The push factors of unemployment and lack of alternative opportunities are often more marked than in urban areas and the positive element of community and family networks is stronger. Women, as in most cultures, are most likely to be involved in maintaining these networks and in preserving traditions. The privatisation of the collectives has to some extent released capital, equipment and agricultural resources in rural areas (Kovács 1996). Many women were employed by the collectives in small manufacturing branch plants, or in services such as childcare or retail stores or book-keeping. These skills can now be transferred to self-employment in the private sector. The availability of shops is more limited in rural than in urban areas and as commuting to towns is reduced by the rising cost of transport, there is an increasing need for local services such as convenience and clothing stores, hairdressers and restaurants. These services are particularly important to women who are least likely to have access to private means of transport and it is logical that women entrepreneurs should respond to these needs. They are also involved in providing secretarial and financial services in small family-owned businesses such as plumbing or pig-rearing.

Szabo (1992) reported that 32 per cent of the owners, managers and members of the new small enterprises created immediately after the fall of communism were women. Their participation rates varied by type of enterprise, being highest (65 per cent) in trading enterprises and in new small co-operative activities (43 per cent). The privatised businesses made use of women's knowledge gained from the skills learned from management of the household economy, their involvement in private or semi-private spheres of production and their high levels of education and training especially in economics and finance (Szabo 1992). Women's role in such enterprises has been encouraged partly because the hotel and catering sector, in which a lot of women are involved, was one of the first to be privatised in 1990 (Groen and Visser 1993). Lengyel and Tóth, in a representative survey of the adult population of Hungary covering 3,000 individuals in 1988 and 1,000 in 1990, found that women's interest in entrepreneurship increased from 16 per cent of those surveyed in 1988 to 37 per cent in 1990 while the parallel increase in male interest rose from 37 per cent in 1988 to 54 per cent in 1990 (Lengyel and Tóth 1994). In general, the 1999 UNICEF report found that women appear to be less inclined or less able to move into self-employment or entrepreneurship than men throughout the ECE and CIS countries, stating that further research into women's role in entrepreneurship is needed (UNICEF 1999: 40).

Regional patterns of post-communist rural entrepreneurship

As Smith and Ferenčíková (1998) point out, it is only recently that attention has turned to the sub-national regional development implications of transition in East and Central Europe. Few such studies in Hungary (Enyedi 1990, 1994, Cséfalvay 1994, Hamilton 1999, Horváth 1999, Momsen 2000) consider the networks and social practices vital to entrepreneurship which are clearly territorially embedded (Smith and Swain 1998). In order to illuminate regional differences we selected one study area on the north-west border with Austria in the county of Györ-Moson-Sopron and one in the south-east in Békés County on the Romanian border (see also Ch. 7 and Figure 8.1). The two areas were chosen to maximise the range of conditions under which rural entrepreneurs operate: the north-western border with Austria is an area of intensive mixed farming and a dense network of nucleated settlements which benefits from flows of capital, ideas and tourists from Western Europe and daily movement of Hungarian workers across the border to better paying jobs in Austria; while in the more thinly populated south-east, where there is extensive grain and livestock production, cross-border contacts with Romania are predominantly in terms of refugees, illegal immigrants and black-market traders seeking opportunities in Hungary. Despite these differences, in both areas rural entrepreneurs are responding to demand for services from local residents and from the externally generated growth of travellers and tourists.

This comparison allows us to take into consideration the effect of the flow of capitalist influences from west to east. The county of Györ-Moson-Sopron was traditionally an area of small peasant farmers while Békés County in the east was traditionally an area of large grain farms worked by an agricultural proletariat. In the Györ area it was predicted that cross-border trade and flows of capital and tourists would encourage the growth of entrepreneurship among a population historically attuned to self-employment, while in Békés County the presence of the border with Romania was expected to have a neutral effect on the growth of small firms. The western study area is described by Enyedi (1994: 242–244) as an area with promising prospects while he sees the eastern area as a crisis region. The north-east has fewer foreign residents than the south-east but both regions have net outmigration (Geographical Research Institute 1994, 1995). There is considerable foreign investment in the west but very little in the east (Berényi 1992) and the rural economy of Györ-Moson-Sopron is more diversified than that of Békés County. Thus the conditions for the development of entrepreneurship are very different in the two regions.

In 1987, 10.5 per cent of the total personal income of all Hungarian households and 18.6 per cent of the personal income of village households came from the agricultural second economy. By 1990, 41 per cent of the total agricultural production was produced by the few private farms and nearly 1.5 million household plots (Andorka 1993). While Szelényi (1988) hoped that a new bourgeoisie would evolve from this rural second economy, after the transformation of the regime in 1989 agricultural activity rapidly declined accounting for only 5 per cent of GDP in 1999 as compared to 7.7 per cent in 1995 (Barclays 2000).

Unemployment is higher in rural areas than in urban areas but even in rural areas the unemployment rate for women is lower than for men. In 1994 male unemployment in villages was 24.6 per cent versus 15.3 per cent in towns while for women the rates in villages and towns were virtually the same, 11.3 per cent compared to 11.4 per cent (Morell 1999). However, for women economic activity rates were much lower in villages (43.9 per cent) than in towns (57.2 per cent) while for men the difference was only seven per cent (58.9 per cent versus 65.6 per cent) (Morell 1999). Overall it appears that rural areas have shouldered the greater part of the burden of economic restructuring since 1990 because of the reduction of government agricultural subsidies, the break-up of co-operative farms and the closure of the industrial enterprises associated with them, and the loss of subsidised transport for commuters to nearby towns. Women, in particular, have become spatially entrapped in the countryside and many villages have a high proportion of elderly women.

The percentage of the national population living in rural areas declined from 41.9 per cent in 1985 to 35.9 per cent in 1995 but has since shown a slow but steady increase to 36.3 per cent in 1998 (World Bank 1999). This counterurbanisation trend reflects the improvement of village infrastructure undertaken by local governments in the last decade and a realisation that property prices and the cost of living are lower in the countryside where it is possible to grow some of one's own food and to heat with cheap wood rather than expensive electricity as in the city. Houses in villages are spacious enough to permit the operation of a small business and over two-thirds of our survey respondents in both east (69.2 per cent) and west (68.4 per cent) Hungary, combined their home with their business premises. Working from home also made it permissible to deduct the expenses of heating and lighting the house as a business expense.

It is only by detailed ethnographic field research that it is possible to examine the extent to which officially registered entrepreneurs have employees, are producing something of true economic value and are engaged in legitimate trading. In other words, how much of the initiative apparently being displayed in the transition economy is merely a tactical response to the crisis of employment and inadequate welfare systems rather than a true flowering of a newly rediscovered culture of enterprise.

We interviewed 30 per cent of the entrepreneurs officially listed in border villages in 1998 for a total of 351 individuals made up of 250 from the west and 101 from the east. The random sample was stratified by gender and by economic sector according to the relative importance of the sectors as shown in Table 8.1. As can be seen, the service sector dominated with four-fifths of the women and about half the male entrepreneurs in both parts of the country in that sector. The primary and secondary sectors were more important for male than female entrepreneurs with manufacturing involving almost three times the number in agriculture in the west while agriculture occupied twice as many as manufacturing in the east. In both areas more than two-thirds of those surveyed did not have employees. In the west 12.4 per cent had one employee and 9.6 per cent had two employees, with the largest firm employing 30 people. In the east 17.8 per cent of those surveyed employed one person with the remaining 15 per cent employing between two and 14 workers.

Table 8.1 Types of entrepreneurial activity in rural west and east Hungary, by gender (per cent of total)

Activity type	West Hungary		East Hungary	
	Women %	Men %	Women %	Men %
Primary Agriculture/ Forestry/ Hunting	5.1	14.9	11.4	28.4
Secondary Manufacturing/ Craft work	9.4	36.0	5.3	13.7
Tertiary Services	85.5	49.1	83.3	57.9
Of which:				
Sales: goods, food and drink	50.8	23.3	65.9	37.9
Personal	18.8	0.0	9.1	0.8
Tourism	2.4	2.8	–	–
Security	–	2.6	–	1.0
Transport	0.0	10.9	1.5	5.4
Professional	13.5	9.5	6.8	12.8

Source: Field data, 1998.

Some have argued that an early start in the private sector matters in terms of current size or success (Webster 1992, Róna-Tas and Lengyel 1997). In our analysis of 1998 data on 456 entrepreneurs drawn from the records of 27 villages in Eastern and Western Hungary[2] we found that only 2.6 per cent of entrepreneurs in eastern Hungary compared to 10.4 per cent in the west had started such work before 1990 and survived to 1998. In western Hungary the peak year for starting as an entrepreneur was 1997 with 20.3 per cent, followed by 1992 with 18 per cent for those still operating in 1998. In eastern Hungary 30 per cent of 1998 entrepreneurs started in either 1993 or 1994 while 19 per cent started in 1997. Dates of first official registration as an entrepreneur were not available for all 1998 entrepreneurs but the numbers for which we had this data in both areas were roughly the same. Thus both before and after the transition villages in eastern Hungary were slower to develop entrepreneurship than those in the west. The east may also have a lower survival rate though our data lack precise evidence for this. Of the seven entrepreneurs surviving from the 1970s all were men, with two working as hairdressers and most of the others having house-building skills.

Those contemporary entrepreneurs who founded their businesses in the 1980s are very different. In the western study area there is an equal number of men and women with most running shops or offering hairdressing, dressmaking or transport skills. In the eastern villages three of the current businesses were started by women in the 1980s. One man set up as a tailor in 1980 and it is only after the changes of 1982 that women appear in the official record. This gender differentiation supports Róna-Tas's (1997) analysis. One man started making and selling whitewash in 1987 after having had to give up carpentry because of injury. His father had been a private carpenter in the 1970s and the son had also continued in this business. His wife had started a business in 1986, on her husband's urging, mixing animal feed because the state cafeteria where she worked as a cook closed. These two are now amongst the most successful people in their village, working long hours and ploughing all their profits back into their businesses in order to expand. Thus they are more like capitalist entrepreneurs than socialist despite being technically forced into this role before the transition. The overwhelming dominance of post-transition start-ups in these rural areas suggests that earlier activities in the private sector are of importance in only a few cases but that these individuals tend to be the most successful, especially in the east.

It is often said that many people are forced into self-employment by the loss of a job. In Békés County border villages 41.6 per cent of entrepreneurs, equally divided between men and women, said that they were forced entrepreneurs. In Győr in the west, only 21.6 per cent of men and 30.4 per cent of women said that they were forced entrepreneurs. In several cases our respondents told us that they had set up a business because their spouse became unemployed or was forced to take early retirement because of disability. In other cases young people were forced to become self-employed when they finished their training as no jobs were available for them in the villages. In both areas village teachers said that they had to take on part-time self-employment in order to earn enough to live, while several retired people were supplementing their inadequate pensions by farming part-time, taking advantage of land returned to them following the break-up of the co-operative farms.

Surprisingly, despite this high level of negative reasons for choosing to become entrepreneurs, 91 per cent of men and 86 per cent of women in both study areas said that they preferred to be self-employed rather than work for someone else. This overwhelming consistency of support for entrepreneurial independence in two regions where the local economy offers very different success rates and opportunities is remarkable. It may well indicate a new attitude to self-employment among the wider population. In further support of this view are the responses of the interviewees to a question about expanding their businesses. Once again regional differences were minimal with 29.7 per cent of village entrepreneurs in the east and 31.6 per cent in the west planning to expand. Such expansion usually involved opening another outlet in the same or a nearby village, increasing the range of goods or services offered, buying more modern machinery to upgrade production or taking on more employees. Reasons for declining to expand were advancing age or health problems, lack of capital, and increased competition in the village. Problems specific to women entrepreneurs were pregnancy or increased household responsibilities for children or the elderly. In the west, where several people ran small businesses on a part-time basis while continuing to work in their main job, lack of time was often mentioned. In rural eastern Hungary no-one complained of lack of time.

In western Hungary, of the 833 registered entrepreneurs in 17 villages surveyed, 36 per cent were women while in the ten border villages in eastern Hungary 39 per cent of the 336 entrepreneurs were women. In both cases women were concentrated in the service sector and the types of business owned by women were less varied than those of men. Most women ran small shops or restaurants while men were more likely to utilise craft skills and work as carpenters or electricians as Table 8.1 shows. Women were also active in providing personal services but these were more common in the west where Austrian tourists and second-home owners provided high-paying customers. In one village in the west there were even two masseuses while in the east few villages had more than a hairdresser and possibly a cosmetician. In the west two women hairdressers were planning to expand their businesses by investing in solariums. Men often drove trucks or buses but one woman in the west had a horse-drawn carriage used by tourists. Tourism also created a demand for souvenirs and small hotels and for security services. In Békés one village had joined the national rural tourism association but had failed to attract tourists although German hunting parties did occasionally visit. In Győr-Moson-Sopron the mayors of the border villages had a conference in June 1998 to discuss ways of joint advertising in the western European press to attract visitors, emphasising especially their local horsemanship.

In both areas there was a surprising range of professional jobs in the villages, from customs officials, and insurance agents to business advisors, doctors, dentists and veterinarians. Professions were also strongly gendered with dentistry, and accountancy as predominantly female occupations. In western Hungary the cheap and excellent dental care attracts people from all over Europe and some of the biggest new houses in the villages are owned by women dentists. In order to serve these foreign clients, people living in western Hungarian border villagers recognised the need to speak other languages, especially German. Among the entrepreneurs surveyed in western Hungary 78 per cent of women and 64 per cent of men spoke at least one language in addition to Hungarian. In the east the gender balance was reversed with 68 per cent of male entrepreneurs speaking another language (either Romanian or German) while only 36 per cent of female entrepreneurs spoke a second language. Most of these women were of Romanian origin and spoke Romanian as their first language.

Austria supplies not only wealthy customers but also opportunities for well paid work which provides start-up capital for businesses, as well as allowing some women to choose to stay home as full-time mothers and housewives or to work only part time. In the west 19 per cent of men and 12 per cent of women entrepreneurs admitted to having worked outside Hungary. It is likely that others have worked and continue to work for short periods illegally, in Austria. In the east such opportunities are less easy to find and only 4 per cent of both men and women entrepreneurs had worked in another country. In a pattern parallel to that in western Hungarian border villages, illegal Romanian workers provide low-cost labour on many eastern Hungarian farms. In both areas the bazaar economy of trade across the border in cheap goods, which had often involved women, is declining.

Conclusion

Small businesses in rural areas of Hungary may be seen as being one part of a complex household jigsaw used to construct a livelihood in a rapidly changing economic environment (see also Chs 11 and 13). We also noted an additional benefit from feelings of well-being or psychic income (Withers 1985) which had not been possible under communism when citizenship was linked to paid employment. The choice to resign from a disliked job, to give up commuting, to move from the city to the countryside, to work part-time or even to stay at home with children beyond the period permitted by the state childcare allowance, were especially important for women. These were often mentioned during our fieldwork in western Hungary. We even met one woman who had moved to rural western Hungary to escape the disapproval of her husband's family who thought he had married beneath him. She had trained as a pilot but had started a business designing flower arrangements which she sold through a German partner. Her business was not only financially successful but also gave her personal satisfaction through her enjoyment of and pride in her artistic creativity. In eastern Hungary self-employment was seen more as part of a very restricted range of livelihood strategies rather than an opportunity which allowed a lifestyle choice.

The family was central to all these small businesses. Most entrepreneurs were cautious about seeking credit from a bank because of high interest rates and feelings of financial insecurity and risk avoidance. They preferred to rely on loans or assistance from family members, or to build up personal capital by working abroad for short periods. Labour also was usually supplied by family members as it was felt that only family could be trusted. This focus on the family may partly be a relic of the situation under communism where the family was seen as a refuge from the state, especially in relation to the second economy. In several cases we found that the official registered entrepreneur was not the person actually running the business. The choice of who took out the licence was a family decision taken to minimise taxes and perhaps to allow the risk of failure to be carried by the family member least likely to be damaged by it (Szelényi 2001). In one case an eighteen-year old woman was the official entrepreneur employing her parents to run the village shop. She had been chosen for this role as taxes were lower for entrepreneurs who had never been employed. Another quite common situation was for agricultural entrepreneurs to use an imaginary subdivision of the family farm. Each family member registered as an entrepreneur and the production value was divided up and portions assigned to each official entrepreneur so that taxes were minimised, although the land was still farmed as a single unit. Such family negotiation made it very difficult to identify clear differences between male and female entrepreneurs and underlined the importance of obtaining village-level survey data.

Self-employment has become a part of rural family livelihood strategies in Hungary and the links with the second economy under socialism are becoming ever less relevant, although the capital, managerial experience and networks built up before the transition were useful in the early stages (Maurel 2000). Such entrepreneurial legacies remain more important in the more difficult economic environment of eastern Hungary than in the west. The newly acquired freedom to develop a business has enabled previously undervalued entrepreneurial skills to be utilised, and encouraged flexible specialisation and contingent labour practices, while bringing greater prosperity and a wider range of services to villages in Hungary.

Notes

1   The research project on which this paper is based, entitled 'Differences in women's entrepreneurship in rural Hungary', was funded by the National Science Foundation (NSF SBR-9710073). It was carried out in collaboration with Dr Irén Kukorelli Szorenyi and Dr Judit Timár of the Centre for Regional Studies of the Hungarian Academy of Sciences. See also Chapter 7 for a discussion of changes in parts of the same regions.
2   Villages surveyed were located close to the international border with Austria in the west and the border with Romania in the east. We surveyed ten villages in the east and 20 in the west but were able to obtain official time series data on entrepreneurs for only 17 of the western villages.

References

Agócs, P. and Agócs, Sándor A. (1993) 'Entrepreneurship in post-communist Hungary', *The Journal of Social, Political and Economic Studies*, 18 (2): 159–179.
Andorka, R. (1993). 'Rural-urban differences in income level and in living conditions in Hungary', *Landscape and Urban Planning*, 27: 217–222.
Barclays (2000) *Country Report: Hungary*, Poole: Barclays Group Economics.
Berényi, I. (1992) 'The socio-economic transformation and the consequences of the liberalisation of borders in Hungary', in Z. Kovács (ed.) *New Perspectives in Hungarian Geography. Human Geographical Studies*, Geographical Research Institute, Hungarian Academy of Sciences, Budapest, pp. 45–58.
Cséfalvay, Z. (1994) 'The regional differentiation of the Hungarian economy in transition', *GeoJournal*, 32 (4): 351–361.
Denich, B. (1990) 'Paradoxes of gender and policy in Eastern Europe: A discussant's comments', *East European Quarterly*, 23 (4): 499–506.
Einhorn, B. (1993) *Cinderella Goes to Market: Citizenship, Gender and Women's Movements in East Central Europe*, New York and London: Verso.
Enyedi, G. (1990) 'New basis for regional and urban policies in East-Central Europe', *Centre for Regional Studies Discussion Paper* No. 9, Hungarian Academy of Sciences.
Enyedi, G. (1994) 'Regional and urban development in Hungary until 2005' in Z Hajdú and

G. Horváth (eds) *European Challenges and Hungarian Responses in Regional Policy*, Pécs: Centre for Regional Studies of the Hungarian Academy of Sciences, pp. 239–253.

Fukuyama, F. (1992) *The End of History and the Last Man*, London: Penguin.

Gábor, I. (1997) 'Too many, too small: Small entrepreneurship in Hungary – ailing or prospering?', in G. Grabher and D. Stark (eds) *Restructuring Networks in Post-Socialism: Legacies, Linkages and Localities*, Oxford: Oxford University Press, pp. 158–175.

Gal, S. (1994) 'Gender in the post-socialist transition: The abortion debate in Hungary', *East European Politics and Societies*, 8 (2): 256–286.

Geographical Research Institute, Hungarian Academy of Sciences (1994) *National Atlas of Hungary*, Supplementary Map Lift-Out Series Part Two: Population and demographic trends, 1980–89. Budapest: Hungarian Academy of Sciences.

Geographical Research Institute, Hungarian Academy of Sciences (1995) *National Atlas of Hungary*, Supplementary Map Lift-Out Series Part Three: International migration, 1980–1992. Budapest: Hungarian Academy of Sciences.

Goven, J. (1993) 'Gender politics in Hungary: Autonomy and antifeminism', in N. Funk and M. Mueller (eds) *Gender Politics and Post-Communism: Reflections from Eastern Europe and the Former Soviet Union*, New York: Routledge.

Groen, R. and Visser, A. (1993) *Development Chances for Békés County (A Terület-Fejlesztés Esélyei Békés Megyében)*, Utrecht and Békéscsaba: Faculty of Geographical Sciences of the Utrecht University and Centre for Regional Studies of the Hungarian Academy of Sciences, Alföld Institute, Békéscsaba.

Hamilton, F.E.I. (1999) 'Transformation and space in Central and Eastern Europe', *The Geographical Journal*, 165 (2): 135–144.

Horváth, G. (1999) 'Changing Hungarian regional policy and accession to the European Union', *European Urban and Regional Studies*, 6 (2): 166–177.

Kovács, K. (1996) 'The transition in Hungarian agriculture 1990–1993. General tendencies, background factors and the case of the golden age', in R. Abrahams (ed.) *After Socialism: Land Reform and Social Change in Eastern Europe*, Providence, RI and Oxford: Berghahn Books, pp. 51–84.

Kuczi, T. (1998) 'The post-communist transformation and the social resources of entrepreneurs', *International Journal of Sociology*, 27 (4): 50–83.

Lengyel, G. and Tóth, I. (1994) 'The spread of entrepreneurial inclinations in Hungary', *Studies in Public Policy* No. 224, Centre for the Study of Public Policy, University of Strathclyde.

Makara, K. (1992) 'A woman's place', *New Hungarian Quarterly*, 33 (126): 100–102.

Matynia, E. (1995) 'Finding a voice: Women in postcommunist Central Europe, in A. Basu (ed.) *The Challenge of Global Feminisms: Women's Movements in Global Perspective*, Boulder, CO: Westview.

Maurel, M-C. (2000) 'Patterns of post-socialist transformation in the rural areas of Central Europe', in G. Horváth (ed.) *Regions and Cities in the Global World: Essays in Honour of György Enyedi*, Pécs: Centre for Regional Studies, Hungarian Academy of Sciences, pp. 141–158.

Momsen, J.H. (2000) 'Spatial transformations and economic restructuring in post-socialist Hungary', in G. Horváth (ed.) *Regions and Cities in the Global World: Essays in Honour of György Enyedi*, Pécs: Centre for Regional Studies, Hungarian Academy of Sciences, pp. 202–219.

Morrell, I.A. (1999) 'Post-socialist rural transformation and gender construction processes', paper presented at the Conference on Gender and Rural Transformations in Europe, Wageningen Agricultural University, Wageningen, the Netherlands.

Quack, S. and Maier, F. (1994) 'From state socialism to market economy: Women's employment in East Germany', *Environment and Planning A*, 26 (8): 1257–1276.

Róna-Tas, Á. (1994) 'The first shall be last? Entrepreneurship and communist cadres in the transition from socialism', *American Journal of Sociology*, 100 (1): 40–69.

Róna-Tas, Á. (1997) *The Great Surprise of the Small Transformation: The Demise of Communism and the Rise of the Private Sector in Hungary*, Ann Arbor: University of Michigan Press.

Róna-Tas, Á. and Lengyel, G. (1997) 'Entrepreneurs and entrepreneurial inclinations in post-communist East-Central Europe', *International Journal of Sociology*, 27 (3): 3–14.

Smith, A. (2000) 'Employment restructuring and household survival in postcommunist transition: Rethinking economic practices in Eastern Europe', *Environment and Planning A*, 32: 1759–1780.

Smith, A. and Ferenčíková, S. (1998) 'Inward investment, regional transformations and uneven development in Eastern and Central Europe: Enterprise case studies from Slovakia', *European Urban and Regional Studies*, 5 (2): 155–173.

Smith, A. and Swain, A. (1998) 'Regulating and institutionalising capitalisms: The microfoundations of transformation in Eastern and Central Europe', in J. Pickles and A. Smith (eds) *Theorising Transition: The Political Economy of Post-Communist Transformations*, London: Routledge, pp. 25–53.

Szabo, K. (1992) 'Small is also beautiful in the East: The Boom of small ventures in Hungary', in B. Katz and L. Rittenberg (eds) *The Economic Transformation of Eastern Europe: Views from Within*, Westport, CT: Praeger, pp. 127–151.

Szelényi, I. (1988) *Socialist Entrepreneurs: Embourgeoisement in Rural Hungary*. Madison: University of Wisconsin Press.

Szelényi, I. (2001) Personal communication. University of California Davis, March.

UNICEF (1999) *Women in Transition*, UNICEF: Florence.

United States Agency for International Development (USAID) (1991) *Hungary: Gender Issues in the Transition to a Market Economy*, Washington DC: US AID, Office of Women in Development, Bureau for Research & Development with the Bureau for Private Enterprise.

Watson, P. (1993) 'Eastern Europe's silent revolution: Gender', *Sociology*, 27 (3): 471–487.

Webster, L. (1992) 'Private sector manufacturing in Hungary: A survey of firms', *Industry Series Papers*, No. 67. Washington DC: World Bank.

Withers, G. (1985) 'Artists subsidy of the arts', *Australian Economic Papers*, December: 290–295.

World Bank (1999) *Hungary: On the Road to the European Union. A World Bank Country Report*. Washington DC: The World Bank.

9   Gender and labour market restructuring in Central and Eastern Europe

Mike Ingham and Hilary Ingham

Introduction

Early predictions that gender bias would pervade the process of labour market transformation in Central and Eastern Europe (CEE) were made in a vacuum, insofar as the move from command principles to market direction had not occurred before. Implicit in the forecasts was an assumption either that women's position was worse previously than some market norm and would deteriorate further, or that women held a favourable position under communism and that this would be lost. However, the usual seeds of female disadvantage – relatively low educational and health status (IBRD 1995) – were largely absent in the communist world. 'Initial conditions' are often held to be important determinants of transformation possibilities, strategies and trajectories, and these varied much more than was commonly supposed in the Soviet realm of influence (Allen 1992). As such, it is a little surprising that identical arguments regarding the negative impacts of change on the position of women have been applied to all transition economies.

A small number of examples must serve to characterise the gloomy prognosis for women pervading the early literature. In the case of Bulgaria it was argued that '[d]espite the disposition to work, in the conditions of mounting unemployment the risks for women are greater than those for men' (Kostova 1993: 104). For the former Soviet Union (FSU) it was maintained that 'the labour market, just being formed, is already two-sided, insofar as a secondary labour market and marginal position has emerged for women' (Posadskaya 1993: 163–164). Hungary's history was rather different to that of the preceding two countries yet, '[a]s the economy moves in the direction of greater reliance on markets under stagnant economic conditions, women are likely to suffer disproportionately' (Weil 1993: 284). Finally, the Polish experience was different again, yet '[t]he transition from a centralized economy to a free market economy, and the accompanying unemployment, has created new problems and particular dangers for women . . .' (Kuratowska 1991: 54). While doubtless deliberate, such predictions are rhetorical in content and the following section of the chapter provides a critique of their underlying assumptions.

Incomplete as reform may be, it is just about possible, ten years on, to begin to think in terms of comparing outcomes across the transition economies, aided by data that has been generated on a reasonably consistent basis. Using an Organisation for Economic Co-operation and Development (OECD) summary database of the western inspired Labour Force Surveys (LFS) that have now become established features in many countries of the region, this chapter takes some initial steps towards establishing what these outcomes have been. This is of course a case of being wise after the event; early commentators did not have such information against which to measure their predictions. However, many of the original beliefs persist and one can still read that '[reform has] contributed to their [women's] exclusion from the labor force . . .' (UNDP 1999: 68); '[d]uring the transition . . . women find it more difficult than men to hold onto paid employment . . .' and '[w]hen it comes to making a choice between men and women, employers usually select men . . .' (UNDP 1999: 70).

The measurement of female labour market disadvantage in what follows is as holistic as possible, given the source employed. The third section provides some background on the major labour market aggregates: employment, participation and unemployment. The fourth section then presents an overview of the evidence on the emergence of more flexible labour markets and the roles that men and women are playing within them. A formal test of the significance of the differences emerging from the preceding discussion occupies the following section.

As the architects of market-oriented reform laid considerable emphasis on the presence of latent entrepreneurship in the communist economies and its potential to advance a virtuous process of wealth creation and improved living standards (Sachs 1990), it is appropriate that the brief discussion of self-employment early in the chapter be developed in more detail, and this forms the focus of the sixth section of the chapter. This is particularly important as the relevant data are here at their most ambiguous, yet could be pivotal to the interpretation of the gendered impacts of reform. This section therefore explores more closely the definition of self-employment adopted by the OECD and its behaviour in the transition economies.

The threat to women on the labour market

That heavy labour market adjustment costs would accompany transition was obvious and the intention here is to appraise the arguments of those who predicted that the penalty would fall disproportionately upon women. The central argument is that gender *per se* is too broad a classification upon which to devise effective, efficient labour market policy.

It has often been suggested that the collapse of planning and the emergence of enterprises motivated by the pursuit of profit would expose a resistance to the employment of women that had been latent during the communist era (Kuratowska 1991, Wolchik 1993). This argument runs the risk of misrepresenting the situation prior to 1989 and of failing to understand the forces that market liberalisation should set in motion. Under communism, the position of women was far from equal to that of men; for instance, there was a list of restrictions placed on the types of employment that women could undertake and this very often excluded them from the most highly paid occupations (Leven 1994). Rather than increasing the potential for employers to indulge any preference they may have for a male workforce, the replacement of plan by market – when profit replaces patronage – should witness less, rather than more, discrimination, given the implied monetary cost of engaging in such behaviour (Becker 1971). Nevertheless, the fear was that women, viewed in prevailing ethos as social rather than economic actors, would be dismissed first by contracting enterprises (Ingham *et al.* 1998). Similarly, it was envisaged that there would be discriminatory behaviour in the filling of vacancies. Theoretically at least, both of these phenomena could prevail only to the extent that budget constraints failed to harden fully or that players in the post-communist environment took time to adapt to the rules of the market.

In principle, women were afforded extensive non-wage benefits by the communist authorities, including maternity and childcare leave and crèche facilities (Hübner *et al.* 1993). The cost was not, however, borne directly by the employing enterprise but by the state. If the wages of men and women were equal in the newly marketised economy, women continued to shoulder the major domestic burden and firms were obliged to provide the same benefits as previously, profit maximising employers would clearly be unwilling to hire women (Kuratowska 1991, Paukert 1991). Yet women were paid less than men (UNDP 1995), the provision of welfare benefits was not as widespread as is sometimes imagined (Ciechocińska 1993) and there was a rapid decline in the provision of non-wage, family-related benefits in the early 1990s (Łobodzińska 1995). It is quite possible that this reduction in the choice set of women would hinder their participation on the labour market. However, of itself, this is not an example of employer discrimination and it does not deny the possibility that more flexible working hours and part-time working in the transforming economies could offset the impact of reductions in state welfare provision.[1] At the same time, one of the underlying reasons behind the rejection of the communist order was its failure to deliver satisfactory standards of living. To the extent that reform makes possible the increases in productivity necessary to achieve this goal, real earnings in the reformed economy should rise, thereby creating a potential demand for private sector provision of welfare facilities.

In a somewhat different vein, it has been argued that, in the new environment, firms do not feel bound by the provisions of the law and that this will therefore operate to the detriment of women (Einhorn 1991). This is a pessimistic vision of how markets function in practice and suggests that early reformers were actually seeking to establish a brand of 'wild capitalism' (Karasimeonov 1998). Of course markets will not function without the rule of law being imposed but, at the same time, it is erroneous to suggest that it prevailed under the previous regime: women may have had rights, but there was usually no mechanism in place by which they could enforce them (Ingham *et al.* 1997).

Seemingly more plausible are those arguments highlighting the gender division of labour in the centrally planned economies. For example, women were heavily overrepresented in administrative functions, and such peripheral activities were often viewed as likely targets of the transformation retrenchment (Budziszewska 1991, Paukert 1991, see also Ch. 5). Also, it was forecast by some that female intensive industries, such as textiles, would be hit hardest by the transition (Janowska *et al*. 1992, Fong and Paull 1993). However, both of these arguments fail to take into account the fact that men predominated in manual occupations in heavy industry, a sector considered to be at least as non-viable as light industry (Hughes and Hare 1991). In fact, the corollary of moves towards western style economies should be the expansion of sectors that are usually observed to be feminised (Fong and Paull 1993). Nevertheless, it is necessary to recall that there was a large, feminised state service sector prior to 1990 and this was potentially under threat from reductions in public budgets and efficiency drives (Ingham *et al*. 1998).[2]

Outcomes

The discussion that follows places heavy reliance on the LFS data held by the OECD for Bulgaria, the Czech Republic, Hungary, Latvia, Poland, Romania, the Russian Federation, Slovakia and Slovenia. These countries had a combined population of almost 250 million in 1995 (Lavigne 1999: 292), or about 65 per cent of the total population in the CEE transition economies. On the whole, the LFS exercises are comparable with those conducted in the west and provide a useful point of departure for comparative studies. However, the survey is a recent innovation in the region; the earliest being conducted in Hungary in the first quarter 1992, while that in Latvia commenced only in November 1995. Therefore, initial brief comment on developments prior to its inception are necessary. Also, the LFS is not conducted with the same periodicity in every country and does not always contain the same degree of detail. Finally, the discussion is limited in its scope by the fact that only certain variables are disaggregated by sex in the OECD database.

Examining changes between 1989 and the first LFS involves the marriage of data from different sources that it would be impossible to render entirely compatible. While being overtly suspicious of the results, the simple expedient adopted here is to compare unmodified employment and participation totals from the LFS with those reported in CEC (1995) for certain countries for 1989. The first caveat is that no breakdown of recorded employment by sex was published in the latter source, so the 1989 figures actually refer to the economically active population. Although the bias this introduces is not great, given that the explosion in open unemployment was still to occur, employment is thereby inflated. Second, the employment component of that data is based on firm survey information, therefore multiple job holders might be double-counted. Third, some women on elongated maternity leave will undoubtedly be included in the 1989 figures. Fourth, other ghost employees, such as pensioners retained on the books of enterprises, may also have been enumerated. Fifth, the data includes only estimates of the size of the private sector workforce. There is no way of knowing how large the combined biases introduced by these considerations might be, or

Table 9.1 Employment and participation change (per cent): 1989 to first LFS

	Employment		Participation	
	Female	Male	Female	Male
Bulgaria (1993.3)	−29.5	−12.4	−9.6	10.7
Czech Republic (1993.1)	−8.4	−10.5	−3.7	−6.8
Hungary (1992.1)	−23.2	−23.7	−16.3	−14.6
Poland (1992.2)	−13.4	−11.9	0.8	−0.0
Romania (1994.1)	2.0	−2.2	11.8	5.9
Slovakia (1993.2)	−21.5	−18.2	−7.7	−6.4

Notes
The date of the first LFS is given in parentheses. The base year for Bulgaria is 1991.

how they are distributed across countries or the sexes. Nevertheless, the presumption must be that, as measures of either employment or participation, the 1989 figures are overestimates.

Table 9.1 provides the percentage changes in employment and participation between 1989 and the first LFS for the six countries for which data is available. Notwithstanding the problems of comparability, significant early employment collapses appear to have occurred in all countries covered, except Romania (see also Ch. 1). Much less clear is whether any gender bias accompanied these losses. With the exception of Bulgaria, where the difference between the employment reductions experienced by men and women in just two years is little short of incredible, all other contrasts would appear to lie comfortably within margins that could be explained by conflicts of definition.[3] The data also suggest that not only did overall participation rise in as many countries as it fell; in certain countries, but particularly Bulgaria and Romania, marked differences in trend were apparent for men and women. Indeed, in Bulgaria, the changes by gender were not only large, they also moved in opposite directions. However, the largest declines were recorded in Hungary, where total participation seemingly fell by 15 per cent between 1989 and the beginning of 1992. At the same time, the apparent increase of almost 12 per cent in female participation in Romania between 1989 and the beginning of 1994 is notable. Only the Bulgarian data would lend any support to a claim that the onset of reform exacted a disproportionate toll on the labour market participation of women (see also Ch. 11). On the understanding that significant shocks pre-dated the introduction of the LFS, more confident attention can now be turned to the era tracked by that survey.[4]

Unemployment

On the basis of the last available LFS for each country, some 13.8 million people, out of a total population aged 15–64 of 167.1 million, reported themselves to be without work at the beginning of 1999.[5] However, even though this jobless tally is based upon exercises that are arguably free from the objections levied against unemployment register data, the count is undoubtedly too low. In particular, it takes no account of the continued existence of large numbers of hidden unemployed in all countries of the region.[6] While the latest reported unemployment rates are below their peaks in six countries, they are also above their troughs in all cases except Latvia and, net of seasonal factors, Hungary. As such, there is no serious evidence of an ongoing improvement in the health of labour markets in the region, with delayed restructuring and the periodic crises in Russia being likely, if partial, explanations.

Gender specific unemployment rates have followed broadly similar cyclical and seasonal patterns within each of the countries, although the ratio between the two has exhibited marked differences across labour markets. The unemployment rate of women has consistently exceeded that of males in the Czech Republic and Poland, and usually has done so in Slovakia. In only one period did the differential fall below 10 per cent in Poland, while in the Czech Republic it was never less than 25 per cent. Arguably, the size of the ratio in the latter case is influenced unduly by the relatively small number of jobless before 1997 and it will be of interest to monitor its future behaviour, given that unemployment in the Czech Republic is seemingly now set to continue increasing (WERI 1999). On the other hand, proportionately fewer women than men were always unemployed in Hungary, as was also usually the case in Latvia and Russia. The average ratio over all available observations was less than unity in Hungary, Latvia, Slovenia and Russia and was precisely equal to one in Bulgaria.

It is with reference to headline unemployment rates that the case for women to be recognised as the major losers from transformation is often made, although *prima facie* evidence that this has occurred in fact could, however, only be made by a judicious sample selection. Indeed, if the Polish evidence of females who are unavailable for work remaining registered as unemployed in the face of the tightening of benefit eligibility criteria (Ingham and Ingham 2001) generalises, and if it is accepted that LFS jobless counts are unlikely to be wholly independent of the criteria attached to registration, the current data might be regarded as representing upper bounds to women's disadvantage. It is though incautious to place reliance on just one indicator in forming conclusions regarding gender bias in transition labour markets. At the very least, some initial unemployment shock was always anticipated and, as such, the question of whether its impact upon particular groups is transitory or more protracted assumes as much importance as its incidence.

Long-term unemployment

The extent of long-term unemployment (LTU) – joblessness for a continuous period of twelve months or more – that has emerged in CEE, together with the speed at which it did so, might frighten those looking for signs that economic, political and social stability are now assured in the region. Over the LFS period, LTU always exceeded half of total unemployment in Bulgaria and Latvia and its mean value was 50 per cent in the case of Slovenia. In addition, on average over 40 per cent of the unemployed in Hungary, Romania and Slovakia were without work for more than one year. Only the Czech Republic and Russia have seemingly been affected less severely by the curse of long-term unemployment, although in neither case is the forecast future scenario optimistic.[7]

With women more prone to LTU in six countries, one might conclude that they are generally exposed to a greater risk of long spells without work than men. Their position was worst in Russia, although female-to-male LTU rates less than unity occurred only once in both Poland and Romania. On the other hand, in Russia there was a strong downward trend in the female-to-male LTU rate from 1994. In no country did women fare consistently better than men, although the average value of the ratio was 0.9 in Slovenia and Hungary. There is though no simple relationship between women's long-term unemployment and either the overall level of unemployment or the female presence in that stock, whether the data is interrogated by correlations of country averages or by pooled regressions across all economies.

Employment

Table 9.2 indicates that the picture of employment change is not always a simple mirror of the unemployment statistics (see also Ch. 1). In only four countries – the Czech Republic, Hungary, Poland and Romania – did the difference between sex specific unemployment rates exceed 1 per cent at the terminal observation point. Cross-reference to the employment changes reveals that this difference had the sign one might expect only in the first case. In Hungary and Romania, female unemployment might have been predicted to exceed that of males when in fact the reverse was true. In Poland, the number of women in work fell slightly less than the number of men in the years from 1992, yet the rate of female unemployment was almost 15 per cent higher than that of males at the beginning of 1999. Employment increases for both sexes were recorded in Latvia and Slovenia, yet the former country recorded the highest average female-to-male unemployment rate in the sample and the third highest ratio at the final observation point. In the case of Slovakia, male employment fell while that of women increased, even though the female unemployment rate exceeded that of males at the beginning of 1999 and, on average, was 11 per cent greater over the data period.

Table 9.2 also disaggregates the data into those sub-periods when employment was falling (column 2) and when it was rising (column 3). In the former case, women clearly fared less favourably than men in the Czech Republic, given that their employment fell continuously throughout the period covered. For those countries which have enjoyed an employment upswing, however, the data provide almost no confirmation of the hypothesis that employers would be unwilling to recruit women: more jobs for females have emerged in the upturns in six of the countries and, in three of these, the gains exceeded those recorded by men by some margin.

Part of the apparent conflict between the employment and unemployment data can be explained by the fact that the LFS did not commence until after the effects of the first transition-related shocks had already been felt. Comparing

Table 9.2 Employment change (per cent): LFS data

Country (Data period)	First to Latest		First to Low		Low to Latest	
	Males	Females	Males	Females	Males	Females
Bulgaria (1993.3–1999.1)	−5.7	−4.3	Last Lowest	Last Lowest	0.0	0.0
Czech Republic (1993.1–1999.1)	1.8	−9.9	First Lowest	Last Lowest	1.8	0.0
Hungary (1993.1–1999.1)	−4.3	−9.2	−9.4	−15.31	4.1	7.2
Latvia (1995.4–1998.4)	3.6	3.5	−2.5	First Lowest	6.2	3.5
Poland (1992.2–1999.1)	−2.1	−1.0	−6.6	−4.9	4.8	4.1
Romania (1994.1–1999.1)	−5.5	−9.5	Last Lowest	−14.0	Last Lowest	5.3
Russia (1992.4–1998.3)	−14.6	−18.8	Last Lowest	Last Lowest	Last Lowest	Last Lowest
Slovakia (1993.2–1999.1)	−0.6	5.8	−1.3	−1.0	0.6	6.9
Slovenia (1993.2–1999.1)	4.7	2.3	First Lowest	First Lowest	First Lowest	First Lowest

Note
Lowest employment levels recorded in: Bulgaria, 1999.1 (females and males); Czech Republic, 1993.1 (males), 1999.1 (females); Hungary, 1996.1 (males), 1997.2 (females); Latvia, 1996.2 (males), 1995.4 (females); Poland, 1994.1 (males), 1995.1 (females); Romania, 1999.1 (males), 1996.1 (females); Russia, 1998.3 (females and males); Slovakia, 1993.4 (females), 1994.1 (males); Slovenia, 1993.2 (females and males).

employment changes with point or average unemployment observations is therefore problematic, as initial unemployment rates were not zero. However, comparisons of changes in both variables do not always help to clarify the picture. In Bulgaria, unemployment rates and employment fell for both sexes, although the number of males in work fell more and their jobless rate fell less than was the case for females. Women have obviously suffered in the Czech Republic, but there the rate of male unemployment rose while the number in jobs was increasing. In Latvia, employment increased roughly equally for both sexes, but the female unemployment rate fell less than that of males. The employment of women fell more than that of men in both Romania and Russia, yet female unemployment declined while that of men rose in the former and rose slightly less than that of males in the latter. Finally, in Slovakia women's employment rose while that of

Table 9.3 Participation changes (per cent)

	1989 to First LFS			First to Latest LFS		
	Total	Males	Females	Total	Males	Females
Bulgaria	0.1	10.7	−9.6	−11.2	−10.9	−11.7
Czech Republic	−5.4	−6.8	−3.7	0.6	5.4	−4.7
Hungary	−15.4	−14.6	−16.3	−8.7	−6.7	−11.0
Latvia	n/a	n/a	n/a	−2.7	−3.9	−1.2
Poland	0.4	−0.0	0.8	−2.0	−2.3	−1.8
Romania	8.6	5.9	11.8	−7.3	−4.1	−10.9
Russia	n/a	n/a	n/a	−8.6	−6.0	−11.3
Slovakia	−8.3	−6.4	−7.7	5.8	2.4	10.2
Slovenia	n/a	n/a	n/a	1.9	2.2	1.6

Notes
Data periods as in Table 9.2. The data for Bulgaria is for 1991.

men fell, yet female unemployment increased more than male. In a world of perfect labour market accounts, the key to such apparent puzzles would lie in the open boundaries of the labour market.

Participation

Table 9.3 reveals that after 1992 there was a large reduction in overall participation in Hungary, although the impact on women was somewhat greater than on men. The same apparent gender imbalance was also observed in the Czech Republic, Romania and Russia, although the movements in the second country merely reversed the changes that seemed to occur at the beginning of the decade. On the other hand, there was a large increase in female participation in Slovakia, which although seemingly only countering an earlier fall, amounted to a much larger correction than that experienced by males. This case is particularly interesting because women endured relatively high unemployment at the same time as their participation increased. In the Czech Republic, by contrast, women experienced both the highest unemployment burden and a declining presence on the labour market.

Towards greater flexibility?

Even though perceptions of the consequences diverged widely, all commentators accepted that greater labour market flexibility would ensue from labour market reform. The demise of central planning in CEE, along with the troubles experienced in recent years in South-East Asia, almost certainly erased the emphasis on 'jobs for life' and full employment in many parts of the world in the post-War era. In this new climate, rigid labour markets are likely to be high unemployment labour markets, as EU experience testifies. The current data does not permit an extensive investigation of the issues involved in the flexibility debate, but it does allow an examination of the behaviour of part-time working and self-employment, both of which are, of course, constituent elements of the employment totals discussed above.

Part-time employment

To preface the examination of current levels of part-time working, it is necessary to cast some doubt on the accuracy of popular accounts of past practice. It is easy to gain the impression that previously there was almost no part-time working under communism, although to accept this as fact is surely to err. Under planning, absences from work for maternity and family-related reasons were an established feature of working life, whether they were officially sanctioned or merely condoned unofficially. Indeed, such absences might be viewed as having been essential to the maintenance of stability in the economic and social system of the time. Equitable or not, the bulk of justifiable leave was taken by women. Furthermore, occupations in which full-time working was more apparent than real, such as school teaching, tended to be highly feminised. One Hungarian study, reported in Fong and Paull (1993: 235), found that mothers worked, on average, 50 per cent of the standard working week. If to this is added the extent of under-employment in communist economies, one might be assured that part-time working in CEE is not a new phenomenon.

Nevertheless, current levels of part-time working, summarised in Table 9.4, appear to be low and only exceed 10 per cent of the employed population in Latvia, Poland and Romania, and are in general no more significant than in Britain in 1961 (DEP 1971: 198 and 275). Also, levels of part-time work have remained more or less unchanged from the time of the first LFS. Overall, and at the risk of being seen to assume an equivalence, this might be regarded as symptomatic of the continued under-development of modern service sectors in the region. Nevertheless, other than Romania, with relatively high levels of part-time working and relatively low levels of unemployment, and Bulgaria, which

Table 9.4 Part-time working: averages

	Part-time as proportion of total employment	Part-time as proportion of total female employment	Female-to-male part-time employment rates
Bulgaria	0.01	0.01	1.56
Czech Republic	0.06	0.10	3.35
Hungary	0.04	0.06	2.73
Latvia	0.13	0.13	1.08
Poland	0.11	0.13	1.56
Romania	0.15	0.18	1.48
Slovakia	0.03	0.04	3.81
Slovenia	0.06	0.07	1.35

Notes
Data periods as in Table 9.2. No data is available for Russia.

exhibits the opposite characteristics, there is little evidence that this particular brand of flexibility translates readily into smaller jobless tallies.

Table 9.4 also makes it clear that part-time working is low for both sexes taken separately, although the tendency remains, as elsewhere in the world, for the majority of part-timers to be female.[8] Two questions are often raised when attempting to interpret this fact. First, is such employment covered by the legal protection afforded to those on regular employment contracts? Second, are those undertaking such work doing so voluntarily? Consideration of the former issue lies outside the scope of this paper, save to remark that the existence of legal protection is one thing, compliance to the law is quite another, as has been argued forcibly in the case of CEE labour law (Budziszewska 1991). The data do, however, allow a little light to be shed upon the latter question.

ILO guidelines define under-employment as 'persons who are working part-time and would like to be working full-time'. With the exception of Russia, for which no data is available, all of the countries in the current sample provide returns from an LFS question that attempts to elicit information on some measure closely related to this concept. The data therefore permit some insight into the question of whether part-time employment represents an enforced margin-alisation of workers, although it is incomplete in as much as it fails to capture under-employed workers who notionally work full time. Accepting this limitation, the overall conclusion must be that under-employment on its current definition is not significant. On average, the proportion of the total workforce under-employed reached a maximum of 8 per cent in Latvia, followed by 3 per cent in Romania. In no other country do more than 2 per cent of workers consider themselves to be constrained in the number of hours they work. In fact, outside Hungary, Latvia, Romania and Slovenia, the number experiencing such a restriction never exceeded 2 per cent of all employees. Using part-time workers rather than total employment as the base reveals more variation across countries, as shown in Table 9.5.

While the underlying series are quite volatile, involuntary part-time working amongst women is on average as low as 15 per cent in Slovenia, but involves over

Table 9.5 Average under-employment figures

	Proportion of female part-time under-employed	Female-to-male part-time under-employment rates
Bulgaria	0.46	0.96
Czech Republic	0.22	1.85
Hungary	0.39	0.57
Latvia	0.52	0.72
Poland	0.15	0.80
Romania	0.15	0.47
Slovakia	0.33	1.80
Slovenia	0.19	0.60

Notes
Data periods as in Table 9.2. No under-employment data is available for Russia.

half of all female part-timers in Latvia. Nevertheless, only in the Czech Republic and Slovakia does the proportion exceed the equivalent figure for men. Given the low levels of part-time working, there is little evidence of binding hours of work constraints and less still that women have been the principal victims of those that do exist.

Self-employment

Although the ubiquity of black markets made a nonsense of the communist drive to eliminate private enterprise, it is important to establish the extent to which genuine entrepreneurship has emerged in the current decade in CEE. To many early reformers and their advisers, an explosion of mass self-employment would attest to the power of the market and the universal existence of a culture of enterprise. With the two major exceptions of Poland and Romania, the self-employed account for between 7 and 17 per cent of all those in work in the economies under study, as shown in Table 9.6.

In every case, however, the numbers involved are sufficient to influence interpretation of other labour market aggregates, as discussed further below.[9] For the moment, it is merely noted that Table 9.6 indicates that, with the exception of Romania, women are considerably less likely than men to be self-employed, as is true in Western Europe also (CEC 1992: 147). In all other cases, the proportion of self-employed women never exceeded that of men at any time in the period covered by the data.

Formal tests of gender bias

A more formal test of gender bias in labour market transitions over the LFS period can be performed by switching attention from averages and changes over relatively long periods of time to a statistical examination of time-series of differences by sex in rates and of differences in rates of change. The first measure

Table 9.6 Self-employment averages

	Self-employed as proportion of total employment	*Female-to-male self-employment rates*
Bulgaria	0.11	0.66
Czech Republic	0.13	0.54
Hungary	0.15	0.63
Latvia	0.16	0.81
Poland	0.30	0.90
Romania	0.37	1.30
Russia	0.13	0.61
Slovakia	0.06	0.42
Slovenia	0.17	0.72

Note
Data periods as in Table 9.2.

is applied to unemployment, long-term employment, self-employment, part-time employment and under-employment, while the second is used for employment and participation.

In the case of rates, the test applied consists of estimating, for each country separately, the simple ordinary least squares equation:

$$R_{iwt} = \alpha + \beta R_{imt} + e_{it}$$

where R_{iwt} and R_{imt} are the values of rate i at time t for women and men, respectively, and e_{it} is an error term. For rates of change, the test applied is similar, taking the form:

$$(I_{iwt} - I_{iwt_{-1}})/I_{iwt} = \alpha + \beta(I_{imt} - I_{imt_{-1}})/I_{imt_{-1}} + e_{it}$$

where the Is are labour market indicators that are not expressed initially as rates.

Estimated values of β in these two sets of equations which are significantly different from unity at the 1 per cent level are taken as either very favourable or very unfavourable to women, depending upon their sign and the particular context. Values that are significant at the lower level of 5 per cent are regarded as either favourable or unfavourable. In some cases, it is not entirely evident what constitutes a favourable outcome for women. While this does not invalidate a finding of non-neutrality, in these instances the conventions adopted below should be regarded merely as expository.

The results of conducting the above tests are presented in the matrix reproduced as Table 9.7, in which outcomes favourable to women are denoted

Table 9.7 Gender bias in labour market outcomes

	1	2	3	4	5	6	7
Bulgaria		− −	− −				
Czech Republic	− −	− −	− −	− −			
Hungary	+ +	+ +	− −	− −	+ +		
Latvia		− −	− −	+ +			
Poland	− −	− −	− −	− −	+ +		
Romania		− −	− −	− −	+ +		
Russia	+	− −	− −	n/a	n/a		
Slovakia	− −	− −	− −	− −	+ +		+
Slovenia		+	− −	− −			

Notes
(1) *Unemployment rate differences.* A low relative female unemployment is favourable.
(2) *Long-term unemployment rate differences.* A low relative female long-term unemployment rate is favourable.
(3) *Self-employment rate differences.* A high relative female self-employment rate is favourable.
(4) *Part-time employment rate differences.* A low relative female part-time employment rate is favourable.
(5) *Under-employment rate differences.* A low relative female under-employment rate is favourable.
(6) *Employment change differences: first to latest LFS.* A smaller female employment loss (greater gain) is favourable.
(7) *Participation change differences: first to latest LFS.* A smaller female participation decline (greater gain) is favourable.

by + and very favourable ones by + +. Unfavourable and very unfavourable outcomes are denoted by − and − −, respectively. Cells in the matrix that correspond to approximately gender-neutral outcomes have been left blank. When interpreting these results, it should be noted that no account is taken of the overall impact of transformation on any particular country's labour market. For example, in the Czech Republic there is a notable difference between male and female unemployment rates, although both sexes were, at least initially, exposed to lower risks of joblessness than in any other country in the sample. On the other hand, overall unemployment has been extremely high in Latvia, but the burden has been borne fairly equally by men and women.

The heavy emphasis placed upon the disproportionate share of the unemployment burden likely to be borne by women finds some support in the case of Poland and the Czech and Slovak Republics, although precisely the opposite conclusion could be drawn by focusing upon Hungary and Russia. There is stronger evidence that women are especially troubled by long periods without work, as the data for Poland, Romania, Russia and Slovakia testify. Once again, however, the findings for Hungary and, on this occasion, Slovenia, invite a contrary reaction. Notwithstanding the observations for these latter two countries, are these unemployment disparities strong enough to support a conclusion that women have been disadvantaged by the transformation?

Column 6 indicates that there were no significant differences in the patterns of employment change exhibited by the sexes. In other words, not only have men and women lost jobs when employment has been falling, they have also found them when it has been rising. Furthermore, there appear to have been no differential movements in rates of labour market participation, except insofar as there is some evidence that the importance of women in the Slovak labour force has been increasing, even though the unemployment statistics would suggest that they face serious difficulties in that country. The emerging picture, at least for some countries, is consistent with the existence of a relatively larger core of women than men who, for reasons that cannot be ascertained precisely with the current data set, fail to engage fully with the labour market once inside its boundaries, although the evidence would suggest that the reason resides less on the demand than the supply side of the market.

The most widespread differences between the sexes relate to the characteristics of their gainful activity. In every country represented in Table 9.7, women are significantly more likely than men to be working part-time (column 4). Nevertheless, there would appear to be significantly less involuntary part-time working amongst females than males in all countries except the Czech Republic (column 5). Be this as it may, the data further indicate that generally women have not entered the ranks of the self-employed to the same extent as men, with the experience in Romania representing the conspicuous exception. However, the behaviour of self-employment in the region is sufficiently important to merit further investigation.

Self-employment: suppressed entrepreneurship?

When using the current database to examine self-employment, it is necessary to inject one vital caveat: under OECD reporting conventions, unpaid family workers are regarded as self-employed. The distortion this imparts will vary from country to country, and over time within the same country. Taking Poland as an example, the LFS has at various times identified more than one million unpaid family workers, of whom women constitute typically 55–60 per cent (GUS 1999). The vast bulk of such workers are found in rural areas, particularly in agriculture. This difficulty, allied to the limited range of variables which are enumerated in the database, imposes clear limitations on what can be concluded with confidence, although certain tests of some fairly general hypotheses regarding the determination of self-employment rates are possible. In particular, by pooling the data, a simple model can be constructed with which to explore the extent to which self-employment depends upon the health of the aggregate labour market and the industrial structure of the economy. The arguments are straightforward.

At least some of the self-employment in the transformation economies undoubtedly takes the form of low productivity, semi-legal alternatives to joining the ranks of the unemployed. Confronted with decreasingly generous benefit regimes, this may be a rational response on the part of those who lose, or are in danger of losing, their attachment to the formal labour market, either for reasons of personal morale or, less convincingly, market signalling. At the same time, the rule of law – in particular, tax law – is still not firmly in place in much of the region and this may represent a further attraction of self-employment. It could also be that growth in the extent of long-term unemployment, presumably implying an increase in the number of benefit recipients at or near the stage of eligibility exhaustion, will be associated with a growth in self-employment. Finally, even though the resources available for active labour market measures have been limited, the higher is the level of unemployment and the number of long-term jobless, the greater are the pressures on the authorities to act to ameliorate the situation; and inducements for the unemployed to work on their own account are one of the weapons in the policy armouries of governments throughout the world. In summary, unemployment and long-term unemployment seem likely to be incubators of self-employment.

The argument for including a measure of the prevailing industrial structure relates back, in part, to the reporting conventions adopted by the OECD; in particular, the requirement that unpaid family workers (sometimes referred to as 'helpers') be classified as self-employed. Such individuals tend to be attached to traditional family enterprises and as such are often to be found in agriculture, especially as the privatisation procedures adopted in the region have frequently involved dismembering the old state and collective farms into much smaller units. What is more, retreat to self-employment on the family farm represents an alternative to unemployment for those dismissed from state industrial enterprises. For both of these reasons, it is prudent in a time-series, cross-national modelling exercise to include a term measuring the importance of agriculture in the overall employment structure.

In summary, the above discussion suggests the following model, here to be estimated in simple linear form:

$$PSE_i = \beta_0 + \beta_1 UR_{-1} + \beta_2 PLTU_{-1} + \beta_3 PAG + D_j + e$$

where:

PSE_i is the proportion of self-employed amongst the total employed of sex i
UR_{-1} is the total unemployment rate, lagged one quarter
$PLTU_{-1}$ is the proportion of the total unemployed without work for over twelve months, lagged one quarter
PAG is the proportion of total employment in agriculture
D_j are country dummies
e is an error term

Data pooling provides the necessary degrees of freedom for the purposes of estimation although, if applied strictly, the model can be analysed only for the Visegrad countries. However, by allowing all regressors to refer to the current period, the fifteen observations available for Romania can be included in a first-round approximation of the model. The results are presented in Table 9.8.[10]

Columns 1 and 2 of Table 9.8 report, for men and women separately (*PSEM* and *PSEW*, respectively), the results of the regression when Romania is included in the sample. While the unemployment rate is insignificant for both sexes, the extent of *LTU* and the size of the agricultural sector increase the importance of self-employment for men and women alike. Excluding Romania from the sample and introducing lagged values of the unemployment terms generates the findings reproduced in columns 3 and 4. In this case, each of the principal regressors acquires the predicted sign and is significant. On the face of it, male self-employment is more sensitive to growing labour market slack while female self-employment is more sensitive to the size of the agricultural sector. These impressions can, however, be subjected to direct test.

Columns 5 and 6 of Table 9.8 adopt the samples and specifications of the above variants of the model to explore the behaviour of the ratio of the self-employment rate of women to that of men (*PSEWM*). Once again, the use of current data and the inclusion of Romania generates less clear findings than when the true lagged specification is adopted and the Romanian data is excluded from the sample. The latter indicates, first, that *PSEWM* is positively related to the extent of agricultural employment, a finding that is here interpreted as an indication of the importance of that sector as an enclave of female unpaid work. Second, *PSEWM* declines as long-term unemployment increases. This is consistent with some fraction of self-employment being simply another buffer against prolonged idleness among men; that is, motivated by essentially negative forces. It might be speculated that as unemployment benefit and registration regimes have been progressively tightened throughout the region, males have been the principal victims and have to some extent been pushed into self-employment as a consequence. While much of this activity is characterised by instability and low returns, male employment

Table 9.8 OLS regression on male and female self-employment

	PSEM (1)	PSEW (1)	PSEM (2)	PSEW (2)	PSEWM (1)	PSEWM (2)
Constant	0.10610 (13.468)	0.01500 (2.429)	0.11513 (20.185)	0.03064 (5.019)	0.49198 (15.539)	0.50387 (18.843)
UR_{t-1}	0.00085 (1.178)	−0.00037 (0.651)	0.00265 (4.276)	0.00141 (2.121)	0.00052 (0.179)	−0.00074 (0.253)
$PLTU_{t-1}$	0.07440 (4.467)	0.06310 (4.832)	0.05850 (4.992)	0.03325 (2.651)	−0.10763 (1.608)	−0.13340 (2.439)
$PCAG_t$	0.48749 (7.730)	0.87905 (17.778)	0.29824 (4.815)	0.63769 (9.619)	1.10985 (4.379)	1.08478 (3.737)
Hungary	−0.00621 (1.135)	−0.00054 (0.127)	−0.00978 (2.527)	−0.00107 (0.259)	0.07265 (3.302)	0.08203 (4.522)
Poland	0.05297 (4.383)	0.04271 (4.508)	0.06964 (7.364)	0.07007 (6.923)	0.18393 (3.787)	0.20379 (4.598)
Romania	0.00451 (0.201)	0.04566 (2.598)			0.38654 (4.292)	
Slovakia	−0.10874 (14.105)	−0.08378 (13.862)	−0.11502 (21.308)	−0.08473 (14.665)	−0.12827 (4.140)	−0.10785 (4.263)
R^2	0.986	0.996	0.992	0.993	0.975	0.966
n	120	120	102	102	120	102

Note
'*t*'-statistics are given in parentheses.

totals have thereby been the subject of an automatic stabiliser.[11] The same tendency would, of course, be evident if males were disproportionately the beneficiaries of schemes to enable the unemployed to become self-employed. However, such speculation merely underscores the need for more detailed analyses in this area at the level of individual countries.

Conclusions

At the onset of the process of systemic transformation there was a widespread belief that the labour market reforms associated with change would impose significantly higher costs upon women than men, and this view persists in many quarters. Given the weak theoretical footing of those who argue that women would be the universal casualties, a contrary expectation might be that, in a region of such heterogeneity, a multiplicity of outcomes would result. Use of what appears to be the most comprehensive comparative database available does indeed highlight a varied experience across countries and some rather surprising developments within particular economies. While it is possible to make a weak case that women have suffered more unemployment and a somewhat stronger one that they have borne the brunt of long-term joblessness, the figures do not have an obvious reflection in the data on employment. Also, even though women are more likely to work part-time than men, the numbers are low in a wider international context and have not grown in a manner that would explain the behaviour of their employment totals. Furthermore, the available evidence does not identify widespread hours constraints.

Although there has not been an explosion of self-employment in the transition economies, the numbers involved could have a significant bearing on the interpretation of aggregate employment levels and unemployment statistics. In particular, to the extent that self-employment is low productivity and dead-end in character it could be seen as simply a buffer against overt unemployment. With considerably more men than women working on their own account, this is clearly an important consideration in the examination of potential gender bias. On the basis of the results reported in this chapter, the self-employment of both sexes is sensitive to the health of the labour market, but is proportionately more so in the case of men. Any evidence that men have relatively low levels of joblessness should be interpreted in the light of this potentially important caveat. On the other hand, the database used in this chapter includes unpaid family workers amongst the ranks of the self-employed. To the extent that such positions are to be found largely in agriculture and are more frequently held by females, some caution needs to be exercised when casting the employment record of women in a favourable light. Further analysis of these neglected issues is required at the national level and, unless such enquiries provide compelling evidence to the contrary, it seems ill-advised to conclude that women have everywhere borne a disproportionate share of the costs of labour market upheaval.

Notes

1 Many view the proliferation of part-time working in western economies in recent years as an employer reaction to the preferred working patterns of married females (e.g. McGregor and Sproull 1991, Meulders *et al.* 1997).

2 It might also be noted that women acquired, perhaps inadvertently, extensive education under the previous regime. This was both less vocationally orientated, and often pursued to a higher level, than that of men. Possession of such human capital could render women more flexible than men and thereby may enable them to adapt more readily to the technological changes accompanying the transformation to a modern economy (Ingham *et al.* 1998, Białecki and Heynes 1993).

3 Given the lack of speed with which serious transformation packages were adopted in all transition countries – including, many would argue, in Poland – the size of the reported collapse in jobs might be seen to invalidate completely the comparisons made here over the pre-LFS years.

4 Even country-specific studies with access to wider information sources tend to place too much credence in early labour market data. The statistical practices of

the communist years did not evaporate with the overthrow of the old regimes, and the move to western conventions, along with adequate monitoring of private sector activity, took some time (Eurostat 1993).

5 The unemployment figures are for the first quarter 1999, except for Latvia and Russia, which are for the fourth and third quarters 1998, respectively. All population estimates refer to the same quarter as the associated unemployment figures.

6 Aspects of this issue are addressed later in the chapter, although the country-specific literature provides greater insights into the nature and scale of the problem in particular economies. For example, see Czaban (1999) on Hungary; Ingham and Ingham (2001) on Poland; Clarke (1998) on Russia.

7 Possible reasons for both of these exceptions are offered in the literature cited in note 2 above.

8 The 1961 Census of Population found that one quarter of all working women in Britain were employed part-time (DEP 1971: 275).

9 By way of comparison, some 16 per cent of all persons in employment in the European Community in 1990 were classified as self-employed (CEC 1992: 147).

10 With the Czech Republic as base, the country dummies have obvious, albeit superficial, interpretations and will not be discussed in what follows.

11 That is, at least some self-employment is disguised unemployment.

References

Allen, M. (1992) 'IMF-supported adjustment programs in Central and Eastern Europe', in G. Winkler (ed.) *Central and Eastern Europe: Roads to Growth*, Washington DC: International Monetary Fund.

Becker, G. (1971) *The Economics of Discrimination*, Chicago: University of Chicago Press.

Białecki, I. and Heynes, B. (1993) 'Educational attainment, the status of women and the private school movement in Poland', in. V. Moghadam (ed.) *Democratic Reform and the Position of Women in Transitional Economies*, Oxford: Clarendon Press.

Budziszewska, G. (1991) 'The role of national machinery for the advancement of women in the changing political and economic situation', in UN (ed.) *The Impact of Economic and Political Reform on the Status of Women in Eastern Europe*, proceedings of a UN regional seminar, United Nations Centre for Social Development and Humanitarian Affairs, Vienna, 8–12 April.

CEC (Commission of the European Communities) (1992) *Employment in Europe 1992*, Brussels.

CEC (Commission of the European Communities) (1995) *Employment Observatory Central and Eastern Europe 8*, Brussels.

Ciechocińska, M. (1993) 'Gender aspects of dismantling the command economy in Eastern Europe', in V. Moghadam (ed.) *Democratic Reform and the Position of Women in Transitional Economies*, Oxford: Clarendon Press.

Clarke, S. (1998) 'Trade unions and the non-payment of wages in Russia', *International Journal of Manpower*, 19 (1–2): 68–94.

Czaban, L. (1999) 'The reorganisation of companies and the transformation of work organisations: Employment strategies in Hungarian firms in the mid-1990s', paper presented to the inaugural seminar of the Restructuring Employment and Work in East-Central Europe series, Centre on European Political Economy, Sussex European Institute, University of Sussex, 18–19 June.

DEP (Department of Employment and Productivity) (1971) *British Labour Statistics: Historical Abstract 1886–1968*, London: HMSO.

Einhorn, B. (1991) 'A comparative analysis of women's industrial participation during the transition from centrally-planned to market economies in East-Central Europe', in UN (ed.) *The Impact of Economic and Political Reform on the Status of Women in Eastern Europe*, proceedings of a UN regional seminar, United Nations Centre for Social Development and Humanitarian Affairs, Vienna, 8–12 April.

Eurostat (1993) *Employment and Unemployment in Economies in Transition: Conceptual and Measurement Issues*, Statistical Office of the European Communities: Paris.

Fong, M. and Paull, G. (1993) 'Women's economic status in the restructuring of Eastern Europe', in V. Moghadam (ed.) *Democratic Reform and the Position of Women in Transitional Economies*, Oxford: Clarendon Press.

GUS (Polish Central Statistical Office) (1999) *Aktywność Ekonomiczna Ludności Polski w Latach 1992–1998* (Labour Force Survey 1992–1998), Warsaw.

Hübner, S., Maier, F. and Rudolph, H. (1993) 'Women's employment in Central and Eastern Europe', in G. Fischer and G. Standing (eds) *Structural Change in Central and Eastern Europe: Labour Market and Social Policy Implications*, OECD, Centre for Co-operation with the Economies in Transition: Paris.

Hughes, G. and Hare, P. (1991) 'Competitiveness and industrial restructuring in Czechoslovakia, Hungary and Poland', *European Economy*, special issue no. 2, pp. 83–110.

IBRD (International Bank for Reconstruction and Development) (1995) *Toward Gender Equality: The Role of Public Policy*, Washington DC: The World Bank.

Ingham, H. and Ingham, M. (2001) *The Gender Dynamics of the Polish Labour Market in Transition*, Basingstoke: Macmillan.

Ingham, H., Ingham, M. and Karwińska, A. (1997) 'Women in the Polish labour market: Facts and perceptions', *ESRI Working Papers in Policy Studies* No. 15, University of Salford.

Ingham, M., Ingham, H., Karwińska, A. and Węcławowicz, G. (1998) 'Women in the Polish labour market: Is transition a threat?', in M. Bull and M. Ingham (eds) *Reform of the Socialist System in Central and Eastern Europe*, Basingstoke: Macmillan.

Janowska, Z., Martini-Fiwek, J. and Goral, Z. (1992) 'Female unemployment in Poland', *Friedrich-Ebert Foundation of Poland, Economic and Social Policy Series* Paper no. 18, Warsaw.

Karasimeonov, G. (1998) 'Conceptions and misconceptions of political change in East-Central Europe', in M. Bull and M. Ingham (eds) *Reform of the Socialist System in Central and Eastern Europe*, Basingstoke: Macmillan.

Kostova, D. (1993) 'The transition to democracy in Bulgaria: Challenges and risks for women', in V. Moghadam (ed.) *Democratic Reform and the Position of Women in Transitional Economies*, Oxford: Clarendon Press.

Kuratowska, Z. (1991) 'Poland: The present situation of women', in UN (ed.) *The Impact of Economic and Political Reform on the Status of Women in Eastern Europe*, proceedings of a UN regional seminar, United Nations Centre for Social Development and Humanitarian Affairs, Vienna, 8–12 April.

Lavigne, M. (1999) *The Economics of Transition*, Basingstoke: Macmillan.

Leven, B. (1994) 'The status of women and Poland's transition to a market economy', in N. Aslanbeigui, S. Pressman and G. Summerfield (eds) *Women in the Age of Economic Transformation*, London: Routledge.

Łobodzińska, B. (1995) 'Equal opportunities: Obstacles and remedies', in B. Łobodzińska (ed.) *Family, Women and Employment in Central-Eastern Europe*, Westport: Greenwood Press.

McGregor, A. and Sproull, A. (1991) 'Employer labour use strategies: Analysis of a national survey', *Employment Department Discussion Paper* No. 83, Sheffield: HMSO.

Meulders, D., Plasman, O. and Plasman, R. (1997) 'Atypical labour market relations in the EU', in G. Dijkstra and J. Plantenga (eds) *Gender and Economics: A European Perspective*, London: Routledge.

OECD (1996) *Lessons from Labour Market Policies in the Transition Countries*, Paris.

Paukert, L. (1991) 'The economic status of women in the transition to a market system: The case of Czechoslovakia', *International Labour Review*, 130 (5–6): 613–33.

Posadskaya, A. (1993) 'Changes in gender discourses and policies in the former Soviet Union', in V. Moghadam (ed.) *Democratic Reform and the Position of Women in Transitional Economies*, Oxford: Clarendon Press.

Sachs, J. (1990) 'Eastern European economies: What is to be done?', *The Economist*, 13–19 January, pp. 23–8.

UNDP (1995) *The Gender Gap in Eastern Europe and the CIS*, New York: Regional Directorate for Europe and the CIS, United Nations Development Programme.

UNDP (1999) *Human Development Report for Europe and the CIS*, New York: Regional Bureau for Europe and the CIS, United Nations Development Programme.

Weil, G. (1993) 'Economic reform and women: A general framework with specific reference to Hungary', in V. Moghadam (ed.) *Democratic Reform and the Position of Women in Transitional Economies*, Oxford: Clarendon Press.

WERI (World Economy Research Institute) (1999) *Poland: International Economic Report*, Warsaw School of Economics.

Wolchik, S. (1993) 'Women and politics in post-communist Central and Eastern Europe', in V. Moghadam (ed.) *Democratic Reform and the Position of Women in Transitional Economies*, Oxford: Clarendon Press.

Part IV

New forms of employment and survival strategies

10 Sources of subsistence and the survival strategies of urban Russian households

Simon Clarke

Introduction

Much recent discussion of household subsistence in the transition economies has been centred on the notion of 'household survival strategies' (Voronkov 1995, Johnson *et al.* 1996, Yaroshenko 1999). The notion of a 'household survival strategy' has been used widely in development studies to draw attention to the diversity of sources of household subsistence and in particular to the role of informal and household economic activity, the domain primarily of women, the young and the old. The notion was important in moving away from the narrow perspective of the wage-earning breadwinner supporting a dependent family that is associated with a one-sided view of the young, the old and women as dependants on the wages of men (Pahl 1984, Chant 1991, Nelson and Smith 1998). This approach provided the basis for powerful critiques of development strategies which had single-mindedly pursued the objective of expanding wage-earning or small business opportunities, even if this was at the expense of the contribution of other household members and of other activities to household subsistence. This is particularly important where households are not fully committed to wage-earning in the market economy, so that subsistence production and engagement in the informal economy play a significant role in the reproduction of household members (Tinker 1990). However, I would suggest that the notion is less appropriate to transition economies for three main reasons.

First, by the 1980s the vast majority of the adult population of the state socialist countries was fully committed to employment in the wage-earning economy, with a continuing role for subsistence agricultural production in some rural districts and a limited amount of moonlighting in the urban economy. Those categories of the population who were not in waged employment (full-time students, the elderly, the chronic sick and disabled, women with young children) were supported by state benefits which, in general, were sufficient to provide for their basic subsistence. Age and gender were significant in determining differential labour market opportunities, not in determining differential commitment to waged as opposed to non-waged employment. With the exception perhaps of Hungary, informal and subsistence activities were of marginal significance to the survival of urban households and the majority of people lacked the skills and resources to engage in such forms of activity.

Second, the notion of a household survival strategy is also misleading in that it implies the determining role of agency (Crow 1989, Morgan 1989, Rodgers 1989: 20): if survival is a matter of strategy more than of resources then households which adopt the appropriate strategies can survive the destruction of jobs and income-earning opportunities and the erosion of welfare benefits that have been a general feature of the collapse of the state socialist economy. It is only a short step from that view to the current attempts, encouraged by the World Bank, to slash welfare spending and to impose punitive systems of social assistance.[1] While it is important to reject the view of the poor as passive victims, it is equally important not to divert attention from what should be the main policy priority of rebuilding the economy to provide new jobs and to finance the benefit system.

Finally, the notion of a household survival strategy presumes that the household is a decision-making unit. Research on household employment decision-making suggests that it is more plausible to think about household members more or less independently taking advantage of such opportunities as may present themselves within the framework of a limited range of opportunities and quite restrictive constraints (Clarke 1998). Prosperity, survival, poverty and destitution are not then the results of more or less successful household strategies, but express the greater or lesser good fortune of household members in the face of radical economic change. In this chapter I want to give some indication of the range of opportunities facing household members by looking at the outcome of their income-earning activities, as indicated by the composition of Russian household income. The paper is based primarily on analysis of the data of a household survey conducted in four Russian cities in April–May 1998,[2] but also draws on the data of the Russian Longitudinal Monitoring Survey (RLMS), the Russian Centre for Public Opinion Research (VTsIOM) and the official Household Budget Survey (HBS).[3]

What are the components of household subsistence?

In the Soviet period household incomes comprised wage income from primary and officially registered secondary employment, monetary social transfers (primarily maternity benefits, child allowances, student stipends, disability benefits and age-related pensions) and private transfers. On the expenditure side, housing, fuel, utilities, transport, leisure activities and food were heavily subsidised, while health care and education and a range of other social and welfare services were provided free so that households could survive on very small monetary incomes. The main problem faced by households was not the shortage of money, but the shortage of goods on which to spend their money.

The collapse of the soviet system was followed by a dramatic and sustained fall in incomes and employment. According to the official estimates, GDP fell by 50 per cent between 1990 and 1998. This reflects a fall in employment of around 25 per cent, with unemployment rising to around 13 per cent and a large number of teenagers and those approaching or beyond pension age withdrawing from the labour force, and a fall in real wages of over two-thirds, to reach a level about that of the mid-1970s (see Clarke 1999c, chapter 1 and appendix, for a review of the data). The real value of the minimum wage and many welfare benefits were also severely eroded. Many households faced a greater loss of income than even these figures indicate, since wage inequality increased from Scandinavian to Latin American levels, while many of those still employed were laid off or put on short-time and wages and benefits have gone unpaid for months or even years on end. On the other hand, the demands for cash payment escalated as subsidies for consumption were removed and services that were formerly provided free are now only available for a charge.

The sources of household subsistence in post-soviet Russia are much the same as those in the soviet period: primary and secondary employment, domestic subsistence production and social and private transfers. The principal change has been in the decline of employment in the state sector and in the real value of social transfers, the growth of the new private sector, predominantly in trade and services, and the legalisation of self-employment, both of which provide much greater scope for casual and informal employment than was available in the soviet period. Social and private transfers may make an important contribution to the survival of a household, but it is difficult to envisage them as being the objects of a household survival strategy. But how extensive are the opportunities provided by informal sources of household income and subsistence?

The elusive hidden economy

According to many commentators, the collapse of incomes in the formal economy has been matched by an explosion of informal economic activity which is not reported in official statistics, so that there has been a substantial growth in unrecorded money incomes in the 'hidden' economy.[4] The proponents of this view typically cite the official data which purportedly show that wages comprise less than half of the money incomes of the population. According to Goskomstat data for 1998, wages comprised 40.5 per cent of money income, social transfers 13.3 per cent, property income 5.6 per cent, entrepreneurial income 16.5 per cent and 'other' income 24.1 per cent (the last category including unreported wage income). However, to cite this data as evidence for the existence of a hidden economy is somewhat disingenuous, since the categories of 'entrepreneurial' and 'other' income are themselves constructed to bring the income data derived from the budget survey into line with estimated macroeconomic aggregates which already include a very substantial but completely arbitrary allowance for unidentified informal economic activity that amounted to 20 per cent of GDP in 1995, 23 per cent in 1996 and 28 per cent of GDP in 1997.[5]

The concept of a 'hidden economy' is a very difficult one with which to engage, since if the economy is hidden there is, by definition, no evidence for its existence. Suffice it to say here that all the evidence is quite consistent in showing that the overwhelming majority of primary employment, including that in incorporated businesses in the new private sector, is registered and so is reported in official statistics and is subject to taxation. Both the employment and the income data derived from all-Russian surveys is very consistent and provides no evidence for the existence of a large amount of hidden primary employment or the large-scale concealment of income by survey respondents. While incomes in the new private sector may not be fully reported, new private sector employment could not be less hidden from view, for it is predominantly to be found in the retail trade and services that line the streets and fill the advertising spaces. Moreover, the earnings reported in surveys by employees in the new private sector are already substantially higher than those reported by employees in the traditional sectors of the economy, while the levels of income inequality are such as to leave little scope for a substantial concealment of income (the distributions in the various data sets are also very similar, and approximately log-linear). If hidden primary employment does exist, then it is extremely well hidden, but the onus is definitely on those who believe that there is a large amount of hidden primary employment to bring forward some hard evidence in support of their arguments.

Secondary employment

While it would seem that there is relatively little unregistered primary employment, the situation with regard to secondary employment is rather different. A much larger proportion of secondary employment is involved in forms of activity which avoid registration: petty trading and the provision of services by individuals or unregistered enterprises. However, the scale of secondary employment has certainly been exaggerated by many commentators.

The consensus that emerges from a review of the extensive survey data is that around 5 per cent of the adult population admits to working regularly in more than one job, with around twice as many people involved in occasional secondary employment in any one month. About the same proportion of those of working age who are not in primary employment are engaged in some kind of supple-mentary income-earning activity. For some people the first job is purely formal, the second job is where they really work, but for most people secondary employment is subsidiary employment, a means of making additional income by working some additional hours – typically two or three hours a day after work, or through the weekend. A substantial proportion of secondary employment takes the traditional soviet forms of an additional job at the main place of work or 'individual labour activity', providing goods and services for friends and neighbours (Klopov 1996, ISEPN RAN 1998, Clarke 1999a).

We would expect people to be liable to under-report secondary employment, even in surveys, since a substantial proportion of secondary employment is unregistered and unreported for tax purposes. In the ISITO household survey comparison of the responses of the head of household and individual household members suggests that the incidence of secondary employment at individual level may be around double that which is reported in the survey data. Nevertheless, this still means that over 80 per cent of the population of working age does not have regular secondary employment while about two-thirds of all households are not involved in secondary employment at all.

Secondary employment tends to be much better paid than primary employment. However, it also tends to be unstable and irregular. This means that a substantial proportion of the adult population may engage in some kind of supplementary economic activity at some time or another but that few households can rely on supplementary earnings to sustain the household budget consistently.[6]

Surveys show that more people would like to have an additional job than in fact have one at present; having a second job is not just a matter of wanting an additional source of income, but it is also a matter of having the opportunity to have one. In the VTsIOM data, a quarter of respondents would like to have additional work, against one-eighth who in fact have it. Of those who say that they do not want additional work only 15 per cent say that it is because they do not need it. Half say that they are not able to take on any additional work and over a third that they cannot get good work or work that brings in enough money. To undertake supplementary work it is necessary to have the time, skills, experience and resources necessary to do so, as well as the personal connections through which to find a supplementary job or, if self-employed, to get premises, find customers, etc.

There is little evidence that secondary employment is a response to economic hardship, it is rather an opportunity for additional earning that is seized by those with the skills and motivation to do so. Those with higher education or professional skills have a wider range of opportunities for secondary employment. Adults of prime working age, having often acquired a variety of skills and experience, are much better placed than are young people. Those on administrative leave and those with flexible working hours are substantially more likely to engage in secondary employment, as are those who work shorter hours in their main job, although in the latter circumstance it is not easy to disentangle cause and effect.

Subsistence production

The impression given by many Russian and western journalistic sources is that Russia has become a nation of urban peasants, city dwellers surviving the crisis by growing a large proportion of their own food on their garden plots.[7] In order to evaluate the 'myth of the urban peasant' in our survey we asked about the use of land and household agricultural production. The findings of this research can be summed up briefly: although a majority of urban households have a plot of land on which they grow fruit and vegetables, and 40 per cent of all household heads in our survey said that such produce was an important source of household subsistence, such horticultural activity makes little or no contribution to the household budget (see also Chs 11 and 12). In particular, the poorest households are the least likely to engage in such agricultural production, while those who do grow their own foodstuffs do not spend any less on food than those who do not use any land, primarily because the crops grown tend to be of low value so that there is very little monetary saving. Moreover, it takes an enormous input of time, and sometimes money, to produce a relatively modest amount of food. Finally, there is no evidence that urban households regard work on the land as a substitute for paid employment; those in paid employment and those with second jobs are significantly more likely to be involved in such work. The domestic production of food by urban households is an historical legacy of the insecurity of basic food supplies in the soviet period and is still more prevalent in regions in which commercial agriculture and the market economy are less highly developed, but it is an extraordinarily inefficient form of agricultural production which is only available to those with the money and the material and human resources required to undertake it. It is best seen as a by-product of a traditional leisure pursuit of the relatively better-off, which enables them to enjoy a more varied and, perhaps, ecologically purer diet, rather than an element of the survival strategies of impoverished households (Clarke *et al.* 2000).[8]

How do Russian urban households survive?

The only way to get a realistic picture of how households survive is by analysis of available survey data on income and expenditure. The principal published sources of such data are the official Household Budget Survey (HBS) and the more or less annual Russian Longitudinal Monitoring Survey (RLMS). The HBS stopped collecting income data in 1996, since when it has imputed household income from the reported household expenditure data. The disadvantage of the RLMS survey is that, although it asks very detailed questions regarding income and expenditure, its questions relate only to the period immediately preceding the survey (7 days, 30 days or three months, depending on the income or expenditure category), which can be misleading when wages and benefits are paid very irregularly and there is very large seasonal variation in incomes. In our household survey we could not ask such detailed questions, but we did ask our respondents to estimate their average levels of income and expenditure under various headings. While such estimates are bound to be approximate, they are consistent with the other sources and we believe that they provide a reasonably accurate impression of the overall picture. I will draw attention to only a few significant points demonstrated by the data presented in the following tables (for a more detailed discussion of poverty see Clarke 1999b).

First, over a third of all households, even in these relatively prosperous regional centres, had an average per capita money income below the local subsistence minimum even before the most recent devaluation crisis, which led to an immediate fall in real wages of one-third, struck in August 1998 (Table 10.1). The subsistence minimum does not appear to be by any means generous: 28 per cent of our household heads said that they did not even have enough money to buy sufficient food for their families. A further 47 per cent said that they had enough to buy food, but it was difficult to buy clothing.

Second, although these cities are relatively prosperous, a lot of households with wage-earners are in poverty. Almost one in five of those in employment earn a

Table 10.1 Percentage of households with money income per head below the official regional adult subsistence minimum

Percent	Samara	Kemerovo	Lyubertsy	Syktyvkar	Total
Total individual incomes this month	36	52	43	44	43
Total average individual incomes	29	37	37	39	35
Reported household income per head	33	43	38	40	38

Note
The first row results from the sum of income received the previous month from all sources reported individually by all household members; the second row results from the sum of the average monthly income reported by all individuals; the third row results from the average monthly household income reported by the head of household. Only households for which we have complete income data on each measure are included in this table. The subsistence minimum used for Lyubertsy is the mean of Moscow city and Moscow region. We have not applied any weighting for children and pensioners, for whom rather lower minima are defined, but the figures are meant only to be indicative.

wage that is less than the subsistence minimum, without taking account of non-payment. Just over half the wage-earners in each city earn less than twice the subsistence minimum, so do not earn enough to support one dependant.

Third, the very high dependence of the majority of households on social transfers is striking (Tables 10.2 and 10.3). The heads of three-quarters of households which had such income reported that it was important for the household's subsistence. According to the RLMS data for 1998, in spite of extensive non-payment, over one-third of households depended on state benefits (pensions, child benefit, unemployment benefit and grants) for more than 50 per cent of their money income.[9] Overwhelmingly the most important benefit is pension income, which accounts for well over two-thirds of the total income from benefits – it is almost as important to have a pensioner in the household as it is to have a wage-earner (households with at least one pensioner but no working member have about two-thirds of the income per head of households with at least one worker but no pensioners – about the same as the differential between men's and women's pay). Pensions are a very effective means of combating household poverty – 20 per cent of households would have had incomes below the poverty line were it not for their pension income – and not only for pensioner households, but also for households with working members; pension payments are sufficient to pull 10 per cent of such households above the poverty line. Without pension payments, half of working households would have had a money income below the poverty line in the month prior to the survey.[10] This is why the issue of pensions is such an emotive one and why the World Bank feels that it is necessary to finance a 'public information campaign explaining the [pension] reforms to the population' (World Bank News Release No. 97/1408 ECA, 26 June 1997), reforms which would reduce the state pension to a minimum, and privatise the provision of compulsory and voluntary earnings-related pensions in a three-tier pension system.

Table 10.2 Components of household income as percentage of total net income of all household members, excluding private transfers

	First decile	Second decile	Second quintile	Third quintile	Fourth quintile	Ninth decile	Tenth decile	Total	N Households
Wage income	48	48	42	51	67	71	74	56	3,669
Entrepreneurial income	1	1	1	2	3	3	7	2	3,669
Income from secondary employment	9	7	5	5	5	6	9	6	3,669
Pensions	30	37	49	38	22	16	7	31	3,669
Grants	0	0	0	0	0	0	0	0	3,669
Benefits	6	4	2	2	2	2	1	2	3,669
Alimony	1	1	1	0	1	0	0	1	3,669
Other	3	1	1	1	1	1	2	1	3,669
Net private assistance	9	6	2	3	2	-2	1	3	2,871

Table 10.3 Components of household income by income group. Percentage of income contributed by each source for those households who have that income source and percentage of households with that income source

		Wage income	Entrepreneurial income	Income from secondary employment	Pensions	Grants	Benefits	Alimony	Other	Net private assistance
First decile	% of income	72	53	39	64	27	23	29	37	24
	% of households	57	2	19	40	2	27	3	6	26
Second decile	% of income	70	47	33	68	11	13	24	26	16
	% of households	63	1	21	50	2	32	4	5	29
Second quintile	% of income	73	60	27	76	14	12	17	31	4
	% of households	55	1	16	61	1	21	3	3	30
Third quintile	% of income	75	68	25	68	14	8	20	36	8
	% of households	64	3	18	54	1	24	2	4	30
Fourth quintile	% of income	77	70	23	46	9	6	21	23	4
	% of households	81	4	20	44	1	25	4	5	38
Ninth decile	% of income	80	62	31	38	31	7	13	18	−4
	% of households	83	5	20	38	1	21	3	5	43
Tenth decile	% of income	82	71	27	24	6	3	13	32	2
	% of households	83	9	30	28	3	14	3	6	44
Total	% of income	76	66	28	61	15	10	20	29	6
	% of households	69	3	20	47	1	23	3	4	34

Fourth, there is a very small contribution made to household money income by other welfare benefits, notably unemployment benefit and child benefit which have shrunk to a derisory sum which is rarely paid (Tables 10.2 and 10.3). However, these benefits do make a significant contribution to the household incomes of those poor households who are fortunate enough to receive them, and are clearly progressive in making a proportionately greater contribution to the incomes of the poor than to the better-off households.

Fifth, secondary employment does not provide a substantial addition to the household budget overall, contributing only 6 per cent of total income when averaged across all households, but it does provide a significant addition to household income for those who have this source (Table 10.2). However, since many of these households are already comfortably off, reported secondary employment only reduces the incidence of poverty by about 2 per cent. If we assume that every household which appears to have undeclared secondary employment earns as much as those who declare such incomes, the effect is to increase the mean household income by about 10 per cent uniformly across all the income groups, reducing the incidence of poverty by about six percentage points; a significant, but not substantial contribution to the survival prospects of the Russian household. Twenty per cent of household heads said that such income was important for the subsistence of their household, 5 per cent that it was not very important and 8 per cent that it was not important, with 67 per cent saying that they had no such income.

Finally, private transfers make a substantial contribution to the income of quarter of the poorest 20 per cent of households which report such receipts (Tables 10.2 and 10.3). Indeed, a quarter of all household heads reported that the help of friends and relatives was important for the household's subsistence. However, richer households are even more likely than poorer ones to be involved in exchange networks – we have found in our analysis of a variety of different aspects of household survival that the density of social networks in which the individual is involved has a very powerful impact on the ability to get a job, to earn more money, to undertake secondary employment and so on. However, net private help was still sufficient to reduce the poverty count by eight percentage points – a more significant contribution than secondary employment and second in importance, after wage income, only to pensions. Moreover, monetary transfers are only a small part of the exchange networks in which our respondents are embedded. While 25 per cent of households gave money and 10 per cent made loans to others during the previous twelve months, 30 per cent gave food and 20 per cent gave goods. Two-thirds of all households reported their involvement in exchange relations, providing help to or receiving help from others, with about 25 per cent giving help but not receiving it, 20 per cent receiving help but not giving it and 20 per cent both giving and receiving help.

According to the RLMS data, people in need are becoming increasingly dependent on private transfers, which made up an average of 4.7 per cent of total money income of all households in 1993, 7.1 per cent in 1996 and 12 per cent in 1998.[11] In 1993 such transfers comprised 20 per cent of the money income of net recipients. In 1996 they comprised almost a third of the monetary income of the one in four households who reported receiving such transfers from friends and relatives, which was sufficient to raise the money incomes of one-third of these people above the poverty line. By 1998 net private transfers accounted for over half the money income (excluding sales of household property) of the quarter of households who received them, but by then money incomes were so low that the transfers took only 15 per cent of their recipients above the poverty line (my estimates from RLMS data). Private transfers are a part of the system of reciprocity between kin and, to a lesser extent, between friends rather than being an informal system of poverty relief. Thus, in the 1998 RLMS data, high income households were more likely than low income households to be beneficiaries of private transfers, and on average net recipient households in the top income decile received almost five times as much as did net recipients in the bottom income decile. The growing reliance of households on private transfers is an indication of the impact of the decline in money incomes on the domestic economy, but at the same time we can expect increasingly asymmetrical relationships to put such support networks under growing strain.[12] Any attempt to incorporate an evaluation of private transfers into assessment of eligibility for social assistance, as is proposed by the World Bank, is likely to be counter-productive in destroying the social networks which play such a vital role in household survival.

The 'reform' of the system of social support

In principle, the traditional system of social support largely remains intact, with the addition of unemployment insurance. However, this system is now in a state of virtual collapse as a result of the budget crisis of central government and regional and local administrations. This has been compounded by the chaotic transfer of assets and responsibilities from enterprises and from trade unions to municipalities which have neither the administrative capacity nor the funds to maintain such responsibilities. The result is that housing construction has ground to a halt, the maintenance of housing and municipal leisure and cultural facilities has stopped, the health service, while nominally free, is increasingly inaccessible to those who cannot pay (even for emergency services), while benefits are distributed haphazardly if at all.

Rather than rationalise the benefits system what in practice has happened has been that local offices have had to manage within the limits of the finance available. In the case of the payment of pensions, disability, child and unemployment benefits, this has led to the widespread non-payment of benefit or payment at reduced rates and/or in kind.

The key problem is that of the budget. The central issue is whether social policy should be reformed so as to reduce its cost to the limits allowed by the current budgetary system, as has been pressed by the World Bank and the IMF as a condition for their loans, or whether the fiscal system should be reformed in order to provide the funding needed to sustain an effective system of social protection. I will not go into the ethical and political aspects of the issue here, nor discuss any of the problems of fiscal reform, but simply look briefly at the practical aspects, using the data of our household survey to get some indication of the costs and benefits of various different welfare reforms, at least as regards the urban population.

Total local and national expenditure on social support is not high. In 1997, according to the official figures, the total cost of social policy to the consolidated budget and off-budget funds, including administration costs, amounted to 10.8 per cent of GDP, comprising budget spending on social policy (2.4 per cent) and spending of the pension fund (6.8 per cent), the social insurance fund (1.2 per cent) and the employment fund (0.3 per cent) (this compares with 19 per cent of GDP in Ukraine and 28 per cent of GDP in Poland devoted to public transfers in 1995 (Milanovic 1998)). According to Goskomstat estimates, social transfers had fallen from 17 per cent of household income in 1993–94 to 13 per cent in 1997, despite the considerable increase in poverty. The World Bank's 1994 poverty assessment noted that social benefits, apart from occupational pensions, were far too low to combat poverty, and since 1994 they have fallen even further in real terms. In 1997 the minimum wage was less than one-fifth of the subsistence minimum and the bottom grade of the public sector wage scale was even lower than this. The minimum pension was one quarter of the subsistence minimum, the highest rate of disability pension was only half the subsistence minimum and child benefit had fallen to 15 per cent of the subsistence minimum.

The most obvious first step in a realistic programme to reform the system of social protection is to make some attempt to restore the value of the social benefits paid to those categories of the population who cannot be expected to provide for themselves: children, the elderly, the chronic sick and disabled. The World Bank has proposed such a programme for Russia, driven primarily by fiscal considerations, the aim being to means-test benefits and move from fiscal to insurance-based financing with the introduction of a new system of rigorously means-tested social assistance to provide the social safety net. The World Bank's $800 million Social Protection Adjustment Loan, announced in June 1997, was designed to support the implementation of a comprehensive package of reforms approved by the Russian government in February 1997. On pensions, the reforms proposed a guaranteed minimum pension of 80 per cent of the subsistence minimum, adjusted for inflation, while shifting the burden of pension finance from the employer to the individual and from the state to the private sector. In relation to unemployment, the reforms proposed a greater degree of regional redistribution of the employment fund, an unemployment benefit of 20 per cent of the regional subsistence minimum (the present minimum benefit is equal to the minimum wage, which is approximately 20 per cent of the subsistence minimum but which is not adjusted to the regional cost of living) but with tighter eligibility conditions. Child allowances would be transformed from a universal entitlement to a form of social assistance, with benefits means-tested for children over three. Finally, sick pay, maternity and childcare benefits would be reviewed, with a cap placed on sick pay. Although all of these measures were agreed by Deputy Prime Minister Chubais on behalf of the Russian government at the beginning of June 1997, as a condition for the World Bank's extending their loan, not one had been through the Duma. When they were put to the Duma later in June, every single proposal was thrown out, except that to tax child benefit, most of which is not paid in any case. This was really an academic question since, with at least the tacit approval of the World Bank, the Russian government immediately spent the first $300 million tranche of the loan to pay off pension arrears and proposed to spend the remainder almost as fast on paying off wage arrears to teachers and health workers (Reuters 1.7.97, 7.7.97). Since then, there has been much talk, much spending of World Bank money, but no reform.

The overall effect of the World Bank's programme would be to reduce the already limited scale and coverage of categorical benefits and to put the main emphasis of social protection on a means-tested social assistance programme, despite the fact that its own Poverty Assessment for Russia concluded that means-testing was impractical (World Bank 1995). In order to try to identify the 'best' system the World Bank has financed three experimental schemes in Russia. Under all three of these schemes social assistance will be paid to households, not to individuals, and eligibility will be based not on actual income but on an inquisitorial assessment of potential income sources, including the sale or leasing of household assets, access to land and potential private transfers (Ovcharova 1997). First results of these experiments indicated that such schemes would substantially reduce the cost of social assistance not by relieving poverty but by sharply reducing the number of people securing assistance; in its first year of operation in the Komi Republic the number of recipients of social assistance fell by 80 per cent.

Building on the past

The alternative approach to poverty relief is to attempt to relieve as much poverty as possible by the allocation of income on the basis of categorical entitlements and minimum income guarantees which minimise the need for inquisitorial and punitive methods of assessment.[13] This can be supplemented by means-tested social assistance or poverty relief to mop up the remaining pockets of hardship. This represents an adaptation of the traditional system of social policy to the conditions of a market economy. Results of estimates of the cost and effectiveness of such policies for the population surveyed in our own project are shown in Table 10.4. Apart from the first column, the poverty line selected for the household is the subsistence minimum for those over 16 and 70 per cent of the subsistence minimum for those under 16. The mean income per head gives a simple indication of the cost of alternative policies, the distribution in relation to the subsistence minimum gives an indication of their benefits from the point of view of poverty relief. We take half the subsistence minimum as the criterion of severe poverty. The income measure used as the reference income in this example is the normal household income declared by the head of household.

The first columns of Table 10.4 show the costs and benefits of the present system of social protection by comparing the distribution of income and the mean income per head with the present system of benefits against those if no benefits at all were

Table 10.4 Percentage of households in poverty with different social policies

Percentage with income per head:	Present income. No weighting	Present income	No benefits	Pension only	Replace occupational by social pension	Replace occupational by social pension non-working only	Minimum pension at subsistence minimum	Existing pension + 50% child benefit	Minimum pension and child benefit	Pension + child benefit + minimum wage	Pension + child benefit + non-employment benefit	Everything
Less than half subsistence[a]	6.3	5.1	33.2	6.7	5.7	7.4	4.1	3.7	2.7	2.2	1.0	0.7
Below subsistence	29.8	26.6	20.0	28.2	23.0	24.0	20.6	25.6	18.1	16.2	16.5	13.8
Between subsistence and twice subsistence	44.5	43.9	30.2	44.6	51.0	50.2	53.7	48.1	55.9	57.6	58.5	61.1
More than twice subsistence	19.4	19.9	16.7	20.6	20.2	18.5	21.6	22.5	23.3	24.0	24.0	24.4
Mean income/head (roubles)	618	618	461	608	608	590	635	640	656	668	677	689

Notes

a   The subsistence level for all but the first column is calculated by weighting all children under 16 as 70 per cent of an adult, using the regional subsistence minima. The individual poverty count would be slightly higher in each case since larger households are more likely to be poor, particularly if they have more than one child.

In these models the pension and minimum wage are set at the subsistence minimum, child and non-employment benefit are set at 50 per cent of the subsistence minimum. The invalidity pension is treated along with the retirement pension for these purposes since there are relatively few people involved.

paid and if only pensions were paid. It can be seen that pensions comprise much the most significant component of the benefit system, as we would expect. Without any benefits one-third of households would be in extreme poverty and over half would be in poverty. The existing pension system takes over a quarter of households out of extreme poverty, it removes almost 20 per cent from poverty and it allows 4 per cent of households to move into relative comfort.

The World Bank, in all of its poverty assessments, makes great play of the fact that pensions are not efficiently targeted on the poor (Milanovic 1998, World Bank 1995) because the pension is earnings-related, because many people in receipt of a pension still work and because many pensioners live in households with wage-earners. Most people still regard their pension as an entitlement that they have earned through decades of hard labour, so as a 'deferred wage' rather than as a welfare benefit. Nevertheless, we can see that replacing the occupational pension by a social pension set at the level of the subsistence minimum does provide some improvement in the targeting of benefits, by coincidence at exactly the same cost. (Six per cent of those of pension age in our sample, most of whom are still working, do not appear to draw a pension. In our simulations we assume that these people will continue not to draw a pension.) If this is paid only to those who are not working, there is a saving of about 12 per cent on the pension bill, if we assume that nobody gives up work to retain their pension, but at the cost of an increase in poverty because so many older people are paid very low wages. It is very doubtful that such a change would be politically possible, and it is hardly worthwhile for what is a relatively small saving, particularly as many old people would give up their jobs to preserve their pension entitlement. On the other hand, raising the minimum pension to the level of the subsistence minimum, without changing any other entitlements, increases the pension bill for our sample population by 18 per cent. The cost across the whole country would be more because pensions paid to the rural population are much lower, but in total we can estimate that it would raise the cost of pensions from 6.8 per cent in 1997 to about 8–8.5 per cent of GDP, with quite a significant impact on the incidence of poverty.

The payment of child benefit at a rate of 50 per cent of the regional subsistence minimum would cost a little more than raising the minimum pension to the subsistence minimum, and, as we would expect, would turn out to be rather less well targeted on poverty, but would have a bigger impact on extreme poverty. Combining the upgrading of child benefit and of pensions shows that the impact of the two is reasonably complementary to one another.

The final two columns consider the impact of a minimum wage, set at the level of the subsistence minimum, and a non-employment benefit paid at the rate of 50 per cent of the subsistence minimum to all those below pension age who have no income from primary employment.[14] The minimum wage turns out not to be very expensive, since many of those on low pay are paid not far below the minimum, but it correspondingly does not have a major impact when added to child benefit and an uprated pension (although its impact is more substantial on its own). It has the advantage of having no immediate fiscal implications, unlike all the other reforms that we have considered. The payment of a benefit to the non-employed picks up well over half the households who remain in extreme poverty after the uprating of pensions and child benefit and is also complementary to a minimum wage in its impact.

This is only an indicative exercise, but the cost of this whole package of welfare reforms would amount to about 3 per cent of GDP, which would be matched by some savings on social assistance, increasing the welfare budget to a not unreasonable 13–14 per cent of GDP, while almost eliminating extreme poverty and cutting the overall poverty headcount by more than half. All of these benefit reforms would be easy to implement and administer, only the benefit to the non-employed involving any innovation, while massively reducing the administrative and financial burden imposed by any effective system of social assistance.[15] The cost of such measures is hardly unreasonable, even in the dire conditions in which Russia finds itself; in total they would only represent an increase in the fiscal cost of cash transfers to a level of those of Ukraine, less than Latvia and little more than half the rate in Poland (Milanovic 1998).

Conclusion

I argued at the beginning of this chapter that the idea of a household survival strategy distracts attention from the principal sources of household subsistence, which are waged employment and social transfers. We have seen that subsistence production and engagement in the informal economy make only a marginal contribution to household survival, tending more to diversify and increase the incomes of the more prosperous households than to lift the less fortunate out of poverty. Moreover, these are retrograde forms of economic activity which should by no means be encouraged by policy-makers. In particular, domestic subsistence agriculture is an extremely inefficient method of agricultural production and distribution whose persistence undermines the development of an agricultural market and so impedes the development of a more efficient system of commercial agriculture. The informal economy is similarly the domain of extremely inefficient forms of economic activity which provide unstable and insecure employment, in which illegal, unsafe and unhealthy working conditions are endemic, in which extortion and other criminal activity is rife and the expansion of which can only exacerbate the fiscal problems of the state, because of pervasive tax evasion in this sector. The priority should, therefore, not be to encourage the persistence and even expansion of such retrograde and unsustainable forms of employment as the solution to the crisis of household subsistence, but to encourage the regeneration of a modern economy and to renew the system of social support.

The World Bank has been pressing all the transition countries to 'reform' their pension and social welfare systems to reduce what is purported to be the excessive fiscal cost of social transfers. However, the fiscal cost of the existing system in Russia is not excessive, while our simulations suggest that even a system of income guarantees oriented to what is a very low subsistence minimum would not impose an excessive burden on the tax system. Whether or not the fiscal cost of a welfare system is excessive is not a technical question to be resolved by the World Bank but a matter for the political judgement of the population, expressed through the democratic system and in their recognition of the legitimacy of the fiscal system.

Notes

1 See, for example, the Letter of Intent sent by Prime Minister Chernomyrdin to the IMF on behalf of the Russian government (April 30, 1997, No. 1348p-P2), which was linked to the conditionality terms of the $800 million Social Protection Adjustment Loan approved by the World Bank on 25 June 1997.

2 The survey was conducted by the Moscow-based inter-regional Institute for Comparative Labour Relations Research (ISITO) in April–May 1998 as part of a project on 'new forms of employment and household survival strategies', funded by the British Department for International Development, within the framework of a larger project on 'employment restructuring and the formation of a labour market in Russia', funded by the Economic and Social Research Council, neither of which bodies is responsible for any of the views expressed in this chapter. The sample was a single-stage probability sample of 4,000 households in four Russian cities (Samara, Kemerovo, Syktyvkar and Lyubertsy, a satellite city of Moscow), drawn from the computerised databases of the city population. Details of the survey, sample evaluation and access to the data and working papers can be obtained from the project website, www.warwick.ac.uk/fac/soc/complabstuds/russia/.

3 I am grateful to VTsIOM for making some of their data available to me. The RLMS data is available for downloading from www.cpc.unc.edu. The recent HBS data is published in Goskomstat 1999a, Goskomstat 1999b, Goskomstat 1999c, Ministry of Labour and Social Development and Goskomstat Rossii 1997. The results reported here are developed in more detail in a forthcoming book, *Making Ends Meet: the Survival Strategies of Russian Households*, to be published by Edward Elgar.

4 An unpublished World Bank 'Labour Market Concept Paper' prepared in Spring 2000 is typical in declaring that 'self-employment income [is] now playing a dominant role in household income', comprising a 'much higher share of GDP in Russia, than in CEE countries'. The authorities cited in support of this assertion are not included in the references at the end of the paper!

5 This leads to massive discrepancies between the income and expenditure estimates, which are then reconciled by Goskomstat estimating savings and financial investments and purchases of foreign currency at between 15 and 25 per cent of income. According to the Goskomstat macroeconomic estimates for the fourth quarter of 1996, the latter supposedly accounted for 4 per cent and 19 per cent of money income respectively, but in the budget survey data for the same period net savings amounted to a total of 1 per cent, including 0.1 per cent accounted for by net purchases of foreign currency!

6 There is also the question of the extent to which secondary incomes are available to the household budget. Culturally, there is a fairly well-established understanding in Russia that secondary earnings are at the disposal of the individual. This practice would appear to be confirmed by the fact that, in the ISITO survey, in households with declared secondary earnings, but not in those without secondary employment, the declared individual incomes of household

members are significantly higher (by almost 20 per cent) than the household income reported by the head of household. This would imply that on average only about a third of individual secondary earnings (of both men and women) are at the disposal of the household.

7   Even the authors of one of the very few serious publications on the subject reproduce without question the typical view that 'the majority of the population now produces its own food supply to a considerable extent' (Seeth *et al*. 1998: 1611).

8   It is important to stress that this analysis relates to urban households: domestic agricultural production is more significant for rural dwellers and the inhabitants of small towns. These results are replicated in the analysis of all of the available data sources. Some surveys (RLMS and the HBS since 1997) include the imputed monetary value of agricultural production (at local market prices) as a part of the household income. This can be very misleading since very little of this production is sold and it is likely that a significant proportion does not contribute to household subsistence because it is given to others, used as seed or goes to waste.

9   According to RLMS, social transfers had amounted to about 18 per cent of household money income in 1996 (30 per cent of the bottom quintile and 40 per cent of the second quintile), which is fairly close to Goskomstat's budget survey data which reported that social transfers amounted to an average 16 per cent of household money income (25 per cent of the bottom decile income group, 22 per cent of the second decile) in the fourth quarter of 1996. As a result of non-payment, in 1996 11 per cent and in 1998 6 per cent of households reported a total money income to RLMS of zero in the previous month. These cases are omitted from the analysis in this section.

10   By the time of this survey pensions were being paid more regularly. In the RLMS survey in the autumn of 1998 85 per cent of pensioners had been paid the previous month.

11   According to the Goskomstat data such private transfers accounted for 4 per cent of total money income and about 9 per cent of the money income of the lowest decile, those in extreme poverty, in the fourth quarter of 1996.

12   This is one of the most seriously under-researched dimensions of the transition. For an analysis of the rather unsatisfactory first phase RLMS data see Cox *et al*. (1995). For a more detailed analysis of the ISITO data see Yakubovich (1999), which has been published in Russian in Kabalina and Clarke (1999).

13   Anders Aslund and Richard Layard, strong supporters of the course of radical reform, noted in 1993 that 'the existing schemes can quite well handle each type of poverty, and a new means-tested benefit would be impossible to administer' (Aslund and Layard 1993: 58). The World Bank at that time also considered that the uprating of some benefits, the addition of a social safety net and the rationalisation of welfare finance could alleviate poverty at the cost of about 3.0 per cent of GDP (World Bank 1994, Vol. 1: 70).

14   Only 10 per cent of the ILO-defined unemployed are entitled to benefit under the present system. Realistically, it is impossible in the Russian context to distinguish the 'deserving' from the 'undeserving' unemployed: in our survey exactly the same percentage of employed, registered unemployed and unregistered unemployed are engaged in secondary activity. We model a universal non-employment benefit as an example only. In practice such a benefit could be more efficiently targeted on those population categories who find it hardest to get work; for example, by providing more grants for young people undergoing education, by providing

more generous and broader maternity and childcare benefits, by providing grants for those with lower educational levels who choose to undergo retraining and by providing benefits for those who choose to retire early.

15 It is not possible realistically to model the impact of such benefit reforms on incentives. However, the willingness of people to continue to work for years on end with low or no pay in no or low productivity jobs has been a major barrier to the restructuring of the economy. This implies on the one hand that not many are likely to leave work because of the small increase in their benefits, but on the other that there is a strong case to be made for encouraging the low paid to leave work.

References

Aslund, A. and Layard, R. (1993) *Changing the Economic System in Russia*, London: Pinter.

Chant, S. (1991) *Women and Survival in Mexican Cities: Perspectives on Gender, Labour Markets and Low-income households*, Manchester and New York: Manchester University Press.

Clarke, S. (1998) *Household Employment Decisions*, mimeo, available from www.warwick.ac.uk/facs/soc/complabstuds/russia.

Clarke, S. (1999a) *New Forms of Employment and Household Survival Strategies in Russia*, Coventry: Centre for Comparative Labour Studies.

Clarke, S. (1999b) 'Poverty in Russia', *Problems of Economic Transition* 42 (5): 5–55.

Clarke, S. (1999c) *The Formation of a Labour Market in Russia*, Cheltenham: Edward Elgar.

Clarke, S., Varshavskaya, L., Alasheev, S. and Karelina, M. (2000) 'The myth of the urban peasant', *Work, Employment and Society* 14 (3): 481–99.

Cox, D., Zereria, E. and Jimenez, E. (1995) *Family Safety Nets During Economic Transition: A Study of Inter-Household Transfers in Russia*, Washington DC: World Bank.

Crow, G. (1989) 'The use of the concept of "strategy" in recent sociological literature', *Sociology* 23 (February): 1–24.

Goskomstat (1999a) 'Osnovnye pokazateli vyborochnogo obsledovaniya byudzhetov domashnikh khozyaistv po Rossiiskoi federatsii v 1998 godu', *Statisticheskii byulleten'* 1 (51) (March 1999): 9–182.

Goskomstat (1999b) 'Osnovnye pokazateli vyborochnogo obsledovaniya byudzhetov domashnikh khozyaistv po Rossiiskoi federatsii v 1998 godu', *Statisticheskii byulleten'* 5 (55) (June 1999): 49–182.

Goskomstat (1999c) 'Osnovnye pokazateli vyborochnogo obsledovaniya byudzhetov domashnikh khozyaistv po Rossiiskoi federatsii vo II kvartale 1998–1999 godu', *Statisticheskii byulleten'* 11 (61) (November 1999): 113–88.

ISEPN RAN (1998) *Rossiya 1997, sotsial'no-demograficheskaya situatsiya*, Moscow: ISEPN, RAN.

Johnson, S., Kaufmann, D. and Ustenko, O. (1996) 'Household survival strategies', *Ukrainian Economic Review* II, 3: 112–6.

Kabalina, V. and Clarke, S. (1999) *Zanyatost' i povedenie domokhozyaistv: adaptatsiya k usloviyam perekhodnoi ekonomiki Rossii*, Moscow: Rossiiskaya politicheskaya entsiklopediya (ROSSPEN).

Klopov, E. (1996) 'Vtorichnaya zanyatost' kak forma sotsial'no-trudovoi mobil'nosti', in L. Gordon, V. Gimpel'son, E. Klopov and V. Komarovskii (eds) *Trudovye peremeshcheniya i adaptatsiya rabotnikou* Moscow: IMEMO.

Milanovic, B. (1998) *Income, Inequality and Poverty during the Transition from Planned to Market Economy*, Washington DC: World Bank.

Ministry of Labour and Social Development and Goskomstat Rossii (1997) *Monitoring of the Socio-Economic Potential of Families for the Fourth Quarter of 1996. Statistical Report*, Moscow.

Morgan, D.H. (1989) 'Strategies and sociologists: A comment on Crow', *Sociology* 23 (February): 25–9.

Nelson, M.K. and Smith, J. (1998) 'Economic restructuring, household strategies and gender: A case study of a rural community', *Feminist Studies* 24 (1): 79–114.

Ovcharova, L. (1997) 'The definition and measurement of poverty in Russia', in S. Clarke (ed.) *Poverty in Transition*. Coventry: Centre for Comparative Labour Studies, University of Warwick.

Pahl, R.E. (1984) *Divisions of Labour*, Oxford: Basil Blackwell.

Rodgers, G. (1989) *Urban Poverty and the Labour Market: Access to Jobs and Incomes in Asian and Latin American Cities*, Geneva: ILO.

Seeth, H.T., Chachnov, S., Surinov, A. and von Braun, J. (1998) 'Russian poverty: Muddling through economic transition with garden plots', *World Development* 26 (9): 1611–23.

Tinker, I. (1990) *Persistent Inequalities*, Oxford: Oxford University Press.

Voronkov, V. (1995) 'Poverty in modern Russia: Strategies of survival and strategy of research', in K. Segbers and S. de Spiegeleire (eds) *Post-Soviet Puzzles: Mapping the Political Economy of the Former Soviet Union*, Berlin: Nomos Verlagsgesellschaft, pp. 23–38.

World Bank (1994) *Russia: Social Protection During Transition and Beyond*, Washington, DC: Human Resources Division, Country Departments III, Europe and Central Asia Region, World Bank.

World Bank (1995) *Poverty in Russia: An Assessment*, Washington, DC: World Bank.

Yakubovich, V. (1999) *Economic Constraints and Social Opportunities: Participation in Informal Support Networks of Russian Urban Households*, Department of Sociology, Stanford University, mimeo.

Yaroshenko, S. (1999) 'Domashnie khozyaistva v usolviyakh perekhodnoi ekonomiki v Rossii: Tipy obespecheniya pitaniya v gorodskikh sem'yakh', in V. Kabalina and S. Clarke (eds) *Zanyatost' i povedenie domokhozyaistv*. Moscow: Rossiiskaya politicheskaya entsiklopediya (ROSSPEN), pp. 156–171.

11 Economic strategies of surviving post-socialism

Changing household economies and gender divisions of labour in the Bulgarian transition

Mieke Meurs

Introduction

Since 1989, East Central European governments have pursued policies to expand markets and shrink the state. According to the neo-liberal model, these policies should result in a significant re-allocation of resources into new, higher productivity uses and, in turn, economic growth. At the household level, the high levels of unemployment and collapsing real wages which have accompanied economic restructuring are expected to provoke the expected re-allocation of labour to new activities. Such changes are central to the outcome of the so-called transition process since, if markets are indeed to become the dominant economic mechanism, households as well as firms must re-allocate resources in response to emerging market signals. But the extent to which households are likely to do so has become the subject of growing debate.

Emerging critical approaches have emphasised that rural populations are not simply passive recipients of state actions (Bridger and Pine 1998). Others have highlighted the limited capacity of the post-socialist state to guide household behaviour effectively in line with market-building objectives (Burawoy and Verdery 1999, Smith 2000), and the existence of important variations in households' abilities to adapt to changing macro circumstances (Smith 2000). These approaches emphasise that households have considerable autonomy in formulating responses to macro changes and that local resources upon which households draw may lend themselves more often to non-market than market uses. The non-market activities of households may, in turn, undermine the market orientation of state policy. In Poland, for example, the private farmers who had long demanded greater market freedoms have responded to free market policies by withdrawing resources from market production, shifting these instead into subsistence agriculture. At the same time, they have become important political opponents of free market policies (Zbierski-Salameh 1999).

In this chapter, I examine patterns of household activity in the Rhodope region of Bulgaria (see Figure 13.1, p. 247) over the period 1986–1996. The Rhodope region is an important contrast to the more frequently studied urban households (see Smith 2001 and Ch. 12, Clarke 1999, Walker 1998), which tended to be closely integrated with the industrialised national economy under state socialism. The examination of households in the rural Rhodope region provides further evidence of the complexity of the relationship between state policy and resource allocation by households since 1989. In particular, the case highlights the important influence of the degree and form of prior integration into the national economy on household responses to macro changes.

Like many rural households in the late-industrialising socialist economies, households in the Rhodope region were only partially integrated into the national, centrally-planned economy prior to 1989. These semi-proletarianised households 'stood on two legs' in the socialist period, depending on both paid labour and subsistence agriculture for reproduction (Figure 11.1). Industry in marginal regions like the Rhodope collapsed particularly quickly and completely in response to macro policy changes after 1989 (Begg *et al.* 1999), bringing the effects of these changes to bear on the vast majority of households. At the same time, however, the limited integration into the national economy meant that other activities continued almost unaffected. Rhodope household economies are thus better characterised as having been *truncated* by the new conditions, than as *adapting* to these. While prior uses of some resources have become impossible, re-allocation of these resources to new activities has been very limited.

This is not to suggest that Rhodope households have found a comfortable means of weathering the post-socialist economic decline. Like rural households from outside the Rhodopes whose members were interviewed during the World Bank's 'Consultations with the Poor' (World Bank 1999), members of Rhodope households emphasise the economic and psychological loss which has accompanied the disintegration of their links with formal employment and the national economy. But at the same time, households report that they are not starving, and this lack of desperation allows such households to avoid the most drastic sorts of re-allocation of resources towards markets, such as prostitution and other types of illegal activity, which have become increasingly widespread among the urban poor in transition economies.

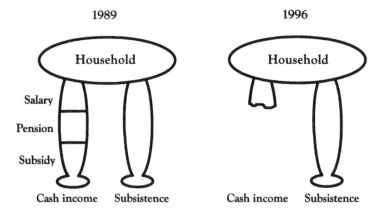

Figure 11.1 The structure of household economies in Bulgaria.

To date, the discussion of household responses or adaptations to macro changes has paid little attention to the implications of these for the gender divisions of labour.¹ The Rhodope experience examined here, however, suggests that impacts may differ significantly by gender. Even in the Rhodope case, where households appear to have engaged in very little *overall* re-allocation of resources, significant re-allocations can be seen between male and female members of households. So, whereas literature to date has highlighted the way that households, extended families, and other networks pool resources and co-operate to overcome economic hardship (Smith 2001) evidence from the Rhodopes suggests that activities during transition may also provoke new conflicts within these groups.

Perspectives on post-socialist households

Initially, household behaviour during economic restructuring was framed as responses to state actions and the economic dislocations resulting from those actions (Bridger and Pine 1998, Seeth *et al*. 1998). More recent work critically examines the premise that households *respond* to macro-structural changes. Burawoy and Verdery (1999) emphasise that such an understanding ignores two important features of the macro environment. First, macro structures of the state collapsed to a great extent in 1989, leaving significant room for autonomous manoeuvre on the part of households – manoeuvre guided by the resources and institutions available to the household at the micro level. Secondly, macro policies are likely to generate a plenitude of unintended consequences, which will themselves influence household behaviour. In this case, changes at the household level are not responses to neo-liberal policy itself but are responses to its unintended consequences in the micro environment. Thus household adaptations in the period after 1989 may have little to do with the specific goals of state policy. Instead, the adaptations must be understood as 'autonomous' (Burawoy and Verdery 1999: 2) actions which may have unexpected impacts on the emerging structures. As chapters in the volume edited by Burawoy and Verdery (1999) show, in many cases the adaptations involve non-market behaviour and shifts in resources away from market transactions (Woodruff 1999, Zbierski-Salameh 1999, Creed 1999).

Smith (2000) also argues that the marketisation process in transition economies is accompanied by significant non-market economic activity at the household level. Since non-market activities develop over the course of the transition and are not just holdovers from a previous system, the transition should thus be understood not as a transition to capitalism but as a transition to a plural economy, consisting of both capitalist and non-capitalist activities. Smith also emphasises the impact of differential access to resources on household behaviour. Surprisingly, it is the households with the most access to emerging (labour) markets which also engage in the most non-market activity (see also Ch. 10). Using a World Bank household survey, Smith finds that households with poor labour market access also tend to have the least access to resources needed for non-market activity. For these households, (labour) resources 'freed' by labour market adjustments could not be readily re-allocated by households to other uses, market or otherwise, due to a lack of complementary resources (see also Ch. 10).

My argument builds on the above points. I begin by noting that many socialist households, especially in rural areas, were far from being fully proletarianised prior to 1989. Like classic semi-proletarian households, they depended on cash inflows from employment (in this case from the state sector), but they also remained heavily engaged in non-socialist activities of simple reproduction. These households might be thought of as 'standing on two legs', as shown in Figure 11.1.

This situation limited the impact of the collapse of the socialist state on many rural households, and particularly on those households in more marginal regions such as the Rhodopes. While cash inflows from employment and the state have been very radically reduced, the second 'leg' of the household remains in place. Few resources have been re-allocated to expanding agricultural activities. Rather, with the disappearance of other activities, the subsistence activities have taken on greater relative importance in the household economy. The increased reliance on simple reproduction is thus not an 'adaptation' driven by new circumstances. Instead, the household economies have simply been 'truncated' – the employment leg has been severed or significantly reduced.

The Rhodope case emphasises the importance of regional context for understanding household behaviour in the context of macro change. Some (especially urban) households, more fully integrated into the socialist economy, will find their economic activities much more strongly affected by the macro changes. At the same time, rural households in land-rich or peri-urban areas may face many more market-oriented adjustment opportunities than those in more peripheral regions. The specific outcomes are important for understanding likely feedbacks into state policy.

The Bulgarian experience

The data used in this section come from two surveys carried out by the Institute of Sociology of the Bulgarian Academy of Sciences. The first, a representative national survey carried out in 1986, was undertaken in conjunction with the national census, includes about 280 Rhodope households, and was funded by the Bulgarian government. The second, carried out in 1996, includes about 85 Rhodope households drawn randomly from the 1986 list and was funded through a grant from the US National Science Foundation.

The Rhodope region in the south east of Bulgaria is geographically marginalised, lying over the Rhodope mountains from the urban centres of Sofia and Plovdiv and along the Greek and Turkish borders (see Figure 13.1, p. 247). Under central planning, the region was an important source of tobacco, which was exported to earn hard currency for the socialist state, and in the 1970s the region benefited from important investments in apparel and electronics assembly firms (Begg *et al.* 1999, see also Ch. 13). These investments helped keep tobacco-producing households in the region, by providing jobs for the families of tobacco workers and for the workers themselves in off season. The region is ethnically diverse, with significant populations of ethnically Turkish Bulgarians and of Bulgarian Muslims.

Household economies under socialism

Prior to 1989, even the marginal Rhodope region was characterised by high rates of labour force participation. Of the surveyed population, 82 per cent of working age men (15–60 years) and 69 per cent of working age women (15–55 years) were employed in the formal labour market. Well over half of employed women worked in the agricultural sector, with the service sector and industry comprising about equal shares of the remainder of female employment (21 per cent). Men were less concentrated in agriculture (48 per cent of employed, working age men). In addition to working in industry (21 per cent) and services (16 per cent), men also worked in construction and as Communist Party cadre (Table 11.1).

Employment was thus one mainstay of the household economy under central planning. The vast majority (71 per cent) of Rhodope households had at least one employed household member, and households which did not have anyone currently employed received state pensions, earned by household members in previous employment. Many of the Rhodope households, which are typically two- or three-generation in composition, received cash income through both earnings and pensions; to this, a number of households added income from seasonal work on state-run collective farms (Table 11.2).

At the same time, nearly all households (92 per cent) supplemented their state earnings with agricultural and livestock production on 'private support plots', averaging 0.3 ha (Table 11.2). These plots supplied the majority of food consumed by the household. Indeed, rural households had little choice but to engage in extensive subsistence production. State shops in the countryside offered few products (mainly staples such as macaroni and salt). Central planners expected households to supply their own milk, cheese, meat, and vegetables, and the households did so. Home production made up an estimated 34 per cent of total income in 1990 (NIS 1991).[2]

Table 11.1 Sector of employment by sex, working age Rhodope population, 1986, 1996 (per cent of total employment)

Sector	Men		Women	
	1986	*1996*	*1986*	*1996*
Agriculture	48	16	64	25
Industry	21	16	16	11
Services	16	36	17	53
Construction	9	16	0	0
Forestry	0	9	0	4
Party cadre	5	0	0	0
Independent	1	7	0	7

Source: Survey Data, 1986; 1996.

Table 11.2 Sources of income, rural Rhodope households, 1986, 1996 (per cent of households)

Income Source	1986	1996
Salary	71	45
Pension	55	64
Own agriculture (cash and kind)	92	93
Own agriculture (cash)	12	63
Other private production	2	6
Other agricultural labour/rent[a]	55	12

Source: Survey Data, 1986; 1996.

Note
[a]   In 1986, these earnings were mainly from seasonal labour on collective farms.

Households were also permitted to sell surplus private production to the state or on 'free' peasant markets, but few did so. Only 12 per cent of households reported earning cash income from agricultural plots in 1986. More common were small-scale, in-kind exchanges with local collective farms. Households often exchanged production, especially of livestock and livestock products, for inputs into the households' subsistence production – seeds, fertiliser, feed for livestock, or young animals. Together, the subsistence production and exchange with collective farms provided a major source of support for rural households. The household economies thus rested firmly on two legs – state employment and eventual pensions produced cash income and private plots provided a significant share of food (Figure 11.1).

Work on the private plots was shared fairly evenly by men and women. In 1986, 8.5 per cent of men interviewed reported that they alone cared for the household plot, while 7.5 per cent of women reported that they took full responsibility for this activity. Most men and women reported sharing the work. Time budget data collected separately reveal a similar pattern.[3] Men working on the plots reported spending an average of slightly more than two hours a day there in 1990, while women working on plots reported just over 1.5 hours (NIS 1990). A greater share of livestock tending was done by women, however. In 1986, 7 per cent of men reported full responsibility for livestock and 9 per cent of men claimed no participation in this activity, whereas 9 per cent of women claimed full respon-sibility and only 1 per cent of women reported no participation. Livestock was the main source of cash agricultural income for households, and as a result, women were more likely than men to report a secondary income from household agriculture in 1986.

Household economies in post-socialism

From one perspective, the macro structural transformation after 1989 was particularly intense in rural areas. Rural industries collapsed quickly (Pickles and Begg 2000), due to their lack of a strong political base in top management and, in some cases, to the high transport costs and other locational problems they faced. As a result, in the Rhodope *okrug* (region) of Smolen, where comprehensive local data are available, employment fell 35 per cent from 1989–1996, compared to a 21 per cent fall in the nation as a whole (TSB 1994: 30). Agricultural employment fell even more rapidly. While privatisation remains minimal in Bulgaria even after ten years of reform, collective farms were quickly dissolved. Land was returned in small parcels to previous owners or their heirs, all other collective farm assets were liquidated, and workers were dismissed. In Smolen, in 1996, reported employment in agriculture fell by 90 per cent (TSB 1994: 30, NIS 1994). The comprehensive agricultural services which collective farms had provided to household production, including tilling of land, veterinary services and sometimes even the working of 'household' plots, were discontinued. Other support from the central state also declined, as the value of pensions, child payments, and educational stipends fell. At the same time, all restrictions on private production, prices and trading were lifted, as were most restrictions on export. It would be hard to imagine a greater change in macro structures.

At the household level, the impact of these changes is mainly seen in a very radical decline in formal employment in the Rhodope. Agricultural employment showed the largest collapse. Whereas 82 per cent of working age men and 69 per cent of working age women were employed in 1986, only 28 per cent of working age men and 19 per cent of working age women reported employment in 1996 (Table 11.3). Industrial employment also declined, falling from 21 per cent of employed men and 16 per cent of employed women to 16 per cent and 11 per cent of employed men and women, respectively. The service sector saw an increased share of the declining number of jobs (Table 11.1).

This change, of course, resulted in a significant decline in cash income generated by salaries. The share of households receiving cash income from salaries declined from 71 per cent in 1986, to only 45 per cent a decade later. In 1996, more households relied on pensions (64 per cent of households compared to 55 per cent in 1986), sales of private agricultural production (63 per cent of households compared to 12 per cent), and other private production (6 per cent compared to 2 per cent) to provide cash income (Table 11.2).

Table 11.3 Employment status of Rhodope working age women and men, 1986, 1996 (per cent)

Status	1986		1996	
	Men	*Women*	*Men*	*Women*
Employed	82	69	28	19
Self-employed			1	0
Own agriculture only			15	20
Pensioner	13	25	25	26
Not employed	2	4	12	16
Studying full time	3	2	19	19

Source: Survey Data, 1986; 1996.

The change in employment status was accompanied by other declines in cash flows to households. Unemployed workers and school leavers must report to the labour bureau monthly, in person, to receive unemployment benefits, child payments and health insurance. But in interviews, a number of households reported that they no longer make the trip to the labour bureau. When contrasted with the minimal benefit payments and futility of the job search, the cost of round trip bus tickets to a neighbouring village or municipal centre seems excessive. As a result, sources of household support that continue to be available in principle, have in fact also been discontinued.

There is little evidence, however, of significant innovation or adaptation in the face of the declining employment and state support and new opportunities for household activity. As salaried employment disappeared and agricultural land and other assets were privatised, rural households did expand agricultural production. But this expansion is minimal and does not represent a significant re-allocation of resources 'freed' by unemployment. In 1996, 93 per cent of households kept livestock, compared to about 85 per cent in 1986, and 97 per cent of Rhodope households cultivated an agricultural plot, farming an average of 0.46 ha, compared to 92 per cent farming an average of 0.30 ha in 1986. This is, of course, more than a 50 per cent increase in the average area of land farmed, but it hardly represents a large-scale shift of resources from the state sector into family farming. Further, only a few households entered into new areas of agricultural production or shifted out of old ones in response to radically shifting relative prices.

Of course, this does not mean that households engaged in no adaptation to the new situation. Nineteen per cent of households earned some income from new forms of private, non-agricultural production in 1996, and the share of households producing some agricultural products for sale rose more than five times. Indeed, a few households expanded the amount of land they used for agricultural production to as much as 1.6 ha. But the majority of household agricultural activity appears to be a continuation of subsistence activity in which the household has been engaged for decades.

Households produce small quantities of a variety of products needed for subsistence – 38 per cent of households met more than three-quarters of their food needs from own production in 1996, while another 33 per cent met between one-half and three-quarters. To meet their most urgent needs for cash income (electric bills, bus tickets, land taxes) and to barter for products they cannot produce themselves, households have begun to grow and market more of those products which are most readily exchanged. In interviews, households reported using their limited cash earnings to obtain only foods they could not produce, such as oil and sugar and bartering potatoes for flour and oil. Replicating a pre-1989 practice, some of the purchasers of household production offer reduced-price goods in exchange. One household reported that the dairy to which it delivers the excess milk from its two cows offers them a discount on purchases of butter and cheese.

Significant expansion of the subsistence 'leg' of the household economy was not a real option for most households after 1989. For one thing, especially in the mountainous Rhodope region, households own only small plots of land, and since each household depends on its land for survival, little additional land is available for rent. Secondly, the Rhodope region is relatively isolated, with poor access to urban markets. Thirdly, as I have written elsewhere, the transaction costs involved in organising a private, commercial farm are large (Meurs 2001). Households often consist mainly of elderly members, incapable of heavy farm work, and households own few machines. Weak development of input and credit markets makes it difficult for households to adjust resources to make a viable farm, and the domination of distribution networks by a few large firms makes profit margins minimal in any case. As one member of a rural household from outside the Rhodope region described it: 'This year we have had almost everything to eat. If the prices were fair, I would have rather sold it instead of having it myself – my son-in-law has a pot belly as big as mine' (World Bank 1999: 14).[4]

Unable to re-allocate resources freed from state firms and collective farms, household economies are increasingly limited to subsistence production. Of course, the extent of 'truncation' of household economies varies. Some households have simply shifted more weight onto their subsistence 'leg', and continued to rely also on (often small and uncertain) earnings in the formal labour market – salaries from private apparel firms, the state sector, or migratory construction labour. But a significant number of other households have lost their link to the national economy and learned to balance on only one leg. One Rhodope woman from the village of Kominiga noted the advantage of having this leg: 'In the village one lives more easily. We can't complain – we'll grow everything, we'll raise livestock – and we'll at least have food'. Still, the shift from industrial society to primitive agriculture is obviously extremely difficult for the Rhodope population. People refer to the loss of employment and the civilised accoutrements which accompanied it under socialism – vacation, broad social contacts, culture – as 'going wild' (World Bank 1999).

The impact of change on gender divisions of labour

While the macro structural changes have not been accompanied by significant re-allocation of household resources in the Rhodopes, they do appear to be associated with a significant redistribution of labour by gender. Here I will examine only changes in the activity of working age men and women, since these seem subject to the greatest post-socialist adjustments.

First, as was seen earlier, a much greater share of women than men have moved out of formal employment.[5] In 1996, only 19 per cent of working age women in the surveyed households reported employment, compared to 28 per cent of working age men (Table 11.3). Women in the Rhodope region were particularly disadvantaged by the dissolution of the collective farms, where 64 per cent of surveyed women had been employed in 1986, and by their weak relative position on those farms, where they worked predominantly in unskilled positions – as field hands and in dairies. When the collective farms were dissolved in 1992, livestock holdings were liquidated. New agricultural co-operatives were less likely to form in the Rhodopes than in other places, and where they did form they have preferred to rely on casual, seasonal labour for field work. Current co-operative staff thus consist mainly of skilled workers – tractor drivers, agronomists and a manager – who are most often male. As a result of this reorganisation, the share of employed women working in agriculture fell from 64 per cent in 1986 to 25 per cent in 1996, and the share of employed men working in that sector fell from 48 per cent to 16 per cent (Table 11.1).

Women were also more likely than men to lose industrial jobs. Whereas only 16 per cent of interviewed women held industrial jobs in 1986, 36 per cent of unemployed women had worked in that sector. Twenty-one per cent of men had worked in industry, while 26 per cent of unemployed men come from that sector. Women who continue to report employment work mainly in commerce and services (including government) (53 per cent), which are also important sources of male employment (36 per cent).

Second, faced with unemployment, men and women have sought new employment in different ways. The majority of both women and men reported to the local labour bureau; men and women also used family and other local contacts to gain employment to a lesser but equal extent. But men were more likely than women to search through other official channels, including local government officials, unions, and state firms. Women were much more likely to seek work directly at new private firms (often cafés). Most importantly, women were more likely than men to report doing nothing to find work. With more men than women finding or keeping formal employment, a greater share of women report helping out on the family's agricultural plot as their main occupation (20 per cent of working age women).[6] Only 15 per cent of working age men reported this as their main occupation (Table 11.3).

So as women have shifted out of the labour market, their work is increasingly limited to the private plot. Women's agricultural work is not solely in the reproductive sphere, however. As was the case prior to 1989, women were more likely than men to report cash income from agricultural products. Of the significant sources of cash income from agriculture – livestock, tobacco and potatoes – both tobacco and potato production were carried out mainly by women. Surprisingly, livestock production no longer appears to be mainly a female job. In over half of households, livestock work is now done mainly by men.

The impact on gender relations within households of women's decreasing employment and increasing focus on (mainly subsistence) agricultural production has yet to be properly evaluated. It is unlikely that this represents an end to the 'double burden' of outside employment and housework, since household plots are often fairly distant from living quarters. Feminist economic theory would suggest that the double burden might even increase. As women's income increasingly comes from household agriculture where multiple family members work, women may lose bargaining power relative to men, who are more likely to bring home an income which they can claim as their own (Roldan 1988, Blumberg 1988). In recent interviews, women did report feeling a particularly strong decline in status as a result of the loss of employment. Their greater relative activity in the informal and subsistence economies may be an attempt to recoup that lost status (World Bank 1999: 90).

One way to examine changes in the relative contributions and bargaining power of men and women is to examine data on the division of household domestic tasks. If changes in women's employment status erode their bargaining position, this may make it harder to distribute housework to male household members. It is thus surprising that, compared to 1986, both working age and post-working age women report doing a significantly smaller share of housework (measured on a four-point scale from 'I do all of the task myself' to 'I do none of it'), and large numbers of women (10–20 per cent, depending on the task) reported that they did not participate at all. Men do not report doing more housework, however, and children report only minimal levels of helping at tasks in either year.

How can these responses be understood? Some of the change may be unrelated to the changing structure of the household economy, and may simply reflect gradual progress in an on-going process toward sharing the burden of household work across the sexes. Another possible interpretation is that with multiple unemployed members in households there is more general sharing of housework. In this case, might men continue to report only 'helping' but women would no longer report that they do the task alone or even mainly. Alternatively, perhaps less housework is being done, as households spend more time in subsistence production, barter, transport and other survival activities.

Further study of the impact of labour market changes on household divisions of labour is clearly needed. These preliminary data suggest that, like other aspects of the transition, its gender aspects are complex. Contrary to some expectations, women's decreased relative access to formal employment does not appear to have resulted in increased specialisation in traditional domestic duties. On the other hand, men's falling employment levels have not resulted in increased reported participation in household work from their very low initial levels. For women more than men, work is increasingly limited to household agricultural and subsistence production. But although men also work in household agriculture, women report the main responsibility for cash crops.

Household members are renegotiating gender divisions of paid and unpaid labour, housework and agricultural work, even as they appear to do little to adjust overall productive activities. Thus whereas the recent emphasis on household strategies tends to highlight the collectivist nature of household and extended family activities in the context of macro changes, this evidence reminds us that the burdens of shocks to households can be shared among members in many ways (Folbre 1982). The outcome of intra-household negotiations will have its own impact on the overall course of the ongoing transformation.

Conclusions

I have argued that the economic activity of rural Rhodope households in 1996 appears to be best characterised as the persistence of activity which was not socialist and is not capitalist, but is geared toward simple reproduction of the household. Because rural Rhodope households were only weakly integrated into structures of central planning prior to 1989, the collapse of state structures left them with both a solid (if limited) economic 'leg' to stand on and limited ability to re-allocate resources freed from the state sector into new activities. While agricultural activity has expanded slightly since 1986, the main change in the household economy is the simple loss of salaried employment – what I refer to as a 'truncation' of the household economy.

Households have found few appealing ways to re-allocate labour freed from the state sector. At the same time, their access to subsistence allows them to ignore the most desperate, market-based options. Many households thus lie outside the state-sponsored transition to markets. They are, instead, part of a significant devolution to the persisting subsistence economy. Importantly, for Rhodope households this is driven by the limited integration of the region into the state economy prior to 1989. The regional concentration of large numbers of households falling outside the expected market-driven re-allocation of resources will heighten their impact on the political and economic[7] course of the ongoing transformation.

While apparently continuing a long-standing tradition of subsistence production, Rhodope households are also engaged in significant re-allocations of labour along gender lines. Whereas men and women previously shared paid and subsistence labour relatively equally, the past decade has witnessed a clear shift in gender roles, with women increasing their relative engagement in household-based agricultural production and decreasing their engagement in the paid labour force. Preliminary evidence suggests that this has not resulted in a significant loss of bargaining power for women within households. But the changes recall the feminist critique that research based on the household as a unit of analysis may limit our understanding of the micro aspects of macro structural changes.

Notes

1 See Bridger (1998) and Pine (1998) for some exceptions to this.
2 This estimate is based on data from Plovdiv and Haskovo oblasts, which include the three okrugs of Kurdjali, Smolen and Haskovo, as well as three other okrugs (Stara Zagora, Plovdiv, and Pazadjik), of which one arguably lies partially in the Rhodopes.
3 See note 2.
4 The World Bank (1999: 48–49) report provides a detailed summary of these issues and an example of the careful calculus which some rural households have made in deciding not to expand commercial production.
5 While in the Rhodopes a greater share of women than men have withdrawn from the formal labour force, this is not the case for the nation as a whole (Giddings and Meurs 2000).
6 Note that they do not report primary responsibility for this task; they rather report sharing in the labour.
7 Alain de Janvry (1981) outlines one set of implications of such an emerging structure, based on the Latin American experience. Specific models addressing the emerging structure in ECE remain to be developed.

References

Begg, Bob, Meurs, Mieke and Pickles, John (1999) 'Peripheral transitions and industrial change in an ethnic region', unpublished manuscript.

Blumberg, Rae Lesser (1988) 'Income under female versus male control: Hypothesis from a theory of gender stratification and data from the Third World', *Journal of Family Issues* 9 (1): 51–84.

Bridger, Sue (1998) 'Tackling the market: The experience of three Moscow women's organizations', in Sue Bridger and Frances Pine (eds) *Surviving Post-socialism: Local Strategies and Regional Responses in Eastern Europe and the Former Soviet Union*, London: Routledge, pp. 203–218.

Bridger, Sue and Pine, Frances (1998) 'Introduction: Transitions to post-socialism and cultures of survival', in Sue Bridger and Frances Pine (eds) *Surviving Post-socialism: Local Strategies and Regional Responses in Eastern Europe and the Former Soviet Union*, London: Routledge, pp. 1–15.

Burawoy, Michael and Verdery, Katherine (1999) 'Introduction', in Michael Burawoy and Katherine Verdery (eds) *Uncertain Transition*, Boulder: Rowman and Littlefield, pp. 1–18.

Clarke, Simon (1999) *New Forms of Employment and Household Survival Strategies in Russia*, Warwick: Centre for Comparative Labour Studies.

Creed, Gerald (1999) 'Deconstructing socialism in Bulgaria', in Michael Burawoy and Katherine Verdery (eds) *Uncertain Transition*, Boulder: Rowman and Littlefield, pp. 223–244.

De Janvry, Alain (1981) *The Agrarian Question and Reformism in Latin America*, Baltimore: Johns Hopkins University Press.

Folbre, Nancy (1982) 'Exploitation comes home: A critique of the Marxian theory of family labour', *Cambridge Journal of Economics* 6 (4): 317–329.

Giddings, Lisa and Meurs, Mieke (2000) 'When the margin becomes the core: Occupational segregation in economic transition', *American University Working Paper*, Washington, DC.

Meurs, Mieke (2001) *The Evolution of Agrarian Institutions: A Comparative Study of Post-Socialist Hungary and Bulgaria*, Ann Arbor: University of Michigan Press.

National Institute of Statistics (1990) *Time Budget of the Population of Bulgaria*, Sofia: National Institute of Statistics.

National Institute of Statistics (1991) *Budget of Households in Bulgaria*, Sofia: National Institute of Statistics.

National Institute of Statistics (1994) *Statistical Yearbook of the Republic of Bulgaria*, Sofia: National Institute of Statistics.

Pickles, John and Begg, Robert (2000) 'Ethnicity, state violence, and neo-liberal transitions in post-communist Bulgaria', *Growth and Change* 31 (2): 179–210.

Pine, Frances (1998) 'Dealing with fragmentation: The consequences of privatization for rural women in central and southern Poland', in Sue Bridger and Frances Pine (eds) *Surviving Post-socialism: Local Strategies and Regional Responses in Eastern Europe and the Former Soviet Union*, London: Routledge, pp. 106–123.

Roldan, Martha (1988) 'Renegotiating the marital contract: Intrahousehold patterns of money allocation and women's subordination among domestic outworkers in Mexico City', in Daisy Dwyer and Judith Bruce (eds) *A Home Divided: Women and Income in the Third World*, Palo Alto: Stanford University Press.

Seeth, H., Chachnov, S., Surinov, A. and von Braun, J. (1998) 'Russian poverty: Muddling through economic transition with garden plots', *World Development* 26 (9): 1611–1623.

Smith, Adrian (2000) 'Employment restructuring and household survival in "post-communist transition": Rethinking economic practices in Eastern Europe', *Environment and Planning A* 32: 1759–1780.

Smith, Adrian (2001) 'Culture/economy and spaces of economic practice: Positioning households in post-communism', unpublished ms.

Survey Data (1996) Survey of Rhodope Rural Households.

Territorial Statistical Bureau (1994) *Statistical Handbook, Smolen 1994*, Smolen, Bulgaria: Territorial Statistical Bureau.

Walker, Michael (1998) 'Survival strategies in an industrial town in East Ukraine', in Sue Bridger and Frances Pine (eds) *Surviving Post-socialism: Local Strategies and Regional Responses in Eastern Europe and the Former Soviet Union*, London: Routledge, pp. 188–202.

Woodruff, David (1999) 'Barter of the bankrupt: The politics of demonetization in Russia's federal state', in Michael Burawoy and Katherine Verdery (eds) *Uncertain Transition*, Boulder: Rowman and Littlefield, pp. 83–124.

World Bank (1999) 'Consultations with the poor: National synthesis report, Bulgaria', available at: http://www.worldbank.org.

Zbierski-Salameh, Slawomira (1999) 'Polish peasants in the "valley of transition": Responses to postsocialist reforms', in Michael Burawoy and Katherine Verdery (eds) *Uncertain Transition*, Boulder: Rowman and Littlefield, pp. 189–222.

12 Rethinking 'survival' in austerity

Economic practices and household economies in Slovakia

Adrian Smith

Introduction: household economies and economic practices after 1989

In East-Central European (ECE) societies that underwent a rapid modernisation under state socialism an important issue concerned the ways in which emergent economic activities, centred on the formal command economy, transformed economic practices that existed prior to the implementation of state socialism. One area of research has indicated how the home and the domestic sphere became an important element in the ways that individuals tried to 'escape' from the economic and political demands of state socialism (Kideckel 1993). The private sphere, it was argued, enabled individuals to find a way of negotiating the rapid transformation of their lives. At the same time, Creed (1998) has argued that the cultures of community practice and organisation in rural Bulgaria provided a basis for sustaining the formal, command economy and represented a way of 'domesticating' state socialism.

Since 1989 an emerging literature has claimed that household and community economic relations and activities are taking on an even more significant role in ECE. The economic crises, felt to varying degrees across the region, the decline of real incomes, and the loss of employment, it is argued, have resulted in households seeking out new opportunities for survival. Household survival strategies, it is argued, are developing in a variety of spheres from the increased domestic production of household food to the increased role of petty commodity production and sale. In this sense, then, household and individual survival strategies are seen as responses to the austerity of transition and structural adjustment.

While most studies recognise that households utilised all kinds of activities under state socialism (such as household food production), a significant emphasis of this emergent research seeks to explain the purported *increase* in domestic subsistence production during transition (see also Chs 10 and 11). For example, a study of three regions in Russia by Seeth *et al.* (1998: 1611) 'addresses the question of how households *respond* to the economic stress of the transition economy' (my emphasis) and seeks to understand how households 'cope with poverty by increasing subsistence food production'. Pine and Bridger's (1998: 11) introduction to their edited collection *Surviving Post-Socialism* also argues for a 'focus on survival strategies which, to a greater or lesser extent, are being developed by local actors and interest groups within the context of displacement, dispossession and exclusion'. And in a different context still, Endre Sik (1994) has argued that the second economy of state socialism has partially become the informal economy of transition. Sik (1994: 68) suggests that 'the informal economy has an increasing importance for the households in making ends meet'. However, as Meurs (1999) has pointed out in another context, relying upon the increased *relative* share of household food production in overall food output does not provide evidence of a *real* increase in the absolute role of household subsistence production (see Ch. 11).

A contrasting perspective, developed from work on households in Russia by Simon Clarke (1999), has claimed that household food production does not represent a significant survival strategy for the losers of transition (the very poor) (see also Ch. 10). Instead, it is argued that domestic food production is more a response to the uneven and irregular availability of agricultural produce in Russian regions (Clarke 1999). In this sense, food production is seen as relatively inefficient, time consuming and undertaken by middle-income groups. It is not therefore a survival strategy in response to employment loss and declining income: 'Against the widespread belief that urban households have become increasingly self-sufficient in food, we show that domestic agriculture cannot be explained as a response to shortages of money income or of limited employment opportunities' (Clarke 1999: 13). Furthermore, '[u]rban households who grow their own potatoes, vegetables and fruit actually spend no less money on food . . . than those who do not' (Clarke 1999: 13). '[O]ur conclusion is that the use of land is not simply a cultural phenomenon, but it reflects uncertainty about the supply of agricultural produce in local markets much more than insecurity at the level of the individual household. Regional variations in the use of the dacha are therefore closely related to the demonetisation of the regional economy, and particularly to the extent of the non-payment of wages' (Clarke 1999: 13–14). However, household food production is still explained as a response mechanism, in this case not to the effects of austerity on household and individual incomes and employment opportunities but as a response to the collapse of the formal agricultural sector. There is little space for thinking of economies as diverse sets of practices often constituted through 'cultural' phenomena. Furthermore, the factors identified by Clarke (1999) in explaining Russian domestic food production may be quite specific to the Russian experience: an agricultural crisis, the demonetisation of regional economies and the non-payment of wages, all of which are of less significance in Central European transitions.

There has emerged, however, a parallel body of research which is attempting to examine the continuities between past and present household activities. This research does so by situating such practices within a framework sympathetic to plural economic formations undergoing complex articulations which are multi-determined and non-reducible to one another (see, for example, Gibson-Graham (1996) and Smith (2000)). For example, Creed (1998) has examined how rural households in Bulgaria 'domesticated' both the workings of Bulgarian communism and transition. Creed's perspective on the rural and household economies of Bulgaria is informed by a position one might call 'interactionism', which provides a quite different set of claims from those that treat household action as survival activity or as responses. For example, in discussing the formal economy and the informal sector, Creed (1998: 185) emphasises 'the continuing interaction between formal and informal sectors. These two worlds were in fact two dimensions of a single reality' and leave open the possibility that informal activities may in fact transform the formal sector (see also Ch. 13). Similarly, Mieke Meurs (1999) has been working on rural households in the Rhodope region of Bulgaria and the continuation of non-socialist, non-capitalist activity in which households have been engaged for decades (see also Ch. 11). She relates these activities to the important dimension of internal gender dynamics within households. Meurs (1999: 15) argues that 'the economic activity of rural Rhodope households in 1996 appears to be best characterised as persistence of activity which was not socialist and is not capitalist. It is activity geared toward simple reproduction of the household'.

Developing a similar line of argument, I have suggested elsewhere that many household economic practices take place outside the commodified and market relations of an emergent capitalist economy, in a kind of decommodified space of non-capitalist/non-market relations (Smith 2000). Such practices are undertaken in complex articulation with 'formal' economic relations, but are constituted differently and are characterised by different class relations concerning the production and appropriation of economic surpluses. Together these practices highlight the diversity and plurality of economic relations in East-Central Europe, that has increasingly been misread as an hegemonic form of capitalist relations. This is not a culturalist explanation but one recognising the plurality and historicity of economic practices.

Households and the articulation of the urban and the rural

The varied debates concerning the relative importance and conceptualisation of 'household survival strategies' has produced a variety of important claims. However, most existing studies (including my own, but excluding the study by Clarke of four Russian cities) either use national-level data or focus on detailed ethnographic studies of rural communities. These empirical foci therefore leave open the question as to whether or not there is a specificity of urban households without direct access to land on the home site, that is, has there been a trans-formation of household economies through the articulation between the urban and the rural after 1989?

Despite the significant levels of urbanisation that accompanied the forced industrialisation of state socialist societies, Szelenyi's work has been important in arguing that ECE societies were fundamentally 'under-urbanised' (Szelenyi 1981, Konrad and Szelenyi 1977, Szelenyi 1996). Under-urbanisation, however, led to the complex articulation between urban and rural societies. Under-urbanisation is defined as the phenomenon by which urban-based extensive industrialisation creating urban industrial jobs was not accompanied by comparable levels of population movement into towns and cities and commensurate growth of urban populations due to under-investment in infrastructure, in particular housing. Instead, Szelenyi argues, the industrial proletariat maintained a significant degree of residence in villages: 'this new class of industrial workers remains a class of village dwellers' (Szelenyi 1981: 194). The consequences were several: increased levels of rural to urban commuting to work (see also Creed 1998); the proletarianisation of villages; and the dualisation of the income earning and 'survival' strategies of households with household food production on village plots by village proletarian families becoming a significant activity. Indeed, Szelenyi goes as far as to suggest that these new class divisions produced a group of 'peasant workers' in which entrepreneurial activity in the second economy through agricultural production became increasingly important as an expression of working class power: it was 'a result of a decades-long struggle by the rural new working class to carve out for itself some autonomy in the "second economy"' (Szelenyi 1996: 299).

After 1989, Szelenyi (1996: 311) goes on to argue that 'under-urbanization continues to be reproduced, even though its socio-economic and political basis has been undermined' for two main reasons. First, new urban based jobs (where they are found) attract the young and better-trained, not the peasant workers of rural settlements. Therefore, there is no large scale 'pull' of population into urban areas. Second, Szelenyi argues that rural communities remain to a large extent attractive to the peasant workers who, even though they may have lost work in industry since 1989, have security in the form of good quality, self-built housing and access to land for domestic food production.

This discussion of rural-urban interactions is centred upon rural societies becoming transformed by urbanisation (or more accurately, under-urbanisation) and extensive industrialisation. What is lacking from such an analysis is a consideration of the structuring of urban-rural interactions by those members of the emergent working class (and others) who *did* move to and reside in cities and towns, but had 'backward' linkages into village life. Creed (1998) has provided some discussion of this in the Bulgarian context of state socialism. But very little work has looked at the ways in which *household plots of urban residents* (which are invariably located in surrounding rural locations and often attached to properties owned by relatives still resident in villages) are utilised.

This chapter therefore examines whether urban households in different income and labour market positions in different regional economies have deepened their reliance upon the rural economy/food production since 1989. One might expect, for example, as much of the literature on the development of household survival strategies does, that urban households, which are witnessing a reduction in income and security, develop ways of responding to these changes through increased reliance upon domestic self-provisioning. Therefore, a central question to be explored concerns how the articulations between urban, peri-urban and neighbouring rural economies have been reconstituted in the recent past. Or are there more significant historical continuities, as seen with research on rural households in Bulgaria (Creed 1998, Meurs 1999)?[1]

The research context

This chapter draws upon research in two contrasting urban-regional economies in Slovakia: Bratislava and Martin (Figure 12.1). The research, which involves collaboration with the Institute of Sociology of the Slovak Academy of Sciences in Bratislava and other Slovak researchers, has involved two rounds of interviewing with households in each region. The first stage, undertaken in 1999, involved in-depth structured interviews with 100 households in the two regions. Households were selected to provide a range of different occupational groups, although there are differences between the two groups in each region. Interviews lasted from just under one hour to two hours and were undertaken in the respondents' homes. As far as was practicable and relevant, interviews were undertaken with adult members of the household together. This raises a number of issues concerning the disclosure of information that may be considered sensitive and contested between adult members of households, but it was the most practicable method of organising interviews. The second stage involved more in-depth and open-ended, semi-structured interviews with a smaller number of households (approximately ten in each area). The purpose of these interviews was to put some qualitative depth on the first round of interviewing.

The research was undertaken with households resident in the largest high-rise urban structures in the two urban areas: Petržalka in Bratislava and Ľadoveň in Martin (Figure 12.2a and 12.2b). The research environments differ considerably. Bratislava, with a population of just under 500,000, has witnessed significant restructuring since 1989. The city has received something in the order of 60 per cent of total inward investment in Slovakia and in 1995 per capita GDP was nearly four times the Slovak average. Unemployment in Bratislava is around 4 per cent and employment levels have increased by 30 per cent between 1990 and 1996 (82,000 jobs). In Martin, by contrast, economic decline has been centred around the crisis of the locally dominant heavy engineering and armaments industry. Per capita GDP in 1995 was approximately equal to the average for Slovakia, and unemployment is around 10 per cent. However, between 1990 and 1996 nearly half of all employment was lost in Martin (24,000 jobs) (see Smith 1998 for more detail).

Both high-rise apartment settlements in these two urban areas were established as large, mass-build estates in the 1970s, and Petržalka became the largest such structure in Slovakia with a resident population in 1991 of just over 128,000. The construction of both settlements was associated with the industrialisation of Slovakia. In Martin, in particular, the construction of the Ľadoveň estate was connected with the expansion of the workforce in the large, locally dominant ZŤS-TEES heavy engineering and armaments plant (Smith 1994, 1998). Both settlements, although quite different in overall population size, became dominant in the urban fabric of their respective cities. In-migrant residents from

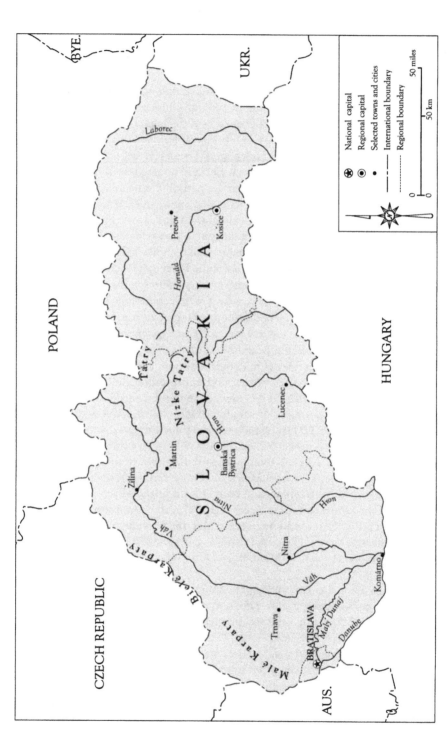

Figure 12.1 The Slovak Republic.

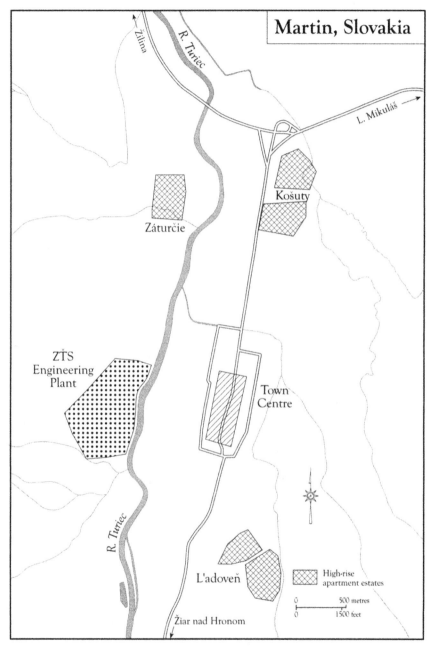

Figure 12.2a High-rise apartment estates in Martin, Slovakia.

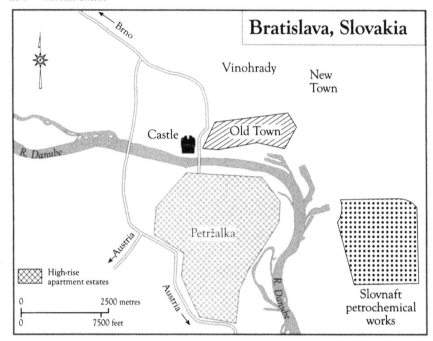

Figure 12.2b Petržalka, Bratislava.

surrounding rural areas, as well as more long-distance migrants, also populated both estates initially. New migrants were often young families with small children, often from rural areas and migration was connected with new employment opportunities for these groups in the expanding industrial base of the two urban areas (see Mládek 1994, Cibul'ková 1994, Miškolci and Mládek 1994, Mládek *et al.* 1998, Smith 1998). Consequently, while households became part of the urban social fabric of these two cities, many retained quite important linkages back into the rural economies in which their relatives often remained, or they developed access to land in the nearby vicinity. For example, one household in Martin who had previously moved from rural East Slovakia utilised a plot of land that was rented from the local gardener's association. The plot is located in a nearby village, some 30 minutes away by bus. Since the death of their parents, who had remained in East Slovakia, the household has also inherited this familial land, and during periodic visits to their parents' former homes in the past they had received various products from the land.

Households and post-communism in Slovakia: an overview

Before examining in detail the changing economic practices of households involved in this study, this section explores the overall changes to household economic life since 1989 in Slovakia. Data from the Slovak microcensus indicate that income differentiation during the 1990s increased (Filipová *et al.* 1998).[2] The difference in the ratio of income accruing to the bottom quintile of households compared to the top quintile increased from 1:2.4 to 1:3.2 between 1992 and 1996. In addition, the proportion of income accruing to the bottom quintile of households fell between 1992 and 1996 from 12.7 per cent to 10.5 per cent of the total. The average incomes accruing to different social groups also underwent a process of polarisation over this period (Table 12.1). Peasants and pensioners saw a relative decline in income while all other groups (especially white-collar, independent productive activity and other household heads) saw a relative increase. Households with heads under the age of 29 and without children also saw a relative increase in income. At the same time, the percentage of households below half of median income has increased to about 6 per cent, while at the top end of the income spectrum the percentage of households has increased to just under 60 per cent (Filipová *et al.* 1998).

While there has been an increase in the levels of household inequality in Slovakia since 1989, the level of inequality tends to be lower in comparison with other ECE countries. The Gini coefficient for household income in Slovakia has increased, but the level of increase and the absolute value place Slovakia below most other ECE countries in the mid-1990s, in terms of household inequality (Smith 2000). Furthermore, the number of individuals and households living in poverty in Slovakia tends to be below levels found in most other ECE countries, except perhaps the Czech Republic (see Smith 2000). However, during 1999 and 2000 a series of price liberalisations have been implemented in Slovakia which have significantly added to the costs of living of households and potentially to the degree of inequality amongst the population (Úrad vlády Slovenskej republiky 2000).

Table 12.1 Average personal income in Slovakia, 1992–6

	1992		1996	
	Sk	*% of average*	*Sk*	*% of average*
All households	2,902	100.0	4,638	100.0
Social groups (defined by household head)				
White-collar workers	3,464	119.4	5,666	122.2
Blue-collar workers	2,732	94.1	4,466	96.3
Independent productive activity	3,765	129.7	6,566	141.6
Peasants	2,700	93.0	4,221	91.0
Pensioners	2,660	91.7	3,824	82.5
Others[a]	1,972	67.9	4,099	88.4

Source: Filipová *et al.* (1998).

Note
[a]   Others include unemployed, 'domestic entrepreneur' and student household heads.

Food production, land and household economic practices

In the context of these transformations, have increasing inequality and declining production and consumption of food resulted in the development and expansion of food production in urban households? For example, in 1998 real gross agricultural output in Slovakia was 60 per cent of the 1989 level and per capita food consumption had declined to levels lower than those reached in the 1986–1990 period (Blaas 1999).

Household food provisioning

Table 12.2 indicates that households surveyed rely quite considerably on the market purchasing of essential food items. The level of reliance varies by type of food item, with dairy and meat products being purchased to a much greater extent than potatoes, fruit and vegetables. There is also quite significant regional variation in the level of self-provisioning of these food items. Households in the region of Martin tend to provision through a lower level of market purchasing of potatoes, vegetables and fruit than households in Bratislava. Indeed, non-market provisioning of potatoes and vegetables in Martin represents an average of over one-quarter of the total, and provisioning of fruit is just over one-fifth. This pattern of provisioning may well reflect the greater use of land by households in Martin: 54 per cent of interviewed households stated that they had used land in the last 12 months, compared to 23 per cent of households in Bratislava.

Table 12.2 Average percentage of food purchased, produced and received by households, 1999

	All households	Martin	Bratislava
Potatoes bought	82	73	91
Potatoes produced	9	14	3
Potatoes received	9	13	6
Vegetables bought	78	72	85
Vegetables produced	17	23	10
Vegetables received	5	5	5
Fruit bought	82	79	84
Fruit produced	14	18	10
Fruit received	4	3	6
Dairy products bought	100	100	100
Dairy products produced	0	0	0
Dairy products received	0	0	0
Meat bought	97	97	97
Meat produced	1	1	0
Meat received	2	2	3
N	100	52	48

Source: household interviews, 1999.

Household income and domestic food production

Given these regional differences, is there any evidence that households in different income positions are more or less reliant upon market exchange to provision food? Is there any evidence to suggest that lower income households rely more upon household food production and exchange than more affluent households as claims over the deepening of household relations with self-provisioning in the context of economic austerity would suggest? Table 12.3 reports data from the interviewed households classified by median income and it is clear that the broad differences between the two regions appear also when median income differences are examined. The most significant income differences are apparent in the provisioning of vegetables, which are the most widely domestically grown food items. Those households below median income levels in Martin tend to rely more fully on domestic production and exchange (31 per cent of average provisioning), while those households above median income levels tend to purchase a greater proportion of vegetables (81 per cent). In Bratislava, however, the reverse is the case. Indeed, in Bratislava there is some evidence across all of these food products to suggest that above median income households rely more on domestic production and receipt of produce than those below the median. These differences may then reflect the different patterns of access to land between these groups.

Table 12.3 Average percentage of food purchased, produced and received by below median income and above median income households, 1999

	Martin		Bratislava	
	Below median income	*Above median income*	*Below median income*	*Above median income*
Potatoes bought	74	70	95	90
Potatoes produced	14	15	0	4
Potatoes received	12	14	5	6
Vegetables bought	69	81	92	82
Vegetables produced	25	17	2	13
Vegetables received	6	2	6	5
Fruit bought	79	80	85	84
Fruit produced	18	18	3	12
Fruit received	3	2	12	4
Dairy products bought	100	100	100	100
Dairy products produced	0	0	0	0
Dairy products received	0	0	0	0
Meat bought	97	95	98	97
Meat produced	2	0	0	0
Meat received	1	5	2	3
N	38	14	12	36

Source: household interviews, 1999.

Unlike in Martin, where land is more fully used by below median income households (68 per cent of households using land in Martin lie below median household income), the situation in Bratislava suggests that relative wealth is important in having access to food production resources. Indeed, only one household using land lies below the median income level.

Household occupational structure and domestic food production

While there is some limited, but variable, evidence to suggest the greater usage of land and production of food for lower income groups in one of our regions, is there evidence that those in lower paid and lower status occupations rely proportionately more on domestic food production?[3] The following analysis uses a classification of occupational groups derived from information provided by interviewed household heads (professional and managerial; technicians and associate professionals; clerks and other service sector workers; industrial and manufacturing workers). There is some evidence that household per capita incomes are affected by job status, however not in a way that indicates poorer/lower-status households using land as a survival strategy. In both Bratislava and Martin households with heads that were in professional and managerial jobs had higher per capita household incomes, although the differences across all of these occupational groups was not great (ranging from Sk 3,808 to Sk 5,078 in Martin, and from Sk 6,484 to Sk 6,871 in Bratislava). In both Bratislava and Martin there is no clear link between households in lower category occupations and the higher usage of land, although in each region the relationship works in different ways. In Bratislava, most of the households that use land had a household head in a managerial or professional occupation (9 of the 11 households). In Martin there was much greater dispersion of usage of land across these occupational groups to the extent that the same number of households used land in the professional and managerial group as did in the lowest paid group of industrial and manufacturing workers.

When one examines the reliance upon the production of food items by households with different occupational profiles the differences between Martin and Bratislava are once again apparent (Table 12.4). In Bratislava, professional and managerial households, which are more engaged in food production anyway, produce a much larger share of their food than all other occupational groups. In Martin, professional and managerial households also produce a variety of food items, but those in service and industrial occupations tend to rely upon domestic food production to a much greater extent (nearly 30 per cent of total sourcing of vegetables and fruit). Consequently, there is no clear evidence that poorer and lower status households in these two regions rely to a greater extent on food self-provisioning than higher income/status groups. Three further questions, however, can be explored.

First, do poorer households and different occupational groups spend on average less income on food as we might expect if household impoverishment leads to increased self-provisioning? In both regions there is very little difference in the

Table 12.4 Average percentage of various foods produced by occupational groups, Martin and Bratislava

	% Potatoes produced		% Vegetables produced		% Fruit produced	
	Martin	Bratislava	Martin	Bratislava	Martin	Bratislava
Professional and managerial	13	7	15	19	15	17
Technical and associate professional	6	2	16	8	13	9
Clerical and service sector	15	–	27	2	17	3
Industrial and manufacturing	13	–	27	–	27	–
Total	14	3	23	10	18	10

Source: household interviews, 1999.

proportion of household per capita monthly income spent on food. In Bratislava, the major difference is that professional and managerial households tended to spend less (32 per cent of average per capita monthly income) on food than all other occupational categories, which no doubt reflects the greater level of land utilisation by this group. In Martin the differences are negligible (averaging around 40 per cent of per capita monthly household income).

Second, do food producers spend any more or less money on buying food than non-food producers? That is, does domestic food production provide some substitution for expenditure on market cash purchasing? There is limited evidence in Martin, but stronger evidence from Bratislava that non-food producers do indeed spend a greater proportion and absolutely more of their income on food (Table 12.5).

Third, of those that do produce food, do those that use land as a leisure activity have a different level of household income from those that use land to produce food as additional food for the household table? Do these different producers spend different amounts of money on food purchases? In Martin, the mean monthly per capita household income of those using land primarily for leisure was higher than for those using land for additional food (Sk 4,574 compared to Sk 3,958). However, there is very little difference between hobbyists and producers of additional food for the household in terms of expenditure on food (38 per cent and 39 per cent of income respectively). In Bratislava, expenditure on food was

Table 12.5 Food expenditure of households, Martin and Bratislava

	Martin		Bratislava	
	With land	*Without land*	*With land*	*Without land*
Mean monthly food expenditure per capita	Sk 1,596	Sk 1,701	Sk 1,841	Sk 2,453
Mean % income spent on food	38%	43%	26%	41%
N	28	24	11	37

Source: household interviews, 1999.

much lower for those households using land to produce additional food (17 per cent of income, compared to 35 per cent of income for hobbyists). Yet at the same time, mean household income for the food producers was much higher than for hobbyists (Sk 8,983 compared to Sk 6,625).

One reason for the apparent differences in land utilisation and food production between households in Martin and Bratislava may lie in the nature of the local economies of these two regions. Even though land utilisation is lower in Bratislava than in Martin, one-half of those using land in Bratislava did so to provide additional food for the household compared to 42 per cent of households utilising land in Martin. In Martin the majority of households both above and below median income levels said that they used land because it was a hobby (53 per cent below median income, 89 per cent above median income), whereas in Bratislava the figure was 40 per cent of those above median income (only one household using land fell below median income levels). The key to the higher utilisation of land for additional food in Bratislava in above median income households may well lie in the differences between the costs of living in these two regions and the pressures that this places on the reasons for household utilisation of land. A household with an above national-median income in Bratislava may still have to rely upon self-provisioning to a much greater extent than in a region such as Martin because of the relatively high cost of living in the capital city compared to that of more provincial regions. However, this does still not provide clear evidence that households use domestic food production as a survival strategy in conditions of austerity. Indeed, it could be argued that such regional, occupational and income differences result from historical continuities rather than responses to transition. This is a point to which I will return.

One of the central issues is the access that households have to land. In Bratislava, where land utilisation was lower anyway, 82 per cent of below median income households not using land and 89 per cent of above median income households not using land suggested that the main reason for not producing food was because they could not get access to land. This is in a situation where households often have direct links back to rural areas from where they originally moved. In Martin problems of access to land were much less acute (reflected in the higher levels of utilisation) but for below median income households without land the main reason was also lack of opportunity to access it. So access is not universal but it does reflect to a certain extent the particular features of urbanisation and rural-urban connectivities in these two regions, which in many ways are a product of the past, not a response to the austerity of transition. What other historical continuities might however be at work?

Historical continuities of food production or land as survival?

In Bratislava, the average length of time that households with access to land have used the land to produce food is 27 years. In Martin, the average number of years using land is 12 and only eight households started to use land since 1989. In Bratislava, only one household has acquired land since 1989. For the majority of households in both regions (and particularly for the majority in Bratislava who are mainly professional and managerial heads), then, the utilisation of land is a household activity preceding 1989. Indeed, it is also an activity that is not undertaken for household survival. For example, in Martin the majority of households both above and below median income levels said that they used land because it was a hobby (53 per cent below median income, 89 per cent above median income), whereas in Bratislava the figure was 40 per cent of those above median income (only one household using land fell below median income levels). Otherwise, households produced food as additional to that which they purchased. For example, one-half of those using land in Bratislava did so to provide additional food for the household compared to 42 per cent of households utilising land in Martin.

However, for those that have started to use land for home food production since 1989, is there any evidence to suggest that they are doing so because of economic hardship? In Martin, average per capita household income levels for 'new users' were below that for those who had a longer history of land utilisation; the majority of new users had experienced significant financial problems in the last two years, and half were not at all satisfied with their household income level. The existence of only one new user in Bratislava suggests that we need to be careful about asserting causality from the results, but overall this household was at a lower status and level of income than those who had used land for quite some time. This suggests, then, that there is some partial evidence of households accessing land because of difficult economic circumstances. Indeed, in Martin, half of those that got access to land since 1989 did so to provide additional food for the household table, but this is not a clear indication of a survival strategy which deepens the relations between urban based households and peri-urban and rural economies. However, the overall level of new acquisition of land is very low and what seems more important is the continuance of practices developed in the past.

Indeed, the overall evidence points to the use of land as the continuation of household practices which may have their own cultural and economic 'logics' not reducible to actions in response to the austerity of transition. Some of our emerging qualitative interview data suggests that this may be the case. Take for instance the case of the Sykora family[4] in Martin who share use of a cottage garden with one of their sets of parents some 20 minutes away from the town by bus. The family have two small children but are relatively secure financially. One partner (the husband) is an accountant, the other is on maternity leave. Work on the plot is shared with their parents, and during summer often involves daily trips. They produce mainly vegetables and potatoes from the plot which allows the household to be self-sufficient in potatoes, garlic, onions and root vegetables. Ms Sykora explained the significance of the household's plot of land as follows: 'We consider our work at our garden mainly as a hobby, but it also provides a useful source of food which helps our family to save money on food expenditure. . . . We also like to grow our own food because it is more healthy and not as chemically treated as products from the shops.'

Such views are not atypical. A second household in Martin provides a clear case of the continuities of food production between communist and post-communist periods. Located in a small village some 30 minutes from Martin by bus, the land used by this household is primarily for the production of food for domestic consumption. But as the household head Mr Murajda explained, the household have used the land since 1982 and 'while the garden is important for us, gardening is more or less a hobby'.

For lower income households the continuities of land usage are also apparent. The Zlatko family, for example, which comprises a retired mother and her 26-year-old daughter who is a teacher, have a piece of land quite close to the town where they grow potatoes. The mother suggested, for example, that 'we make good use of the land and what we produce helps our family budget. But for retired people like me gardening is mainly a hobby and we have always used it that way'.

Conclusions

There are several themes that stand out from this research in Slovakia. First, there is overall a relatively high level of reliance upon market provisioning of food, but there is also a greater level of domestic food production of some food items in one of our regions, Martin, which is reflected in the higher levels of land usage.

Second, there are quite significant regional differences in the type of households producing food and utilising land, which reflects certain specificities of these local economies. Lower income households and households across the occupational profile in Martin tend to produce more food and have more usage of land than in Bratislava. Higher income and professional households in Bratislava tend to produce more food and have more usage of land.

Yet, third, there is little overall evidence of food production and land usage as a survival strategy. While food production plays a role in helping households to provide additional food (especially in more expensive locations such as Bratislava and for lower income households in Martin) there are very important continuities with past practices. This suggests that relations between city and country continue to be important but have not necessarily deepened as a response to the austerity of capitalist transition. The number of households acquiring new land is relatively small and the usage of land as a hobby or to provide some additional food for the table is predominant. Equally, however, the relations between town and country are differentiated by regional context. In Martin, there is a closer relationship with the surrounding rural area concerning land utilisation, which may reflect the relatively close (geographically) family and land ties, than those in Bratislava where residents originate from further afield.

Consequently, as Meurs (1999: 11) has argued within the context of Bulgarian rural households, much of the food production activity of households appears 'to be a fairly pure continuation of non-socialist, non-capitalist activity in which the household has been engaged for decades'. In other words, household food production activity is 'geared toward simple reproduction of the household' (Meurs 1999: 15). In this sense then, we should avoid reading such household practices as responses to austerity – which is not to argue that the impacts of transition have not been profoundly negative for many households. But such practices have their origins elsewhere and are constituted by different kinds of economic relations from those of the 'formal economy'; relations of domestic self-provisioning and mutuality. This suggests then that it is important to think beyond the binary oppositions of socialist economic relations replaced by post-socialist/transition economies, and to consider some of the ways in which significant household practices constitute partially separate spheres of activity not reducible to capitalist transition.

Acknowledgements

An earlier version of this chapter was presented at the ESRC-funded research seminar on 'Households and survival strategies in transition', University of Warwick, February 2000. I am very grateful to the participants at that seminar for discussion of the issues raised, and especially to Adam Swain and Orjan Sjoberg. The research reported in this chapter arises from a project examining household 'survival strategies' and regional economic change in Slovakia. I am very grateful to the Nuffield Foundation for funding the project. I would also like to thank Zuzana Kusa of the Institute of Sociology, Slovak Academy of Sciences for her assistance with this project. Andrea Gonová provided valuable research assistance both in the UK and Slovakia.

Notes

1   This chapter does not consider other aspects of what have been conceived as survival strategies (e.g. networks, secondary employment, etc.) (see Smith 2001). Rather, the focus is on household food production and land utilisation.
2   The microcensus of 1996 involved a survey of 16,336 households by the Slovak Statistical Office (see Štatistický úrad Slovenskej republiky 1997).
3   Between these occupational groups there is some variability in per capita household incomes. Average monthly incomes tended to be higher for those in professional and managerial positions (Sk 5,078 in Martin and Sk 6,871 in

Bratislava) than for all the other categories of occupation. Indeed, average per capita monthly household income in Martin for industrial and manufacturing occupations was as low as Sk 3,808.
4   All names have been changed to protect the identity of respondents.

References

Blaas, G. (1999) 'Transformation of agriculture in Slovakia', paper presented to the conference on Transitional Societies in Comparison, Prague, May. Available from the author at: Research Institute of Agricultural and Food Economics, Trenčianska 55, 824 80 Bratislava, Slovakia.

Cibuľková, J. (1994) 'Migration movements of Petržalka population', *Acta Facultatis Rerum Naturalium Universitatis Comenianae, Geographica* 34: 61–70.

Clarke, S. (1999) *New Forms of Employment and Household Survival Strategies in Russia,* Institute for Comparative Labour Relations Research, Moscow and Centre for Comparative Labour Studies, University of Warwick, Coventry.

Creed, G. (1998) *Domesticating Revolution: From Socialist Reform to Ambivalent Transition in a Bulgarian Village,* University Park, PA, Pennsylvania University Press.

Filipová, J., Valná, S. and Myslíková, I. (1998) *Analýza prímovej situácie domácností Slovenskej republiky v r. 1992 a v r. 1996 (na základe výsledkov Mikrocenzov)* (Analysis of the Incomes of Slovak Households in 1992 and 1996 (on the basis of the Microcensus)), Research report 31, Employment, Social and Family Research Institute, Bratislava.

Gibson-Graham, J.K. (1996) *The End of Capitalism (As We Know It): A Feminist Critique of Political Economy,* Oxford: Blackwell.

Kideckel, D. (1993) *The Solitude of Collectivism: Romanian Villagers to the Revolution and Beyond,* Ithaca, NY, Cornell University Press.

Konrad, G. and Szelenyi, I. (1977) 'Social conflicts of underurbanization', in M. Harloe (ed.) *Captive Cities,* London, Wiley, pp. 135–147.

Meurs, M. (1999) 'Economic strategies of surviving post-socialism: changing household economies and gender divisions of labor in the Bulgarian transition', unpublished manuscript, Department of Economics, American University, Washington DC.

Miškolci, A. and Mládek, J. (1994) 'The basic characters of population structure of Petržalka', *Acta Facultatis Rerum Naturalium Universitatis Comenianae, Geographica* 34: 83–93.

Mládek, J. (1994) 'Petržalka – development and transformation of urban structure', *Acta Facultatis Rerum Naturalium Universitatis Comenianae, Geographica* 34: 3–12.

Mládek, J., Kovalovská, V. and Chovancová, J. (1998) 'Petržalka – demografické, najmä migračné špecifiká mladej urbánnej štruktúry', *Geografický časopis* 50 (2): 109–137.

Pine, F. and Bridger, S. (1998) 'Introduction: Transitions to post-socialism and cultures of survival', in S. Bridger and F. Pine (eds) *Surviving Post-Socialism: Local Strategies and Regional Responses in Eastern Europe and the Former Soviet Union,* London, Routledge, pp. 1–15.

Seeth, H.T., Chachnov, S., Surinov, A. and von Braun, J. (1998) 'Russian poverty: Muddling through economic transition with garden plots', *World Development* 26 (9): 1611–1623.

Sik, E. (1994) 'From the multicoloured to the black and white economy: The Hungarian second economy and the transformation', *International Journal of Urban and Regional Research,* 18 (1): 46–70.

Smith, A. (1994) 'Uneven development and the restructuring of the armaments industry in Slovakia', *Transactions of the Institute of British Geographers* 19: 404–424.

Smith, A. (1998) *Reconstructing the Regional Economy: Industrial Transformation and Regional Development in Slovakia*, Cheltenham: Edward Elgar.

Smith, A. (2000) 'Employment restructuring and household survival in "post-communist transition": Rethinking economic practices in Eastern Europe', *Environment and Planning A* 32 (10): 1759–1780.

Smith, A. (2001) 'Culture/economy and spaces of economic practice: Positioning households in post-communism', unpublished manuscript.

Štatistický úrad Slovenskej republiky (1997) *Mikrocenzus 1997: údaje o prímoch domácností za SR*, Bratislava: Štatistický úrad Slovenskej republiky.

Szelenyi, I. (1981) 'Urban development and regional management in Eastern Europe', *Theory and Society* 10: 169–205.

Szelenyi, I. (1996) 'Cities under socialism – and after', in G. Andrusz, M. Harloe and I. Szelenyi (eds) *Cities After Socialism: Urban and Regional Change and Conflict in Post-Socialist Societies*, Oxford: Blackwell, pp. 287–317.

Úrad vlády Slovenskej republiky (2000) *Komuniké z rokovania vlády Slovenskej republiky 26. Januára 2000*. Available at: http://www.government.gov.sk/MATERIALY_U... MUNIKE/2000/sk_komunike20000126_78.shtml. Accessed on 28 January 2000.

13 Gulag Europe?

Mass unemployment, new firm creation, and tight labour markets in the Bulgarian apparel industry[1]

John Pickles

Introduction

Until recently, the overriding experience of liberal adjustment policies throughout Central and Eastern Europe (CEE) has been the rapid collapse of industrial capacity, the weakening of social infrastructure, the emergence of widespread long-term unemployment, and household economic restructuring. In some peripheral regions, historical patterns of uneven development have been compounded by the emergence of region-wide mass unemployment. Post-1989 labour market restructuring has thus been one primarily of economic and social adjustments to plant closure, job loss, and changes in the sources, amount and structure of household incomes.

Largely hidden by this more general crisis, some enterprises in traditional sectors were able to sustain minimal levels of state underwriting, contracting, and production. In some cases, these 'resources' permitted state and former-state firms and managers to struggle along in generally unfavourable circumstances, often under conditions of branch-specific forms of re-monopolisation and regional re-concentration, dependent largely on national markets (see Begg and Pickles 1998). In other cases, new small private locally owned enterprises were able to emerge based on *ad-hoc* contracting or new buyer-relationships. This chapter focuses on the situation in one oblast (Kurdjali) and one branch of manufacturing (apparel) in the Rhodope region of Bulgaria (Figure 13.1), where this kind of 'defensive restructuring' occurred in conditions of extreme fiscal and financial difficulty.

The chapter also focuses on new forms of economic adjustment that have arisen because of this 'defensive restructuring', but are now also producing parallel and spatially contiguous forms of what might be thought of as 'offensive restructuring' (see Burawoy 1996 and Smith 2000b for discussion of these forms of restructuring in Eastern Europe). Particularly after the currency crisis of 1996–97, a new round of internationalisation has emerged alongside plant closure and small-scale persistence. Established apparel firms have restructured production towards export markets and reduced their dependence on domestic markets, and new firms are emerging at a rapid rate. One consequence has been an increase in demand for female factory workers in a region still typified by mass unemploy-

Figure 13.1 Map of Bulgaria.

ment, high levels of discouraged and 'retired' workers, and lack of formal waged work in most households. Low-wage, relatively skilled industrial labour pools are driving this resurgence, with all the consequences so frequently associated with despotic production systems (Burawoy 1985, Gereffi 1999). In particular, the demand has increased for workers with sewing skills who will work long hours for low wages on relatively insecure and 'flexible' work contracts. The resultant tightening of such locally circumscribed labour markets, combined with highly differentiated and competitive market conditions, has forced some firms to turn to higher-value production and compete more vigorously for 'skilled' reliable workers who can meet the demands of such higher quality work (see Lovasz 2000 for a similar argument about Hungarian clothing firms). The implications of such labour market segmentation are unclear, particularly as the bulk of the population still experiences conditions of mass unemployment. Clearer are the ways in which newly internationalising production facilities are articulating in diverse ways with locally existing social conditions. In turn, these social conditions affect the competitive success of firms. This chapter focuses on the social conditions for accumulation in apparel firms in one region of Bulgaria, and shows how local circumstances actively shape the diversity of organisational forms and work practices that are emerging.

Industrial collapse and mass unemployment in peripheral regions

From the 1960s, the Bulgarian space economy was dominated by large-scale, fully integrated production units concentrated in core industrial regions (the 'commanding heights' of the economy, see Begg and Pickles 1998). Typically, this 'combinat' space comprised ferrous metallurgy, petrochemicals, heavy equipment, armaments, transportation equipment, and the larger consumer goods factories. Mining and metallurgy were also important in some mountain and peripheral regions, such as Kurdjali oblast,[2] but generally such areas received lower levels of state investment and had only limited manufacturing capacity organised in small enterprises. Major urban areas contained 59.2 per cent of the population, but in them 'the concentration of funds in production and material infrastructure [was] 4.3 times higher than the national average' (MRDC 1996: 17). By contrast, mountainous regions had 'funds in material production and infrastructure three times lower than the national average' (MRDC 1996: 27) and included some regions classified as of 'most depressed' status.[3] The first years of economic restructuring were, therefore, also years of major regional change as these historical patterns of uneven development shaped local paths of transformation.

While the first years of transformation after 1989 resulted in loss of markets, tightening budget constraints, and plant closure in all sectors of the economy, in practice, the degree of decline was sectorally and regionally differentiated. For example, between 1989 and 1996, Bulgaria's 'central districts' experienced slower declines than peripheral regions.[4] Characterised by continued soft budget constraints and struggles to maintain employment levels and wage bills (Bristow 1996, ILO 1994, Pickles 1995), 'commanding heights' industries (and the regions in which they were concentrated) were able to maintain levels of state investment and avoid lay-offs longer than other sectors of industry as the economy declined after 1989 (Table 13.1). In these other sectors and in those regions whose economic structure was dominated by agriculture and branch plants, declines were much sharper and the ability of branches and enterprises to protect themselves politically was much weaker (Begg and Pickles 1998).

In Kurdjali, tobacco farming was an important part of the regional economy, but unlike commanding heights industries it had remained loosely structured with co-operatives operating more as buying co-operatives than collectivised production units, farmers retaining greater levels of private control over their land and work-time, and households controlling more of their production than in the state sector (Begg and Meurs 1998). In such mountain, border, and ethnic regions, small-scale workshops and branch-plants, referred to as 'daughters of the mother

Table 13.1 Decline in employment by sector: Kurdjali 1991–8

	1991	*1998*	*% Change*
Total	75,364	38,840	−48
Agriculture	27,816	2,065	−93
Manufacturing	19,950	12,969	−43
Metallurgy and mining	4,329	3,899	−10

Sources:
National Statistical Institute (1997a) *Statisticheski Sbronik Kurdjali 1996.* Sofia: 30.
Territorial Statistical Office Kurdjali. Mimeo No. 220, 247.

plant', had been developed by the state as a direct employment strategy (Pickles and Begg 2000). Ostensibly, the wives of miners, metallurgy workers and tobacco farmers were to be provided with employment opportunities in the workshops, often on a seasonal basis.

From their inception, mining, tobacco farming and workshop production thus functioned as linked elements of an articulated (if not integrated) production system providing limited economic support to the rural population of the Kurdjali region. State contracting in the small workshops was both intermittent and 'flexible' (see Pickles 1995), but in part this was because workshops had to adjust their work and production schedules to the seasonal demands of agriculture and mining, ceding to workers some bargaining powers even under state management. However, because such employment was always seen as a secondary source of income for female household members, it tended to maintain their status as low-wage workers.

The most important of the light industries distributed under the late socialist economy to mountain, border, and ethnic regions such as Kurdjali was apparel assembly. Apparel was a traditional industry in the Rhodopes, beginning with home production of woollen products using local wool derived from a transhumant pastoral economy that linked the Rhodopes with the Aegean to the south. Apparel later emerged in elaborate networks of putting-out that linked ethnic villages across the region with the manufacturing and trade centres such as Plovdiv. The introduction of state apparel firms in the region in the early 1980s was part of a national strategy to deepen textile production by creating local demand for cloth and to support peripheral regions at a time when new markets were opening in Western Europe. From 1980 to 1995, countries like West Germany responded to market pressures in textile and apparel industries by 'off-shoring' production to Eastern Europe (Dicken 1998: 307), with 'the most rapid growth in clothing production in Eastern Europe [occurring] in Bulgaria and Romania' (Dicken 1998: 291). During the latter years of the command economy, the apparel sector grew rapidly as Bulgaria became part of the international production network supplying department stores, mass merchandisers, and discount chains in Europe and the United States.

The apparel industry (and the mountain, border, and ethnic regions in which it was concentrated) also experienced the fastest and most serious declines after 1989 (Table 13.2).[5] With land restitution and privatisation of co-operative farm property, agricultural employment collapsed. With loss of CMEA markets and political struggles over control of enterprise resources, branch plants and workshops were also closed quickly (see Begg and Pickles 1998, Pickles and Begg 2000). Villages experienced the most serious declines in access to waged income and state disbursements. For many years, co-operatives and workshops had offered the primary and, in some villages, the only sources of waged employment. In 1996, the Ministry of Regional Development and Construction (1996: 22) argued that it was precisely these branches and regions that were most exposed to the critical events of transition: 'The affiliate economy existing there was the first to sustain the economic crisis. The affiliates and departments of large

Table 13.2 Production and employment in apparel, 1980–96

Year	1980	1989	1990	1991	1992	1993	1994	1995	1996
Production Index (1990 = 100)	66	90	100	87	74	62	75	63	71
Employment	64,448	80,467	83,259	67,483	57,354	54,024	48,535	47,014	41,381

Sources:
Production
    National Statistical Institute. *Statisticheski Godizhnik* 1991: 168; 1995: 223.
    National Statistical Institute. *Statisticheski Spravochnik* 1997b: 90.
Employment
    National Statistical Institute. *Statisticheski Godizhnik* 1991: 147; 1995: 89.
    National Statistical Institute. *Statisticheski Spravochnik* 1997b: 42.

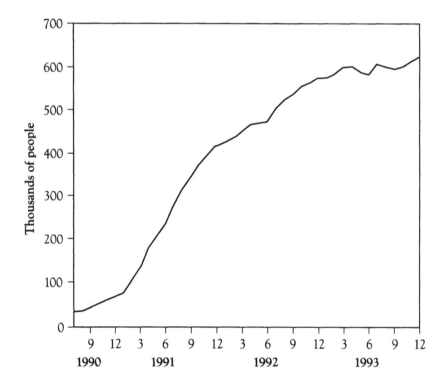

Figure 13.2 Unemployment levels in Bulgaria, 1990–3.

Source: Avramov and Antonov 1994: 126.

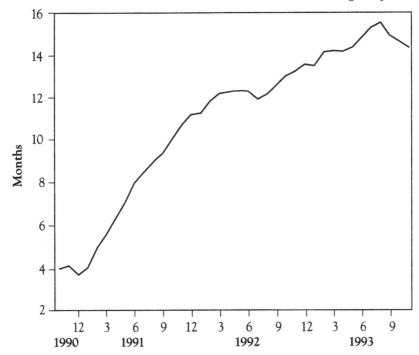

Figure 13.3 Average duration of unemployment in Bulgaria, 1990–3.

Source: Avramov and Antonov 1994: 130.

enterprises from central districts have been closed nearly 100 per cent.' Massive labour shedding occurred as a consequence of rapid de-collectivisation of state farms, loss of CMEA markets for apparel, textiles and tobacco, and the peripheral nature of workshops and branch plants within the command economy structure. Between 1990 and 1993, for example, Kurdjali lost 70.3 per cent of its jobs compared to 21.3 per cent for Bulgaria as a whole, and in 1992, 69 per cent of Kurdjali's labour force was classified as unemployed or economically inactive (NSI 1996: 135). One immediate consequence was that unemployment rates increased rapidly (Figure 13.2) and short-term unemployment was replaced by long-term, chronic unemployment (Nenova-Amar and Radeva 1994: 130) (Figure 13.3).

Throughout the 1990s, regional unemployment rates in Kurdjali remained extremely high (Begg and Pickles 1998, Wyzan 1997) and labour costs continued to drop. Dicken (1998: 296) has estimated that already by 1995 wages in the clothing industry in Bulgaria (0.2 DM/minute) (and elsewhere in eastern Europe) had dropped substantially below those for workers in Germany (0.741 DM/minute) and south-east Asia and were only marginally above those of the Yucatan (0.12 DM/minute). One consequence was that the proportion of Bulgarian

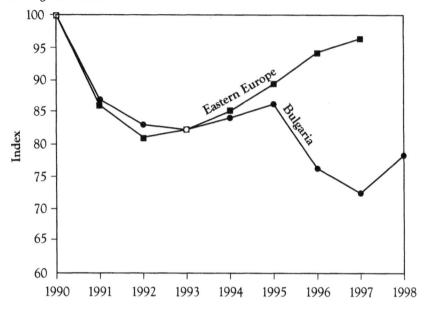

Figure 13.4 Index of real gross domestic product, Bulgaria and Eastern Europe (1990–8).
Source: World Bank 1999: 1.

households with low incomes and those in poverty increased rapidly, as did household income inequality. Indeed, drawing on UNICEF data, Smith (2000a) shows that between 1990 and 1994 the percentage of low-income households increased from 13.6 per cent to 67.1 per cent while households in poverty increased from 2.1 per cent to 32.1 per cent.[6] Wage levels, industrial output, and GDP per capita declined even further with the currency crisis of 1996–97, when the Bulgarian *lev* collapsed against other currencies (Bristow 1996, ILO 1996/97) (Figure 13.4). The UNDP's *Poverty in Transition* (1998) reported that, as a result, by the end of 1996 the proportion of the population living below subsistence levels had risen to over two-thirds. As agricultural production declined, unemployment increased, and consumer prices soared, total daily food supply in calories per capita also declined quickly (National Statistical Institute 1997b: 507). In turn, death and infant mortality rates increased quickly (National Statistical Institute 1999). The overall result was the creation of pools of impoverished relatively skilled potential workers desperately needing to find new sources of income.

Industrial resurgence and tightening labour markets in regions of mass unemployment

Between 1992–1998, apparel employment in the Kurdjali region increased by 164 per cent, compared to a 52 per cent increase in the nation as a whole as local and foreign entrepreneurs moved swiftly to take advantage of contracting opportunities (Table 13.3). Thus, from the early 1990s on, initial small-scale industrial

Table 13.3 Per cent change in manufacturing employment by selected branch 1992–8

Branch	Bulgaria	Kurdjali
Food, beverage, tobacco	−5%	44%
Textiles	−46%	−90%
Wearing apparel	52%	**164%**
Leather and footwear	0%	−28%
Total	−10%	2%

Sources:
National Statistical Institute. *Statisticheski Sbronik Smolyan* 1995. Sofia: 30.
National Statistical Institute. *Statisticheski Sbronik Kurdjali* 1997a. Sofia: 30.
Territorial Statistical Office Kurdjali. Mimeos Nos. 220, 247, 1999.
National Statistical Institute. *Stasticheski Godishnik* 1994: 187; 1999: 46, 47.

persistence was complemented by a process of further internationalisation resulting in a wave of new firm creation and established firm restructuring geared towards export markets. Indeed, the restructuring of the regional economy as a result of the emergence of the new private firms has been so rapid in recent years that it is referred to locally as 'Klondike capitalism'.

Several processes created this turnaround. First, there has been a change in the structure and operations of the global apparel industry (see Dicken 1998). Second, the regulatory environment for apparel exports and imports has changed, particularly as a result of European Union (EU) regulations (see Snyder 1999). And third, combined these two have resulted in new production systems and geographies of apparel across Eastern Europe and increasingly beyond, based in large part on small-scale apparel assembly for export (known in southern Bulgaria by the Turkish word *ishleme*). *Ishleme* specifically refers to assembly production using imported materials, local labour and production facilities, for re-export, and it is enabled under EU Outward Processing Trade (OPT) agreements allowing duty free import into European Union member countries under specified quota restrictions of goods assembled using previously exported raw materials.[7]

In these highly advantageous regulatory circumstances, local conditions of mass unemployment in traditionally skilled apparel and textile producing regions resulted in attractive labour market conditions for Bulgarian and foreign producers. The legacy of a flexibly organised and spatially distributed structure of plants and workshops provided a basis for growth: many small workshop sites were available, managerial and worker skills remained resident in the community, and established supplying, transport and marketing systems were still in place. State socialist regional investment policies during the 1980s had bequeathed an uneven mix of older and newer equipment to the small village workshops, and some of this equipment provided necessary capital for newly established workshops supplying new markets in Western Europe. Kurdjali's border location was also attractive to foreign investors, being within trucking distance of other factories and port facilities in Turkey, Greece and other parts of Bulgaria.

These conditions were compounded by the financial crisis of 1996–1997 in which the Bulgarian *lev* fell in value from 70.4 to the US$ to 2,045.5 to the US$. As a result, the official dollar value of the average monthly wage collapsed from over $127 to under $25, during a brief period of hyper-inflation. Although a new government introduced a Currency Board in July 1997 and the currency subsequently stabilised, GDP fell by another 7.2 per cent in 1997.[8] Registered unemployment remained high throughout the period and real unemployment figures were much higher.[9]

In these circumstances, some enterprises remained open, sustained by minimal levels of state underwriting, contracting, and production. In some cases, these 'resources' permitted state and former-state firms and managers to struggle along in generally unfavourable circumstances, often under conditions of branch-specific forms of re-monopolisation, dependent largely on national markets. In some cases, firms were able to continue operations through manager privatisation. These took several forms. Some larger firms were 'simply transferred' to former managers or went through formal privatisation procedures. In some cases, closed workshops were re-opened by former managers producing for niche markets, based on former international contacts and contracts. Other privatised units were able to establish new markets, usually on contract basis, either through national buying organisations, international distributors, or direct brand name marketers, with smaller workshops surviving off *ad-hoc* and uncertain contracting. The new small and medium-sized assembly operations work under short-term contracts to supply international buyers and marketing firms geared to new geographies of consumption, and are driven largely by cheap and relatively disciplined labour pools. As the Central and East European Business Center (US Department of Commerce) currently argues on its webpage for Central and Eastern Europe generally: 'Unemployment should continue to grow as the government closes unprofitable enterprises. This means good news for foreign investors who now face a job market rich with eager and skilled labour' (http://www.mac.doc.gov/eebic/countryr/bulgaria/market/macro.htm). Indeed, many workers have been so eager for work of any kind that, with deterioration of state oversight mechanisms, the practice of paying part or all of the wage 'in hand' has become quite common. Such 'in-hand' wages reduce social taxes for the firm and income taxes for some workers, but also maintain uncertainty of labour contract for many.[10]

In fact, in many villages where workshops were closed in 1989, existing conditions have produced strong and growing demand for labour and workshops and new firms have emerged producing for foreign markets. Many small villages in Kurdjali again seem to have a functioning apparel workshop economy and, in some cases, the resurgence of demand for skilled sewers has created local labour shortages (Table 13.4). One result is the re-working of state socialist practices of flexible labour arrangements within factories. As managers did under state socialism, current managers struggle to orchestrate production under conditions of labour shortage and seasonal competition for labour time. Managers continue the long-standing practice of permitting female workers to schedule work time around the seasonal demands of agricultural production, especially tobacco. For

Table 13.4 Apparel employment and unemployment by obstina

	Total population 1995	Apparel employment 1998	Percent of manufacturing employment in apparel (excl. metallurgy) 1998	Unemployed (%) 1999
Kurdjali Oblast	213,806	4945	48	14.1
Ardino	18,174	27	8	26.8
Djebel	10,994	361	51	16.8
Ivailovgrad	10,555	52	14	17.7
Kirkovo	33,112	384	75	13.8
Krumovgrad	31,268	1	0	14.4
Kurdjali	76,155	3,612	60	11.7
Momchilgrad	20,836	365	27	14.9
Chernoochene	12,712	143	83	9.7

Sources:
Kurdjali Labor Office. *Ravnishte na bezrabotitsa, predlagane i turcene na trudoviya nazar*, 1999.
Territorial Statistical Office Kurdjali. Mimeo Nos. 220, 247, 1999.
National Statistical Institute. *Oblasti i Obstini* 1988: 37–45.
National Statistical Institute. *Statisticheski Sbornik Kurdjali* 1997a: 115–116.

the female workers, flexible labour time means that they can maintain formal and informal work regimes and rely on multiple economic strategies in situations where other forms of household income (particularly male wages) have been declining or may not be available (see Ch. 11). Indeed, as international marketers and name-brand buyers demand higher quality production under strict supply deadlines, the ability of some workers to maintain flexible labour-time arrangements and even to leverage increases in wages and improvements in working conditions has increased within the context of locally tight labour markets (see Begg *et al.* 2000).

In some enterprises, efforts to restructure work practices in order to meet international quality controls, to retain workers, to ensure workers remain on premises, or to capture some portion of wages back from workers have resulted in the expansion of services for workers on site. In enterprises with strong orders, strict quality demands, and fixed deadlines, managers and owners are adding coffee bars, restaurants, shops, and other facilities to the factory. In other enterprises, where workers have been hired from a wide area and therefore must travel long distances to work, providing free or heavily subsidised food and transport has become an essential pre-requisite for maintaining quality production throughout the working day. Reminiscent of integrated state socialist firms, these socialised factory operations nonetheless represent new forms of factory regime.[11]

It is certainly tempting to characterise these emerging assembly operations as a form of 'maquila' production based on cheap labour pools, as Pavlínek (1998) has suggested for new German and Austrian assembly operations along the Czech border (see also Pavlínek and Smith 1998). The London *Sunday Times* (September 26, 1999) has even suggested that Western buyers privately refer to these burgeoning industrial regions as 'gulag Europe', where wages of 20p (about 32c) an hour are common and where in at least one 'Bulgarian factory making Levi Strauss clothing for sale in British stores, more than 100 female textile workers are being forced to strip naked by their bosses at the end of their shifts – ostensibly to check they have not stolen anything.'

In the Bulgarian case, however, while *ishleme* production explicitly refers to export processing based on cheap and initially abundant, 'disciplined,' female labour, such generalisations obscure the actual variety of industrial forms that are emerging, the ways in which particular industries have themselves restructured their production logics and geographies in the past decade, the complexity of labour market dynamics emerging within the region, and the important roles played by culture and ethnicity in shaping regional transformation. They also run the risk of rendering workers as docile and reactive, and regions as little more than cheap labour reserves. This view overlooks the many ways in which the politics of production and community are contested and carefully negotiated (albeit under unequal conditions and constraints) (for similar arguments in different contexts see Gibson-Graham 1996, Smith *et al.* 2002, and Pavlínek and Pickles 2000).

In practice, the new firms exhibit a range of organisational forms, varying levels of capitalisation, and multiple and changing labour demands and practices. They are variously articulated with, and dependent upon, broader social conditions and practices and differ in having a long pre-capitalist history in the region. Some are small operations run on short-term and uncertain contracts usually by local, former state firm employees capitalising on their previous experiences and contacts. Some are more substantial enterprises employing from 20–150 workers and also drawing on equipment, workers and contacts developed in the state system. Still others are new factories built with or by foreign firms who have strong links with international retailers, wholesalers or name-brand companies (such as Nike, Fila and Adidas). The main foreign investors have been Turkish, Greek and Italian, often in joint agreements with Bulgarians. All firms produce for foreign markets and few do more than assemble imported cut pieces to order, although for a significant number national suppliers and markets remain important, and some are experimenting with local design and dyeing operations. All are, in different ways, now integrated into the commodity circuits of global apparel assembly (see Gereffi 1999). All depend on low wage, ethnic, female workers in a variety of contractual arrangements, including putting-out, short-term contract home work, and factory employment, although some are now upgrading their technologies, work regimes and training programs, and are attempting to build into the enterprise more than mere assembly operations. In a few cases, enterprises with design functions that can sell through buyers and agents have established contacts in fashion lines with international or national marketers. In other cases, manufacturers supply national markets (usually of lower quality) to maintain production runs between international contracts. (See Begg *et al.* 2000 for further details of firm structure and their embeddedness in global commodity chains.[12])

What at first appeared to have been a form of defensive restructuring in a regional branch plant economy now appears more complex, as ownership and organisational forms diversify, work regimes are transformed, and some workers seem better positioned to bargain for better working conditions and some manufacturers are better positioned, and have good reasons, to deliver on those demands. Labour markets and enterprise behaviour show signs of increasing differentiation as enterprises articulate in different ways with national and international suppliers and markets and with local social conditions. Where new economic opportunities have emerged, they have done so almost exclusively for female workers and, as a consequence, household and gender relations are also being restructured. At least relative to others in the region, whose primary experience of transition has been unemployment and economic hardship, female apparel workers are finding employment, receiving benefits, and increasingly seem to be gaining marginal advantages in bargaining power.[13] What emerges is a picture of industrial restructuring that is both a product of, and a problem for, the thesis that Eastern Europe is emerging as a 'cheap labour gulag' region.

Domesticating *ishleme*

Each of these 'experiments' in the structure and practices of private production have depended in varying degree on the ability of managers to articulate production, quality and wages with the constraints of international contracting and the broader social conditions of workers' lives. These forms of constraint are not entirely new, but have emerged as reworkings of state socialist practices. Gerald Creed (1998) has shown how formal economic relations under state socialism were 'domesticated' through village and household economies, and it is this domestication of the transitional economy and of capitalist economic practices that occurred in Kurdjali in response to post-1989 economic decline. In a sense, deep economic decline has been 'absorbed' (with great hardship) by the multiple and adaptive nature of village economies and marginal household practices and budgets. But it has also produced new conditions within which transformation is occurring. It is to the nature and role of these 'productive adaptations' that I now turn.

As Smith *et al.* (2002: 20) have recently suggested, commodity chain analysis has 'simply accepted that female workers tend to be a source of cheap labour without developing any adequate analysis of why this should be so.' Specifically, they argue, such analyses of international divisions of labour in the apparel industry have failed adequately to focus on and account for the role of non-wage labour in shaping the nature of production relations and the ways in which regions are located within international systems of production and consumption. Instead, they argue, 'we must have a more sophisticated form of analysis of the relationship between welfare systems, the domestic division of labour and the form and function of the family...' (Smith *et al.* 2002: 21). One of the more complex stories of the transition in Kurdjali has to do with precisely these patterns of employment, welfare, and allocation of labour, and particularly the gendered nature of each.

These social legacies and practices are important elements in the ability of new and existing firms to operate effectively in a rapidly changing and highly competitive international contracting environment, and at the same time they structure and domesticate the ways in which new regional production systems emerge in a region such as Kurdjali. Indeed, these articulations are so important that I will now turn to some of the key forms of the 'social economy' with which production is being articulated. In so doing, I do not assume that household economies and practices are merely reacting to conditions of shortage. Indeed, the extent to which household practices are adaptive to or actually shape those processes is precisely at issue. Instead, and more important for our understanding of new enterprise creation in peripheral ethnic regions, this section focuses on the ways in which social networks have functioned historically as channels for economic and political survival in response to the rigors of economic marginality, political uncertainty and economic competition. Under these conditions, the ethnic Turkish population has drawn on its pre-existing social networks and linkages, and these have proven to be crucial in at least two ways to the kinds of economic adjustments that have emerged.

In this section of the chapter, I focus on three primary ways in which people in the region are multiplying their economic practices in adjusting to transformation in a manner that has direct consequences for the emergence of industrial capitalism in the region: (i) deepening social networks; (ii) increasing household dependence on alternative forms of cash income generation, such as migrant labour remittances, pensions and petty-commodity trading; and (iii) re-peasant-isation, deepening of subsistence production, and growing dependence on natural resource extraction. These are, I argue, crucial elements of any understanding of the ways in which labour market flexibilities are being structured in apparel firms and how the new industries have become embedded regionally and socially.

Deepening social networks

Extended family networks have always been a common feature of daily life in ethnic Turkish communities. As in Bulgarian families generally, 'close' networks or *bliski* are structured in terms of family and locality networks, age, school, army and marriage cohorts, and even year-of-birth affiliations (see Cellarius 2000, Creed 1998, and Ledenova 1998). These networks (and many others) operate as stronger or weaker functioning systems of reciprocity, trust and debt that individuals, families and whole communities use on a regular basis, but can call upon to a greater extent in times of difficulty and need (Czako and Sik 1995). Besides providing material and social support, such *bliski* also operate as channels of communication and exchange, providing opportunities for learning and increasing the chances of interaction, contact and support to a degree not possible for individuals who are not so 'networked'.

Early reforms in Kurdjali led to what elsewhere Michael Burawoy (1996: 1109) has described as 'economic involution'; 'a process of economic degeneration in which the economy feeds on itself' through a reworking of exchange relationships instead of a fundamental change in the relations of production. In this process, the role of powerful economic actors in orchestrating relations of exchange and the social networks that support them was crucial. This was certainly the case in the large state enterprises in the commanding heights of the economy and in many core enterprises of lower-value added branches in Bulgaria. These were effectively 'privatised' in ways that are now well known, involving little public participation: branch plants were closed to protect the jobs and wage bills of core enterprises and workers, the resources of state enterprises were 'pirated', and viable enterprises were 'taken over' by manager privatisations of one kind or another. These social networks were extremely powerful and effective. But, in the early stages of transition they disadvantaged Kurdjali and ethnic Turks who, because of their already marginalised socio-economic status, were unable to benefit from such rapid and large-scale forms of primitive accumulation (Pickles 1995, Begg and Pickles 1998, Begg *et al.* 1999).[14] Only in public sector employment did ethnic Turkish employment increase in absolute and relative terms after 1989, and this occurred in large part because of the local power of the Movement for Rights and Freedom (MRF). For the general population, regional economic decline and mass unemployment mobilised kinship, friendship and social networks to sustain family and community members.[15] Social networks have been particularly important in the circulation and distribution of remittance and pension incomes, and non-commodified food supplies. These have been important in shaping the re-emergence of industrial capital in the region. It is to these social networks that I now turn.

Alternative forms of cash income

During the period of the command economy, Kurdjali's economy relied on the trinity of tobacco, mining and apparel. After 1989, employment for men in agriculture and manufacturing collapsed quickly, and mining slowly declined. Enterprise closure was especially swift and definitive in those branches of industry typically employing male workers. Unlike apparel workshops, where managers and workers held out hope for at least short-term contracts and a limited return to work, other sectors were closed permanently and often machinery was sold off or shipped out to core enterprises in urban areas (Begg and Pickles 1998). With employment declines in agriculture, manufacturing and mining, male workers were particularly hard hit by recession. The number of ethnic Turkish men working on migrant labour contracts (especially in construction) increased substantially, and as a result these men are absent from towns and villages for long periods during the year. One important consequence has been the institutionalising of a household economy based on migrant male labour remittances, which in turn has contributed to changes in basic gender roles and work responsibilities within the household.

With men unemployed or absent from the villages, women have been forced to deepen their historical reliance on agricultural work and off-farm employment. Under state socialism, women were already heavily involved in off-farm

employment and this seems to be continuing, with women comprising one-half of
the formal labour force (National Statistical Institute 1996, 1998a). Because
agricultural labour is seasonal, workshops (especially apparel assembly)
absorbed the surplus labour of the village. In what follows, I want to suggest some
of the ways in which this articulation has been important in shaping the specific
pathways and industrial forms emerging in the resurgence of the apparel industry.

In some cases, households have little or no access to land or resources or ability
to farm whatever land is available to them, and only a minority has access to
formal or informal sources of income. In these situations state pensions and
time-limited unemployment benefits provide the only source of income (see also
Ch. 10). As in post-colonial economies, remittances and pensions support large
numbers of people beyond the immediate recipients. In one context, however,
transition opened up new avenues for ethnic Turks, and the region more generally,
through the emergence of forms of merchant capitalism. The mass emigration/
expulsion of ethnic Turks in 1989 and the subsequent return of some of those who
left created exchange and trading networks that have had profound effects on the
regional economy. With the advent of more liberal social and economic policies,
borders have been opened and traders have been able to normalise trade relations
that were once seen to be illegal. Throughout the 1990s, traders travelled regularly
between Bulgaria and Turkey exchanging goods and money legally and illegally,
and maintaining links among family and village networks. The 'Turkish trader' is
now a well-known figure throughout rural Bulgaria (Chevalier 1999), supplying
low-cost imported consumer goods to all areas of the country. Because of
language, proximity and this history of cross-border contact, the border to Turkey
has emerged as an important trading zone and the local economy has become
further enmeshed in broader national and international networks of exchange,
movement and association. Neighbourhoods and even entire villages in Turkey
were settled by Bulgarian Turks. Many maintained contacts with family members
in Bulgaria and refugees and labour migrants often entered Turkey with their
assistance. Such flows of refugees, emigres and returnees consolidated and
extended the trans-border reach of these families, creating new diasporic and
trans-national geographies of movement and exchange and opening
opportunities for new kinds of investment (see Zhelyazkova 1998).

After 1989, legal and illegal imports of consumer goods across the border from
Turkey boomed. 'Turkish traders' selling imported low cost clothing, shoes, toys
and appliances were quickly able to establish their position in the Bulgarian
market. Managers of Bulgarian apparel firms, particularly those competing for
national markets, complained bitterly that this competition hurt local producers.
Certainly, Turkish social and cross-border networks and experiences fostered the
rapid emergence of a petty merchant class among Turkish traders, and some of
these were able to leverage their positions and markets into substantial sources of
accumulation. Moreover, such patterns of migrant work and trading also seem to
have played a role in shaping the actual paths of entry of new cross-border apparel
contracting and direct investment, with Turkish and Greek firms predominating
in the start-ups of the early 1990s (see Pickles and Begg 2000). Turkish entre-

preneurs and traders, in particular, were among the first international investors involved directly in the region's apparel industry, either through the establishment of new factories or in trading and labour arbitraging for locally owned firms.[16] As with initial Greek investments in the western part of the country, the first Turkish[17] 'entrepreneurs' tended to work on short time horizons, extracting profit from short-run contracts and sometimes deploying highly exploitative, even illegal, work practices. As one informant explained, 'They take in young girls, work them long hours six or seven days a week until their eyes or their fingers fail, and then they throw them out.' These entrepreneurs were also among the more 'creative' in the production systems they were willing to deploy to 'make contract'. In one case, a Turkish contractor arranged with a local mayor to establish a village-wide 'putting-out' system, in which cloth and patterns were supplied to women in the village who worked piecework from their homes. The mayor operated as the clearing agent and subcontractor. In another case, a 'Turkish' investor had managed to set up a sweatshop in former office space rented from a local authority. The 'enterprise' closed within weeks and 'local lore' had it that it had re-opened in a neighbouring village. A third case is, perhaps, more typical. Here a Bulgarian Turkish man had opened a small workshop employing half a dozen sewers, mainly from his own extended family, fulfilling contract orders for uniforms from the German army, contracts he had learned about while previously working in a large state apparel enterprise.

As apparel enterprises become increasingly linked to larger national and international buying chains, the importance of these kinds of locally specific linkages and legacies may diminish. Certainly, the period when 'fly-by-night' contractors can profitably operate in the region has, in all probability, already passed, although low-cost operators are still an important part of the regional economy. However, the cultural practices of the broader economy are becoming more important determinants of struggles over wages, contracts and the competitive position of regional producers. It is to these broader social conditions that I now turn.

Re-peasantisation, the deepening of subsistence production and natural resource use?

In what more generally Smollet (1989) has called 'the economy of jars', rural and urban Bulgarians have long supported each other through informal kin exchanges. Indeed, Chevalier (1999: 11) found that all forms of village exchange, including monetary, now operate largely within family and village networks: 'several changes have occurred which provoke a new expansion of the familial and personal spheres, a withdrawal into kinship and local identity.'[18] Produce, including large quantities of jarred preserves, continues to make its way (as it has for many years) from village to city, and children and grandchildren contribute with occasional weekend and summer-time farm labour. Money is increasingly important to the pensioned villager in these village-city exchanges (Chevalier 1999), but for many whose access to money is restricted to welfare distributions, pensions and remittances, subsistence production, food gathering and networks of reciprocal exchange have also remained important.

Clarke (1997) has argued that in Russia and Eastern Europe more generally labour market flexibility brought about by neo-liberal employment policies promoted a reversion 'to subsistence production as wages fall below the minimum necessary for physical survival' (Clarke 1997: 25). Thus, one response to economic immiseration is a return to the land, an effective re-peasantisation or the production of a rural proletariat. Under conditions of mass unemployment, rural dwellers have drawn more heavily on the resources available to them (land, social connections, natural resources) as survival strategies. The *Development Cooperation Report* for 1998 also suggested that during the 1990s a 'majority of Bulgarians became reliant on survival strategies, such as household/urban agriculture' (p. 11), with more than one-third of households producing their own fruits, vegetables and preserves on small plots. But, Meurs (1999 and Ch. 11) has argued that this 'strategies of survival' argument misreads the historical importance of private production for domestic household consumption (see also Smith 2000a and Chs 11 and 12). In her view, subsistence production never did cease being an important element in household economies throughout the period of communist rule. While neo-liberal adjustment policies resulted in unemployment rates of over 90 per cent in some villages and land restitution broke up the co-operative farms and returned title over small parcels of land to farmers, there is little evidence of an increase in subsistence production. Instead, as total household budgets declined after 1989, the relative importance of subsistence production from small-plot farming increased. Between 1989 and 1996, while income from household plots rose from 14.7 per cent to 22.6 per cent of average income, the contribution of salaries and wages fell from 55.9 per cent to 39.5 per cent (National Statistical Institute 1998b). This is what Meurs (see Ch. 11) calls a 'truncated transition'.

Clarke (1999) has also questioned the 'myth of the dacha', arguing that there is no general return to the land in similar circumstances in Russia, in part because access to land and the ability and resources to farm it was uneven. In short, those with resources have been able to farm while those in greatest need as a result of loss of employment income have been unable to either gain access to sufficient land or, where land is available, do not have the resources or know-how to cultivate it. In this sense, there has been a differentiation of the population based on access to resources and know-how. Those with access to land and resources to farm have increased their levels of activity and dependence on production. Those most in need and lacking access to land and resources have, for the most part, been unable to compensate for loss of waged income by turning to agriculture. Instead of a re-peasantisation or a deepening of subsistence production as a survival strategy, people without land and resources have been forced to survive at much lower levels of economic well-being and are, as a result, much more at risk of illness and malnutrition.

Meurs (see Ch. 11) seeks to provide an even more nuanced reading. Instead of a de-monetisation occurring in the rural economy, to which rural households must adapt, Meurs argues that rural households have 'a logic of their own, distinct from the neo-liberal logic of macro policies'. That is, household processes are not responses to state policies, but instead are adaptations originated by autonomous households which were only weakly integrated into the macro-structures of central planning in the first place. Pre-socialist and now non-capitalist agrarian practices suffuse the rural household economy and cannot be reduced to either. In Smith's (2000a) terms, since these are non-market processes, the current transformation must be seen as consisting of a plurality of economic practices, both capitalist and non-capitalist. In this view, as with Meurs, households were differentially integrated into state structures prior to 1989 and these differences provide the legacies and conditions from which current adjustments to economic crisis are occurring. For Meurs (1999: 6), since rural households were heavily engaged in non-socialist production prior to 1989, with large amounts of household time spent in simple reproduction, we cannot see current subsistence production either as a 'distinct survival strategy' in the face of economic crisis or a non-capitalist agrarian holdover from socialism. Instead, she suggests, they are continuations of earlier forms of simple reproduction and are not adaptations or forms of resistance to new circumstances.

These arguments are important correctives to the too easy characterisation of agrarian production as reactive to economic crises, but they also need to account more fully for the meaning of 'continuity'. For Burawoy and Verdery (1999) such explanations depend on notions of culture and history as static, failing adequately to account for the 're-workings' and 're-articulations' present in apparently similar practices at different times and in distinctly different social and economic circumstances. Further, in postulating autonomous and parallel forms of economic practice (socialist and non-socialist, capitalist and non-capitalist), both Meurs and Smith may not pay sufficient attention to the ways in which such modes of production may be historically and regionally articulated, and the ways in which such semi-autonomous spheres were *always* also articulated in rural household economies – what Holmes (1989: 9), in the context of north-eastern Italy has called the 'liminal' status of the 'worker-peasant' household economy:

> The members of each liminal group employ a mosaic of productive arrangements in their day-to-day lives and over the course of their labor careers. In rural households, individuals engage in agrarian and industrial wage work, mining, construction, and a range of scavenging activities, as the family moves through the domestic cycle ... ties among family and kin to a common round of agrarian activities make the rural household the center of peasant-worker livelihood and society. Thus, worker peasantries are sustained by individuals who, in their efforts to secure a livelihood, create linkages between rural households and the wage nexus.

In our present case, this points again to the importance of a consideration of the flexibilities workers have constructed for regulating their entry and exit from waged employment, whether under state socialism or emergent peripheral capitalism, and the ways in which seasonal availability of 'free' household labour, remittance and pension economies, and home production have historically been important for the forms and practices of industrial employment. The fact that labour shedding after 1989 could occur on such a scale and at such a rapid pace without corresponding labour or social unrest can only be understood, I argue, in terms of this legacy. The loss of jobs brought serious economic hardships to many families of workers, but households had long been used to extended periods of lay-off and non-work followed by calls to return to work as orders came in. In this sense, too, the rapid return to work as new factories opened in the 1990s was a form of business as usual, building into the new private factories the very same flexibilities (and powers) that such labour contracts presuppose.

As a result of employment uncertainties for all household members, food production and *bliski* have been intimately related in Bulgarian social and economic life. In relative terms households have become more dependent on non-formal sector sources of subsistence, exchange and income. These include land-use and natural resource extraction practices such as collecting on common lands and public forests, hunting, free-range grazing of sheep and goats, and wood gathering for heating and construction, along with associated wood and leather craftwork (Cellarius 1999, Chevalier 1999, Pickles *et al.* 2001). As wage income and state benefits declined, these – like subsistence farming and gardening – became relatively more important.[19]

It is, I suggest, the complexity (and social and historical depth) of 'peasant-worker' household economies that have played an important role in the particular form of cheap wage economy that has emerged in Kurdjali; wages and uncertain work regimes are underwritten by other forms of family income. But it is these same complex patterns of alternative though limited livelihoods, and their necessary demands on flexible time, that suggest that there are limits to efforts that seek to generalise 'gulag' production in the region. First, the diversity of production forms and relations in the region is hard to capture under the rubric of low-wage assembly production (although more than any other single descriptor, this is an accurate one). Second, low wages and despotic work practices are already being met, albeit on a limited scale, by worker resistance and pressure for better conditions. And third, these very conditions of social reproduction are now producing capital deepening and higher value production, as manufacturers realise the marginal utility and practical necessity of improved wages and working conditions for a relatively well trained, disciplined, and highly flexible workforce.

Local apparel producers are adjusting quickly to make use of whatever resources they have at their disposal to maintain their position in a highly competitive industry. For some, this still means taking every advantage of desperate workers who will work long hours for low wages. In other cases, new imperatives are forcing trade-offs with wage costs. First, workers themselves are increasingly resisting the exploitation they face. They do this in many ways, but one way is through their defence of seasonally flexible work arrangements. In some cases, workers have attempted (often unsuccessfully) to form trade unions and (more successfully) to push for higher wages and better working conditions. For those firms that are increasingly constrained by international buyer demands for higher quality and quick turnover times, workers are becoming a more important resource than just 'nimble fingers'. They are being asked to take responsibility at each stage of production for quality control and to agree to the kind of 'storming' practices long familiar under state socialism, in which contract deadlines are met through extra work hours (see Pickles 1995). Where higher quality and higher value are involved, sweatshop arrangements can only work for short periods of time, although there are clear efforts by some manufacturers to sustain them. Indeed, in several cases where high quality international buyers carefully regulate the working environments in firms with which they deal, managers have been found to be subcontracting work from the monitored and sanctioned 'clean' factory to 'hidden' sweatshops nearby (Georgieva 2000).

In other cases, however, even where production is directed almost entirely to export-processing and assembly of imported materials on contract to international buyers, the needs of the industry may be congruent with at least marginal pressure from workers to increase wages and conditions. While low wages are the primary driving force behind the geographical relocation of apparel production to Eastern Europe (especially under European Union OPT regime arrangements), competitive pressures within the industry and their articulation with specific regionalised social formations are giving rise to a wide diversity of industrial forms and workplace arrangements on the ground.

Together these provided the conditions for the emergence of new firms in a highly competitive international industry. But the new firms have had to adjust to the social conditions in which they have emerged, and in many cases have found those conditions valuable in their own efforts to manage costs and deal with uncertainty in contracting and pricing. Seasonal agricultural labour demands necessitate flexible labour contracts, but also result in greater willingness among workers to tolerate variable working hours and periodic lay-offs. Traditional and new natural resource uses are crucial elements of many household budgets, but they also reduce pressure on wages. Pensions, remittances and petty trading similarly inject new, albeit limited resources into the household economy, but remittance and trading economies also provide opportunities for learning about other economic opportunities that might otherwise not be available to village communities. In this sense, at least, village life is 'remote' only in the sense of distance from urban centres. Culturally and economically villagers tend to be highly integrated into national, and in some cases international, circuits.

Conclusion

Neo-liberal structural adjustment in Bulgaria occurred in two phases. A period of rapid and intense economic decline after 1989 was followed by the financial crisis of 1996–1997 and the subsequent period of macro-economic stabilisation. While each phase has involved different mixes of macro-economic and political policies, each has resulted in a deepening crisis of infrastructural provision and economic opportunity, in which income levels collapsed and education, health and social well-being deteriorated. The consequences have been particularly severe in marginal rural, mountain and 'ethnic' regions.

Under state socialism, employment and subsistence practices embedded in family and village relationships marginalised the ethnic Turkish population of Kurdjali. This marginalisation deepened even further with neo-liberal economic adjustment policies, resulting in the collapse of employment and the rise of mass unemployment after 1989. These conditions, and responses to them, have led to the re-emergence of apparel production using primarily imported raw materials for re-export to European Union countries. These have in turn further differentiated traditionally segmented labour markets creating limited increases in bargaining power for female apparel workers in regions where male unemployment is high. One consequence is a deepening articulation of a dynamic industrial branch that is increasingly tied to international marketing structures with formal and non-formal household economic practices geared to economic survival. Apparel enterprises experiencing an industrial boom in a regional context of mass unemployment, household poverty and predominantly female wage-earners are, thus, reworking state socialist forms of 'domestication' and producing new forms of industrial organisation and practice.

Elsewhere, Smith (2000b) has shown – drawing on Lipietz (1992) – that 'defensive restructuring' (involving low-wage, cost advantages and large-scale worker flexibility) is the norm for peripheral regions in Slovakia, especially in those with a substantial minority population. This has also been the story of economic change in the peripheral regions of Bulgaria with substantial ethnic Turkish populations. Georgieva (2001) has recently argued that 'the domestic market offers no survival chances to producers', that the 'only chance of survival is working with materials for their foreign clients', and that 'Bulgarian producers have to resort to exporting working clothes, aprons, linens, etc'. But there are signs that small and medium size firm creation is increasing, that highly segmented labour markets are tightening, that firms are investing in capital deepening and better working conditions, wages and benefits are improving, and that local linkages to support training programmes and worker retention are being developed. That is, that a form of 'offensive' restructuring in the apparel industry – however tentative and small-scale – might be emerging. If this is the case, then one reason lies in the demands for quality, speed and flexibility within the global apparel industry. But one reason also lies within the capacities of local people to shape regional futures and to domesticate capitalism in ways that are similar to their domestication of socialism.[20]

Ishleme contracts must be constantly renewed and new contracts and buyers found. Competition in the industry is extremely strong. As a result, product lines change frequently to accommodate buyer specifications, and buyers are themselves constantly involved in predicting, matching and creating consumer demand for material, design, style and quality of clothing. In this situation, flexibilities in production and labour are increasingly important to the success of a new enterprise. Export processing industries currently benefit from comparatively low wages in regions of high unemployment and proximity to major markets in Western Europe. But, low wages are sustained only to the extent that household budgets are supplemented by complex non-formal economic practices. *Ishleme* firms thus articulate in diverse ways with the labour demands of household economies. Insofar as they do, they reproduce and reconfigure the broader social and economic flexibilities that sustained Turkish households during the worst years of state socialist political and economic dislocation and that are now necessary under conditions of highly segmented processes of labour market restructuring. 'Export processing' captures an economic aspect of this emerging regional development model, but it is a form of assembly for global markets predicated on pre-existing industrial structures and social networks, and is articulated with flexible household economies. Insofar as these articulations are resources for social action, the question of regional economic futures will also be open to transformation of one sort or another.

Notes

1   This chapter is based on research supported by the Geography and Regional Science Division of the National Science Foundation (Award #SBR-9515244). It draws on a survey of 80 firms carried out in November 1999 in collaboration with researchers at the Institute of Geography, Bulgarian Academy of Sciences, and field interviews with managers carried out between 1995 and 1999 with Robert Begg, Mieke Meurs and Poli Roukova. Parts of the argument developed here are reworked from Pickles and Begg (2000) and Begg *et al.* (2000). I am grateful to the editors of *Growth and Change* and *Problemi na Geographi*, for permission to reproduce some details here, and particularly to Robert Begg, Mieke Meurs and Poli Roukova whose influences run throughout the chapter. Svetla Anechkova provided valuable research and translation assistance, Jayme Walenta and Josh Lepawksy worked with the survey data, and Grigor Gradev shared some of the findings from his own research on emerging industries in Bulgaria. I am grateful to Adrian Smith and Adam Swain for insightful review of an earlier draft of the chapter. Final editing on the chapter was facilitated by a Fulbright award to the Dipartimento di Scienze Geografiche e Storiche, l'Universita degli Studi di Trieste, where Gianfranco Battisti kindly provided the opportunity for reflection and writing.

2   Bulgaria has a complex hierarchy of regional administrative divisions and responsibilities. About the size of Pennsylvania, it is made up today of 278 *obstini*, roughly counties, and nine *oblasti*, roughly states. The 28 *okrugi* administrative units were eliminated in 1987, but were reformed in 1999 as the basis for future territorial administration and planning.

3   Those regions classified as 'most depressed' were Pernik, Vidin, Kurdjali and Smolyan.

4   'Central districts' were Sofia, Burgas, Plovdiv, Stara Zagora, Pleven, Varna, Veliko Turnovo and Vratza.

5   In the early 1970s, the central government acknowledged significant differences in the economic status of Bulgarian regions (MRDC 1996) and in the 1979 'New Economic Programme' deliberate efforts were made both in agriculture and in industry to make rural areas of the country more self-sufficient (Koulov 1992). Three related policies were designed to slow rural to urban migration, raise the rural standard of living, and address the needs of the most disadvantaged communities. The first was the Border Regions Policy, which encouraged industrial branch plants and infrastructure investment in 97 *obstini* along the southern and western borders of Bulgaria (MRDC 1996). The second was the Mountain Regions Policy that included, additionally, some of the more remote

Balkan *obstini*. The third, the Social Industries Policy, targeted *obstini* with high concentrations of Muslims and Roma.

Together, these policies of industrial allocation, credits and financial supports constituted an explicit industrial location policy that, beginning in 1981, began to decentralise small assembly operations to border, mountain and ethnic villages. In what, elsewhere, we have called 'branch plant' and 'workshop' space (Begg and Pickles 1998), textiles, electronics, leather, wood products and apparel industries were organised as a set of dispersed, smaller factories, branch plants and workshops located in district capitals and villages. Employing 20 to 50 people, the village workshops did simple assembly work for core plants located in district capitals. They, in turn, took orders from larger regional factories and ultimately operated within a unified combinat national structure. The regional head-quarters, through which workshops received orders, enjoyed some level of autonomy and engaged in specialised production for both CMEA markets and markets outside the CMEA system. In 1988, the policies covered 54 *obstini* along the western and southern borders of Bulgaria and affected 570,000 people in 1,028 settlements (Koulov 1992: 397).

6   Low-income households are defined as those earning 45 per cent of the average wage. Poverty households are defined as those with per capita income below 60 per cent of the low-income threshold.

7   OPT regime quotas are governed under EU regulations and are being phased out in stages. Phase three for 2002 permits 18 per cent of imports to be tariff free and phase four (coming into effect in 2004–5) will open the EU entirely to foreign imports (DG Trade 2000, European Commission 2000, Snyder 1999).

8   The Currency Board Arrangement (CBA) was established in July 1997, at which time the Bulgarian lev was pegged to the Deutschmark (1,000/1).

9   In a 1996 household in rural villages in the Rhodope region, Meurs (see Ch. 11) found that only 29 per cent of working-age men and 19 per cent of working-age women were engaged in wage employment, while most were surviving on income earned from farming their personal plots of land.

10 I am grateful to Grigor Gradev for this insight.

11 Labour shortage in a growing industry combined with the permeability of the Bulgarian-Turkish border has provided some Bulgarian Turkish women with a different option. Highly educated and well-trained workers in Kurdjali apparel firms migrate to equivalent firms in Turkey where they can command higher wages and, because of their skill levels, have better opportunities for promotion. Such labour migration further diminishes the bargaining power of firms located in Kurdjali.

12 The boom in assembly operations is not unique to Kurdjali or Bulgaria more generally. In Bulgaria all border regions in the Rhodopes have experienced a rapid increase in assembly operations for apparel, and leather and footwear.

13 This issue has recently been at the heart of arguments, particularly in the US, over appropriate forms of analysis and politics for dealing with the globalising of low-wage apparel and footwear assembly production. For a discussion of the debate over the economics and politics of sweatshop production and the anti-sweatshop campaign see Featherstone and Henwood (2001).

14 The people of the region are predominantly Turkish-speaking Muslims who have been subject to repeated nationalist efforts to assimilate, punish or expel them. The most recent of these policies culminated in the 1989 expulsion and migration

to Turkey of over 360,000 ethnic Turks and Roma, over 100,000 coming from the Kurdjali region itself. While many of those who left subsequently returned, the loss of population has left a deep scar on the social and economic fabric of villages throughout the region. See Eminov (1997), Brunnbauer (1999), and Pickles and Begg (2000).

15 Not all these 'mobilisations' involve direct financial or material support, although often they do. The 'mobilisation' of such support networks can just as easily involve the deepening of already existing masculinist and patriarchal practices. Certainly in non-Muslim Bulgarian households such *bliski* have probably contributed as much to increases in alcohol and cigarette consumption as they have to direct economic or material subventions of the household. In ethnic Turkish Bulgarian households such *bliski* networks also contribute to marital conflict in situations in which (as wives describe them) unemployed husbands and sons 'sit around' as wives and daughters go out to work.

16 Larger-scale Turkish investment has also entered the region, notably in the planned Turkish hydro-electric and recreation complex in the hills above Kurdjali.

17 There were examples of both Turkish and Bulgarian nationals in this category.

18 The role of social networks in fostering responses to the economic crisis wrought by liberalisation is, however, far more complex than can be captured by categories such as 'networks of support,' remittances, subsistence agriculture and natural resource extraction practices. In one particularly interesting example, lacking few effective economic options, leaders in one Rhodope village have drawn upon family and other social networks to develop a particularly novel and, in the short term, effective collective response to economic crisis. Contacts were used, familial and friendship ties were mobilised, and resources were pooled to send 'starter families' to emigrate to Germany and the United States. Initial immigrants overseas and family and professional contacts in Sofia provided the necessary legal assistance, return remittances, and jobs for family members. Villagers provided local support for families to relocate to take up these opportunities. Over sixty families from this village have already moved to the United States in this way. The precise and manifold ways in which 'social adjustment' is occurring remains an issue for further investigation.

19 This is particularly the case where new markets have also opened up for the products of forest gathering. Three examples are notable: international markets for local mushrooms are managed through travelling buyers often supplying markets in Italy, the war in Kosovo increased demand for cut timber, and (in the absence of any other economic opportunities in 1997 and 1998) Rhodope households pushed the limits of potato cultivation in order to have some commodities for barter. The growing dependence on forest resources is well illustrated by the case of one village in a rural district of the Western Rhodopes. Here 100 per cent of respondent households now depend upon locally collected firewood for heat, 50 per cent collect herbs, 42 per cent use 'common' forest lands for pasturing cattle and sheep, and 27 per cent use them for collecting foodstuffs (Staddon 1999).

20 Whether and to what extent 'offensive restructuring' is occurring in the region is, in many ways, still an open empirical question in need of further research. But, in this chapter I am also concerned with the epistemologico-political implications of a discursive framing of the question of cheap labour production only in terms of docile labour and reactive manufacturers responding to a single 'capitalism' (see

Smith (2000a) and Smith *et al.* (2000) for similar arguments). Instead, with Pred and Watts (1992), I seek a rendering of regional economic change that is both responsive to and transformative of the conditions that give rise to it, that incorporates the symbolic discontents of local people, and situates formal economic processes within the broader social economies with which they are articulated or from which they are disarticulated. That is, with Gibson-Graham (1996), I seek a non-essentialist analysis of the cultures of economic transformation that is attentive to the openings and possibilities of post-socialist transformations.

References

Avramov, R. and Antonov, V. (1994) *Economic Transition in Bulgaria.* London: Agency for Economic Coordination and Development.

Begg, R. and Meurs, M. (1998) 'Writing a new song: Path dependency and state policy in reforming Bulgarian agriculture', in I. Szelényi (ed.) *Privatizing the Land: Rural Political Economy in Post-communist Societies.* London: Routledge, pp. 245–270.

Begg, R. and Pickles, J. (1998) 'Institutions, social networks and ethnicity in the cultures of transition: industrial change, mass unemployment and regional transformation in Bulgaria', in J. Pickles and A. Smith (eds) *Theorising Transition: The Political Economy of Post-Communist Transformations.* London: Routledge, pp. 115–146.

Begg, R., Meurs, M. and Pickles, J. (1999) 'Regional economic change and ethnicity in post-communist transitions: The case of Southern Bulgaria'. Unpublished manuscript.

Begg, R., Pickles, J. and Roukova, P. (2000) 'A new participant in the global apparel industry: The case of Southern Bulgaria', *Problemi na Geographi*, (Sofia), September/October, 3(4), in press.

Bristow, J. A. (1996) *The Bulgarian Economy in Transition.* Cheltenham: Edward Elgar.

Brunnbauer, U. (1999) 'Histories and identities: Nation-state and minority discourses. The case of the Bulgarian Pomaks.' Unpublished Mimeo.

Burawoy, M. (1985) *The Politics of Production.* London: Verso.

Burawoy, M. (1996) 'The state and economic involution: Russia through a China lens', *World Development*, 24 (6): 1105–17.

Burawoy, M. and Verdery, K. (1999) *Uncertain Transition: Ethnographies of Change in the Postsocialist World.* New York: Rowman and Littlefield.

Cellarius, B.A. (1999) 'Global Priority, Local Reality: Rural Communities and Biodiversity Conservation in Bulgaria'. Unpublished PhD Dissertation. Lexington: University of Kentucky.

Cellarius, B.A. (2000) ' "You can buy almost anything with potatoes": An examination of barter during economic crisis in Bulgaria'. Working paper of the Max Planck Institute for Social Anthropology, Halle-Saale.

Chevalier, S. (1999) 'Value, social identity and household consumption practices: A Bulgarian case study', http://www.human-nature.com/hraj/chavalier.html

Clarke, S. (1997) *Poverty in Transition.* Final report for the Department for International Development, December.

Clarke, S. (1999) 'New forms of employment of household survival strategies in Russia'. A report on a project funded by the Department of International Development. Coventry and Moscow: ISITO/CCLS.

Creed, G. (1998) *Domesticating Revolution: From Socialist Reform to Ambivalent Transition in a Bulgarian Village.* University Park, PA: Penn State University Press.

Csako, A. and Sik, E. (1995) 'The role of networks in post-communism', in M. Mendell. and

K. Nielsen (eds) *Europe Central and Eastern*, Montreal: Black Rose Books.

DG Trade (2000) 'Textiles trade must be a two-way street.' *DG Trade* June 2000.

Dicken, P. (1998) *Global Shift*. 3rd Edition. New York: Guilford.

Eminov, A. (1997) *Turkish and Other Muslim Minorities in Bulgaria*. New York: Routledge.

European Commission (2000) 'Report on market access. Background Note 2.' Brussels: European Commisssion: Directorate D: Sectoral trade questions, market access, 12.07.2000.

Featherstone, L. and Henwood, D. (2001) 'Clothes encounters: Activists and economists clash over sweatshops.' *Lingua Franca*, 11 (2), March.

Georgieva, M. (2000) 'Ishleme: The last life-belt for the poor', *Capital* (newspaper). Issue 3, 22–28 January.

Georgieva, M. (2001) 'Bulgaria's textile branch – survival at any cost.' *Capital* (Newspaper), 3–9 February.

Gereffi, G. (1999) 'Industrial upgrading in the apparel commodity chain: What can Mexico learn from East Asia?' Paper presented at the International Conference on Business Transformation and Social Change in East Asia, Tunghai University Institute of East Asian Societies and Economies, Taichung, Taiwan, June 10–11, 1999.

Gibson-Graham, J.K. (1996) *The End of Capitalism (as we knew it): A Feminist Critique of Political Economy*. Cambridge, MA: Blackwell.

Holmes, D.R. (1989) *Cultural Disenchantment: Worker Peasantries in Northeast Italy*. Princeton: Princeton University Press.

International Labour Organization (ILO) (1994) *The Bulgarian Challenge: Reforming Labour Market and Social Policy*. Budapest: ILO.

International Labour Organization (ILO) (1996/97) *Yearbook of Labour Statistics*. Geneva: ILO.

Koulov, B. (1992) 'Tendencies in the administrative territorial development of Bulgaria', *Tijdschrift voor Economishe en Sociale Geografie* 83 (5): 390–401.

Kurdjali Labor Office (1999) *Ravnishte na bezrabotitsa, predlagane i turcene na trudoviya nazar*. Kurdjali.

Ledenova, A.V. (1998) *Russia's Economy of Favours: Blat, Networking and Informal Exchange*. New York: Cambridge University Press.

Lipietz, A. (1992) *Towards a New Economic Order: Postfordism, Ecology, and Democracy*. Oxford: Oxford University Press.

Lovasz, A. (2000) 'Triumphal march: Hungary's clothes-makers move up the value chain.' *Business Central Europe*. June: 24.

Meurs, M. (1999) 'Economic strategies for surviving post-socialism: Changing household economies and gender divisions of labor in the Bulgarian transition', a paper presented to the Conference on 'Gender and Rural Transformation in Europe.' Wageningen, the Netherlands, October.

Ministry of Regional Development and Construction (MRDC) (1996) *Regional Policy in the Republic of Bulgaria*, Sofia.

National Statistical Institute (1991–1999) *Statisticheski Godizhnik (Statistical Yearbook)*, Sofia: Republic of Bulgaria.

National Statistical Institute (1995) *Staticheski Sbornik Smolyan 1994*. Sofia: National Statistical Institute.

National Statistical Institute (1996) *Socialno-Demografski Harakteristisci na Naceleneto i Hilishten Fond: Kurdjali*. Sofia: National Statistical Institute.

National Statistical Institute (1997a) *Staticheski Sbornik Kurdjali 1996*. Sofia: National Statistical Institute.

National Statistical Institute (1997b) *Statisticheski Spravochnik*. Sofia: Republic of Bulgaria.

National Statistical Institute (1998a) *Oblasti i obstini*. Sofia: National Statistical Institute.

National Statistical Institute (1998b) *Household Budgets in the Republic of Bulgaria, 1989–1996*. http://w3.nsi.bg/cgi-bin/sel.cgi/publ/chapt/?FPUBL=12

National Statistical Institute (1999) *Statisticheski Spravochnik*. Sofia: Republic of Bulgaria.

Nenova-Amar, M. and Radeva, E. (1994) 'Wages and employment'. In R. Avramov and V. Antonov (eds) *Economic Transition in Bulgaria*. Sofia: Agency for Economic Coordination and Development, pp. 109–134.

Pavlínek, P. (1998) 'Foreign investment in the Czech Republic', *The Professional Geographer*, 50: 71–85.

Pavlínek, P. and Pickles, J. (2000) *Environmental Transitions: Post-Communist Transformations and Ecological Defence in Central and Eastern Europe*. London: Routledge.

Pavlínek, P. and Smith, A. (1998) 'Internationalization and embeddedness in East-Central European transition: The contrasting geographies of inward investment in the Czech and Slovak Republics', *Regional Studies* 32 (7): 619–638.

Pickles, J. (1995) 'Restructuring state enterprises: Industrial geography and Eastern European transitions', *Geographische Zeitschrift* 83 (2): 114–131.

Pickles, J. and Begg, R. (2000) 'Ethnicity, state violence, and neo-liberal transitions in post-communist Bulgaria', *Growth and Change* 31 (Spring): 179–210.

Pickles, J., Nikolova, M., Velev, S., Mateeva, Z., Staddon, C. and Popov, A. (2001) 'From rectifying revolution to democratic revolution: A decade of environmental change in post-communist Bulgaria', in F.W. Carter and D. Turnock (eds) *Environmental Problems in Central and Eastern Europe*. London: Routledge, forthcoming.

Pred, A. and Watts, M.J. (1992) *Re-Working Modernity: Capitalisms and Symbolic Discontent*. New Brunswick, NJ: Rutgers University Press.

Smith, A. (2000a) 'Employment restructuring and household survival in "post-communist transition": Rethinking economic practices in Eastern Europe', *Environment and Planning A* 32 (10): 1759–1780.

Smith, A. (2000b) 'Ethnicity, economic polarization and regional inequality in southern Slovakia', *Growth and Change* 31 (2): 151–178.

Smith, A., Rainnie, A., Dunford, M., Hardy, J., Hudson, R. and Sadler, D. (2002) 'Networks of value, commodities and regions: Reworking divisions of labour in macro-regional economies', *Progress in Human Geography* 26 (1), forthcoming.

Smollet, E. (1989) 'The economy of jars', *Ethnologie Europa* 19 (2): 125–140.

Snyder, F. (1999) 'Globalisation and Europeanisation as friends and rivals: European Union law in global economic networks.' European University Institute Working Paper LAW 99/8. Florence: European University Institute.

Staddon, C. (1999) 'Economic marginalisation and natural resource management in Eastern Europe', *The Geographical Journal* 165 (2): 200–208.

Sunday Times (London) (1999) 'Top shops use Europe's "gulag" labour', *Sunday Times*, September 26.

United Nations Development Program (UNDP) (1998) *Poverty in Transition*. Sofia: United Nations Development Programme.

World Bank (1999) *World Development Report 1998*. New York: Oxford University Press.

Wyzan, M. (1997) 'Economic transformation and regional inequality in Bulgaria: In search of a meaningful unit of analysis', in D. Jones and J. Miller (eds) *The Bulgarian Economy: Lessons from Reform during Early Transition*. Aldershot: Ashgate.

Zhelyazkova, A. (1998) 'The social and cultural adaptation of Bulgarian immigrants in Turkey', in A. Zhelyazkova (ed.) *Between Adaptation and Nostalgia: The Bulgarian Turks in Turkey*. Sofia: International Center for Minority Studies and Intercultural Relations, pp. 11–45.

Index

Amsden, A.: on East Asian model 11
apparel industry: in Bulgaria 246–73
Aslund, A.: on economic transformation
    36
automobile industry: component
    producers 83–5; in GDR 80–4; in
    Germany 85–92

Bacon, Francis 35
Barnes, T.: on political economy 12, 28
bazaar economy 166
Beck, U.: on the 'Brazilianization' 9; on
    work 30
BEIN (Basic Income European
    Network) 51
'big bang' 7, 36
Bratislava, Slovakia 231–44
Braverman, H.: on Soviet labour process
    13
Bridger S. and Pine F.: on 'survival
    strategies' 213, 215, 227–8
Buck-Morss, S.: on capitalism 28; on
    economic transition 7
budget deficit 38, 204
Bulgaria 247; Rhodope region 213–24
Burawoy, M.: on Soviet labour process
    13–15
Burawoy, M. and Vedery, K.: on market
    behaviour 213, 215

capitalism 7, 10, 92; 'Klondike
    capitalism' 253; plurality of economic
    practices 25, 28–9, 30
Carrier J and Miller D.: on 'virtualism'
    75, 78
Clarke, S.: on economic change 17; on
    Soviet labour process 14–15; on
    survival strategies 228, 262
class structures 230

clothing industry in Bulgaria 246–73
collective bargaining 62
collective farms 221
commodification 17–18; of labour 11,
    25
co-operative agriculture 221–2, 248
Creed, G.: on 'domestication' 16, 227,
    230–1, 257
culture and economy 227–45

de-industrialisation in Germany 75–80
despotic factory regimes 13–14, 247
Dicken, P.: on clothing industry 251,
    253
domestic division of labour 123–6, 148,
    223
domestic economy 21

ECE: economic change 17
economic democracy 50
economic justice 38, 50
economic practices 227–9
Elster, J et al.: on East European
    capitalism 9
employment: in Bulgaria 247–9; change
    in ECE 18–22, 173–4, 176–8;
    conditions of 255; and gender
    105–112, 135–41, 171–3; and
    household division of labour 134; job
    security 112; loss of 18–20, 174, 194,
    219; part time 179–80; secondary
    196–7; underemployment 180–1
entrepreneurship: and forced self-
    employment 164–5, 184–6; and
    gender 158–60; in Hungary 155–66;
    and regional development 161–6;
    self-employment 181
equality 35
ethnicity 216–17, 258–67

EU (European Union) 38; accession into 134; and apparel industry 253; Hungarian accession 150–1
evolutionary theory 11–12

flexible specialisation 167
foreign direct investment 100–16; employment 102; industrial relations 26–7; Poland 103
Fukuyama, F.: on 'end of history' 155

GDP: in Bulgaria 252; change in ECE 9, 252; and tax 38
GDR (German Democratic Republic) 74; automobile industry 80–92; de-industrialisation 75–7; privatisation 77–9
gender 2–3, 16–17, 20, 99–190, 213–26, 249; double burden 17, 126–7, 157, 222; and employment 20; and entrepreneurship 158–65; and EU accession 150–1; and geography 135–41; in Hungary 135–49; and households 123–6, 221–3; ideologies of 117–33; and labour market 102; in Russia 117–18; and Soviet system 16–17; and transformation 99–100; and work 121–3, 126–7
gender orders 117–33
Gereffi, G.: on apparel commodity chains 256
Gibson-Graham, J.K.: on capitalism 12, 28–9, 30, 228; on East European capitalism 7
global commodity chains 256, 257
Grabher, G.: on East Germany 74; on networks 79

Haraszti, M.: on piece rates 14
'hard budget constraints' 10, 37
Havel, V. 27
health: declining standard of 45
hidden economy 195–6
household economies 213–26, 227–45, 258–67
household subsistence 193–212, 213–26, 227–45, 261–5
'household survival strategies' 193–4; in Bulgaria 216–21; food provisioning 236–42; and gender 221–3; in Russia 198–203; in Slovakia 234–42;
Hungary: entrepreneurship 155–8; EU accession 150–1; gendered

employment in 135–45; gendered segregation in 142–5; gendered unemployment in 145–9; workers' councils 18

industrial relations: East Germany 89–92
industrial restructuring 85–92, 246, 257, 266
inequality 35, 37, 45, 234–5, 252
informal bargaining 13
'informal economy' 16, 21, 22, 40, 42, 47, 49, 193, 195–6; articulation with formal economy 1–2, 3, 11, 12, 16, 227–45, 259–67
international financial institutions 38–9, 40, 43, 51, 57, 59–60, 62, 63, 65–6, 69, 203

Kornai, J.: on the Soviet sytem 10
Krakow, Poland 100–16

labour codes 69, 100
labour costs in Bulgaria 251
labour force participation 20–1, 178, 195
labour markets 9, 11, 170–90, 246–7; effect on women 170–3; exclusion 22–5, 49; flexibility 178–81, 254–5, 262; gender bias 181–3; gender segregation 142–5; policy 44, 89–90; position of women in 170–90, 247; post-socialist 10; Russia 11; segmentation of 247; withdrawal from 20
labour process 11; Soviet 13–15
'lean production' 83–4, 92
legacies 74, 258
liberalisation 36–7
life expectancy 45
Lipietz, A.: on 'defensive' and 'offensive' industrial restructuring 266

management: change 107–9; education 29
Martin, Slovakia 231–44
Marxism: political economy 28–9, 36
means testing of benefits 48–9, 204, 205
Meurs, M.: on household survival strategies 243, 263
minimum wage 43
motherhood and gender 120

neo-liberalism 2, 7, 9, 10–12, 15, 23–5, 26, 35–51, 62–3, 76, 213, 262;

alternatives to 11; and labour market reform 23–5, 46; and SMEs 26; and social policy 46

networks: 'disintermediation' and 'reintermedition' 78–80; ethnic 260–1; industrial 77– 80, 90; informal 14, 202–3; social 203, 258–9

new firm formation 246–73

Offe, C.: on ownership 60; on privatisation 77; on Soviet system 28

outward processing 246–73

part-time work 179–81

patriarchy 117, 134

Pensions 199, 204, 205–7; Chilean model of 46; non-payment of 203

Perrons, D.: on patriarchy and geography 134, 135, 137

piece rates 14

Podkrepa, Bulgaria 58, 59, 60, 70

Poland: economic change 99; labour market 104–5; Solidarity 15–16, 60; Soviet system 15–16; unemployment benefit 47; women and work in 99–116

Polanyi K. 2; on commodification 17–18; on embeddedness 35–6; on social integration 45–6

Pollert, A.: on Czech labour movement 64; on industrial relations 26; on transformation 15

poverty 48, 202–3, 235, 252; calculation of 48

privatisation 37–8, 60, 74–96, 160, 254; of GDR automobile industry 81–4

reciprocity 14–15, 48, 202–3

retailing: employment relations in 108–10, 111–12; in Poland 103–4

rethinking economy 28–30

Rhodope region, Bulgaria 3, 213–16, 246–73

rural households 213–26

Russian Federation: gender and work in 117–33; unemployment 40, 41; workers movement 58–9

'second economy' 14, 16, 167; in Hungary 157–8

secondary employment 196–7, 202

security of employment 112

self employment 181, 183, 184–6

'shock therapy' 11, 36–9, 51, 60, 76, 99

Slovak Republic: Bratislava 231–4; household strategies 234–5; Martin 231–4; unemployment 25

small firms 26, 155–69

Smith, A.: on household economies 215–16; on plural economic practices 16

Smith, A. and Swain A.: on territorial embeddedness 161

Smith, A. *et al*.: on commodity chains 257

social capital 39

social networks 202, 258–67

social policy 37, 44–51, 62–3, 66; benefits 199; dis-embedded 44–5; means testing 48–9; privatisation of 37, 49; re-embedding 49–51; in Russia 203–8

social reproduction 13

social safety net 37, 204

social wage 110–12

Solidarity 15, 16, 58, 59, 60, 67, 69, 100

Soviet system 10, 16; employment in 9, 13–18; and entrepreneurship 157–8; and gender 119–20; and household subsistence 194–5, 217–18, 241–2

stabilisation 37

Stark, D.: on 'path dependence' 58 ;on soviet labour process 14

Stark, D. and Bruszt, L.: on property ownership 77

state desertion 37

state-owned enterprises (SOEs) 37, 101–4; conflict in 15; social functions of 13, 103, 110–12

strikes: by miners in Russia 58

subsistence production 197–8, 217–18, 220–4, 236–45, 261–5

survival strategies 3–4, 139, 167, 193–273, 261–5; irrelevance to transition economies 193–4

sweatshop production 246–73

Szelenyi, I.: on 'second economy' 161; on under-urbanisation 229–30

tabula rasa 74, 75, 76, 80, 85

team working 90

THA (*Treuhandanstalt*) 77–9, 86, 88

'third way' 35

Thrift, N.: on 'soft capitalism' 29

tobacco production in Bulgaria 248

trade unions 2, 25–7, 50, 57–73, 88–92,

108; fragmentation of 63; IG Metall 89–92; and identity 68–70; and inward investors 26–7; and politics 66–7; and small firms 26; during Soviet period 16; and the state 27; and transformation 25–7, 57–61

transformation 10, 11, 12, 15, 36, 39; evolutionary approaches 11–12

'transition to capitalism': 7, 10, 25, 39; in GDR 74, 76; and survival strategies 194 transition model 9, 10–11; and trade unions 59–61, 63–4

transition theory 9–12

Treuhandanstalt 76–93

'tripartism' 26–7, 50, 61–3, 69; in Bulgaria 65–6; in Czech Republic 64, in Hungary 64–5; in Slovakia 65

Turks in Bulgaria 246–73

Ukraine: unemployment 40

unemployment 18, 21–2, 22–5, 39–41, 145–50, 161–2, 174–5, 194, 246–73; benefit 47–9, 204, 212, 220; in Bulgaria 250–1; change in ECE 22–5, 39–41, 174–5; hidden 41; long term 23–5, 175–6

uneven development 134–54, 248

urban and rural interactions 229–31, 242–3

urbanisation: urban-rural links 230–1; under-urbanisation 229–30;

VEB-Sachsenring 85–92

VW (Volkswagen) 85–8, 90–2

wages 11, 45, 195; minimum wage 43; social wage 110–12; wage arrears 42

'Washington consensus' 39

welfare 110–12; benefits 172, 193, 199; declining standard of 45

'*Wende, die*' 76

Williams, R.: on 'key words' 35

womanhood: notions of in Russia 117–33

women: attitude to men 127–9; and work 99–116, 117–33;

work 12; change in ECE 9; 'end of work' 30; flexibility 109–10; future of work in ECE 27–30; and gender 107–12, 121–3; in Poland 107–12; and regional change 114–15

works councils 61, 70, 89–92; East Germany 8

World Bank: in Russia 204–5

Wroclaw, Poland 100–16

For Product Safety Concerns and Information please contact our EU
representative GPSR@taylorandfrancis.com
Taylor & Francis Verlag GmbH, Kaufingerstraße 24, 80331 München, Germany

www.ingramcontent.com/pod-product-compliance
Ingram Content Group UK Ltd.
Pitfield, Milton Keynes, MK11 3LW, UK
UKHW040836280425
457818UK00024B/31